PENGUIN BOOKS

LITERARY LONDON

Ed Glinert was born in Dalston. His fascination with people and place, coupled with his expert knowledge of his city's history and his forensic gift for digging out obscure stories, have made him one of the most acclaimed writers about London. He is the author of *The London Compendium*, *East End Chronicles* and *West End Chronicles* and leads a variety of walking tours around the city.

LITERARY
LONDON

A street by street exploration of the capital's literary heritage

Ed Glinert

PENGUIN BOOKS

PENGUIN BOOKS

Published by the Penguin Group
Penguin Books Ltd, 80 Strand, London WC2R ORL, England
Penguin Group (USA) Inc., 375 Hudson Street, New York, New York 10014, USA
Penguin Group (Canada), 90 Eglinton Avenue East, Suite 700, Toronto, Ontario, Canada M4P 2Y3
(a division of Pearson Penguin Canada Inc.)
Penguin Ireland, 25 St Stephen's Green, Dublin 2, Ireland
(a division of Penguin Books Ltd)
Penguin Group (Australia) Ltd, 250 Camberwell Road, Camberwell, Victoria 3124, Australia
(a division of Pearson Australia Group Pty Ltd)
Penguin Books India Pvt Ltd, 11 Community Centre, Panchsheel Park,
New Delhi – 110 017, India
Penguin Group (NZ), 67 Apollo Drive, Rosedale, North Shore 0632, New Zealand
(a division of Pearson New Zealand Ltd)
Penguin Books (South Africa) (Pty) Ltd, 24 Sturdee Avenue, Rosebank,
Johannesburg 2196, South Africa

Penguin Books Ltd, Registered Offices: 80 Strand, London WC2R ORL, England

www.penguin.com

First published as *A Literary Guide to London* 2000
Reissued under the present title 2007
2

Typeset by Rowland Phototypesetting Ltd, Bury St Edmunds, Suffolk
Printed in England by Clays Ltd, St Ives plc

ISBN: 978–0–141–02624–4

www.greenpenguin.co.uk

Penguin Books is committed to a sustainable future
for our business, our readers and our planet.
The book in your hands is made from paper
certified by the Forest Stewardship Council.

CONTENTS

LIST OF MAPS

ACKNOWLEDGEMENTS

Margaret Bluman and Faith Evans (for their unstinting support and enthusiasm), Marian Walsh (many miles of driving and pages of checking), Tim Perry, Cecilia Boggis, John Nicholson, Roger Wells, Andrew Barker and Irene Evans. Many thanks to Charles McKee Books, New Westminster, British Columbia, Canada.

Permissions

Thanks are due to the executors of the John Betjeman estate/John Murray publishers; Faber & Faber (T. S. Eliot, Ezra Pound and W. H. Auden); and David Higham Associates (Louis MacNeice).

Enfield

Lower Edmonton

Walthamstow

Stoke Newington

Hackney

Clerkenwell   The East End
The City

The Borough
Camberwell   Deptford   Isle of Dogs
Peckham   Greenwich
Brixton

Dulwich

Norwood   Beckenham
                   Bromley

INTRODUCTION

There are countless guidebooks on London and countless books on literary London but few, if any, guidebooks on literary London. Guidebooks on the capital invariably have little room to treat literature other than in the most rudimentary fashion, with the occasional passing reference to Shakespeare or Dickens; while some of the more ambitious ones give a cursory nod to Virginia Woolf in Bloomsbury, perhaps Dylan Thomas in Fitzrovia, or Peter Ackroyd in the East End. A few specialist guides treat literature in some depth but pay too little attention to the geographical details, so that the reader, though presented with interesting information, is given little help in exploring the settings.

Then there are the books on literary London. These range from academic tomes of little practical use to lightweight volumes that contain too little information; from those over-laden with colour photos to those that are too heavy to lift off the coffee table; from those that have taken the easy option by listing authors alphabetically or chronologically (which usually means nothing more recent than the era of Virginia Woolf) to those full of long narrative idiosyncratic text that says more about the author than the subject.

This guide is different because it tells the story of the capital's literature – from Chaucer to Iain Sinclair, through Shakespeare, Samuel Pepys, Dr Johnson, Charles Dickens, H. G. Wells, T. S. Eliot, Virginia Woolf, Somerset Maugham, George Orwell, Graham Greene, Anthony Burgess and everybody else of note in between – with precise locational settings, page by page, area by area, street by street, landmark by landmark, in a way that allows the reader to walk from site to site (geographical directions have been given where necessary). The book has not been presented entirely as a walkers' guidebook, and it can be read in its own right; nevertheless, for readers who do want to see the places mentioned and walk the routes, geographical pointers have been provided.

The structure of the book needs a little explaining. It has not been divided around some arbitrary set of boundaries but according to a long-standing system that is of immense practical use to the London explorer, the capital's postal districts. As Philip Larkin put it in *The Whitsun Weddings*: 'I thought of London spread out in the sun/Its postal districts packed like squares of wheat', and nearly every London street displays the local postal district number – E1, SE2, EC2, W1, SW3 etc. – on its nameplate, which is of immense help for those who don't know London intimately, and reassuring for those who do.

First, London has been divided into Central London and Outer London, then central London has been subdivided according to its postal areas: Bloomsbury (WC1), the City of London (EC1–4), Clerkenwell (EC1), Covent Garden (WC2), next the four territories radiating from Oxford Circus that comprise the heart of the West End – Soho, Mayfair, Fitzrovia and Marylebone (all W1) – plus Westminster (SW1). Outer London, similarly, has been broken up into the six territories analogous to the postal districts E, N, NW, SE, SW and W: East London, which incorporates areas with an E1–E17 postcode; North London (N1–N19); North-West London (NW1–NW8); South-East London (SE1–SE25); South-West London (SW1–SW19); and West London (W2–W14). (The authorities, in devising the postal district system, helpfully set out most of the Outer London districts in alphabetical order, so that North London, for instance, comprises N1 (Angel/Islington), N2 (East Finchley), N3 (Finchley), N4 (Finsbury Park), N5 (Highbury), N6 (Highgate), N7 (Hornsey), and so on. Other regions of the capital largely follow the same pattern.)

Despite the simplicity and clarity of this system, there are anomalies because London – unlike, say, New York – does not have a rigid geometric shape so that while Bloomsbury, for instance, falls entirely within WC1, the City of London has been divided quite arbitrarily into EC1, EC2, EC3 and EC4. This book circumvents that problem by cutting up the City into areas based around the eight medieval gates – Aldgate, Aldersgate, Bishopsgate, Cripplegate, Ludgate, Moorgate, Newgate and Temple Bar – which, though long demolished, have in the majority of cases left their identity in the names of well-known City streets.

Clerkenwell, to the north of the City of London, while technically part of the borough of Islington, has an EC1 rather than an N1 postcode and, since it cannot be described as north London, comes under the Central London heading for the purposes of this book. Covent Garden is in WC2, a territory that also includes the Strand (logically) and Leicester Square (illogically). A small section of Marylebone, the streets around Marylebone station, lies north of Marylebone Road, the main road through the area, and has an NW1 postcode. It has been included with the rest of Marylebone under Central London rather than under North-West London. Westminster has an SW1 postcode (even though it is wholly north of the river), but SW1 itself stretches west into what is better described as Belgravia than as Westminster. Since Belgravia is not in central London, it comes under South-West London.

East London has the quirk that is the East End (E1, E2, E3 and E14 – the ancient Tower hamlets) which here have been grouped together. North London is one of the most logical and ordered in all the capital so needs little extra explanation, save to say that a northerly area like Enfield, being in Greater London but outside the London postal district belt, has been included at the end of the North London section and that other Middlesex villages have been dealt with in similar fashion in subsequent sections. In South-East London, Bankside, The Borough and Waterloo are close enough to the City and West End to argue a case for inclusion under Central London. Nevertheless, one can't escape the fact that London is not a city that rests easily either side of its major river (Angela Carter asked in *Wise Children* 'Why is London like Budapest? Because it is two cities divided by a river'). Not only do the two halves have unequal status, but the North dominates to an almost immeasurable extent. All the great buildings of state, government and religion lie north of the river, as do nine-tenths of the areas of interest to the literary explorer; so, in this guide, all south-of-the-river sites feature in either South-East or South-West, rather than Central, London. South-West London has some inconsistencies: a size-able chunk – Belgravia, Chelsea – lies *north* of the river and the border between those areas and the adjacent parts of West London follows no logical pattern. Finally, West London presents no problems except that W1 (the West End) has, of course, been moved to Central London.

Having explained the geography of the book, now for the lay-out. Areas are broken down by postal district and then into streets which, to avoid any confusion, have been set in a different typeface. Entries are then listed in a logical geographical order that can be walked, and the names of the nearest tube (underground) or rail (overground) station given (usually at the beginning of the route). Of course those readers who know London well, or who want to make up their own route combining several different parts of the book, can easily do so. Suffice to say that any attempt to follow the route of the book on foot will need an A–Z map of some kind.

Finally, a word on the text. Each area begins with a general introduction, followed by an explanation on exploring the area, and then a list of useful local bookshops, the emphasis being on independent establishments and the best second-hand shops. Interspersed between the Central London areas are six walks devoted to individual authors: Shakespeare (to represent the era up to the Renaissance); James

Boswell (the Augustan age); Charles Dickens (Victorian London); Sherlock Holmes (fictional characters, he being the best known); Virginia Woolf (early twentieth century); and George Orwell's _1984_ (mid- and late twentieth century). Other authors have been honoured with walks within sections (William Blake in Fitzrovia, even though some of the sites fall just outside Fitzrovia's boundaries) and, in the case of T. S. Eliot, a trawl through the City locations of his epic threnody _The Waste Land_. There is also a section on the River Thames.

But the hardest task for the author of any literary guide is how to decide which authors deserve more space than others. Some anecdotes are so good that they deserve mention in their own right, even though the protagonist, Richard Dadd for instance, is obscure; but how does one choose between, say, Jonathan Swift and Ben Jonson, or Anthony Trollope and Thackeray? A book which included appropriate entries on every great London writer, or every writer on London, would be too heavy to carry around; so much, inevitably, has been omitted. There can be little disagreement however over the merits of Shakespeare and Dickens, the two major pre-twentieth-century English writers, both of whom devoted considerable amounts of their work to London. However, it is their characters' movements rather than their own lives that continue to interest successive generations, so their presence dominates much of central London.

Invariably other choices will be idiosyncratic. This book has given space to twentieth-century writers at the expense of Victorian ones, so there is more on Joseph Conrad, H. G. Wells, Ezra Pound and Somerset Maugham than on Trollope and Thackeray – which at least makes a change from most literary guides – and much more on George Orwell than almost anybody else with the possible exception of Shakespeare and Dickens. As things move closer to the present day it becomes harder and harder to decide who gets space and who doesn't. Some guidebook writers would have given a fuller account of Nigel Williams's Wimbledon, but this book has gone for the bizarre and the fascinating over the fashionable and transient so there is much on Iain Sinclair, slightly less (and probably not enough) on Peter Ackroyd, and perhaps one entry too many on Nick Hornby.

CENTRAL LONDON

Bloomsbury, WC1

'Find a place with a bath and no bugs in Bloomsbury, and be happy there'
Dylan Thomas, letter to Caitlin Macnamara, 1936

Elegant Georgian squares and black brick terraces of hotels and university buildings dominate Bloomsbury, but in literary circles the area is best known for the Bloomsbury Group, London's most influential and best-known early-twentieth-century intellectual clique, whose members, often described as 'Bloomsberries', included Virginia Woolf, Lytton Strachey and E. M. Forster.

Bloomsbury takes its name from Blemonde, a baron who was given land by William the Conqueror in the eleventh century. The land came into the hands of the earls of Southampton (hence Southampton Row, the name of the busy road that bisects Bloomsbury east–west), and the Duke of Montague built a house on the estate which was taken over by the British Museum in 1755. In the nineteenth century Bloomsbury, being near the Inns of Court, was popular with lawyers, but by the beginning of the twentieth century it was no longer quite so fashionable, as the family of Virginia Stephen (later Woolf) pointed out to her when she moved here in 1904. Bloomsbury's fortunes revived as the University of London grew, and expansion has usually involved retaining the Georgian façades and renovating from within. Until recently Bloomsbury was a magnet for publishers, who set up shop in the big squares, but many have since been pushed out by the high rents and only a few names remain: Faber, Souvenir and Thames & Hudson.

Exploring Bloomsbury

The area's boundaries are roughly Euston Road (to the north), Gray's Inn Road (east), High Holborn (south) and Tottenham Court Road (west). For easy exploring in this book, Bloomsbury has been divided into four sections in this book: Gower Street and west; Between Gower Street and Woburn Place; East Bloomsbury; and Great Ormond Street to Gray's Inn.

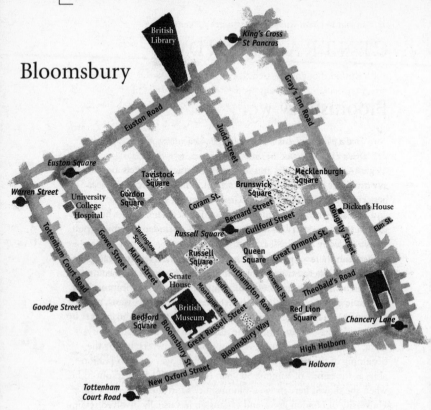

Bloomsbury

GOWER STREET AND WEST

- Landmarks to the north can be reached from Euston Square tube; those further south from Tottenham Court Road tube.

Bookshops

Bookmarks, 1 Bloomsbury Street, tel. 020 7637-1848, is London's leading socialist bookshop. Note the phone number, which cleverly coincides with that of the nineteenth-century so-called year of revolution.

Unsworth's, 101 Euston Road, tel. 020 7383-5507, is excellent for literature.

Euston end to Great Russell Street: north to south

Gower Street

John Ruskin thought the architecture of this University-dominated street particularly ugly. Famous past residents include the young Charles Dickens, the painter Millais and the economist and Bloomsbury Group member John Maynard Keynes.

Site of Charles Dickens's address (1823–4), no. 147 (west side)
Dickens's family moved here at Christmas 1823 when Charles was 11. With his father, John, in debt, Dickens's mother tried to make some money by opening the house as a school, 'Mrs Dickens's Establishment' (the model for Mrs Micawber's Boarding Establishment for Young Ladies in *David Copperfield* (1850)) but there were no takers, and in February 1824 John Dickens's debts had mounted so high that he was jailed in Marshalsea, south-east London (see p. 334). The family joined him there – apart from Charles, who moved to nearby lodgings at 37 Little College Street (the house has since been demolished and the street renamed College Place), and his sister Fanny. Charles then took rooms in Lant Street in The Borough, to be nearer the prison. When his father was released, the family moved from their Gower Street address (which has since been demolished).

University College Hospital, west side Gower Street, at Grafton Way
George Orwell died in a *private* room in the College Hospital on 21 January 1950 when his lung burst. A few weeks before his death Orwell married Sonia Brownell in the hospital, believing that he would soon be returning to live in the countryside where neighbours would disapprove of an illicit liaison. Because of an ancient law protecting dying millionaires from gold-diggers, Orwell and Brownell needed permission to marry from the Archbishop of Canterbury.

University College, east side Gower Street, south of Gower Place
> *'I am Griffin, of University College, and I have made myself invisible. I am just an ordinary man . . . made invisible'* from *The Invisible Man*, H. G. Wells, 1897

University College was founded by Jeremy Bentham, the eighteenth-century philosopher and founder of economic utilitarianism, who bequeathed the institution a large sum of money on condition that his own skeleton be preserved and displayed every year at the annual general meeting. For decades the authorities have duly taken the mummified Bentham (enclosed in a mahogany case with folding glass

---

The Bloomsbury Group

The legendary intellectual circle – or, to complete the geometric analogy, 'couples who live in squares with triangular relationships' – had its origins in a male-only early twentieth-century Cambridge University society called the Apostles, led by Thoby Stephen (Virginia Woolf's brother who died of typhoid at 26). After Stephen left Cambridge he began hosting Friday night art discussion groups at 46 Gordon Square where Virginia Woolf (then Stephen) and her sister, Vanessa, lived (see below) and from this grew the Bloomsbury Group – the name first appeared around 1910 and Virginia Woolf began using the term in 1914 – whose number went on to include: Clive Bell, whom Vanessa Stephen married (the two of them put on Britain's first exhibition of Impressionist paintings); Lytton Strachey; his sister, Marjorie; the critic Roger Fry; Gwen Darwin, granddaughter of the famous anthropologist; John Maynard Keynes; and E. M. Forster. Unlike other contemporary bodies, such as the Vorticists, the Bloomsbury Group had no formal membership and published no manifesto. Instead it followed the teachings of the philosopher G. E. Moore

---

doors and seated in an armchair holding his favourite walking-stick) to the AGM. Bentham's underclothes were changed in 1935 after a visiting academic insisted on it before giving a lecture, and his head is a wax model, the original being stored in the College safe. The late philosopher, who resides in a prominent public position in the South Cloister, is also carted off to the board of governors' meeting once a week, where he is registered present but not voting.

Victorian poet Arthur Hugh Clough taught here, 1849–51, before going to America. In 1878 University College became the first in Britain to enrol women. In *The Invisible Man* (1897), H. G. Wells's hilarious send-up of scientific progress, Griffin, a College student 'who won the medal for chemistry', devises a method for making himself disappear and goes on the run in London and Sussex.

Dillon's, no. 82

In this bookshop in the 1950s Edith Sitwell would give impromptu recitations from her poems to startled customers.

Lady Ottoline Morrell's address (1924–35), no. 10

Lady Ottoline moved here in 1924 after running a famous literary salon in the years leading up to the First World War in her house in Bedford Square (see below). Graham Greene used the address as the home of Lady Caroline Bury in *It's a Battlefield* (1934). The Pre-Raphaelite Brotherhood was founded in the house opposite in 1848.

– that the appreciation of art and beautiful things is the key to social progress. But the Group's self-righteousness and risqué lifestyles – Virginia Woolf had a relationship with Vita Sackville-West; Lytton Strachey with Dora Carrington and Ralph Partridge – repelled many figures. Rupert Brooke spoke of the 'rotten atmosphere in the Stracheys' treacherous and wicked circle'; D. H. Lawrence denounced 'this horror of little swarming selves'; Wyndham Lewis called them 'elitist, corrupt and talentless' and satirized them mercilessly in *The Apes of God* (1930); and Osbert Sitwell mocked their mannerisms with phrases like 'how simply too extraordinary' and 'exquisitely civilized'.

Woolf herself was not particularly enamoured of the Group. In her first novel, *The Voyage Out* (1915), the character Evelyn talks of 'a club in London. It meets every Saturday, so it's called the Saturday Club. We're supposed to talk about art, but I'm sick of talking about art – what's the good of it?', and at a 1921 Bloomsbury Group meeting at Gordon Square she read out a memoir written in 1905 in which she had described the men of the group as 'shabby, ugly, ungracious, sitting about for hours in complete silence'.

Bedford Square

Bloomsbury's only remaining complete Georgian square, Bedford Square was the first example of a London square with houses built in the same style; it is now taken up mainly with professional practices. Publishers Bodley Head, Jonathan Cape, Chatto & Windus and Hodder & Stoughton were based here but have now left for other parts of London.

Weedon Grossmith's address (1902–19), no. 1
Ten years after the publication of *The Diary of a Nobody* (1892) Weedon Grossmith, its co-author, was living in Bloomsbury and enjoying a relatively successful career as a playwright.

Robert Bridges' address (1877–81), no. 52
The future poet laureate (1913–30) lived here with his mother when he was in his early thirties and a physician at Bart's Hospital in the City. Visitors included Gerard Manley Hopkins, who was a priest in Farm Street, Mayfair, at the time. In 1918 Bridges was responsible for publishing the first collected edition of Hopkins's work.

Cyril Connolly's address (1940s), no. 49

Connolly, the arch-critic and literary editor, lived in a flat on the top floor of no. 49 during the Second World War. One day in September 1940 when Connolly had invited friends for tea, an air raid took place. The host was so impressed he took the party on to the roof and, gesticulating at the fires all around, announced: 'It's a judgement on us. It's the end of capitalism.' It wasn't.

Lady Ottoline Morrell's address (1910s), no. 44

Lady Ottoline's famous pre-First World War literary salon at 44 Bedford Square was regularly attended by Aldous Huxley, Lytton Strachey and D. H. Lawrence, who liked the idea of the common man (him) mixing with the aristocracy. T. S. Eliot was introduced by Bertrand Russell to the salon in 1916 but Lady Ottoline found him 'dull, dull, dull. He never moves his lips but speaks in a mandarin voice.' Few figures have been characterized in novels as many times as Lady Ottoline Morrell. She is the horrendous Hermione in D. H. Lawrence's *Women in Love* (1920), Mrs Wimbush in Aldous Huxley's *Crome Yellow* (1921), Mrs Aldwinkle in *Those Barren Leaves* (1925) and Caroline Bury in Graham Greene's *It's a Battlefield* (1934). (Also, see 10 Gower Street.)

Anthony Hope Hawkins's address (1903–17), no. 41

Hawkins, better known as Anthony Hope, moved here ten years after writing his best-known work, *The Prisoner of Zenda* (1894).

Bloomsbury Street

Former *Adelphi* offices (1923–30), no. 52

Adelphi, where George Orwell began his professional writing career, was set up by the publisher John Middleton Murry and edited by Richard Rees, a friend of Orwell. In *Keep the Aspidistra Flying*, his 1936 diatribe against advertising and 'the money god', Orwell cast Rees as the genteel, wealthy socialist Ravelston, 'editor of Antichrist', a magazine modelled on *Adelphi*.

Great Russell Street

W. H. Davies's address (1916–22), no. 14

Davies, the hobo poet who inspired George Orwell to sample the low life, was dubbed 'super tramp' on account of his train-jumping across America at the end of the nineteenth century. While crossing the Canadian border one day Davies mistimed his jump and injured his right foot so badly it had to be amputated. Back in Britain, he tramped around the country, slowly, and eventually his book of poems, *The Soul's Destroyer* (1905), caught the eye of George Bernard Shaw, who took him under his wing. Davies, by now in more congenial surroundings, then wrote what became his most famous work, *The Autobiography of a Super-Tramp* (1908), and by the time he came to Bloomsbury in 1916 was more or less rehabilitated into society.

- In Charles Dickens's 'The Bloomsbury Christening' from *Sketches by Boz* (1837) Charles Kitterbell lives at no. 14.

BETWEEN GOWER STREET AND WOBURN PLACE

The area around the 250-year-old British Museum in Great Russell Street is filled with antiquarian bookshops, most of which are listed below. The museum, which contains the country's largest store of antiquities, was until autumn 1997 also the home of the British Library.

- Landmarks to the north can be reached from Euston Square tube; those further south from Russell Square tube.

Bookshops

More than a dozen bookshops just south of the British Museum, many of which specialize in the classical world and antiquities.

west to east

London Review Bookshop, 14 Bury Place, tel. 020 7269-9030
Gosh!, 39 Great Russell Street, tel. 020 7636-1011, specializes in children's classics and comics.
Arthur Probsthain, 41 Great Russell Street, tel. 020 7636-1096, has some second-hand works but specializes in the Orient and Africa.
Jarndyce Antiquarian Booksellers, 46 Great Russell Street, tel. 020 7631-4220, specializes in eighteenth- and nineteenth-century works.
Fine Books Oriental, 38 Museum Street, tel. 020 7242-5288, is filled with unusual books on Asia.
Quinto, 63 Great Russell Street, tel. 020 7430-2535, antique and second-hand books with a wide range of war and military titles.
Ulysses, 40 Museum Street, tel. 020 7831-1600, stocks many interesting modern first editions.

Bookmarks, 1 Bloomsbury Street, tel. 020 7637-1848, specializes in left-wing titles.

Gordon Square to Bloomsbury Way: roughly north to south

Gordon Square

The commemorative plaques in Gordon Square are confusing. The one at no. 46 celebrates John Maynard Keynes but fails to mention Virginia Woolf's residency. There is also a general dedication to the Blooms-bury Group at no. 50. Many Gordon Square buildings are now occu-pied by London University.

Site of *Action* headquarters (1930s), no. 5
The Fascist magazine *Action*, edited by Oswald Mosley, with the help of Sir Harold Nicolson (husband of Virginia Woolf's occasional lover, Vita Sackville-West), was based here.

Virginia Stephen's address (1904–7), no. 46
The Bloomsbury Group (see box, above) was founded in this tall, five-storey terraced house which was occupied by Virginia Stephen (later Woolf), her sister Vanessa, and brothers Adrian and Thoby in the early years of the twentieth century. Gordon Square was Virginia's first address in Bloomsbury, then a far from fashionable area, and she felt miserable, writing to a friend that 'it seems so far away, and so cold and gloomy'. After Thoby died in 1906 – he caught typhoid in Greece – sister Vanessa and her husband Clive Bell took over the property. Virginia and Adrian then moved to Fitzrovia but regularly returned here for the Bloomsbury Group's discussions and soirées. A decade after Virginia Woolf moved out, the economist and Bloomsbury Group acolyte John Maynard Keynes moved in. The windows of the house were blown in during an October 1940 air raid but the property escaped serious damage.

Lytton Strachey's address (1919–24), no. 51
Strachey moved here shortly after writing *Eminent Victorians* (1918), his controversial critique of Victorian values which set new parameters in the art of biography. In Gordon Square Strachey produced its follow-up, *Queen Victoria* (1921), another debunker of Victorian myths.

east to Tavistock Square

Tavistock Square

The east side of the square is dominated by the grotesque brickwork of the British Medical Association headquarters, built on the site of the house where Charles Dickens once lived.

Site of Virginia Woolf's address (1924–39), no. 52

Woolf wrote *Mrs Dalloway* (1925), *To the Lighthouse* (1927), *Orlando* (1928), *A Room of One's Own* (1929) and *The Waves* (1931) after moving into no. 52 with husband Leonard in March 1924. When not publishing books on their Hogarth Press (which was situated in the building), Leonard spent much of his time tending to the garden. One day while he was planting irises Virginia called him inside to listen to Hitler's ranting on the wireless. Leonard declined the invitation: 'The irises will be there when Hitler is dead and buried,' he replied. They may still be, but the house isn't, having been destroyed in the Blitz on 16 October 1940, a year after the Woolfs had moved to Sussex. Virginia took the destruction badly, writing to Angelica Bell how there was now 'open air where we sat so many nights, gave so many parties'. The ruins of the house lay untouched for many years, and passers-by were able to gawp at the half-standing drawing-rooms with their slowly deteriorating paintings and scorched books. The site is now occupied by the Tavistock Hotel.

Site of Charles Dickens's address (1851–60), east side

Tavistock House, the British Medical Association headquarters, stands on the site of the eighteen-room house into which Charles Dickens and family moved in November 1851 when the lease expired on their Marylebone house near Regent's Park. Dickens became impatient with the work that needed to be done on the property before he could write in comfort, and he noted in his diary: 'Curtains and carpets, on a scale of awful splendour and magnitude, are already in preparation and still – still – NO WORKMEN ON THE PREMISES.' The problem was soon solved and Dickens was able to set to work on his ninth novel, *Bleak House* (1853), followed by *Hard Times* (1854), *Little Dorrit* (1857) and parts of *A Tale of Two Cities* (1859).

Hans Christian Andersen, who stayed here while on holiday, wrote how he had a 'snug room looking out on the garden, and over the tree-tops . . . saw the London towers and spires appear and disappear as the weather cleared or thickened'. At the back of the house was a large room where Dickens and friends such as Wilkie Collins staged plays and shows for their amusement; one of their favourites was Fielding's *Tom Thumb* (1730). However, at Tavistock Square relations between

Dickens and his wife, Catherine, deteriorated. After one row Dickens became more and more angry, jumped out of bed at two in the morning, and walked more than thirty miles to his other home, in Gad's Hill, Kent. The Tavistock Square house was demolished in 1901.

head back to the western end of Gordon Square

Torrington Square

Christina Rossetti's address (1877–94), no. 30
One of Rossetti's regular visitors when she first moved here was Charles Cayley, a would-be suitor whom she refused to marry on religious grounds. Rossetti wrote the poems *By Way of Remembrance* for Cayley, but he never knew as she hid them in her desk and they were found years after both had died. The terrace where Rossetti lived is intact but Torrington Square is now a sorry affair, marred by the expansion of London University.

head west to Malet Street

Malet Street

Senate House, opposite Keppel Street
George Orwell, Evelyn Waugh, Graham Greene, Dylan Thomas and John Betjeman are among the scores of writers connected with this brute of a 1930s building, the University of London's main administrative block, which towers over Bloomsbury and stands on the site of the Montague Place address where Arthur Conan Doyle wrote some of the early Sherlock Holmes stories.

When it was built in the 1930s Senate House was just about the only skyscraper in London and so provided George Orwell with a suitable model for *1984*'s towering Ministry of Truth, 'Minitrue', on which the Party's three slogans 'WAR IS PEACE. FREEDOM IS SLAVERY. IGNORANCE IS STRENGTH' are highlighted. Orwell chose Senate House because during the Second World War it was used to house the Government's Ministry of Information, a magnet for writers looking for easy war work or, as Dylan Thomas put it, for 'all the shysters in London . . . all the half-poets, the boiled newspaper men, submen from the island of crabs . . . trying to find a safe niche'.

One of the Ministry's tasks was to censor literature, and a regular target was Orwell's 'London Letters', written for the American magazine *Partisan Review*, one of which discussed the lynching of German airmen who had baled out of planes over Britain. Orwell later discovered that the Americans were unaware there had been any cuts. As a Ministry, Senate House was not quite as efficient as Orwell's model. After a false air-raid warning was sounded one day in October 1939, reporters who telephoned the building received no reply; all the staff had taken shelter. Evelyn Waugh satirized the place ('that great mass of masonry . . . the vast bulk of London University insulting the autumnal sky') in his 1942 novel about the Phoney War, *Put Out More Flags*, which has one major character, Ambrose Silk, using the offices not to further the Allied cause but to publish a literary magazine, *Ivory Tower*.

Graham Greene, another on-site propagandist, claimed staff often had to wait up to twenty-four hours to receive replies to memos, and that the building was like a beacon 'guiding German planes towards King's Cross and St Pancras stations' (although it was possibly spared because Hitler wanted it as his post-conquest London HQ). Greene's first task on joining the Ministry team in 1940 was to write a patriotic story for US magazine *Collier's* which would promote the plucky British and convince sceptical Americans that their best interests lay in fighting alongside the Allies. Greene came up with *The Lieutenant Died Last*, best remembered now as the eerie film *Went the Day Well?* On first reading, the story seems to fit the bill admirably. A sleepy English village is overrun by German commandos, who lock the inhabitants in the pub and blow up the railway line. The unlikely hero, Old Purves, stalks the infiltrators and shoots them down one by one. But on closer inspection *The Lieutenant Died Last* comes across as more helpful to the Nazis than to the Allies. Old Purves is not brave, just drunk. When the raid is over he is locked up for being a poacher. The village is a dump, peopled by oafs whose first acquaintance with good manners comes courtesy of the Germans. And the title is taken from the scene in which Purves, rather than taking the German lieutenant prisoner, shoots him in cold blood.

An even less suitable propagandist who nearly got a job at the Ministry was Dylan Thomas, who admitted that being ignorant of foreign languages and incapable of deciphering other people's poems – let alone encoded Nazi messages – he was of little use to the Government's war machine and so was given a job with Strand Films in Soho instead. John Betjeman secured a Ministry post in the films division thanks to Kenneth Clark, the art historian. Here, as Humphrey Carpenter in *The Brideshead Generation* later explained, Betjeman was 'in his element, gazing at sports girls in the canteen'. Chief object of his desire was Joan Hunter Dunn, who inspired one of his most famous poems, *A Subaltern's Love-song*, in which she is the tennis-playing goddess 'furnish'd and burnish'd by Aldershot sun'. In 1943 Betjeman was nearly sacked from the Ministry for mocking a colonel, but Kenneth Clark spoke up for him and convinced officers to keep him on.

In John Wyndham's *The Day of the Triffids* (1951) Senate House is briefly taken over as London headquarters by the few sighted survivors.

head east towards Russell Square

Russell Square

> *'I've never heard a grouse/Either from Russell Square or Random House'*
> from *Letter to Lord Byron*, W. H. Auden, 1936

London's second largest square has featured in a number of novels, including Thackeray's *Vanity Fair* (1848) and Virginia Woolf's *Night and Day* (1919) in which the women's suffrage office is based here.

Former Faber & Faber office (1925–65), no. 25

T. S. Eliot worked for nearly forty years for publishers Faber & Faber (originally Faber & Gwyer), first as literary adviser, then as editor, helping turn the newly formed company into the most important poetry publishers in Britain with volumes by W. H. Auden, Stephen Spender, Louis MacNeice, Ted Hughes and Thom Gunn.

Behind the scenes, things weren't always so successful for Eliot. In the mid-1930s Eliot's wife, Vivien, from whom he had separated and who later joined the British Union of Fascists, tormented him by parading outside the Faber & Faber office bearing a sandwich board proclaiming 'I am the wife that T. S. Eliot abandoned'. During the Second World War Eliot often slept in the office, especially on Tuesday nights when he was on fire-watching duty, and put some of his experiences to use in *Little Gidding* from *The Four Quartets* (1943).

In 1944 Eliot turned down George Orwell's *Animal Farm* which publisher after publisher had rejected for fear of upsetting Stalin, then a wartime ally. But Eliot appeared to have no such political motive. He wrote to Orwell: 'Your pigs are far more intelligent than the other animals and therefore best qualified to run the farm . . . what was needed (someone might argue) was not more communism but more public-spirited pigs.' Perhaps Eliot had an ulterior motive. Orwell had described him – albeit tongue-in-cheek – as one of the 'squibs of the passing minute' in *Keep the Aspidistra Flying* (1936), and in the same book twisted the knife by having his absurd anti-hero, Gordon Comstock, read a copy of *The Adventures of Sherlock Holmes* 'because he knew it by heart' – this being another dig at Eliot, who could also recite chunks of Holmes from memory.

Those who visited Eliot here included Dylan Thomas, who came for advice and was amazed to receive it, and Philip Larkin, who dropped by in 1959 for what was the two poets' only meeting. Eliot later remarked: 'Larkin often makes words do what he wants.' Despite the solemnity of his verse Eliot was an inveterate practical joker and lover of comedy. He let off a firecracker during a board meeting one Fourth of July and in later years proudly displayed a photograph of Groucho Marx, with whom he had become pen-pals, on the mantelpiece next to photos of W. B. Yeats and Paul Valéry.

The building is now occupied by London University's School of African and Oriental Studies.

no. 35
In Graham Greene's *The Confidential Agent* (1939) the hero, D., returns to London and makes for Bloomsbury where 'there was no sign of a war – except himself'. Entering a 'big, leafless Bloomsbury Square', which is meant to be Russell Square, he contemplates his pre-arranged destination: 'Well he [D.] remembered the number – 35. He was a little surprised to find that it was a hotel – not a good hotel.' 35 Russell Square is now occupied by offices.

Site of Mrs Humphry Ward's address (1880s), no. 61
Ward, a niece of Matthew Arnold, and aunt of Aldous Huxley, is remembered more for being president of the Women's *Anti*-Suffrage League than for her novels. No. 61 has since been demolished.

Site of William Cowper's address (1750s), no. 62
Cowper lodged here when he was a law student in the 1750s. In Thackeray's *Vanity Fair* (1848) the Sedleys live at the same number, with the Osbornes opposite at no. 96.

Site of Ralph Waldo Emerson's address (1833), no. 63
Also now demolished, a house on this site was briefly occupied by the American essayist and philosopher.

Hotel Russell, east side
The hotel has a Virginia Woolf Burger Bar and Grill.

head west

Great Russell Street

While fleeing down Great Russell Street, Griffin's cover as the Invisible Man in the H. G. Wells novel of the same name is blown for the first time when a couple of urchins notice that footprints which can only have been made by a barefoot person have appeared as if by magic in the mud.

British Museum, Great Russell Street at Bloomsbury Street, tel. 020 7636-1555. Open: Mon.–Sat. 10–5, Sun. 2.30–6. Admission: free.

> *'The inevitable sequel to lunching and dining at Oxbridge seemed, unfortunately, to be a visit to the British Museum'* from *A Room of One's Own*,
> Virginia Woolf, 1929

The British Museum, founded in 1753 for storing the art collection bequeathed to the state by the physician Sir Hans Sloane, contains one of the greatest collections of antiquities in the world: the Rosetta Stone, key to Egyptian hieroglyphics; surviving copies of the Magna Carta; the manuscripts of Beowulf (*c.* 1000); the Lindisfarne Gospels; *The Canterbury Tales*; the first folio editions of Shakespeare's plays; the manuscript of James Joyce's *Finnegans Wake*; and Lewis Carroll's hand-written *Alice In Wonderland*.

Scores of writers have come here for inspiration, most famously Shelley and Keats. Shelley visited the Museum with Horace Smith, the stockbroker-poet, in 1818 at a time when many Egyptian artefacts, including the granite statues of Rameses II, were being added to the collection. Smith suggested they both write a sonnet about their visits and Shelley obliged with *Ozymandias*. Keats wrote *Ode to a Grecian Urn* (1820) after seeing what he thought was a Greek vase at the Museum. Keats didn't realize that the vase was a Wedgwood copy of a Roman copy of a Greek urn – in other words it was made at Etruria, Staffordshire, rather than in Etruria, Italy – and was no more Greek than he. Some 150 years later, Dylan Thomas wasn't quite as inspired. Taken here on his first visit to London in 1932, he began waxing lyrical over a piece of 'abstract sculpture', only to be told that he was looking at a meteorite.

The British Library at the British Museum

Shortly after the Museum opened, the novelist Tobias Smollett complained that it lacked a good book collection. Over the next two centuries it more than made up for any shortcomings by fastidiously collecting a copy of every book, newspaper and magazine published in Britain. By this century the stock had grown so vast it had to be spread over several sites around the country, and in the 1970s the authorities decided that a new purpose-built place for what had become the British Library was needed. An empty lot in St Pancras was selected but the project was beset by delays, the budget overran by millions, and the sorry saga became the source of scores of mind-numbing tales of incompetence, before opening – several years late – in 1997 (see p. 289).

Yet problems beset the Library from the beginning. At first, borrowing books was a bureaucratic nightmare. Visitors were obliged to apply in advance to the chief librarian, who would only deal with ten people at one go. And the building had no artificial light, so readers would be ejected in the middle of the afternoon during the winter. Things did improve, though, and before long writers were flocking to the Library to research, write, work or look for inspiration.

- Charles Dickens obtained a reader's ticket on his 18th birthday in February 1830 and set himself a taxing schedule researching the history of England and the complete works of Shakespeare.
- Coventry Patmore, who wrote *The Angel in the House* in the 1850s, worked in the printed books department around that time.
- Karl Marx put in more labour than most. Month after month in 1857 he would arrive at nine in the morning and leave at seven in the evening after researching what became *Das Kapital*.
- Algernon Swinburne had a seizure in the reading room in July 1868.
- During the 1880s Eleanor Marx (youngest daughter of Karl) came here to translate Flaubert and Ibsen and write socialist pamphlets with her partner, Edward Aveling. Marx, Aveling, George Bernard Shaw, Havelock Ellis, Olive Schreiner and others (known as the Bohemian Socialists) also used the Museum as a meeting place, sometimes ending the day with informal play-readings.
- At the beginning of *Three Men in a Boat* (1889) Jerome K. Jerome explains how he went to the museum 'to read up the treatment for some slight ailment of which I had a touch – hay fever'.
- George Gissing is one of the many authors who have used the Reading Room as a setting. In *New Grub Street* (1891) Marian Yule describes a library official as a 'black lost soul doomed to wander in an eternity of vain research among endless shelves'.
- According to Max Beerbohm, the obscure 1890s poet Enoch Soames was so upset at lack of popular recognition for his work that he sold his soul to the Devil in return for the chance of being projected 100 years into the future into the Reading Room of 1997. Beerbohm wrote how Soames, arriving in the library of the future, looks himself up in the catalogue but finds only a brief mention of his 1890s work and no trace of himself in the *Dictionary of National Biography*, or in any encyclopedia. In despair Soames turns to an assistant, who reveals that the poet is mentioned in a 1990s article which tells how Max Beerbohm wrote a story about an imaginary poet called Enoch Soames who sells his soul to the Devil in exchange for the chance of being projected into the future to find out what posterity thinks of him.

- Bram Stoker has Jonathan Harker, the main narrator in *Dracula* (1897), visit the Reading Room to 'search among the books and maps of the library regarding Transylvania'.

- Lenin followed in Karl Marx's footsteps some fifty years after his mentor, signing himself in as Jacob Richter and taking seat L13. He was spotted by the young John Masefield, later to become poet laureate, who 'wondered who that extraordinary man was'.

- George Bernard Shaw gave the library the royalties from his play *Pygmalion* (1913) after writing much of it in the Reading Room in the early years of the twentieth century.

- Arthur Conan Doyle had Sherlock Holmes come to the Reading Room to consult Eckermann's *Voodooism and the Negroid Religions* in the short story 'The Adventure of Wisteria Lodge' from *His Last Bow* (1917).

- Bertrand Russell had a recurring nightmare in which a library worker meticulously worked his way through the library, discarding or saving copies of books, before alighting on the world's last copy of Russell's own *Principia Mathematica*. Russell kept waking up before finding out whether the librarian thought the work worth saving or not.

- Wyndham Lewis claimed that during the 1920s he was 'always underground . . . buried in the Reading Room'.

- Virginia Woolf immortalized Anthony Panizzi's sumptuous oak-panelled 1857 Reading Room, 'the vast dome . . . the huge, bald forehead which is so splendidly encircled by a band of famous names', in her 1929 essay *A Room of One's Own*.

- Louis MacNeice's poem *The British Museum Reading Room* (1939) tells how 'under the hive-like dome . . . haunted readers go up and down the alleys'.

- Angus Wilson based some of his characters in *Anglo-Saxon Attitudes* (1956) on those who used the Reading Room. Wilson joined the library staff in 1937 and one of his wartime jobs was to remove treasures from the building for safety. He recounted those days in *The Old Men at the Zoo* (1961) but failed to mention his escapades among the stacks with a male librarian many years his junior.

- Colin Wilson wrote much of his once-controversial, now rather dated, first book, *The Outsider* (1956), in the Reading Room.

- David Lodge came up with an irreverent novel about Catholics and contraception in pre-Swinging Sixties London called *The British Museum is Falling Down* (1965).

- Malcolm Bradbury, best known for *The History Man* (1975), began an affair with *Daily Express* gossip columnist Jean Rook after passing her notes in the Reading Room. Bradbury claims that their love notes can be found in some editions of T. S. Eliot's *The Cocktail Party*.

- John Stewart Collis, in *Bound upon a Course* (1971), is impressed about spending all one's weekdays in the Reading Room – 'provided you can justify a claim to receive a ticket of admission' – and thinks it wonderful that 'you can get out any book that has been published in the English language, even R. Zon's brochure on *Forests and Water in the Light of Scientific Investigation*, the last in the catalogue's alphabetical list.
- Peter Ackroyd set part of his 1995 novel, *Dan Leno and the Limehouse Golem*, in the Library.

The Reading Room closed in October 1997 and the last book ordered was the nineteenth-century work *A General View of the Agriculture of Kent* by John Boys. The final day was marked by a speech from the chief librarian, a minute's silence and a small party. The room is now being converted into a museum attraction-cum-general readers' library.

head east

Montague Street

In the Sherlock Holmes story 'The Musgrave Ritual' (1893) Holmes reveals that when he first came to London, before meeting Watson and moving to Baker Street, he 'had rooms in Montague Street, just round the corner from the British Museum', where he took on his first cases. Conan Doyle fails to state at which number in Montague Street Holmes lives, but in the 1870s a real-life Mrs Holmes took a lease out on no. 24 (now the Ruskin Hotel). Montague Street is a barely spoilt Georgian terrace.

Bedford Place

T. S. Eliot's address (1914), no. 28

Eliot came to London as a student (in between stints at Harvard and Oxford) just after he had written *The Love Song of J. Alfred Prufrock*. He had shown the poem to the already established Ezra Pound who, though difficult to please, had confided to a friend in Chicago: 'He has sent in the best poem I have yet had or seen by an American.' Pound took the unknown Eliot under his wing and convinced him to take up poetry seriously. Ironically, it was Eliot not Pound who came to be accepted as the foremost practitioner of modernist poetry, and it was left to Eliot to rescue Pound's reputation in later years. But why did Eliot, who didn't like or know London in 1914, choose an address in Bedford Place? He probably wanted 'rooms in Montague Street', like his great hero, Sherlock Holmes, as revealed in 'The Musgrave Ritual', but, being unable to find any, settled for the adjacent street.

• Eliot owed another debt to 'The Musgrave Ritual', the tale of a cryptic proclamation handed down by members of a long-standing English family which Holmes unravels. He was so taken with the ritual itself he based an entire speech around it in *Murder in the Cathedral*, his 1935 play about the life of Thomas à Becket.

Bloomsbury Square

Bloomsbury Square was created in the eighteenth century in an unusual style: featuring housing for wealthy families on three sides and servants' houses on the fourth. Over the years the square has attracted its share of writers, including Sir Charles Sedley, the seventeenth-century wit and raconteur, who lived and died in a long-demolished Bloomsbury Square house. King James II fell in love with one of Sedley's daughters and made her Countess of Dorchester, but as the Catholic king was known to fall only for ugly women, Sedley took his revenge by becoming a leading supporter of William of Orange, who seized the throne from James in 1688. Bloomsbury Square still retains some of its grandeur, despite being a major traffic route on one side.

Benjamin Disraeli's address (1817–24), no. 6
The future prime minister and novelist was 13 when the family moved to Bloomsbury Square. His father, Isaac D'Israeli, wrote *The Curiosities of Literature* here.

Gertrude Stein's address (1902), no. 20
Stein stayed here with her brother Leo after failing her medical degree, and spent her time in the British Library reading Trollope's novels.

Site of Lord Mansfield's address (1780s), no. 29
Charles Dickens wove into the story of *Barnaby Rudge* (1841) the story of the Gordon Riots, a violent uprising against Catholics which took place in London in summer 1780 following government plans to repeal anti-Catholic legislation. In the novel (as in real life) a group of Prot-estant militants besiege Newgate Gaol, demanding the release of pris-oners who have burnt down a Catholic church, and set the prison

ablaze. They then charge almost a mile west into Bloomsbury Square to wreck no. 29, the home of Lord Mansfield, the Lord Chief Justice, but, finding him absent, burn down the house and destroy his renowned law library. Rudge, the half-witted hero, is due to be hanged in the square for his part in the riots but wins a last-minute reprieve and instead two crippled boys are hanged and made to face the house as the noose is tightened. James Boswell, in his *Life of Johnson* (1791), described the riots as 'the most horrid series of outrage that ever disgraced a civilised country', while Anthony Burgess, 200 years later, claimed they were one of the most shameful episodes in England's history.

head south on to Bloomsbury Way

Bloomsbury Way

from Southampton Place heading west

Site of Colly Cibber's birthplace (1671), Bloomsbury Way at Southampton Place
Cibber, the actor, playwright and poet laureate, was born in a house which stood by this site in 1671. When he was in his fifties Cibber was appointed poet laureate, but few thought his work merited the title and he himself admitted he only got the job on account of his Whig connections. Henry Fielding wanted Cibber tried for murdering the English language, and Alexander Pope cast him as King of the Dunces in *The Dunciad* (1743). Graham Greene revived the name in *Brighton Rock* (1938) but changed the C's to K's and came up with Kolly Kibber, the trade name of the murdered Hale.

E. M. Forster's address (1902–4)/Kingsley Hotel, between Museum Street and Bury Place
Forster and his mother occasionally lodged at this now rather forlorn-looking Edwardian hotel (named after *Water Babies* author Charles Kingsley) as it was near the Working Men's College in Great Ormond Street, where he taught Latin. At the Kingsley, Forster wrote parts of his early 'Italian' novels, *Where Angels Fear to Tread* (1905) and *A Room with a View* (1908), which were based on his experiences travelling throughout that country with his mother in the early years of the century. In *A Room with a View* Bloomsbury is remembered in the often-quoted line: 'And even more curious was the drawing room which attempted to rival the solid comfort of a Bloomsbury boarding house. Was this really Italy?'

St George's, between Museum Street and Bury Place

This grimy Hawksmoor church has fascinated writers since it was erected in 1731. The eighteenth-century aesthete Horace Walpole, son of Robert Walpole, the first prime minister, wrote an amusing ode to the church's rooftop statue of the non-English-speaking monarch George I (the only statue of the king in Britain) which runs: 'When Henry VIII left the Pope in the lurch/The Protestants made him head of the church/But George's good subjects, the Bloomsbury people/Instead of the Church, made him head of the steeple.' Dickens used St George's as a setting in 'The Bloomsbury Christening' from *Sketches by Boz* (1837) in which Nicodemus Dumps, who 'adored King Herod for his mass-acre of the innocents', ruins his great-nephew's christening by making a tactless remark. Iain Sinclair dedicated his 1975 *Lud Heat* collection of poems and essays to the mythical patterns by which Nicholas Hawksmoor supposedly set the locations of his churches.

New Oxford Street

Former Vienna Café, nos. 24–28

In 1910 Ezra Pound met Wyndham Lewis for the first time in the tri-angular upstairs room of the Vienna Café, a favourite meeting place for British Museum Reading Room users. After the outbreak of the First World War, during a wave of anti-Teutonic feeling, it closed.

George Orwell's Chestnut Tree Café no. 40

'Haunt of painters and musicians', the Chestnut Tree Café where Winston Smith has become a fixture after his 'conversion' at the end of *1984* was loosely based on the Bloomsbury branch of the Express Dairy Company chain. Being so near the British Museum and its surround-ing bookshops and artists' studios, the Express attracted a fair number of writers, artists and intellectuals. Orwell used the place regularly. It is now a branch of McDonalds.

EAST BLOOMSBURY

East of Upper Woburn Place (the main road which divides Blooms-bury in two) and its continuations, university buildings give way to mainly small hotels and student accommodation. In the heart of this district stands the 1960s Brunswick Centre, Bloomsbury's only mall, its stepped concrete lending it an Italian futurist look. To the east is the area's biggest green space, Coram Fields.

- Landmarks can be reached from Russell Square tube, except where stated.

Bookshops

north to south

The Marchmont Bookshop, 38 Burton Street, tel. 020 7387-7989, is dark and dusty but packed with interesting finds on most subjects.

Judd Two, 82 Marchmont Street, tel. 020 7387-5333, is Bloomsbury's best bookshop, well stocked on London, local history, architecture and travel books. There are many bargains to be had too.

Gay's The Word, 66 Marchmont Street, tel. 020 7278-7654, is a major gay meeting place and café as well as a bookshop. The Vice Squad famously raided it a few times in the 1980s.

Woburn Walk to Mecklenburgh Square: roughly west to east

Woburn Walk

Woburn Walk was built by canal and railway engineer William Cubitt as London's first pedestrianized street in 1822.

W. B. Yeats's address (1896–1917), no. 5, Euston Square tube
Yeats shared this flat (then 18 Woburn Buildings) with his mistress, the novelist Olivia Shakespear, and here wrote poems found in the collections *The Wind Among the Reeds* (1899) and *The Green Helmet* (1910). Every Monday in the years just before the First World War Yeats was visited at 8 p.m. by a group of fellow poets including T. S. Eliot, the then unknown Ezra Pound, and John Masefield who described the sitting-room as 'the most interesting in London'. Dubbed 'the toff wot lives in the Buildings' by locals, Yeats cut a strange figure locally and could often be seen walking the surrounding streets swinging his arms wildly. In Dublin, where he was better known, people realized he was possessed by the muse, rather than by drink, but in London passers-by were a little concerned. The poet spent much of his time in the British Museum Reading Room where, on account of his delicate constitution, he would dread lifting the heavy catalogues. After Yeats moved out, the rooms were taken by the poet's unrequited love, Maud Gonne, whom he had described as the most beautiful woman in Ireland.

head south along Upper Woburn Place and its continuations

Coram Street

When he was being treated at a local hospital for various tropical diseases in the 1950s, Anthony Burgess used to sneak out and visit an illegal drinking club on the street. The experience provided the basis for his comic novel *The Doctor Is Sick* (1961).

head south along Marchmont Street

Bernard Street

Site of Peter Mark Roget's address (1808–43), no. 39
After retiring from his practice as a physician in 1840, Roget began compiling his eponymous and renowned thesaurus in Bernard Street.

head east

Brunswick Square

In Jane Austen's *Emma* (1816) Isabella defends the healthiness of Brunswick Square, announcing: 'We are so very airy. I should be unwilling to live in any other part of town.' She wouldn't be so keen these days. Excessively rebuilt since the Second World War, Brunswick Square now ranks as the least attractive of Bloomsbury's many squares. E. M. Forster moved into no. 27 in 1925 and after five years went next door, where he stayed for ten years indulging himself away from his mother's disapproving eye. Both houses have since been demolished. Also gone is no. 38 which Virginia Stephen (later Woolf) shared with John Maynard Keynes, Duncan Grant and Leonard Woolf before moving to Richmond (see p. 389) when she married Woolf in October 1912.

Lansdowne Terrace

Former *Horizon* office (1930–49), Selwyn House, no. 2
> *'Have you seen the new monthly magazine,* Horizon, *that Cyril Connolly & Stephen Spender are running? They are trying to get away from the bloody political squirrel-cage, and about time too'* George Orwell, letter to Geoffrey Gorer, 1940

Cyril Connolly started *Horizon* in September 1939, a bad time for a new venture, with the Second World War having just broken out and other magazines, such as *Cornhill*, *Criterion* and *New Verse*, closing down, but he wanted *Horizon* to keep culture alive at a time when intellectuals were worried about a possible totalitarian future and the subjugation of creativity. Connolly made Stephen Spender his editor, but perhaps his most inspired move was to give an old school friend, George Orwell, a platform for what became some of his best essays. One of Orwell's most famous essays was one on comics, *Boys Weeklies*, in which he praised the Billy Bunter stories in the *Magnet* and those on St Jim's school in the *Gem* and marvelled how the two authors, Frank Richards and Martin Clifford, could maintain the same style and characters week after week for thirty years. He was then amazed to receive a response from Richards revealing that he was both authors. Orwell was rather attached to the premises, sleeping in the office during wartime despite noise from the anti-aircraft battery in nearby Brunswick Square, and marrying *Horizon*'s secretary, Sonia Brownell, in 1949 shortly before he died, the same year that Connolly folded the magazine.

continue east

Guilford Street

In Graham Greene's *The Ministry of Fear* (1943), 'Arthur Rowe lived in Guilford Street. A bomb early in the Blitz had fallen in the middle of the street and blasted both sides but Rowe stayed on.'

Coram's Fields
Coram's Fields, a large, oddly-shaped expanse of greenery in an otherwise heavily built-up area, stands on the site of the Foundling (orphans) Hospital which Captain Thomas Coram opened in 1739. Around a hundred years later Charles Dickens publicized the work of the hospital with an article in his *Household Words* magazine and featured it in *Little Dorrit* (1857) in which Harriet Beadle (Pet Meagles' servant) goes by the nick-name of Tattycoram, having been brought up in the hospital. 'A sullen passionate girl, at one time she was Tatty and at one time she was Coram until we got into a way of mixing the two names together and now she is Tattycoram.' The hospital moved to Surrey in the 1920s (it has since closed) and only the gateway now survives but a successful campaign resulted in the land on which it stood being converted to a park which is governed by the unusual rule that adults are allowed entry only if accompanied by a child.

Mecklenburgh Square

The square's unusual title came courtesy of George III's wife, Princess Charlotte of Mecklenburgh-Strelitz. Graham Greene hated home life in Clapham so much that he did much of his writing around the time of the Second World War in a now demolished house in the square. There are no reports of his running into Mecklenburgh's other famous resident-writer of the time, Virginia Woolf. R. H. Tawney, the pioneering social historian, lived at no. 21 during the 1940s.

John Masefield's address (1932–5), no. 18
Masefield was poet laureate while living here.

Site of Virginia Woolf's address (1939–40), no. 37
The Woolfs, Virginia and Leonard, moved to a house in Mecklenburgh Square in August 1939 when the noise from the building work on the new Tavistock Hotel made conditions at their Tavistock Square place (see above) intolerable. The rooms at Mecklenburgh Square were bigger than they were accustomed to and there was more space for their Hogarth Press publishing concern which was installed in the basement. But it was a difficult time for the couple. Leonard's mother had died at a London clinic after falling downstairs at her home, and Leonard's book, *Barbarians at the Gate*, was turned down by publisher Victor Gollancz, who didn't approve of its anti-Soviet stance.

While living here Virginia Woolf wrote the last chapters of her biography of Roger Fry, but she claimed fears about the impending war with Germany made it hard for her to concentrate. Later, during bombing in September 1940, Mecklenburgh Square suffered much damage. The windows of no. 37 were blown out, rendering the house uninhabitable, and the Woolfs spent the next couple of weeks rescuing the books, most of which had remained on their shelves. Two months later, a land mine fell at the back of the property and the Woolfs were obliged to move their possessions to the countryside. The house no longer stands and has been replaced by a university block.

No. 44
Three writers have lived at this Mecklenburgh Square address. D. H. Lawrence and his wife Frieda stayed here in November 1917 during the First World War, having been forced out of Cornwall, where their anti-war sentiment and predilection for singing German *lieder* convinced locals that they were spies. Here Lawrence wrote some of *Women in*

Love (1920). The Lawrences were invited to stay at no. 44 by Dorothy Yorke (mistress of writer Richard Aldington, then away at the war), who shared the house with Aldington's wife, the poet Hilda Doolittle (HD), recovering at no. 44 from a miscarriage. Doolittle was a pioneer of imagism which, Ezra Pound explained, aimed to show 'an intellectual and emotional complex in an instant of time', and she was briefly engaged to Pound in 1905. Dorothy L. Sayers created her best-known character, Lord Peter Wimsey, while living at no. 44 in 1918, but soon grew disgruntled living in what she considered to be a rough part of town where 'drunks and wife-beatings are pretty common' and moved to nearby Great James Street in 1921.

GREAT ORMOND STREET TO GRAY'S INN

• Landmarks can be reached from Holborn tube.

Queen Square to Gray's Inn Road: west to east

Queen Square

Dedicated to Queen Anne, this beautiful secluded square contains a number of attractive hospital buildings and the so-called chimney sweep's church, St George the Martyr, where William Cowper worshipped.

Site of William Morris's address (1865–71), no. 25
Fed up with commuting to central London from the Red House in Bexleyheath, Morris moved back to Bloomsbury and set up a decorator's shop – Morris, Marshall, Faulkner & Co. – on the ground floor of no. 26. In his rooms above he found time to write interminable amounts of verse, including the monumental *Life and Death of Jason* (1867) – all 42,000 rhyming lines of it – and *The Earthly Paradise* (1868–70). When Henry James came to dinner one night, he was much taken with Morris's wife, Janey, who was lying on the sofa with a handkerchief over her face to soothe her toothache, but it was with Dante Gabriel Rossetti that she later had an affair. The National Hospital for Neurology now occupies the site of Morris's house.

• Jerome K. Jerome lived in Queen Square towards the end of the nineteenth century but claimed he could never remember at which number (it was no. 29).

Neurological Institute, Queen Square at Great Ormond Street
Anthony Burgess, being treated for a tropical illness in the late 1950s
at this hospital, was attended to by none other than Dr Roger
Bannister, the athlete who had broken the four-minute mile. Asked
by Bannister in a psychological test to explain the difference between
the words 'gay' and 'melancholy' Burgess, with typical pseudishness,
replied that 'gay' had a French etymology while that for 'melancholy'
was Greek.

Boswell Street

Site of the Poetry Bookshop (1913–28), no. 35

The day in 1913 when Harold Monro opened his Poetry Bookshop,
Robert Frost (then more of a farmer than a poet, having never been
published) wandered past the window and, enticed by the books of
obscure poetry on display, went inside to find out more. When Frost
asked if he could come back later that evening for the official opening,
the shopkeeper, R. S. Flint (also an occasional poet) warned him that it
was by invitation only but that he might get in if he tried. Flint looked
at Frost and asked him if he was American. 'Yes,' Frost replied. 'How
did you know?' 'Shoes,' Flint declared. He then asked Frost if he'd ever
heard of a 'fellow countryman', Ezra Pound. When Frost admitted that
he hadn't, Flint warned that 'if you ever meet him, you won't be fool-
ish enough to say that to his face'. Elizabeth Bowen, who regularly
went to readings at the shop, remembered Ezra Pound reading out
stuff that was 'hypnotically unintelligible'. Monro himself wasn't the
shrewdest judge of verse. When T. S. Eliot passed him an early copy of
The Love Song of J. Alfred Prufrock in 1914, he handed it back claiming
that it was 'absolutely insane'.

detour south to Red Lion Square

Red Lion Square

Run-down and marred by a hotch-potch of awkward-looking buildings, Red Lion Square has a long history of violent demonstration.
It was the setting for a number of executions in the Middle Ages
and Oliver Cromwell's body when exhumed from its grave in
Westminster was left here overnight before being reburied. In the
late seventeenth century workmen developing the square were attacked
by lawyers from nearby Gray's Inn who were annoyed about losing
their green views. In Dorothy L. Sayers's *Strong Poison* (1930) Joan

Murchison, who had been planted in the law office of Norman Urquhart to watch out for anything suspicious, walks around the square after the office closes in order to kill time before returning to burgle the office safe.

Arnold Bennett's address (1908), 7 Halsey House
Bennett, on returning to London from Paris, wrote some of *Clayhanger* (1910) in a flat in this tall red-brick block.

Dante Gabriel Rossetti's address (1851)/William Morris's address (1856–9), no. 17
When Rossetti and the painter Walter Deverell moved in, the landlord warned them not to succumb to the temptations of the models they would be inviting up to their first-floor flat. A few years after moving out, Rossetti heard that the rooms were available and thought they would make ideal accommodation for William Morris. The latter moved in but, as the place was unfurnished, he and Edward Burne-Jones made their own medieval-style furniture. From this Morris developed his domestic design aesthetic which was based around the concept of one huge living-room – a 'noble, communal hall' where everything was done – and the axiom 'have nothing in your houses that you do not know to be useful, or believe to be beautiful'. Morris moved out after marrying Jane Burden.

return north to Great Ormond Street

Great Ormond Street

Hospital for Sick Children, opposite Barbon Close
J. M. Barrie donated royalties from *Peter Pan* (1904), which is set in Bloomsbury, to this famous children's hospital in 1929, and the hospital has a Barrie wing and a Peter Pan ward. The hospital had previously benefited from Charles Dickens's largesse and is where 'with a kiss for the Boofer lady' Johnnie dies in *Our Mutual Friend* (1865). Robert Bridges, poet laureate during the First World War and publisher of Gerard Manley Hopkins's poetry, was a physician here.

Site of the Working Men's College, no. 46
William Morris, Dante Gabriel Rossetti, John Ruskin and E. M. Forster all lectured at various times at the Working Men's College. Thomas Hughes, author of *Tom Brown's Schooldays*, was principal in the late nineteenth century.

William Morris's address (1859–60), no. 41

Morris lived here for a year after getting married, until the Red House in Bexleyheath was ready for him.

Site of Wyndham Lewis's Rebel Arts Centre, no. 38

The American painter and novelist set up a centre for the short-lived avant-garde Vorticist movement here in 1914. Lewis was intent on waging war on contemporary culture and planned for the centre to host exhibitions, lectures and demonstrations and to issue a periodical, *Blast*. Things went according to schedule for a time, but while Ford Madox Ford was speaking here one day a Lewis painting, *Plan of War*, fell off the wall and the frame lodged itself around Ford's neck. He never spoke at the Centre again. The Centre dissolved after the poet T. E. Hulme seduced Lewis's lover, Kate Lechmere.

turn right at the end of Great Ormond Street

Great James Street

Gerald Brenan, Hispanophile and novelist, who lived at no. 14 (1927–9), described Great James Street as 'the most beautiful in London', a rather strange claim. Apart from the addresses below, the street has been home to David Garnett, who wrote *Pocahontas* in 1933 and ran the Nonesuch Press from no. 16, and Frank Swinnerton, critic and prolific novelist, who lived at no. 4 in the middle years of the twentieth century.

Dorothy L. Sayers's address (1921–41), no. 24

When Sayers moved here she was working at an advertising agency in Holborn. Success via the Lord Peter Wimsey books soon followed, but she kept on this address as her town house after moving to the country. No. 24 is easily identifiable by its eighteenth-century doorcase of a phoenix rising from the ashes which was moved here from another property in 1965.

George Meredith's address (1840s), no. 26

Meredith may have been described by Oscar Wilde as a 'prose Browning', and by the end of the century had become one of the grand old men of English letters, but Arthur Conan Doyle correctly forecast in his autobiography that 'his worst [writing] is such a handicap that I think it will drag four-fifths of his work to oblivion'.

Algernon Charles Swinburne's address (1874–5, 1877–8), no. 3

When the solicitor, critic and minor novelist Theodore Watts-Dunton, who lived at no. 15, called on Swinburne one day, he found the outrageous poet 'stark naked with his aureole of red hair flying round his head performing a Dionysiac dance'. Swinburne promptly chased Watts-Dunton out into the street; but that didn't put Watts-Dunton off getting to know Swinburne, and he lived with him for thirty years in Putney (see p. 386).

Theobald's Road

After suffering a bad injury to a kidney in a football match, H. G. Wells came to London in 1888, penniless, and for a short while lived in this busy road in dire lodgings (now demolished) where he claimed the walls were so thin it was impossible to hold a private conversation.

Benjamin Disraeli's birthplace (1804), no. 22

Disraeli was never certain during his lifetime whether or not he was born here, but it has been verified since. The property is now offices for solicitors and architects.

head east along Theobald's Road and turn left at John Street, which leads to Doughty Street

Doughty Street

'*Gordon took a furnished room in Doughty Street (he felt it vaguely literary living in Bloomsbury)*' from *Keep the Aspidistra Flying*, George Orwell, 1936

A sumptuous stretch of Georgian terraced houses built between 1792 and 1822, Doughty Street was blocked at each end by security gates in the days when Dickens lived at no. 48 (now the home of the Dickens Museum). Although Doughty Street was an elegant setting, it was only a few minutes' walk away from the Saffron Hill slums where Dickens set Fagin's lair in *Oliver Twist* (1839). Harriet Vane, the fiancée of Lord Peter Wimsey in Dorothy L. Sayers's stories, lives at no. 100 Doughty Street, a fictional address.

The *Spectator*'s address, no. 56

The famous high-minded weekly magazine dates back to 1711, when it was founded by Richard Steele and Joseph Addison in Little Britain, Smithfield. Hundreds of writers have contributed to the *Spectator* over the centuries but few have worked harder than John Buchan who, at the beginning of the twentieth century, was writing the weekly leader and around ten political pieces for each issue. Graham Greene was film editor in the 1930s, and a recent literary editor was Peter Ackroyd.

Henry Havelock Ellis's address (1890s), no. 49

Ellis, the late nineteenth-century pioneer of sexual freedom, established his Co-operative Residence of the Fellowship of the New Life at this address (now offices for the University of Delaware) in the 1890s. Ellis courted controversy and in the US opponents burnt copies of his 1898 work, *Studies in the Psychology of Sex*.

Charles Dickens's address (1837–9)/The Dickens House, no. 48, tel. 020 7405-2127. Open Mon.–Sat. 10–5. Admission £3.50 (£2.50, £1.50).

This plain four-storey Georgian house, wrongly cited by many as the writer's only surviving London address, is now home to the Dickens Fellowship and the well-crafted Dickens Museum. Charles Dickens moved here in March 1837 when he was 25 and just beginning to make his name as a novelist, and in the two years here his output was prodigious. He finished the final pages of *The Pickwick Papers* (1837), wrote *Oliver Twist* (1839), most of *Nicholas Nickleby* (1839), the opening of *Barnaby Rudge* (1841), and edited the memoirs of the clown Grimaldi. He also found time to throw dinner parties which were attended by literary colleagues Harrison Ainsworth, Leigh Hunt and John Forster, who became his biographer.

Dickens's wife Catherine, whom he had married shortly before moving in, gave birth to two children at Doughty Street. But the author preferred her sister, Mary, who lived with them but soon afterwards died from heart failure aged only 17. Her death moved Dickens so much he wrote: 'I solemnly believe that so perfect a creature never breathed,' and he used her to symbolize innocence and an almost implausible purity in the guise of Rose Maylie in *Oliver Twist* (1839), Little Nell in *The Old Curiosity Shop* (1841), whose death is modelled on her demise, and Florence in *Dombey and Son* (1848). Dickens even requested that he be buried next to Mary (he is buried in Westminster Abbey instead) and wore her ring all his life.

At the end of 1839 the Dickenses moved to Devonshire Terrace, near Regent's Park, and this building was procured by the Dickens Fellowship in 1922 when demolition loomed. Money was raised to convert it into a museum and the owners have admirably resisted the temptation to turn the house into a Dickens theme park. Instead the emphasis is on the more scholarly aspects of Dickens's work, with a number of first editions, original manuscripts, signed letters and personal papers among the artefacts. Also on display are books which the author used for his dramatic productions and which contain his own hand-written stage directions, the velvet-covered desk Dickens designed and took

Gray's Inn

'. . . Gray's Inn, gentlemen. Curious little nooks in a great place, like London, these old Inns are' Mr Pickwick from *The Pickwick Papers*, Charles Dickens, 1837

Gray's Inn is one of the four Inns of Court (along with Lincoln's Inn, the Middle Temple and the Inner Temple) where lawyers have traditionally lived and studied. It dates back to the fourteenth century and occupies what is now a surprisingly peaceful green site on the Holborn–Bloomsbury border. Shelley, when he was severely in debt, used to meet Mary Godwin, daughter of Mary Wollstonecraft, here in secret on Sunday afternoons, as debtors could not be arrested on a Sunday.

Charles Dickens's workplace (1827), 6 Raymond Buildings

When he was 15 Dickens worked as a solicitor's clerk for the firm Ellis and Blackmore, who were based on the second floor of this block. He used to amuse himself by dropping cherry stones on to passers-by and later in *Uncommercial Traveller* (1860) described the place as 'one of the most depressing institutions in brick and mortar known to the children of men'.

Charles Dickens's workplace (1827), 1 South Square

Dickens worked for Ellis and Blackmore as office boy at no. 1 South Square (then Holborn Court) in 1827 before they moved to nearby Raymond Buildings.

Gray's Inn Hall

Shakespeare's *Comedy of Errors* (1594) had its premiere in Gray's Inn Hall, South Square, on 28 December 1594. The building, badly damaged during the Second World War, has since been rebuilt. T. B. Macaulay, the great historian, took chambers at no. 8 South Square (demolished, replaced by a library) after being called to the Bar in 1826.

with him on his travels, and the grille from the Marshalsea prison where his father was imprisoned for debt. The drawing-room, with its rosewood furniture and large table, has been carefully reworked into its original condition, and in the basement there is a reproduction of the Dingley Dell kitchen from *The Pickwick Papers*. There is also a reading room and facilities for research.

Sydney Smith's address (1803–6), no. 14

Smith, a nineteenth-century clergyman and author, well known for his indecipherable handwriting and his outlandish claim, 'Who reads an

American book?', first lived at no. 8 in 1803 and then moved the same year to no. 14. Smith described his own sermons as 'long and vigorous, like the penis of a jackass'.

turn right at Guilford Street and right at Gray's Inn Road

Elm Street

Katherine Mansfield's address (1911–12), Churston Mansions
Mansfield shared a flat in this block with her lover, Ida Constance Baker, and decorated it with oriental wares, bamboo matting and a stone Buddha. Mansfield's mother didn't approve of their liaison and cut Katherine out of her will. In 1912 John Middleton Murry (whom Mansfield later married) became a lodger. On his first day in the flat he found a note in the kitchen next to an egg which read: 'This is an egg. You must boil it. K.M.' When another of Mansfield's (male) admirers threatened to shoot himself if she didn't respond to his approaches, she replied: 'Oh do have some melon first.'

A Walk Through Virginia Woolf's London

'One of these days I will write about London and how it takes up the private life and carries it on without any effort' *Virginia Woolf, from her diary, 26 May 1924*
Virginia Woolf not only lived in London most of her life – mainly in Blooms-bury – she wrote incessantly about the city.

Fleet Street to St James's Street: roughly east to west

Fleet Street
'I have seen violinists who were obviously using their instruments to express something in their own hearts as they swayed by the kerb in Fleet Street,' Woolf wrote in an article for the National Review *in 1905.*

Bolt Court, *off Fleet Street, north side, halfway between Fetter Lane and Shoe Lane*
Orlando in the novel of the same name watches 'three shadows on the blind drinking tea together in a house on Bolt Court', two of whom turn out to be James Boswell and Dr Johnson who lived on Bolt Court from 1776 to 1784.

Site of Ye Old Cocke Tavern, *190 Fleet Street*
At the Cocke, which then stood on this side of the road (the modern-day pub is opposite), Orlando meets the poet Nicholas Greene, who relates the story of a drunken night at the tavern with Christopher Marlowe and Shakespeare in which the former announces, 'Stap my vitals, Bill . . . there's a great wave coming and you're on the top of it.'

Temple Bar, *junction Fleet Street and Strand*
Orlando, in London in Elizabethan times, notices the heads on the pikes at Temple Bar 'like a grove of trees stripped of all leaves save a knob at the end'. In Night and Day Katherine and Ralph take a bus from Chelsea to Temple Bar, where they alight and 'the splendid race of lights drawn past her eyes by the superb swerving and curving of the monster on which she was sat was at an end'.

head north-west up Aldwych

Kingsway
Katherine in Night and Day leaves Lincoln's Inn Fields and turns into Kingsway, where the 'blend of daylight and lamplight . . . gave the people who passed her a semi-transparent quality'. Terence, while in South America in the same novel, dreams of 'walking down Kingsway, by those big placards and turning into the Strand'.

head north

Southampton Row
Woolf spent much time strolling up and down the main road through the heart of Bloomsbury, describing it in her diary for 26 May 1924, as being 'wet as a seal's back or red and yellow with sunshine'.

turn left at Bloomsbury Place

British Museum, *Great Russell Street, between Bloomsbury Street and Montague Street*
Woolf regularly wrote about the Museum which in her day was home of the British Library, but never more so than in A Room of One's Own in which she immortalizes Anthony Panizzi's sumptuous oak-panelled 1857 Reading Room – 'the vast dome . . . the huge, bald forehead which is so splendidly encircled by a band of famous names'. In Jacob's Room the hero reads Marlowe in the Library and watches other readers, including the atheist Fraser and the feminist Julia Hedge, and thinks of the British Museum as an enormous mind. When he goes back to his room the author's voice contemplates the night watchmen 'flashing their lanterns over the backs of Plato and Shakespeare . . . neither flame, rat, nor burglar was going to violate its treasures'.

head south

(Covent Garden) Royal Opera House, *Bow Street at Floral Street*
In The Years *Woolf writes about 'men and women in full evening dress [who] looked uncomfortable as they dodged between costers' barrows' making their way to the Opera House. The market moved out in the 1970s.*

head south-west through the back streets

St Paul's (Covent Garden), *Bedford Street*
Woolf belatedly discovers this church for the first time in March 1937 and, entering, hears the old char singing as she cleans.

head south along Bow Street to the Strand and turn right

Charing Cross station
In The Years *Eleanor reads a placard outside the station which proclaims 'Parnell dead', and recalls her sister Delia's passionate support for the nineteenth-century Irish patriot.*

Eleanor's Cross, *Strand at Charing Cross station*
Early in Orlando *the hero/heroine muses on an 'evening of astonishing beauty' in Elizabethan London, noticing the 'fretted cross at Charing', Eleanor's Cross.*

Admiralty Arch, *The Mall at Charing Cross*
In A Room of One's Own *Woolf writes about 'walking through the Admiralty Arch or any other kind of avenue given up to trophies and cannon, and reflecting upon the kind of glory celebrated there'.*

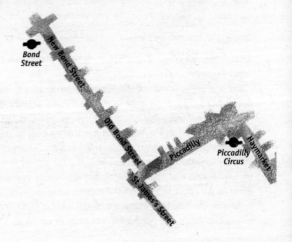

head north

Piccadilly Circus

Orlando and Alexander Pope come across 'two wretched pigmies on a stark desert land' by what is now Piccadilly Circus. In Between The Acts *Mrs Swithin thinks of rhododendron forests in Piccadilly and elephant-bodied seal-necked monsters. Jinny in* The Waves *stands in the tube station and considers that she is standing 'where all that is desirable meets – Piccadilly South Side, Piccadilly North Side, Regent Street and the Haymarket'.*

head west along Piccadilly

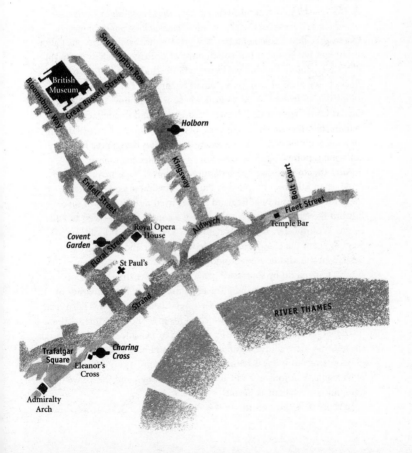

Old and New Bond Streets

'Bond Street fascinated [Mrs Dalloway]. Bond Street early in the morning in the season; its flags flying; its shops; no splash; no glitter; one roll of tweed in the shop where her father had bought his suits for fifty years.'

Site of the Cocoa Tree Coffee House, *64 St James's Street*

As Orlando passes the nearest point on the river to St James's Street the captain points out to her Joseph Addison taking his coffee alongside John Dryden and Alexander Pope, a near impossibility given that (a) St James's Street would never have been visible from the Thames, and (b) Pope was only 12 when Dryden died (as Woolf herself remarks in the footnote).

The City, EC1–EC4

The world's best-known and perhaps greatest financial centre, the City of London is a compact one square mile of ancient churches, medieval alleyways, sombre-looking banks and granite-and-glass hi-tech office blocks based around London's Roman birthplace. The Romans founded a settlement in AD 43 near where St Paul's now stands, choosing the north bank of the Thames because the land was higher and less marshy than that on the south side. They called the settlement Londinium and built a bridge near modern-day London Bridge, the lowest convenient point.

After the Romans left, the settlement declined, but a turning point came when Ethelbert founded St Paul's Cathedral in 604 on the site of the present-day building. England's kings lived nearby until in 1060 Edward the Confessor moved the palace a couple of miles west to what is now Westminster. London's status was saved when, a decade or so later, William the Conqueror founded the Tower and London's eastern border. In the Middle Ages London became a major commercial centre, spurred on by successive generations of dynamic merchants and their trading companies, and attracted almost every English writer of that and following eras including Geoffrey Chaucer, who was born near the Tower and lived locally for much of his life; Thomas More, author of *Utopia* (1516) and Henry VIII's ill-fated Lord Chancellor; Shakespeare, who arrived in London around 1585 and here wrote most of his plays, premiered in local venues; Shakespeare's great contemporary playwrights, Ben Jonson and Christopher Marlowe; and the essayist and philosopher Francis Bacon.

In those days the majority of the City's population was crowded into rickety hovels and tenements overrun with rats. These conditions led to the plague of 1665, described by Harrison Ainsworth in *Old St Paul's* (1841) as 'like a hideous platform stalking the streets at noonday and scaring all in its path' and whose full horrors were best evoked in Daniel Defoe's *A Journal of the Plague Year* (1722). The Great Fire of London, which began in a bakery in Pudding Lane (to the north-east of London Bridge) on 2 September 1666, wiped out the plague. The fire was not taken seriously at first – the Mayor, Sir Thomas Bloodworth, dismissed it with a curt 'Pish! A woman might piss it out!' – but the month had been dry and it soon spread around the wharves, fuelled by their wood and coal, and along the narrow streets. The anonymous ballad *London Mourning in Ashes* tells how it 'swallow'd Fishstreet hil, and straight/it lick'd up Lombard-street/Down Cannon-street in blazing State/it flew with flaming feet'. In his diary Samuel Pepys wrote how when he met the Mayor in Cannon Street the latter had by now woken to the seriousness of the blaze. The Mayor cried: 'Lord! What can I do? I have been pulling down houses, but the fire overtakes us faster than we can do it.' John Evelyn, in his contemporaneous diary, described 'the miserable and calamitous spectacle . . . like the top of a burning oven'. A day after the fire started, most of Cornhill and Cheapside were still aflame.

In all, 400 acres were destroyed, with St Paul's Cathedral, the Guildhall, Custom House, the Royal Exchange, 87 churches and nearly 15,000 homes burnt down and the last embers still burning in parts of the City the following March. The fire inspired more than thirty long poems, including Dryden's *Annus Mirabilis* (1666). Rebuilding London began immediately and the city soon regained its place as a leading centre for trade . . . and ideas. The post-fire period was dominated by the towering personality of Samuel Johnson, who lived at a number of City locations including the surviving No. 17 Gough Square (now a museum).

By the nineteenth century the old city was the commercial heart of the world's greatest empire, with the newspaper industry clustered on and around Fleet Street (to the west) and the banks around Threadneedle Street and Cornhill (to the east). The City's greatest chronicler in this period was Charles Dickens, most of whose novels are crammed with city life, many of the locations he used still intact. As the railways began to take the resident population off to the new suburbs with their own systems of local government, so the City became isolated as a commercial centre, inhabited by a declining population and run by a largely symbolic form of government, the Corporation of London. The Second World War brought more destruction

'Unreal City' – T. S. Eliot's Square Mile Waste Land

Cited by many critics as one of the century's greatest works, Eliot's 1922 poem *The Waste Land* is filled with London references and locations. The poet drew a number of connections between 1920s' London and Dante's Hell – some lines were adapted from the Italian's works – seeing the City as a modern-day Inferno, the streets flowing with the living dead.

'A crowd flowed over London Bridge, so many/I had not thought death had undone so many'

Eliot is comparing the bankers and clerks, pouring across the bridge each morning on their way from London Bridge station to the City's finance houses, with the lost souls in Dante's *Inferno*. Eliot, who lived north of the Thames, wouldn't have taken this route to work.

the crowd flowing along King William Street

King William Street is a short street linking Monument and Bank tube stations and is the route to work for most of the London Bridge commuters.

'To where Saint Mary Woolnoth kept the hours/With a dead sound on the final stroke of nine'

Ezra Pound, when editing *The Waste Land*, suggested taking out these lines which refer to the church Nicholas Hawksmoor rebuilt in 1717. Eliot ignored him and left a note at the end of the poem stating that the St Mary Woolnoth sound was 'a phenomenon which I have often noticed'.

'Sweet Thames, run softly, till I end my song'

The line is lifted from Edmund Spenser's 1596 poem *Prothalamion*.

Leman Street

A 'leman' is a prostitute and the phrase 'the waters of Leman' is associated with the fires of lust, the line being included in the section of the poem called *The Fire Sermon*. It also recalls the well-known biblical phrase, 'By the rivers of Babylon, where we sat down, yea we wept, when we remembered Zion'. Leman Street runs south from Aldgate East tube towards the former London Docks.

Lunching at the Cannon Street Hotel

In 1920 Eliot used to go to the station pub for a pint of Bass, often with the critic Conrad Aitken. The Cannon Street Hotel, birthplace of the British

Communist Party that year, was demolished during post-war redevelopment of the station.

Strand and Queen Victoria Street

Strand and Queen Victoria Street are two of the major routes carrying traffic east–west through central London. The Strand is just outside the City, west of Fleet Street. Queen Victoria Street connects Blackfriars and the junction by the Bank of England.

Bars in Lower Thames Street

None of the bars to which Eliot alludes can still be found on this busy highway near the Tower.

'The walls/Of Magnus Martyr hold/Inexplicable splendour of Ionian white and gold'

The church of St Magnus Martyr was a particular favourite of Eliot, who said that 'the interior is to my mind one of the finest among Wren's interiors'. In 1926, four years after *The Waste Land* was published, the authorities threatened to sell the building. Eliot and others led a protest through the nearby streets singing Christian hymns.

'The river sweats/Oil and tar/The barges drift/With the turning tide/ Red sails/Wide'

A description of the Thames based upon an extract from the opening section of Joseph Conrad's *Heart of Darkness* (1902), the story of which is told on a cruising yawl in the Thames further downstream.

Moorgate

Eliot used Moorgate station when working in the City. The *Norton Anthology of English Literature* erroneously describes Moorgate as a 'slum area in the East End of London' – Moorgate isn't a slum, and it isn't in the East End of London.

'London Bridge is falling down'

A line taken from the seventeenth-century nursery song 'London Bridge is Falling Down'.

The poem also mentions a number of sights beyond the City, including Greenwich Reach, Highbury, Richmond, Kew and Margate, Kent, where Eliot began writing the poem while convalescing from an illness.

than the Great Fire, particularly in the north of the City which was rebuilt in the 1960s as the skyscraper- and walkway-dominated Barbican, now just about the only residential community in the area; and in the 1980s the newspapers left Fleet Street for Docklands, further east. Yet the City remains as a financial powerhouse into the twenty-first century as well as being the most fascinating place in the capital.

Exploring the City

The City covers the two miles or so between Waterloo and Tower bridges and reaches north from the Thames for about half a mile. Its boundaries are roughly Charterhouse Street–the Barbican–Liverpool Street station (to the north), Middlesex Street–Minories–Tower Hill (east), the River Thames (south) and the Temple–Chancery Lane (west). All City streets – there are no 'roads' as such – bear the Corporation of London red sword on their nameplate. For easy exploring, in this book the City has been divided into areas roughly corresponding to the site of the original eight City gates – Aldgate, Aldersgate, Bishopsgate, Cripplegate, Ludgate, Moorgate, Newgate and Temple Bar – plus the Temple. For convenience, Shoreditch landmarks and the Tower have been included under the City.

ALDGATE, EC3

Aldgate (the old gate) led from the City east to Essex and is remembered in the name of a small stretch of main road and two tube stations (Aldgate and Aldgate East). Daniel Defoe's narrator in *A Journal of the Plague Year* (1722) recalls how 'there was no parish in or about London where [the plague] raged with such violence as in . . . Aldgate'. Pits were dug for fifty or sixty bodies, but by August 1665 larger holes were needed to cater for some 200 burials a week. The authorities were unable to dig the pits larger 'because of the order of the magistrates confining them to leave no bodies within six feet of the surface'. Alfred, Lord Tennyson, in his 1848 poem *Black Bull of Aldgate*, waits for 'this lousy coach that runs to Epping' outside the Black Bull pub (now demolished) in Aldgate.

- The Aldgate section includes the area immediately to the north and west of the Tower. Landmarks can be reached from Aldgate, Aldgate East or Tower Hill tubes and Fenchurch Street railway station.

clockwise around Aldgate and the Tower, from Bevis Marks

Bevis Marks

A common misconception about this road is that it's named after the founder of the Bevis Marks Synagogue; but Bevis Marks is a corruption of 'Buries Marks', the burial limits for the area on land once owned by the abbots of Bury St Edmunds. In Dickens's *The Old Curiosity Shop* (1841) no. 10 Bevis Marks is the home of Sampson Brass, 'an attorney of no very good repute'. Dickens recalled in a letter to his biographer, John Forster, in 1840, that when he came to the street to find Brass a suitable home, he got 'mingled up in a kind of social hash with the Jews of Houndsditch and roamed among them till I came out in Moorfields'.

Bevis Marks Synagogue, 2 Heneage Lane, off Bevis Marks
After a quarrel with the synagogue authorities in 1813 Isaac D'Israeli, Benjamin's father, decided to forsake Judaism and have his children baptized. This was how Benjamin Disraeli managed to enter Parliament at a time when Jews were not allowed in the House, and eventually become prime minister.

Aldgate

Aldgate Pump, junction of Aldgate, Fenchurch Street at Leadenhall Street
Dickens mentioned the pump in several works: there's a brief reference in *Uncommercial Traveller: Wapping Workhouse* (1860); in *Sketches By Boz* (1837) he talks of 'shabby gentility . . . as purely local as the statue at Charing Cross or the pump at Aldgate'; the connection is again made in *Nicholas Nickleby* (1839) in which the 'statue of Charing Cross' might be walking 'arm in arm with the pump from Aldgate'; and in *Dombey and Son* (1848) Mr Toots leaves 'the little company that evening . . . to take a little turn to Aldgate Pump and back'.

Aldgate High Street

Site of Geoffrey Chaucer's address (1374–86), no. 2
While engaged in customs duties for the Government at the nearby Port of London, Chaucer was allowed to live in the twin-towered gatehouse rent-free in return for allowing troops use of the fortification in time of attack. Soon after he moved in, the threat of invasion from the French saw Aldgate fortified with portcullises and a barbican. Chaucer

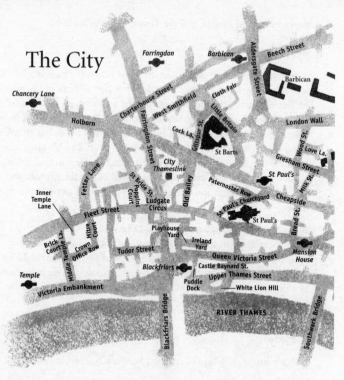

The City

wrote *Parlement of Foules* (1381), *Hous of Fame* (1385), *Troilus and Criseyde* (1385) and the *Legend of Good Women* (1391) while living here.

south along Mansell Street

Mansell Street

Former Royal Mint, Mansell Street at Royal Mint Street
Daniel Defoe sought sanctuary here for a month in 1692 after being involved with some businessmen who unsuccessfully insured ships during the war with France and were then declared bankrupt. After a month he fled to Bristol.

Tower Hill

Traitors imprisoned in the Tower were executed on Tower Hill; the most famous of these was Thomas More, who refused to accept the Act of Supremacy which made Henry VIII head of the English church and

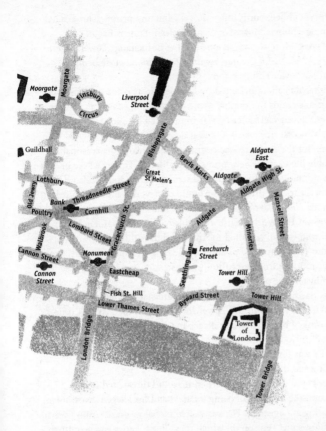

who was beheaded in 1535. More remained stoical to the end. On his way to the execution block a woman offered him a glass of wine and he replied: 'Marry, good woman, my master, Christ, had vinegar and gall and not wine given to him to drink.' As he was about to be beheaded More asked the axeman to be careful with his beard: 'That has not committed treason.'

Tower of London

'. . . and, if you can, burn down the Tower too' Jack Cade, from *Henry VI Part II*, William Shakespeare, 1591

The world-famous Tower of London, home of the Crown Jewels and one of Britain's most visited tourist attractions, began in 1078 as William the Conqueror's palace (Shakespeare erroneously thought it dated back to Julius Caesar's time). It has since served as a fortress, observatory, public records office, Royal Mint and prison. Those jailed here include Thomas More, Sir Walter Ralegh, Francis Bacon and Samuel Pepys. More was imprisoned in the Beauchamp Tower, where he wrote *A Dialogue of Comfort Against Tribulation* before being beheaded on Tower Hill (see above).

Sir Walter Ralegh, imprisoned by Elizabeth in 1592 for seducing one of the queen's maids of honour, wrote *Cynthia, the Lady of the Sea* in the Tower. Eleven years later he was imprisoned here for treason by Elizabeth's successor, James I. On that occasion he was threatened with execution, but the sentence was commuted and he lived a reasonably comfortable life in furnished rooms in the Bloody Tower, where he was joined (voluntarily) by his family and servants. Here Ralegh also had a laboratory for testing drugs and he wrote poetry, much of which is lost, although his *History of the World* (or, as Dante Gabriel Rossetti put it, 'Here writ was the World's History by his hand') survives. On his release in 1616 Ralegh returned to America, but within two years was back in the Tower, accused of abusing the king's confidence. This time the earlier reprieve from execution was rescinded and he was beheaded in Westminster (see p. 227).

Francis Bacon, the Elizabethan essayist and statesman, was sent to the Lieutenant's House in the Tower for bribery in 1621. At that time certain forms of bribery weren't illegal and Bacon thought he was safe. But he had misjudged the situation. Too ill to attend his own court hearing, he was fined £40,000 in his absence and imprisoned in the Tower for a few days.

Samuel Pepys was confined here in 1679 and threatened with execution on the grounds of being a Papist and for alleged involvement in murdering a magistrate. He was visited by fellow diarist John Evelyn, who brought some venison on which they dined. Pepys was acquitted the following year.

The Tower has featured as a setting in a variety of works. In Shakespeare's *Henry VI Part I* (1590) Edmund Mortimer, incarcerated in the Tower, tells Richard Plantagenet that he should have been king and that Richard is his rightful heir. Shakespeare made a mistake with his history and is confusing Mortimer with his uncle, also Edmund Mortimer. In *Henry VI Part III* (1591) Henry hands over the government to Warwick in the Tower and, while praying, is murdered here by Gloucester (the eventual Richard III). In the play of that name Richard is responsible for several deaths in the Tower: his older brother, Clarence, whose body is dropped into the malmsey (sweet wine); Lord Hastings after he refuses to help Richard seize the throne ('Thou art a traitor: off with his head'); and the so-called 'Princes in the Tower' – Edward V and the Duke of York, murdered by Dighton and Forrest on Richard's orders.

Other works which use the Tower as a setting include Christopher Marlowe's *Edward II* (1594), Walter Scott's *Peveril of the Peak* (1823) and Harrison Ainsworth's *The Tower of London* (1840), which is based on the nine-day reign of Lady Jane Grey between those of Henry VIII's heirs, Edward VI and Mary Tudor.

head west from the Tower along Byward Street

Byward Street

All Hallows Barking

Founded in the seventh century and built on land owned by an abbey in Barking, this church, which has since been rebuilt several times, is where Henry Howard, Earl of Surrey, the poet who introduced blank verse into English literature, was buried in 1547. William Penn, founder of Pennsylvania, was baptized here in 1644. During the Great Fire of London in 1666 Samuel Pepys climbed the steeple of this church and 'saw the saddest sight of desolation that I ever saw'.

head north along Seething Lane

Seething Lane

Site of Samuel Pepys's address (1660–73), Seething Lane at Pepys Street

One night in September 1666 Pepys was awakened by 'a great fire . . . in the City'. He wasn't particularly alarmed and went back to sleep for a few hours, but his attempt to ignore what became the Great Fire of London wasn't successful. Over the next few days the fire raged uncontrollably and eventually wiped out much of the city.

St Olave's, Seething Lane at Hart Street

Samuel Pepys and his wife are buried in the crypt of the church where he worshipped. The bust of Pepys's wife in the church nave was sited so that he could see it from his pew. To Charles Dickens, St Olave's was 'my best beloved churchyard – the churchyard of ghastly grim', and in *Uncommercial Traveller: City of the Absent* (1860) he described its 'ferocious strong spiked iron gate like a jail ornamented with skulls and cross bones'. John Betjeman thought St Olave's was 'like a country church in the world of Seething Lane'.

head back to Byward Street and west

Lower Thames Street

Custom House, Lower Thames Street opposite St Dunstan's Hill
Burnt, blown up and bombed over the centuries, Custom House was
where Geoffrey Chaucer worked as controller of export tax on wool,
appointed by Edward III in 1374 on an annual salary of £10. In
Anthony Trollope's *The Three Clerks* (1858) Scatterall yearns to secure
an appointment here. Custom House features a number of times in
Dickens's novels. Pip in *Great Expectations* (1861) leaves a boat on the
Thames outside Custom House as part of his plan to get Magwitch out
of the country.

Former Billingsgate Market, Lower Thames Street opposite St Mary at
Hill
George Orwell, in the early 1930s, used to work in the fish market that
was then situated here, starting at five in the morning as a 'scat' – push-
ing trolleys of fish to Eastcheap – and was paid the standard 'twopence
an up'. He wrote about how the work 'knocks it out of your thighs and
elbows' but that there were never enough jobs to tire one out. The fish
market is now situated in the Isle of Dogs and the building has since
been renovated into offices.

ALDERSGATE, EC1

The name Aldersgate derives from Ealdred's Gate and the route
through the gate used to lead into Watling Street, the Romans' Dover
to St Albans road. Much of the locale was destroyed in the 1940s but
some of the medieval street pattern of alleyways and passages remains;
John Betjeman when he lived here claimed that 'everything could be
reached on foot, down alleys and passages'.

• The Aldersgate section follows the route south from the medieval gate
  to the river. Landmarks to the north can be reached from Barbican
  tube; those nearer the cathedral from St Paul's tube and those further
  south from Mansion House tube.

Aldersgate Street to the river: north to south

Aldersgate Street

Site of John Milton's address (1660), between Beech Street and London Wall
Milton lived and wrote much of *Paradise Lost* (1667) in a house in Jewen Street which was destroyed in the Second World War. The Barbican block, Thomas More House, stands close to the site.

Site of Aldersgate, between Beech Street and London Wall
In the sixteenth century John Day, who introduced Anglo-Saxon type and italics to Britain, printed an early copy of the Bible, *The Folio Bible*, from a room above the gate. Samuel Pepys, in his 1660 diary, commented on the limbs of traitors hanging from Aldersgate. The gate was demolished in 1761. Thomas More House stands close to the site.

St Martin's-le-Grand

Site of General Post Office, east side, between Gresham Street and Cheapside
Before going to work in the Post Office that then stood on this site, the young Anthony Trollope would get up at 5.30 a.m., rigorously pen his target 250 words every 15 minutes for an hour or so before breakfast, and then set off for St Martin's-le-Grand. In 1841 after seven years of this ordeal he suffered a nervous breakdown which was also brought about by an accumulation of bad debts and, after recuperating, was transferred to Ireland. Trollope's major achievement as a post office worker was to invent the pillar box, and the authorities later also thanked him for 'regulating foreign mails and country deliveries'. Trollope's 1858 novel, *The Three Clerks*, is based on his Post Office experiences.

Paternoster Row

This hellish concrete precinct to the north of St Paul's Cathedral, probably London's ugliest post-war redevelopment, was one of the capital's major publishing areas until the Second World War, when it was destroyed in the 1940 Blitz (as covered by Anthony Powell in *The Military Philosophers* (1968) from the series *A Dance to the Music of Time*). In the eighteenth century Paternoster Row was home to the Chapter Coffee House, as patronized by James Boswell, and was where the ill-fated Thomas Chatterton was a regular, knowing 'all the geniuses there', as he claimed in a letter to his mother. The Chapter was the first place the Brontë sisters, Anne and Charlotte, stopped at on their initial trip to London in 1848.

St Paul's Churchyard

When Paternoster Row (and Paternoster Square, to the west) were leading publishing areas, St Paul's Churchyard was a centre for second-hand bookselling (also bombed to pieces in the Second World War). The original St Paul's school, where Leland the antiquarian was a student in the 1520s, Milton in the 1620s and Pepys in the 1640s, stood in St Paul's churchyard, to the east of the cathedral. In 1884 the school moved to Hammersmith and is now in Barnes.

St Paul's Cathedral

'He came out into what seemed the vast and void of Ludgate Circus, and saw St Paul's Cathedral sitting in the sky' from The Man Who Was Thursday,
G. K. Chesterton, 1908

Built on a prominent site at the top of Ludgate Hill, St Paul's was originally a seventh-century wooden church which burned down and was rebuilt several times before becoming the third biggest cathedral in Europe (after St Peter's, Milan, and Seville). After the Reformation St Paul's lost its status, and in its new role as a centre for every imaginable local venture the nave, Paul's Walk, came to be used as a market, with stalls selling groceries and animals, delivery boys cutting through to avoid the traffic and prostitutes touting for business.

In 1666 St Paul's burned down in the Fire of London. Samuel Pepys recalled in his diary 'the miserable sight of Paul's church with all the roofs fallen' and his contemporary, John Evelyn, watched the blaze and described how 'the stones of St Paul's flew like grenades'. St Paul's was rebuilt by Christopher Wren, aided by Evelyn and heralded by many as the finest example of Renaissance architecture in Britain – although, as Daniel Defoe explained in *A Tour Through the Whole Island of Great Britain* (1724–6), the building 'however magnificent in itself, stands with the infinite disadvantage as to the prospect of it'.

St Paul's in its former and current guise features in a host of books and plays: in Shakespeare's *Henry VI Part III* (1591) the king's funeral takes place here; Ben Jonson's *Every Man out of his Humour* (1599) is partly set in Paul's Walk (see above); and Harrison Ainsworth's *Old St Paul's* (1841) describes how the Fire wrecked the cathedral. 'The flames were descending the spiral staircase and forcing their way through the secret doors . . . white fluid streams of smoke crept through the mighty rafters of the roof.' In the book, Solomon Eagle walks on a cathedral parapet carrying his brazier of blazing charcoal and shouting warnings of doom over the city.

The 15-year-old Katherine Mansfield, on a visit to London in 1903, wrote home complaining about 'the pigeons that are constantly flying about'. She did however find the service 'fearfully impressive'. Evelyn Waugh revealed in a letter to his wife Laura that, despite taking his young son Auberon (minor novelist and major satirist) 'up the dome of St Paul's', giving him a packet of triangular stamps, and then taking him on to 'luncheon' at the Hyde Park Hotel one day in August 1945, the ungrateful mite told his grandmother that the day was 'a bit dull'. A furious Waugh Senior vowed that this was the 'last time I inconvenience myself for my children', with Laura given the onerous job of having to 'rub that in to him'.

St Paul's has memorials to:
- John Donne (1572–1631), 'alias Jack Donne, alias the Dean of St Paul's', as Angela Carter notes in *The Magic Toyshop* (1967). Donne was Dean from 1621 to 1631 and is remembered by a memorial in the south choir aisle, which shows him wrapped in a shroud standing on an urn awaiting his own resurrection. It was the only memorial to survive the 1666 Fire of London.
- Dr Samuel Johnson (1709–84), the Dictionary compiler and leading eighteenth-century man of letters.
- Sir Joshua Reynolds (1723–92), the painter and founder member of Dr Johnson's Literary Club.
- William Blake (1757–1827), poet, painter and mystic.
- Walter Besant (1836–1900), London historian and founder of the Society of Authors.
- Max Beerbohm (1872–1956), 'the incomparable Max', cartoonist and essayist.
- Walter de la Mare (1873–1956), poet and short story writer.
- T. E. Lawrence (1888–1935), 'Lawrence of Arabia' and chronicler of service life.

head south along Godliman Street

Queen Victoria Street

Site of Doctors' Commons, Queen Victoria Street opposite White Lion Hill

Dickens worked as a shorthand reporter in an office to the north of the long-demolished college for doctors of law that stood here, and gave

David Copperfield a job here as an articled clerk in the semi-autobiographical novel of the same name. In *Sketches by Boz:* 'Doctors' Commons' (1837) Dickens describes it as 'the place where they grant marriage-licences to love-sick couples, and divorce to unfaithful ones'.

White Lion Hill

St Benet's Church

Now rather forlorn-looking and located by some hideous concrete roadways, St Benet's is the Wren church where Henry Fielding married his first wife's maid, to hoots of derision from London society, in 1747.

Castle Baynard Street

Site of Baynard Castle

> '*If you thrive well, bring them to Baynard's Castle*' Richard, Duke of Gloucester, from *Richard III*, William Shakespeare, 1594

It was in this huge palace, once the alternative to the Tower on the west side of the City, that Richard of Gloucester was crowned Richard III in 1483, as Shakespeare records in the play of the same name. Baynard Castle was destroyed in the Great Fire (1666). A pub in nearby Queen Victoria Street has cleverly been named the Baynard Castle.

Upper Thames Street

Site of the Bar of Gold, south of Upper Thames Street and St Benet's Church

The Sherlock Holmes story 'The Man with the Twisted Lip' (1891) opens in an opium den, the Bar of Gold, where Watson, looking to rescue a friend, inadvertently discovers Sherlock Holmes who is investigating the mysterious disappearance of Neville St Clair, a city businessman last spotted (by his wife) supposedly screaming for help at a window above the den. In the story Conan Doyle describes the Bar of Gold as standing in (the fictitious) Upper Swandham Lane, 'a vile alley . . . east of London Bridge . . . near the corner of Paul's Wharf'. Holmes scholars have expended considerable energy trying to locate the den and the fictitious surrounding streets named in the story, but few have spotted that Paul's Wharf (until its recent demolition) was situated immediately south of St Benet's Church and St Paul's Cathedral, i.e. *west*, not east, of London Bridge; Conan Doyle, not for the first time, made a mistake with his London settings.

BISHOPSGATE, mostly EC3

In medieval times the bishops of London made hinges for the Bishops' Gate (which stood by Camomile Street, opposite the massive present-day NatWest Tower) in return for which they received one stick from every cart of wood passing through. To the north of Bishopsgate is Shoreditch, the setting for Henry Fielding's 1752 *Enquiry into the Causes of the Late Increase of Robbers*, in which he wrote about the 'destruction of all morality, decency and modesty; the swearing, whoredom and drunkenness' in the area. These days Shoreditch, though run-down and impoverished, is a less frenetic place and its dingy warehouses have recently started to prove popular with artists looking for cheap premises.

- The Bishopsgate section includes landmarks in Shoreditch and those further south in or near the road Bishopsgate and its continuations to the river. Landmarks to the north can be reached from Old Street tube; those further south from Monument tube (except where stated).

Bookshops

East Side, 116 Brick Lane, tel. 020 7247-0216, specialists in East End works.

Shoreditch end to the river: roughly north to south

Curtain Road

Site of The Theatre (1576–98), Curtain Road at Great Eastern Street, EC2

London's first theatre, designed as an amphitheatre with galleries and a one penny entrance charge, was opened by James Burbage, one of Lord Leicester's players, at the back of the George Inn on this site in 1576. Shakespeare is believed to have acted here and it is possible that the premiere of *Romeo and Juliet* was held at The Theatre in 1598. When the lease expired that year the landlord, Giles Allen, threatened to pull it down, citing the trouble that accompanied the shows, or, as he put it, 'the great and greevous abuses that grewe by the Theater'. But Cuthbert and Richard, Burbage's sons, who by then had succeeded their late father, were wise to Allen and in January 1599 took down the building, plank by plank, and carted it off to Bankside, south of the Thames in Southwark (the lease allowed the tenant to remove any theatrical buildings on the site). There they rebuilt it as the Globe, which lasted till the 1640s and has recently been rebuilt nearby (see p. 328).

- There is a plaque for The Theatre at no. 86 Curtain Road.

Site of the Curtain Theatre (1577–c. 1610), Curtain Road at Hewett Street, EC2

Opened to compete with James Burbage's theatre (see above), Henry Lanman's venue took its name not from the theatrical curtain but from the curtain wall of the nearby Holywell Priory. The premiere of Ben Jonson's *Every Man in his Humour* by the Lord Chamberlain's Company was held here in September 1597, with Shakespeare allegedly taking one of the roles. A car park now stands on the site.

Bishopsgate

Dirty Dick's, nos. 202–204, EC2, Liverpool Street tube

Dirty Dick was the sobriquet of Nathaniel Bentley, a local ironmonger who preserved the unused wedding breakfast that was left when his fiancée died on the eve of their marriage and who, despite the success of his ironmongery business, spent the rest of his life in squalor. Charles Dickens loosely based the post-nuptial fate of Miss Havisham in *Great Expectations* (1861) on the tale of Bentley. When the latter died, the landlord of the pub that stood here (not the present building) bought the contents of his shop and house – including what remained of the wedding breakfast – as well as the bodies of Bentley's dead cats, and they were displayed here until the 1980s.

Great St Helen's

Site of William Shakespeare's address (1598)

Records of the time show that a William Shakespeare lived in this passageway in 1598, although there is no proof that this Shakespeare was the playwright. Great St Helen's, which can be found between the huge NatWest Tower and the church of St Helen Bishopsgate, contains that City rarity – a house.

Crosby Square

Site of Crosby Place

'Presently repair to Crosby House . . . I will with all expedient duty see you'

Richard, Duke of Gloucester, from *Richard III*, William Shakespeare, 1594

Home to Richard in the 1480s before he became Richard III, some forty years later Thomas More moved in and here, ironically, wrote his censorious *History of King Richard III* (1518) as well as much of *Utopia* (1516). When it was demolished in 1908, the bricks were saved and in the 1920s the old hall was rebuilt into a student hostel in Chelsea (see p. 373). Crosby Square is now two small granite-walled alleyways.

Gracechurch Street

P. G. Wodehouse's workplace (1900–2), Hong Kong and Shanghai Bank, no. 9

Wodehouse recalled in his autobiography how he used to run from his Chelsea lodgings to the bank and, as he neared Gracechurch Street, would speed up and charge flat out through the entrance doors and up the stairs, cheered on by groups of clerks, so that he could clock in on time and save his bonus. Wodehouse's departure from the bank was nowhere near as impressive as his daily entrances. He resigned after admitting tearing out a page from a new ledger to write out one of his short stories. He might have got away with the misdeed, but after the head cashier had accused the head stationer of supplying defective materials the latter replied that only an imbecile would tear out the first page of a ledger. After a moment's thought (if the story can be believed) the cashier realized that he did in fact have an imbecile working under him – Wodehouse – who was summoned and interrogated and who admitted blame. This probably explains why Wodehouse later claimed he was the 'worst bungler ever to have entered the portals of the Hong Kong and Shanghai Bank'. Nevertheless his experiences at the bank (now closed) provided appropriate material for *Psmith in the City* (1910).

Leadenhall Market, 4 Bull's Head Passage

The Green Dragon pub (now demolished and replaced by a hairdresser's) gave Charles Dickens his model in *The Pickwick Papers* (1837) for the Blue Boar, the tavern in which Sam Weller wrote his famous 'Valentine'. The preserved, covered Leadenhall Market, with its sweeping arches and ironwork, also features in *Dombey and Son* (1848) and

Nicholas Nickleby (1839), although the present structure is not the original and dates from 1881.

Eastcheap

A far more important thoroughfare in medieval days than now, East-cheap, which runs east from Monument tube, was home to the Boar's Head Tavern, a medieval gathering place for writers. In Shakespeare's *Henry IV Part I* (1598) Falstaff and Prince Hal drink here, and Mistress Quickly, the landlady, described as 'a poor widow of Eastcheap', is derided in the line 'Doth the old boar feed in the old frank? . . . at the old place my Lord in Eastcheap'. Shakespeare was using a small measure of poetic licence in setting these scenes. Although the inn existed in his day, it had not when the royal party were supposed to have used it. So much for Oliver Goldsmith's claim about visiting the Boar's Head, using Hal's chair and 'sitting before the fire in the room that Falstaff had used'. The inn, which stood near where Monument tube can now be found, burned down in the Great Fire of 1666, was rebuilt, but was finally demolished during an early nineteenth-century road-building programme, as Washington Irving discovered to his chagrin when looking for the place during a visit to London.

Fish Street Hill

> *'Up Fish Street! down Saint Magnus' Corner! kill and knock down! throw them into Thames'* Jack Cade from *Henry VI Part II*, William Shakespeare, 1591

Shakespeare made a mistake in setting the scene containing the above line in Southwark. Fish Street (now Fish Street Hill) and Saint Magnus Corner are on the northern bank of the Thames and not in Southwark, south of the river. Oliver Goldsmith began his working life as a chemist in this street, once the main route leading to London Bridge.

The Monument, Fish Street Hill at Monument Street

The Monument was built by Christopher Wren as a memorial to the Great Fire of 1666 (which started in a baker's in nearby Pudding Lane) and should have sported a statue of Charles II at the top, but the king refused the honour, telling Wren, 'I didn't start the Fire.' A now largely forgotten conspiracy theory claimed that the fire was started deliber-ately by Catholics to purge the City of sin, and so in 1681, four years after the Monument was erected, its inscription was altered with the words 'But Popish frenzy, which wrought such horrors, is not yet quenched'. This led the Catholic Alexander Pope to write the lines:

'London's column, pointing at the skies/Like a tall bully, lifts the head and lies' in *To Lord Bathurst* from *Moral Essays* (1735). The 'Popish' reference was removed in 1831. The Monument features briefly in Dickens's *Martin Chuzzlewit* (1844), in which the doorman laughs at a couple who pay to ascend the 311 steps.

Lower Thames Street

St Magnus Martyr, Lower Thames Street opposite Pudding Lane
A favourite church of T. S. Eliot, who mentioned it in *The Waste Land* (see box, p. 30), the position of St Magnus Martyr shows how greatly the landscape has changed: the churchyard formed part of the roadway approach to London Bridge between 1176 and 1831. Miles Coverdale, the first person to translate the Bible into English, was Rector here in the sixteenth century and is buried in the church, which was rebuilt by Wren after the fire.

London Bridge

Sir Thomas More's head was displayed on London Bridge after he was executed at the Tower for treason in 1535, and a scarcely believable story has it that one of his daughters, passing under the bridge one day, saw the head and cried out, 'Oh how many times it has lain on my lap; oh God if only it could now fall into my lap!' – which of course it instantly did. She then safeguarded the skull and sent it to Canterbury Cathedral, where it has remained ever since. The arches that supported the old London Bridge (transported to Arizona in the 1970s) caused the Thames often to freeze in winter, allowing fairs to be held on the ice. John Evelyn in his diary for January 1684 wrote of people setting up stalls and even a printing press on the frozen waterway. Virginia Woolf picked up on the theme in *Orlando* (1928) and described the horror of a thaw which left people stranded on lumps of melting ice in the middle of the water. (Also, see River Thames, p. 242.)

CRIPPLEGATE, EC2

The least known of the old city gates stood at the north end of Wood Street and took its unusual name either from a cripples' hospital which once stood nearby or from the cripples who gathered by the gate to beg.

- The Cripplegate section includes the Barbican and the area immediately south as far as the river. Landmarks to the north can be reached from Barbican or St Paul's tubes; those further south from Mansion House tube.

Barbican to Southwark Bridge: north to south

Beech Street

The Barbican, around Beech Street
Central London's largest housing development, the Barbican, which is named after an ancient City fort, covers a huge area that had been bombed during the Second World War and consists of block after block of brutalist concrete skyscrapers, connected by walkways and labyrinthine paths; when built, they were the tallest in Europe. The towers are named somewhat desperately after the greats of early English literature – Daniel Defoe (Defoe House), Shakespeare (Shakespeare Tower), Ben Jonson (Ben Jonson House) and John Bunyan (Bunyan Court) – and dominate what is essentially a wealthy estate where social life revolves around the excellent Barbican Arts Centre, home of the Royal Shakespeare Company, an art-house cinema and art gallery. Elsewhere the Barbican is devoid of conspicuous life and is eerily quiet, but is the most densely populated area in the City.

head for St Giles's Church at the north-west end of Wood Street in the heart of the Barbican

Wood Street

St Giles Cripplegate, Wood Street, north-west end
An incongruous sight in its pedestrianized courtyard amid the Barbican towers, St Giles Cripplegate is not only the oldest building in the area but is just about the only remaining local property built before the Second World War. John Milton was buried here in 1674, and about a hundred years later his body was exhumed when the authorities were trying to find the grave so that they could place a bust of the essayist Francis Bacon nearby. When workmen discovered what they believed to be Milton's grave – no one was sure if it was his – they opened the coffin, disturbed the shroud (which caused the corpse's ribs to collapse) and then knocked out some teeth, which they kept as souvenirs. When William Cowper heard about this, he angrily wrote the poem *On the Late Indecent Liberties Taken with the Remains of Milton*. There is now a lifesize statue of the poet near the pulpit.

London Wall

Site of Shakespeare's address (1598–1600), south of London Wall, between Wood Street and Noble Street
No trace remains of the house or the street (Silver Street) where Shakespeare probably lived at the end of the sixteenth century and where he wrote a number of plays, including *Much Ado About Nothing* (1600) and *As You Like It* (1600). The property burned down in the Great Fire and was replaced by a pub, the Cooper's Arms, which attracted literary tourists until it was destroyed in the Second World War. Subsequent rebuilding wiped out almost every trace of the Cripplegate area.

Love Lane

Shakespeare statue, Love Lane at Aldermanbury
There is a bust of Shakespeare, who is thought to have lived nearby (see above), in the gardens that mark the site of the church of St Mary Aldermanbury (destroyed in the Second World War). The bust also commemorates Shakespeare's actor colleagues, Henry Condell and John Heming, who edited the First Folio (1623) and are buried in the churchyard.

continue along Wood Street until Gresham Street, then turn left

Gresham Street

St Lawrence Jewry, Gresham Street at Guildhall Yard
This exquisite Wren church, restored in the 1860s by the architect Blomfield, for whom Thomas Hardy then worked, features a stained-glass window of Thomas More, who was born in nearby Milk Street and who lectured here on St Augustine's *De Civitate Dei*. Samuel Pepys commented in his diary for 12 February 1664 that St Lawrence was 'a very fine church'.

Guildhall Yard

Guildhall
Now the setting for the presentation of the annual Booker Prize, the best-known literary prize in Britain, the Guildhall is the ancient seat of government for the body which runs the City of London. Pepys mentions in his 1663 diary how he attended a banquet for the French ambassador, who turned up the worse for wear. For centuries the Guildhall held trials; Henry Howard, Earl of Surrey, who introduced

blank verse into English poetry in the sixteenth century, was charged with treason here in 1547, and in Dickens's *The Pickwick Papers* (1837) the Bardell vs. Pickwick trial takes place here. Within the grounds is an excellent public library, which has a copy of a deed signed by Shakespeare for buying a house in Blackfriars.

return to Wood Street and turn left

Wood Street

Wordsworth's corner, Wood Street at Cheapside
William Wordsworth recalls in *The Reverie of Poor Susan* (1800) how 'At the corner of Wood Street, when daylight appears/Hangs a thrush that sings loud, it has sung for three years'. The corner in question is the western junction of Wood Street and Cheapside and is marked by the churchyard of St Peter West Cheap, which was destroyed in the Fire.

turn left at Cheapside

Cheapside

> 'For whan ther any ridyng was in Chepe/Out of the shoppe thider wolde he lepe' from *The Canterbury Tales (The Cook's Tale)*, Geoffrey Chaucer, *c.* 1392

Linking St Paul's and the area by the Bank of England, Cheapside was the chief market of medieval London and home to the long-gone pub, the Mitre, mentioned by Ben Jonson in *Every Man out of his Humour* (1599) in the lines 'No better place than the Mitre, that we may be spectators with you, Carlo'. In Martin Amis's *London Fields* (1989) Guy Clinch takes a bijou flat in Cheapside, 'trying to keep tabs on the proliferating, the pullulating hydra of Clinch money'.

Bread Street

John Donne was born in Bread Street in 1571, as was John Milton in 1608 in a long-gone house on the east side, about three doors down from Cheapside.

Milk Street

Thomas More was born on 7 February 1478 in the long-gone family home in this tiny street north of Cheapside.

Cheapside

Site of John Keats's address (1817), no. 76
Keats lived with his brothers in a house on this site when he was working as a dresser at Guy's Hospital, just south of the river. On Cheapside
he wrote *Ode to a Grecian Urn* before moving to Hampstead.

St Mary-le-Bow Church, Cheapside at Bow Lane
According to London legend, only those born within the sound of
these church bells are authentic cockneys. In Charles Dickens's *Dombey
and Son* (1848) 'the offices of Dombey & Son were within the liberties
of the City of London, and within hearing of Bow Bells'. In the vestibule there is a model of the city ablaze during the Great Fire.

head south along Bow Lane and west along Cannon Street

Cannon Street

Site of the Mermaid Tavern, south-west junction Cannon Street and
Bread Street
> *'What things have we seen/Done at the Mermaid!'* Francis Beaumont, letter
> to Ben Jonson, *c.* 1610

The Mermaid Club, founded by Ralegh in 1603 and whose members
included John Donne, Ben Jonson and Shakespeare, used to meet
regularly in the pub that stood here. In his poem *Lines on the
Mermaid Tavern* (1818) Keats asks 'Souls of poets dead and gone/What
Elysium have ye known/Happy field or mossy cavern/Choicer than the
Mermaid Tavern?' The Mermaid burned down in the Great Fire of
1666.

head south to Upper Thames Street and turn left

Upper Thames Street

Vintners' Hall, no. 68
During a dinner at the Hall in the 1930s thrown by the Saintsbury Club
literary group, Hilaire Belloc, somewhat overcome by the occasion,
downed a bottle of 1878 Latour, rose to make his speech and shouted in
the direction of one guest, Maurice Healey: 'Healey, Healey, this is
wine [which it was], I am drunk [which he was],' and slumped back
into his chair. He eventually pulled through and made a decent speech.

Southwark Bridge

In Charles Dickens's *Little Dorrit* (1857) John Chivery proposes to the heroine of the novel while 'putting his penny on the toll plate of the iron bridge'.

LUDGATE, EC4

Legend has it that Ludgate was built by the first-century BC warlord, King Lud, inspiration for Iain Sinclair's 1975 collection of poems, *Lud Heat*, and *King Lud* by the unrelated Andrew Sinclair (1988). It is remembered in the names of Ludgate Circus, Ludgate Hill and the pub, the Old King Lud.

• The Ludgate section includes the area from Holborn Viaduct south along Farringdon Street to the Thames. Landmarks can be reached from Blackfriars tube/City Thameslink railway station.

Holborn Viaduct end to the Thames: roughly north to south

Farringdon Street

Site of the London Coffee House (1731–1868), no. 42
In Dickens's *Little Dorrit* (1857) Arthur Clennam sits here out of the rain watching people while the church bells ring 'come to church, come to church . . . they won't come, they won't come'. The London Coffee House was a favourite of James Boswell's and stood roughly where Holborn Viaduct crosses Farringdon Street.

Site of Fleet Prison, between Fleet Lane and Ludgate Hill
John Donne was incarcerated in Fleet Prison in 1601 after being convicted of marrying a minor. Two lesser-known writers who spent time here were Thomas Nashe and John Cleland. Nashe was imprisoned a few years before Donne for writing the supposedly seditious and obscene play *The Isle of Dogs* (1597), now lost. Cleland, in the Fleet for debt, spent his time writing the risqué *Memoirs of a Woman of Pleasure* (1748), better known as *Fanny Hill*. Some scenes from Dickens's *The Pickwick Papers* (1837) were set in the prison: Mr Pickwick does a short stretch inside after refusing to pay costs and damages awarded to Mrs Bardell in the breach of promise case. The Fleet was pulled down in 1846.

Ludgate Circus

Edgar Wallace played truant from school when he was 11 to sell newspapers from a kiosk at Ludgate Circus.

head east along Ludgate Hill

Limeburner Lane

Site of *Woman's World* office

Oscar Wilde edited the magazine *Woman's World* in the late 1880s
from an office in this lane then exotically named La Belle Savage Yard
and until recently known by the more prosaic Seacoal Lane. Wilde's
hours, or rather hour, meant that he had to come to the office three
days a week at noon. After a few weeks this became too much for him
and he cut out one of his days. He also refused to answer his correspondence. 'I have known men come to London full of bright prospects and
seen them complete wrecks in a few months through a habit of answering letters.'

head south through the side streets to Ireland Yard

Ireland Yard

It is believed that Shakespeare in 1613 moved into a house in Ireland
Yard which he bought for £140. It was later destroyed in the 1666 Fire.
A small portion of the wall of the old Blackfriars Monastery remains in
Ireland Yard in the churchyard of the demolished St Ann's.

head west to Playhouse Yard

Playhouse Yard

Site of Blackfriars Monastery and Playhouse

Blackfriars, the area, station and bridge, are named after the Domini-
can monastery which stood roughly on the site of the modern-day
Playhouse Yard by the now-culverted River Fleet, and was broken up
in 1538 following Henry VIII's dissolution of the monasteries. Around
forty years later some of the buildings were used as a playhouse, and
towards the end of the century James Burbage, who had opened
London's first theatre in Shoreditch, bought the buildings. In 1608 a
new Burbage Company, the King's Men, whose number included
Shakespeare, took it over and early performances of the playwright's
Cymbeline (1611) were performed here. Burbage's theatre was closed by
the Puritans in 1642 and demolished thirteen years later. Ben Jonson,

who lived in the area from 1607 to 1616, set much of *The Alchemist* (1612) locally. Virginia Woolf featured Blackfriars in *Orlando* (1928); when Orlando returns to her Blackfriars home after an absence of a hundred years or so, she discovers that she faces a number of lawsuits, including one for being dead and one for being a woman 'which amounts to much the same thing'.

head south along Blackfriars Lane and turn left at Queen Victoria Street

Queen Victoria Street

Site of *The Times* office, no. 162

Graham Greene joined *The Times*'s staff as a sub-editor in 1927 when he was in his early twenties and later recalled in his autobiography, *A Sort of Life* (1971), that he was enraptured by the 'slow burning fire in the sub-editors' room, the gentle thud of coals as they dropped one by one in the old black grate'. He later claimed he could have happily spent his entire working life there 'had I not in the end succeeded in publishing a novel' – *The Man Within* (1929) – which was mostly written in Room 2, where the sub-editors sat. The site is now being redeveloped.

Puddle Dock

Geoffrey Chaucer is believed to have been born in 1343 or 1344 in a house that stood where Puddle Dock can now be found. Puddle Dock is now the location of the Mermaid Theatre, which was the City's first new theatre in 300 years when it opened in 1959.

MOORGATE, EC1

Moorgate was the City gate leading to the fens, high enough to allow soldiers to pass through with their pikes upright and 'very beautiful', according to Daniel Defoe in *A Tour Through the Whole Island of Great Britain* (1726). When it was demolished in 1762 the stones were used to secure London Bridge, which was then in danger of being washed away by the tides. Moorgate is now the name of a tube station and a traffic-laden street to the north of the Bank of England.

- The Moorgate section includes the area from Moorgate tube station south to the Bank of England and around Cornhill. Landmarks to the north can be reached from Moorgate tube; those further south from Bank tube.

Moorgate station end to Cannon Street: roughly north to south

Moorgate

Site of John Keats's birthplace and address (1795–1804), no. 85
Keats was born on 31 October 1795, in his father's livery stables next to the Swan and Hoop inn. A modern-day pub on the site has been thoughtfully titled John Keats at the Moorgate.

Finsbury Circus

Site of Bethlehem (Bedlam) Asylum, Finsbury Circus at Circus Place
> *'Of Bedlam beggars, who, with roaring voices,/Strike in their numb'd and
> mortified bare arms/Pins, wooden pricks, nailes, sprigs of rosemary . . .'*
> Edgar, from *King Lear*, William Shakespeare, 1605

Nathaniel Lee, the playwright and actor who quit performing with severe stage fright, was twice incarcerated in the asylum which stood here in the late seventeenth century. Lee once asked a visitor to leap off the roof with him to 'immortalise ourselves'. The visitor convinced Lee that it would be more immortalizing to leap up on to the roof, thereby saving the writer's life. In 1815 the asylum moved to Lambeth (see p. 345).

Lothbury

Ben Jonson described this small street as being 'possessed for the most part by founders that cast candlesticks, chafing-dishes, spice mortars and such like copper or laton works . . . making a loathsome noise to the by-passers . . . and therefore by them disdainfully called Lothberie'. The turning is now dominated by the back of the Bank of England and the Wren church of St Margaret, under which the Wallbrook stream flows.

head west along Gresham Street to Old Jewry

Old Jewry

William Caxton lived from 1438 to 1446 in an Old Jewry house (long gone) that belonged to mercer Robert Large and had previously been a synagogue. In 1446 Caxton left London for Bruges, where he learned about printing, and, on returning to England in 1476, he set up his first press in Westminster. Ben Jonson set some of *Every Man in his Humour* (1597) on the street. The Sherlock Holmes short story 'The Sussex Vampire' (1924) opens with the detective receiving a letter from the firm of Morrison, Morrison and Dodd of 46, Old Jewry.

head south along Old Jewry to Poultry

Poultry

Site of Thomas Hood's birthplace (1799), no. 31
Hood wrote the poem which went 'I remember I remember/The house where I was born'. Lutyens's Midland Bank now stands on the site.

head east

Threadneedle Street

Bank of England, Threadneedle Street at Princes Street
Hard though it may be to imagine a link between *The Wind in the Willows* and the Bank of England, the author of the former, Kenneth Grahame, had a senior role at the Bank at the end of the nineteenth century, rising in eighteen years from a lowly clerk's position to become Secretary between 1898 and 1908. Grahame's tenure was marked by a bizarre incident in 1903 when a customer handed him some documents and then fired a revolver at him. Some of the bullets turned out to be blanks and Grahame fled. The gunman then rushed into the Director's Library where the key was turned on him and he was eventually disarmed by the fire brigade with a powerful jet. He claimed he pulled the trigger only because Grahame had chosen documents bound with black ribbon – a sign that he was doomed. Grahame resigned in 1908, four months before *The Wind in the Willows* was published.

It was the playwright Richard Brinsley Sheridan who gave the Bank its famous nickname, 'the old lady of Threadneedle Street'.

Hugh Boone's patch, no. 51
In the Sherlock Holmes story 'The Man with the Twisted Lip' (1891) Hugh Boone, an irascible beggar with a shock of red hair, hideous features and boorish manners, sits by 'a small angle in the wall' on Threadneedle Street (which can only be at no. 51) and makes a fortune from sympathetic passers-by. Boone, however, is the *alter ego* of Neville St Clair, a supposedly respectable businessman who has lost his City job but now earns more as a beggar; his double life comes to an end when his wife inadvertently spots him in the window of an opium den,

the Bar of Gold (see p. 50). With this story some critics denounced Conan Doyle for peddling the middle-class conspiracy theory that beggars choose to beg because it pays, being more rewarding than 'real work'.

head south to Cornhill

Cornhill

> 'Thus I awoke and found myself on Cornhill' from *Piers Plowman*, William Langland, 1387

It's hard to appreciate nowadays that Cornhill is the highest hill in the City, which is why in medieval times it was the setting for the pillory, into which Daniel Defoe was placed in 1703 for writing a seditious pamphlet about the government (see Newgate Prison, p. 72, and Temple Bar, p. 75). A few years previously, London's first coffee house opened in St Michael's Alley, off Cornhill; such places subsequently became the hub of eighteenth-century literary life. In Charles Dickens's *A Christmas Carol* (1843) Scrooge's counting-house is in a courtyard off Cornhill facing 'the ancient tower of a church, whose gruff old bell was always peeping down at Scrooge out of a Gothic window in the wall'. The courtyard is probably Newman's Court, the church St Michael's Cornhill. The long-defunct *Cornhill* magazine turned down the first Sherlock Holmes story, *A Study in Scarlet*, in 1886.

west to east

Lloyd's Bank, no. 17

> 'It is a crime against literature to let him [T. S. Eliot] waste eight hours per diem in that bank' Ezra Pound, letter to John Quinn, 1920

When by 1917 T. S. Eliot felt that he would never succeed as a full-time professional writer and needed a day job that wasn't too physically exhausting, he took a post in the Colonial and Foreign Department of Lloyd's Bank. Yet only a few months after he started, *The Love Song of J. Alfred Prufrock* was published and a fellow bank worker professed himself amazed that the author was the banker in the 'immaculate black jacket and sponge-bag trousers and large tortoise-shell rimmed glasses'. Ezra Pound, Eliot's close friend, confidant, tireless promoter and occasional editor of his poems (the latter described Pound as *il miglior fabbro*, 'the better craftsman', in his dedication to *The Waste Land*) thought that Eliot's 'employment in a bank the worst waste in contemporary literature'. But Eliot claimed he needed the formal 9.30–5.30 work schedule to put him in the required frame of mind to produce poetry.

Over the next few years Eliot devised much poetry, including most of *The Waste Land*, while working here, jotting down notes in the office and taking inspiration from the surrounding streets and buildings (see box, p. 38). His habit of taking a shortcut between the bank and the church of St Mary Woolnoth along a tiny passage called Pope's Head Alley may have led to his being given the nickname 'the Pope'. In 1920 Eliot moved to Lloyd's head office at nearby 71 Lombard Street, returned here in 1923, and left finally in 1925 for a job with the publishers Faber & Gwyer (now Faber).

Former Royal Exchange, Cornhill opposite Change Alley
The first Royal Exchange opened in 1567, showing that London had arrived as a major trading city. Thomas Dekker, Shakespeare's contemporary, noted how when walking in the Exchange 'a man is put in mind of Babel, there is such confusion of languages'. The building closed as an Exchange in 1939 and is now offices.

Former Smith, Elder offices, no. 32 (formerly no. 65)
'We found 65 [Cornhill] to be a large bookseller's shop in a street almost as bustling as the Strand' Charlotte Brontë, letter to Mary Taylor, 1848
The Brontë sisters – Anne, Charlotte and Emily – passed themselves off as Acton, Currer and Ellis Bell in their correspondence with their publishers so as to avoid preconceived prejudice. When they visited Smith, Elder in person in 1848, Charlotte fished out a letter addressed to Currer Bell (herself) in front of Smith, and the latter retorted, 'Where did you get this?' She then explained what had happened. The Brontës later met William Makepeace Thackeray here but their encounter got off to a bad start. Charlotte turned up an hour late, complaining of a severe headache, and Thackeray's attempt to cut the ice fell flat when he asked Charlotte whether she had 'perceived the scent of their cigars'. Charlotte replied that she hadn't smelled any cigars, thereby failing to spot a line from her own *Jane Eyre*, and she then made things worse by pointing out Thackeray's literary shortcomings to him. He defended himself, she later explained, 'like a great Turk at a heathen'. A carved panel on the street door at no. 32 features a relief of the Brontë/Thackeray meeting and portrays the now defunct Garraway's Coffee House, a local favourite of Dickens.

Site of Thomas Gray's birthplace (1716), no. 39
Although best known for the rustic *Elegy Written in a Country Churchyard* (1751) Thomas Gray was born in 1716 in a house which stood at what is now 39 Cornhill. A bank can now be found on the site.

head south-west to Lombard Street

Lombard Street

St Mary Woolnoth, Lombard Street at King William Street
Hawksmoor's only City church, St Mary Woolnoth, is mentioned in
T. S. Eliot's *The Waste Land* (1922, see box, p. 38) and features in Peter
Ackroyd's 1985 mystery, *Hawksmoor*.

head west to Bank tube

Mansion House Place

Mansion House
For over two hundred years Mansion House has been the home of the
Lord Mayor of London, nowadays a purely decorative post and not to
be confused with the newly created political post of *Mayor* of London.
In George and Weedon Grossmith's *The Diary of a Nobody* (1892) a
wonderful scene of one-upmanship and class envy takes place here
when Charles Pooter, the laughable hero of the book, turns up at the
Lord Mayor's Ball and finds to his horror that his ironmonger,
Farmerson, has also been invited. Farmerson, to Pooter's horror,
knows one of the sheriffs, which prompts Pooter to enter in his diary:
'To think that a man who mends our scraper should know any
member of the aristocracy.' The line not only encapsulates Pooter's
snobbishness, it also reveals his ignorance: sheriffs are appointed and
are no more aristocratic than Pooter, whose discomfort continues
throughout the evening, climaxing in a humiliating scene in which he
falls over in front of all the guests while dancing. In 1880 the *Diary*'s
main author, George Grossmith, had himself attended a Mansion
House function at which he met Mark Twain.

Walbrook

St Stephen Walbrook, Walbrook at St Stephen's Row
Considered by many to be Wren's masterpiece but bombed during the
Second World War, St Stephen Walbrook is the burial place of the
playwright-architect Sir John Vanbrugh, who died in 1726.

Cannon Street

London Stone, no. 111, Cannon Street tube

> *'At length he sat on London Stone and heard Jerusalem's voice'* from *Jerusalem*, William Blake, 1820

In Shakespeare's *Henry VI Part II* (1591) Jack Cade, the Kent rebel who led a band of men to London in 1450 to try and seize control of the city, stops for a rest by the ancient monument of London Stone (which may have been the Roman milestone for all British distances) and orders the 'pissing-conduit [the poor people's well] run nothing but claret wine this first year of our reign'. Cade saw off the unpopular Lord Treasurer, James Fiennes, but was routed a few days later when Londoners tired of the rebellion. In 1742 London Stone was built into St Swithin's Church, which stood at this site until it was bombed in the Second World War. A fragment of London Stone is now encased at this spot.

NEWGATE, EC4

Probably the earliest of the city gates, and the biggest, Newgate was used as a prison until a purpose-built gaol was constructed on the site of the present Central Criminal Court (the Old Bailey) in the 1420s. John Gay's *Beggar's Opera* (1728), the first ballad opera and a satire of government corruption, is set in the Newgate underworld.

- The Newgate section includes Smithfield. Landmarks to the north can be reached from Barbican tube; those further south from St Paul's tube.

Smithfield Market to Ludgate Hill: roughly north to south

Charterhouse Street

Smithfield Meat Market, north side West Smithfield roundabout
The well-known Smithfield meat market dates back to 1638 and somehow struggles on despite draconian EC legislation. In Dickens's *Oliver Twist* (1839) Oliver passes by during the morning when the market is in full swing and is amazed how the ground is 'covered nearly ankle-deep with filth and mire; a thick stream perpetually arising from the reeking bodies of the cattle'. Pip in Dickens's *Great Expectations* (1861) describes the market as a 'shameful place, being all asmear with filth and fat and blood and foam'.

West Smithfield

West Smithfield – the name Smithfield is a corruption of smooth field – is the name of the roundabout to the south of the Smithfield meat market and the street that leads west from there to Farringdon Street. In the Middle Ages it was an open space regularly used for jousting and other sports and for executing martyrs. In Shakespeare's *Henry VI Part II* (1591) Jack Cade and his gang come to Smithfield to plot their eventually unsuccessful revolt against high taxes and political incompetence.

Site of Bartholomew Fair, south-east side West Smithfield roundabout

> '*The Fair/Holden where martyrs suffered in past time/And named of*
> *St Bartholomew*' from *The Prelude*, William Wordsworth, 1805

Bartholomew Fair, best known from the Ben Jonson play of the same name which follows the fortunes of characters at the event, was a medieval fair and cattle market held every year from 1133 until 1855 on land to the west of where St Bartholomew's Hospital stands. Samuel Pepys wrote about the wrestling at the fair in his diary, and in Defoe's *Moll Flanders* (1722) the heroine attends the fair, where she meets 'a gentleman extremely well dressed and very rich'. In the seventh book of *The Prelude* (1805) Wordsworth rails against the 'anarchy and din' of the fair, and mentions the 'Albinos, painted Indians, Dwarfs, the Horse of knowledge, and the learned Pig'. Wordsworth also refers to the Protestant martyrs who were executed here during Queen Mary's reign.

Cloth Fair

The name of this small but attractive street recalls the origins of Bartholomew Fair as a cloth fair.

St Bartholomew-the-Great

When the poet Vernon Watkins married Enigma code-breaker Gwen Davies at what is London's oldest parish church during the Second World War, he unwisely chose Dylan Thomas to be best man. Thomas failed to turn up and took two weeks to apologize. Nevertheless Watkins forgave him and after Thomas's death edited a collected edition of his poetry. In 1972 he was pipped to the poet laureate position by John Betjeman. It was probably outside St Bartholomew's church that Peasants' Revolt leader Wat Tyler was stabbed to death in 1381.

John Betjeman's address (1955–77), no. 43

Betjeman began using this address as his London base when his marriage fell apart and around the same time he began writing his popular

Spectator column, 'City and Suburban', an affectionate lament about the supposed horrors of modern life – concrete lampposts, haphazard growth of the suburbs – which became instrumental in creating a nostalgia for Victoriana and Edwardiana. Betjeman moved out of Cloth Fair in the 1970s, claiming that 'the noise of articulated lorries coming in from Europe in the small hours drove me out'. The downstairs area is now a restaurant, named, predictably, 'Betjeman's'.

head south

Bartholomew Close

John Milton took refuge in a friend's house in this close in the 1650s, fearing for his life following the restoration of the throne. The painter William Hogarth was born in a house which stood at no. 58 in 1697.

follow Bartholomew Close round to Little Britain

Little Britain

In the late fifteenth century, following the success of William Caxton's printing press in Westminster, printers began setting up hand-presses in the maze of streets around Smithfield's Little Britain. In a bookshop here, around two hundred years later, a bookseller implored the Earl of Dorset to take as many copies of Milton's *Paradise Lost* (1667) as he could carry: no one wanted to buy them. (Ironically, Milton had lived in the street in 1662.) Forty years later, the three-year-old Samuel Johnson came with his mother to London so that his skin disease could be cured. While in the capital they stayed in Little Britain. When Pip arrives in London for the first time in Charles Dickens's *Great Expectations* (1861), he makes for the lawyer Jaggers's office in Little Britain, 'a most dismal place', to hear about his 'great expectations'.

return to West Smithfield and head south along Giltspur Street

Giltspur Street

St Bartholomew's Hospital

Sherlock Holmes meets Dr Watson for the first time at this famous hospital (better known as Bart's) in the first Sherlock Holmes story, *A Study in Scarlet* (1887, see the Sherlock Holmes Walk, p. 172). In Dickens's *The Pickwick Papers* (1837) Jack Hopkins tells of a boy who comes here for treatment after swallowing a necklace which 'makes such a devil of a noise when he walks about they're obliged to muffle him in a watchman's coat for fear he should wake the patients'. Robert

Bridges graduated from the medical school in 1874 and then became a physician at Bart's. (He was appointed poet laureate in 1913.) Aldous Huxley briefly had a part-time job in the 1930s distributing books to patients in the male ward. He used to complain that he had to remember everyone's requests by heart as there was no time to write them down.

The hospital was founded in 1123 by Rahere, jester to Henry I, who was taken ill on a pilgrimage and vowed to found a hospital dedicated to St Bartholomew if he survived. An angel then supposedly appeared before Rahere and demanded a church as well. Rahere founded an Augustinian Priory, the only surviving section of which is the church of St Bartholomew the Great (see below).

- Tours of the complex taking in the churches of St Bartholomew the Great and St Bartholomew the Less, the local alleyways, and the hospital Great Hall with its original Hogarths, take place every Friday at 2 p.m. For details tel. 020 7837-0546.

Cock Lane

In the fourteenth century Cock Lane was the only place in London where licensed prostitutes could solicit for trade. In 1762 there were reports that a ghost had manifested itself to a girl at no. 33. Thousands came by to verify the claim, including Dr Johnson, who wrote an *Account of the Detection of the Imposture in Cock Lane*. A cherub at the corner of Cock Lane and Giltspur Street (Pie Corner, as featured in Ben Jonson's *The Alchemist* (1610)) marks what is believed to be the most westerly spot reached by the Great Fire of 1666.

head south

Giltspur Street

The Church of the Holy Sepulchre

A plaque on the east wall of this church (from where the Crusaders left for Jerusalem) is dedicated to Charles Lamb, the essayist who was a Bluecoat boy at Christ's Hospital which once stood here; it hopefully describes him as 'perhaps the most loved name in English literature'. Lamb wrote about drinking egg-hot, an unlikely concoction made from beer, eggs, sugar and nutmeg, with Coleridge and Southey at the Salutation and Cat, a long-gone pub which stood just south of the church.

Old Bailey

Site of Newgate Prison, Old Bailey at Newgate Street
Some of Britain's greatest pre-modern-day writers – Sir Thomas
Malory, Ben Jonson, Christopher Marlowe, Daniel Defoe, John Milton
and William Cobbett – spent time in the prison that stood on this site
(now occupied by the Central Criminal Court). Malory wrote *Morte
D'Arthur* (1485) inside while serving a term for murder from 1469–1470
and, though mystery surrounds his identity, he is believed to have died
in the prison. Ben Jonson was imprisoned here for killing a man in a
duel in Hoxton (see p. 269). A later inmate was Christopher Marlowe,
remanded while awaiting sentence on a murder charge. He was
acquitted.

Daniel Defoe was particularly unlucky to be sent to Newgate after
getting caught up in the political fall-out following the removal of the
Catholic/High Church/Tory King James II who was replaced by the
Protestant William of Orange in 1689. Although Defoe was a dissenter
and a William III supporter, in 1702 he published an anonymous satirical pamphlet, *The Shortest Way with the Dissenters*, written from the
point of view of a High Church Tory but so fulsomely that it ridiculed
the Tories' arguments. It was too clever; many people took it seriously
and, when it transpired that the author was Defoe, he was cast into the
pillory in Cornhill and Temple Bar (see p. 75) and sent to Newgate. He
used the experience to write the prison scenes in *Moll Flanders* (1722),
the heroine of which is born here.

In 1727 the poet Richard Savage was jailed in Newgate after killing a
man in a tavern brawl but claimed to be enjoying himself 'with much
more tranquillity than I have known upwards of a twelve month past',
as Samuel Johnson recounted in *The Lives of the English Poets* (1781).
When Milton was here prison officers burned his books – those that
advocated freedom against the Stuart doctrine of the divine right of
kings – in the prison yard. William Cobbett spent two years in Newgate (1810–12) after publishing an article on flogging in the army which
annoyed the authoritarian prime minister, Lord Liverpool. The jury
took only five minutes to find Cobbett guilty and fined him the then
punitive sum of £1,000. He was however granted ten hours of visiting
time a day and was able to continue publishing his radical journal, *The
Political Register*. One of its last inmates before the place was demolished was Oscar Wilde, who spent a short time here in 1895 after being
found guilty at the Central Criminal Court (see below) of gross
indecency.

Dickens, fascinated as a young man by the sight of the bodies of recently executed prisoners on display outside, featured Newgate in several novels. He included the story 'A Visit to Newgate' in *Sketches by Boz* (1837). In *Oliver Twist* (1839) Fagin is tried, sentenced and executed here. In *Barnaby Rudge* (1841) Dickens tells how prisoners who had escaped during the Gordon Riots returned the next day, 'drawn back to their old place of captivity by some indescribable attraction', and were flung back into their cells. Rudge, the simpleton hero of the novel, is imprisoned in Newgate for taking part in the Riots and is freed by the mob. The prison was demolished in 1902.

Central Criminal Court, Old Bailey at Newgate Street
Better known as the Old Bailey (the name of the road which runs alongside), the Court has witnessed the trials of some of the most infamous criminals of recent decades, including the murderer Dr Crippen, the Second World War traitor Lord Haw-Haw and the gangland leaders Reggie and Ronnie Kray. Occasionally literary figures who have fallen foul of the law have ended up here. In 1895 Oscar Wilde was tried in the old courts that stood on this site after his libel suit against the Marquess of Queensberry collapsed. The Marquess had intimated in a postcard that Wilde was a homosexual (see Mayfair, p. 190) – Wilde *had* been conducting an affair with the Marquess's son, Lord Alfred Douglas – but he sued the Marquess for criminal libel. At the time, before his downfall, his wit was in fine form and, on leaving court one night, he proclaimed to the press: 'the working classes are with me . . . to a boy'. Eventually his case collapsed and he was then open to prosecution on the grounds that the Marquess had alleged, sodomy. Wilde was found guilty on six counts and given two years' hard labour in Reading gaol. Outside the gaol Wilde, watched by a large crowd which included W. B. Yeats, was led away in chains and taunted by a gaggle of prostitutes, one of whom shouted, ''e'll 'ave 'is 'air cut regular now!'

In 1932 Compton Mackenzie was tried at the 'Bailey for breaching the Official Secrets Act in his book *Greek Memories*. In 1960 Penguin Books were accused of obscenity over the publication of D. H. Lawrence's *Lady Chatterley's Lover*. One of the witnesses for the defence was E. M. Forster, who, asked how he would rate D. H. Lawrence, replied: 'I would place him enormously high. The greatest imaginative writer of his generation.' Penguin were cleared. Various mystery/thriller/crime writers have set stories here, including Margery Allingham's *Flowers for the Judge* (1936), Josephine Tey's *The Man in the Queue* (1953), Julian Symons's *The Blackheath Poisonings* (1978) and, of course, countless John Mortimer *Rumpole of the Bailey* episodes.

head east along Ludgate Hill

Stationers Hall Court

Stationers' Hall, Stationers Hall Court, north off Ludgate Hill
A 1557 charter awarded to the Stationers' Company ruled that all published work be registered here. The law was dropped in 1911 as so many publishers were ignoring it.

TEMPLE BAR, EC4

Temple Bar at the junction of Strand and Fleet Street was the City's traditional western barrier and was originally a chain tied between two posts. A gate with prison above was built in 1351 and then rebuilt by Christopher Wren in the 1670s, before being taken down in 1878 and eventually moved to Theobald's Park, Hertfordshire. The site is now marked by Charles Birch's bronze griffin, the City's unofficial emblem. North of Fleet Street the City's greatest concentration of medieval alleyways can still be found. Samuel Johnson once said that to get to know London 'you must not be satisfied with seeing its great streets and squares but must survey the innumerable little lanes and courts'.

● Landmarks to the west can be reached from Temple tube; those further east from Blackfriars tube.

Chancery Lane to Ludgate Circus: roughly west to east

Fleet Street

> *'The man must have a rare recipe for melancholy who can be dull in Fleet-street'* from *Essays of Elia*, Charles Lamb, 1823

Until the late twentieth century Fleet Street was the home of Britain's newspaper industry, and the name is still used as a catch-all term for the press even though papers are no longer based here. Publishing first came to the area around 1500 when Wynkyn de Worde, a former apprentice of William Caxton, moved his printing press to the area on account of its good location between Westminster and the centre of the City. Fleet Street's first newspaper was *The Daily Courant*, which appeared on 11 March 1702. It was followed by a host of titles, and by the late nineteenth century most of the present-day nationals were based in or around Fleet Street, making the area one of the most exciting in London, with journalists, printers and compositors rushing from office to drinking club. In his biography of G. K. Chesterton, Dudley

Barker described the roaring discussions in the taverns 'that went on hour after hour' and of articles 'scribbled on odd sheets of paper wedged on the pub table'.

Hundreds of writers have worked in Fleet Street. Samuel Richardson was a printer here before becoming a writer and pioneering the English novel. William Cobbett started *The Political Register* while living locally from 1802 to 1835. Raymond Chandler, Evelyn Waugh and Graham Greene worked as sub-editors in the early years of the twentieth century. Hilaire Belloc was literary editor on *The Morning Post* but he could never take orders from a superior, or keep regular hours, and was sacked for disobedience. Many novels have attempted to portray Fleet Street as a newspaper centre, the most famous of which is Evelyn Waugh's *Scoop* (1938) in which *The Daily Beast* is based at Copper House, nos. 700–853 Fleet Street (the real numbers don't quite reach that high). The exodus of titles to Docklands began in the mid-1980s when Rupert Murdoch's News International group (*The Times, Sunday Times, Sun* and *News of the World*) suddenly left for Wapping amid much controversy. Fleet Street is still busy but a shadow of its former self.

- Anthony Hope Hawkins worked out the plot for *The Prisoner of Zenda* (1894) while walking along Fleet Street *en route* to his chambers in the Temple.

Temple Bar, junction Fleet Street and Strand
In medieval times heads of those executed were displayed in Temple Bar, as Orlando notes in the Virginia Woolf novel of the same name. Alongside Temple Bar in medieval times stood the pillory into which Daniel Defoe, as part of his punishment for writing a supposedly seditious pamphlet about dissenters, was placed in 1703 (see Newgate Prison, p. 72). The punishment backfired: Defoe was cheered by supporters, who chanted his poem *Hymn to the Pillory* and sold copies of it in the surrounding streets, and in the pillory he was pelted not with the usual eggs but with flowers thrown by flower girls.

Site of Tellson's Bank, no. 1
In 1678 John Dryden deposited £50 with the bank which then stood here as a reward for anyone who could give him information regarding the thugs who beat him up in Rose Alley, Covent Garden. (They were in the pay of the Earl of Rochester, who wrongly believed that Dryden had written an essay satirizing him and the king.) Charles Dickens sited Tellson's Bank, 'very small, very dark, very ugly, very incommodious', in *A Tale of Two Cities* (1859) at no. 1 Fleet Street.

Site of the Devil's Tavern, no. 2

The Apollo Club, one of London's first literary groups and founded by Ben Jonson, began meeting in the mid-sixteenth century at the Devil's Tavern which was destroyed in the Great Fire of London (1666) and rebuilt. Later patrons included Alexander Pope and Dr Johnson. The building was demolished in 1787.

Prince Henry's Room, no. 17

This first-floor room with its preserved Jacobean ceiling, named after James I's elder son who died at 18 before being able to take the throne, has a permanent exhibition devoted to Samuel Pepys, who may have used the place when it was a tavern in the seventeenth century. No. 17 later housed Mrs Salmon's Waxworks, as visited by Boswell, and mentioned by Dickens in *David Copperfield* (1850).

Former *London Daily News* office, nos. 19–22

In 1906 a *Daily News* journalist, Arthur Machen, was fired from the paper for writing an obituary on Lord Alfred Douglas (Oscar Wilde's lover) which called him a 'degenerate'. There was one slight problem: Douglas was still alive. He sued, won £1,000, and got Machen fired.

Ye Old Cock Tavern, no. 22

T. S. Eliot used to lunch here in the 1920s with the art critic Herbert Read and Harold Monro from Bloomsbury's Poetry Bookshop while planning the launch of the literary magazine *Criterion*. Despite the name, the pub is barely a hundred years old, having replaced the original Cock which stood opposite.

Site of the Cocke Taverne, no. 190 (north side)

> 'O plump head-waiter at the Cock. To which I most resort/How goes the time? Tis five o'clock. Go fetch a pint of port' from *Will Waterproof's Lyrical Monologue*, Alfred, Lord Tennyson, 1842

It was at the Cock that Samuel Pepys 'drank and ate a lobster and sang, and mightily merry' before carrying Mrs Pierce home. In Virginia Woolf's *Orlando* (1928) the hero/heroine meets the poet Nicholas Greene at the Cock and the latter relates the story of a drunken night at the tavern with Christopher Marlowe and Shakespeare in which Marlowe tells Shakespeare, 'Stap my vitals, Bill . . . there's a great wave coming and you're on the top of it.' The pub, which entertained Dr Johnson, Dickens and Tennyson, was demolished in 1887 and rebuilt opposite, where it still stands (see above).

Clifford's Inn, Fleet Street at Clifford's Inn Passage
Featured by Dickens on several occasions, this former Inn of Chancery,
home of Leonard and Virginia Woolf from 1912 to 1913, was almost
entirely demolished in 1934. The passage from Fleet Street remains.

Former Harrison's Toy Shop, no. 31
In Dickens's *David Copperfield* (1850) the hero stops outside this now
rebuilt shop to see the giants of the St Dunstan clock opposite strike
the bells at noon.

Former *Quarterly Review* headquarters, no. 32
It was here in 1809 that publisher John Murray founded *The Quarterly
Review*, a Tory alternative to the Whig *Edinburgh Review*. One of the
publication's driving forces was Walter Scott, who once reviewed his
own *Tales of My Landlord* in its pages. The *Review* also made a scathing
attack on Keats's *Endymion*, which some allege contributed to the
poet's death.

St Dunstan-in-the-West, Fleet Street at Hen and Chickens Court
> '*Strike me ugly, if I should not find as much pleasure in choosing my mistress
> by the information of a lamp under the clock of St Dunstan's*' from The
> Vicar of Wakefield, Oliver Goldsmith, 1766

John Donne was the seventeenth-century rector of this church, best
known for its unusual clock which features two burly figures who
strike the bells on the quarter-hour. William Tyndale, whose translations of the New Testament from the Greek provided the basis for the
King James Bible, preached here in the sixteenth century. The church
has a memorial tablet on an outside wall to its best-known warden,
Izaak Walton, whose fishing bible, *The Compleat Angler*, was first published on the church's press in 1653. Pepys turned up here in 1667, a
year after the Great Fire, to hear a sermon, but was distracted by the
sight of a 'pretty, modest maid' who, rather than succumb to the
diarist's charms, moved further and further away from him and took
pins out of her pocket with which she could jab him if he strayed too
near. Not giving up, Pepys went for another maid (all this while the service continued), who also moved off once Pepys approached. In
Charles Dickens's *Barnaby Rudge* (1841) Maypole Hugh hears the
church clock's giants striking upon the bell before knocking at Middle
Temple Gate. Three years later, Dickens dedicated his Christmas story,
The Chimes, to St Dunstan's.

Site of the Mitre, no. 37
Samuel Johnson, who lived at various addresses a few hundred yards
from the Mitre, claimed that a seat here was 'the throne of human

felicity', and it was here in 1763 that he and Boswell cemented their relationship after meeting for the first time in a Covent Garden book-shop (see p. 115). After Johnson died, successive landlords made the most of references Boswell had made to the tavern in his biography of the dictionary compiler and they kept a cast of Johnson and a plaque above his seat. The Mitre was demolished in 1829.

El Vino, no. 47

The newspaper world's favourite wine bar in Fleet Street's hey-day remains largely unchanged physically, despite the departure of its bed-rock clientele, but socially it has joined the modern world: women are no longer obliged to sit down and be waited upon (even though they must still wear skirts) and men must be wearing ties and jackets. (Lord Marsh was once ejected for wearing a safari suit, despite being chair-man of the Newspapers Publishers' Association at the time.) The one writer particularly associated with El Vino's is G. K. Chesterton, who came here for what he called 'hard drinking and hard thinking' in the early years of the twentieth century. Chesterton would toil away at a table hour after hour despite being completely drunk, and would receive a visit at around six in the evening from friends such as Hilaire Belloc. Chesterton always used to take a hansom cab on leaving the place, even if he was only going to newspaper offices a few hundred yards away, such was his drunken state.

Fetter Lane

Lemuel Gulliver, hero of Jonathan Swift's *Gulliver's Travels* (1726), lives in Fetter Lane.

Site of the Old Curiosity Shop, no. 24

It was a shop which stood on this site in the nineteenth century, as opposed to the so-called Old Curiosity Shop on Portsmouth Street, Holborn, that Dickens probably used as the model for the shop after which his 1841 novel is named. An alternative theory has the original Old Curiosity Shop based at 10 Orange Street, by Leicester Square.

back to Fleet Street and head east along the north side of the road

Johnson's Court

Samuel Johnson lived in a now demolished house at 7 Johnson's Court from 1765 to 1776 and there wrote *A Journey to the Western Isles of Scot-land*. In 1833 Charles Dickens mailed his first story 'in a dark letter-box in a dark office in a dark court in Fleet Street' – the offices of the long-defunct *Monthly Magazine* which stood here.

Bolt Court

Johnson moved in 1776 to 8 Bolt Court, where he died in 1784. The house burned down in 1819. In Virginia Woolf's *Orlando* (1928) the hero/heroine of the novel stands beneath the window of no. 8 watching the outline on the blind of three shadows – Johnson, James Boswell and Mrs Williams – drinking tea. (See Virginia Woolf walk, p. 32.)

head up Hind Court to Gough Square

Gough Square

Dr Johnson's address (1748–58)/Dr Johnson's House, no. 17, tel. 020 7353-3745, Open 11–5 Mon.–Sat. Admission charge.
Johnson wrote his ground-breaking *Dictionary* (1755) in this large brick Georgian house north of Fleet Street, which he bought for its spacious attic and proximity to his printers and which is now a museum dedicated to him. Although over six foot, a giant for his time, Johnson was worried about being attacked, and fixed to the door a heavy chain which is still there. Soon after moving here, Johnson began producing a twice-weekly periodical, *The Rambler* (1750), most of which he wrote himself; in 1752 when his wife, Tetty, died he turned his attention to the *Dictionary* for which he is still best known, compiling it in the garret along with six, mostly Scottish, clerks who worked standing up. Lonely at night with Tetty gone, he would wander the streets looking for prostitutes. When the *Dictionary* was finished, Johnson moved to nearby Staple Inn. Some time after he died the house became a hotel

---

Johnson's *Dictionary* wasn't the first dictionary in the English language, but it was the first with etymologies and examples of usage. It also contains a few errors. He defined pastern (the part of a horse's foot between the fetlock and the hoof) as the knee, and, when asked why, explained, 'Ignorance, madam, pure ignorance.' Then there was the odd verbose definition. Network is defined as 'Anything reticulated or decussated, at equal distances, with interstices between the intersections.' Better remembered is the trenchant wit. Lexicographer is 'A writer of dictionaries; a harmless drudge', and, most memorably of all, Oats: 'A grain, which in England is generally given to horses, but in Scotland supports people.'

and was in a state of near collapse when it was rescued by Lord Harmsworth in 1910. The museum contains a number of the doctor's personal artefacts, a first-edition copy of the *Dictionary*, his 'gout' chair from the Olde Cock Tavern designed to ease the weight from the legs, and various portraits of Johnson and contemporaries such as Kitty Fisher, Drury Lane singer and mistress to many, but not to Johnson.

head east to Wine Office Court, past the statue of Johnson's cat Hodge, 'a very fine cat indeed'

Wine Office Court

Site of Oliver Goldsmith's address (1760–62), no. 6

Although Goldsmith had two rooms in a house at this address he could barely afford the rent, much to the displeasure of the landlady, who threatened to have him arrested for non-payment. Things improved when Dr Johnson intervened and offered to sell one of Goldsmith's manuscripts to a publisher and raise some money. The manuscript was that of *The Vicar of Wakefield* (1764), the sale of which raised 60 guineas for the impoverished author, and which is still one of the best-known works of the period.

Ye Olde Cheshire Cheese, Wine Office Court at Fleet Street

According to Dylan Thomas's biographer, Constantine Fitzgibbon, American tourists can often be found scouring this much-loved antiquated-looking pub searching for the ghost of Dr Johnson, who may have used it as his local and who is remembered by a plaque on a seat in the ground-floor restaurant which he supposedly used. The Cheshire Cheese was the first new building to be built locally following the Fire of London which destroyed most of the City in 1666. In the 300-odd years since, it has acquired a strong literary legacy, attracting Oliver Goldsmith (who lived nearby, see above), W. B. Yeats, Oscar Wilde, G. K. Chesterton and Dylan Thomas, who would come here not least of all to partake of its excellent chop room.

In the 1890s the Cheshire Cheese was home to the Rhymers' Club, whose members and visitors – Yeats, Wilde (who didn't really like the place) and Richard Le Gallienne (who wrote one of the definitive accounts of the era, *The Romantic '90s*) – would meet in an upstairs room and recite their poetry aloud to each other. Another member, John Davidson, published two sets of poems, *Fleet Street Eclogues*, in 1893 and 1896. A few decades later G. K. Chesterton would dress up as Dr Johnson at the Cheshire Cheese's period costume dinners dedicated to the dictionary compiler (Chesterton never needed much excuse to don eighteenth-century gear and always carried a sword-stick). On another occasion Chesterton, needing to work up the courage to visit publishers who might be persuaded to commission his *Napoleon of Notting Hill*, came to the Cheshire Cheese, ordered a huge lunch of his favourite dishes and a bottle of wine, gobbled down the lot, and then hawked round the Fleet Street offices, demanding £20 to begin writing the tome. Despite his inebriated state, he was eventually successful.

In Dickens's *A Tale of Two Cities* (1859) Sydney Carton takes Charles Darnay 'down Ludgate Hill to Fleet Street . . . up a covered way into a tavern' – supposedly this – after the latter is acquitted of high treason at the Old Bailey.

head up Shoe Lane to St Bride Street

St Bride Street

Site of *Daily Express* building, no. 23
Raymond Chandler, who worked as a reporter for the *Daily Express* in his early twenties in 1908, claimed he was a 'complete flop' as a journalist, 'the worst man they ever had'. Nor did another would-be novelist, Evelyn Waugh, fare any better after being taken on by the *Express* in the 1920s. Sent to report on a fire in Soho, Waugh decided there was no story and took a female colleague to the Savoy for lunch instead. Waugh was sacked after two months in the job but put some of his experiences to use when writing *Scoop* (1938), still the best-known Fleet Street novel. A less celebrated but more convincing work based on the *Daily Express* came courtesy of Alan Moorhead, who joined the paper in 1936 as one of a number of Australians seeking glory in the Street of Ink and four years later was sent to cover the war in North Africa. Out of his experiences he produced *African Trilogy* (1944) which sent up the British officers fighting the German desert army leader Rommel.

head south along St Bride Street to Poppin's Court

Poppin's Court

Possible inspiration for Arthur Conan Doyle's 'Pope's Court'
In the Sherlock Holmes story 'The Red-Headed League' (1891) ginger-haired pawnbroker Jabez Wilson sits in an office in the fictitious Pope's Court (probably based on Poppin's Court) copying out the *Encyclopaedia Britannica* for the then grand sum of £4 a week. Wilson is being paid by a shadowy organization called the Red-Headed League, supposedly set up by a wealthy red-head who wants to reward people with similarly coloured hair in return for simple work, but which is really a

cover for crooks who are planning to rob the bank next to Wilson's pawnbroking business. When the crooks, in the guise of the Red-Headed League, first advertise their well-paid vacancy at their Pope's Court office, 'Fleet Street was choked with red-headed folk, and Pope's Court looked like a coster's orange barrow.'

return to Fleet Street

Fleet Street

St Bride's, Fleet Street at St Bride's Avenue

> *'The bells of St Bride's church rung their merry chimes hard by'* from *Boswell's London Journal*, James Boswell, 1763

Richard Lovelace, the Cavalier poet, and Samuel Richardson, the prolix eighteenth-century novelist, are buried in what is still known as the journalists' church. Samuel Pepys, who was born a few doors away, was baptized here in a font which is still in place. In 1664 Pepys had to bribe the grave-digger to 'jostle together' bodies so that he could make room for his brother, Tom. Other writers connected with St Bride's include John Milton, who lived in a house in the churchyard; John Dryden, who wrote his ode, *Alexander's Feast*, for the church; John Evelyn; and Izaak Walton who worshipped here. Wynkyn de Worde, Caxton's assistant, who brought the first printing press with movable type to Fleet Street in 1500, is buried in the chapel. When an American scholar of Samuel Richardson heard of the damage caused to the church during the Second World War, he rushed over from the USA to save what he could, found the coffins and corpses stacked to one side awaiting reburial, and claimed to have touched Richardson on the nose.

Site of River Fleet, Fleet Street at New Bridge Street

Fleet Street was named after the River Fleet, which once flowed from Hampstead to the Thames by what is now Blackfriars Bridge. Its valley accounts for the different levels of the roads around Holborn Circus. In *The Dunciad* (1728) Pope wrote how 'Fleet Ditch with disemboguing streams/Rolls the large tribute of dead dogs to Thames'. The Fleet is now entirely culverted and used as a sewer.

THE TEMPLE

The Temple, at the south-west of Fleet Street, consists of the Middle Temple and the Inner Temple, two of the four remaining Inns of Court (along with nearby Gray's Inn and Lincoln's Inn) where lawyers have traditionally lived and studied. The Inns were established during the reign of Edward I, the name 'Temple' coming from the Order of Knights Templars who occupied the site in 1162, and some of the oldest surviving City buildings can be found among the maze of alleyways and courtyards that comprise the area.

Scores of literary figures have lived in the Temple, dating back to Sir John Paston, whose letters give an interesting insight into fifteenth-century life here, especially his warnings to his aunt not to bring any money with her because of robbers. Members of the Inner Temple over the years have included James Boswell, Compton Mackenzie and Richard Brinsley Sheridan. Members of the Middle Temple have included Sir Walter Ralegh, seventeenth-century chroniclers John Evelyn and John Aubrey, William Congreve, Henry Fielding, Edmund Burke, William Cowper and John Buchan, who came to the Temple at the end of the nineteenth century after coming down from Oxford where he had already been published and been included in *Who's Who* at the age of 23.

In *The History of Pendennis* (1850) Thackeray, another one-time resident, writes of Old Grump 'of the [Temple's] Norfolk circuit', who rails against the 'absurd, new-fangled practice of . . . washing. He had done without water very well, and so had our fathers before him.' Dickens used the Temple as a setting in various novels, including *Great Expectations* (1861) in which Magwitch reveals to Pip that he is his benefactor in the Temple (Pip has chambers in Garden Court). In Virginia Woolf's *Mrs Dalloway* (1925) Elizabeth, the heroine's daughter, walks in the Temple thinking 'of shops, of business, of law, of administration'.

The Temple, a maze of courtyards, does not lend itself to easy exploration; however, there are helpful maps on the walls (one by the porch in Middle Temple Lane and one by Carpmael Buildings) which are marked with sites of literary interest.

- Landmarks can be reached from Temple tube.

roughly west to east

Garden Court

Oliver Goldsmith lived at 2 Garden Court, above the Middle Temple Library, in 1768.

Essex Court

John Evelyn, the diarist, lived in Essex Court in 1640.

Brick Court

Anthony Hope, author of *The Prisoner of Zenda* (1894), who had been called to the Bar seven years earlier, lived in Brick Court. He is supposed to have dreamed up the story of the prisoner while walking back to his chambers after a successful case. Oliver Goldsmith lived at no. 2 from 1765 until he died in 1774, writing *The Deserted Village* (1770) and *She Stoops to Conquer* (1773) here. Thackeray moved into the rooms below in 1855. Most of Brick Court was flattened by a Second World War bomb.

Fountain Court

Henry Havelock Ellis, the sexual freedom pioneer, and W. B. Yeats stayed in rooms in Fountain Court which belonged to Arthur Symons, like Yeats a member of the Rhymers' Club. Symons sublet the rooms to Ellis, but because he spent much of his time in Cornwall the rooms were let in turn to Yeats during the winter of 1895 and 1896. The French symbolist poet Paul Verlaine stayed briefly in a flat in this Court in 1879. In Dickens's *Martin Chuzzlewit* (1844) John Westlock romances Ruth Pinch by the small fountain.

Middle Temple Lane

Middle Temple Lane, which originally ran down from Fleet Street to the river, divides the Inner and Middle Temple.

Middle Temple Hall, Middle Temple Lane at Fountain Court
The premiere of Shakespeare's *Twelfth Night*, possibly staged by the playwright's own company, took place here before Elizabeth I on 2 February 1601. The Queen had opened the building in 1576.

Goldsmith's Buildings

Mortimer Lightwood in Dickens's *Our Mutual Friend* (1865) lives here.

Hare Court

William Makepeace Thackeray lived at 1 Hare Court when he entered the Middle Temple in 1831. He moved to the nearby 2 Crown Office Row when he was called to the Bar in 1848.

Inner Temple Lane

From 1760 to 1765 Dr Johnson lived at no. 1 (now demolished and replaced by Johnson's Buildings) in 'total idleness' off a pension which the newly crowned George III had awarded him. Charles and Mary Lamb moved to no. 4 (now demolished) in 1809, describing the lodgings thus: 'I have two sitting rooms: I call them so par excellence, for you may stand, or loll, or lean, or try any posture in them.' On moving in, Lamb, then in his early thirties, announced, 'Here I mean to live and die,' but eight years later moved to Islington.

Temple Church, south end Inner Temple Lane
A lawyers' church since 1608, Temple Church was where Goldsmith was buried in 1774. In 1842 the Benchers of the Temple banned more burials and paved over the churchyard. Goldsmith's tomb was erected in 1860 but the site of his grave is unknown.

Pump Court

Henry Fielding lived at no. 4, up three flights of stairs, in the 1740s.

Crown Office Row

Site of Charles Lamb's birthplace and address (1775–94), no. 2
The essayist was born in this now rebuilt block on 10 February 1775. His father was legal clerk to Samuel Salt, whom Lamb wrote about in his *Essays of Elia* (1823). Lamb loved the place and wrote: 'cheerful Crown Office Row (place of my kindly engendure) . . . a man would give something to have been born in such places'. He and his sister, Mary, lived here until 1794, when they moved to 7 Little Queen Street, Holborn. The Inner Temple Garden has a fountain dedicated to Lamb and a stone boy inscribed with a quote from an essay which contains his best-known line, 'Lawyers were children once.'

Inner Temple Garden

In Shakespeare's *Henry VI Part I* (1590) Richard Plantagenet and the Earls of Somerset, Suffolk and Warwick take a stroll in the Inner Temple Garden and, while arguing about the rights to the throne of the Houses of Lancaster and York, choose the coloured roses that still identify the counties of Lancashire and Yorkshire: Warwick and Plantagenet choose white (for Lancaster), Somerset and Suffolk red (for York) and battle lines are drawn for the forthcoming War of the Roses which sends 'a thousand souls to death and deadly night'. In William Makepeace Thackeray's *The History of Pendennis* (1850) the hero of the novel walks around the Inner Temple Garden, which he claims 'only antiquarians and literary amateurs care to look at with much interest'.

Mitre Court

Site of Charles and Mary Lamb's address (1801–10), no. 16
Moving here in his twenties, Lamb wrote to a friend, 'I shall be as airy up four flights of stairs as in the country'. He spent Wednesday nights at Mitre Court with Coleridge, Hazlitt and Wordsworth. His and Mary Lamb's *Tales from Shakespeare* (1807) were written here.

King's Bench Walk

Oliver Goldsmith lived at no. 3 of this mostly Wren-designed block in the 1770s. Other King's Bench Walk residents have included H. Rider Haggard and Harold Nicolson and Vita Sackville-West.

Walking Shakespeare's London

Mystery surrounds much of the playwright's life, but there is no shortage of Shakespeare London associations. He is believed to have lived in Ireland Yard in Blackfriars, Silver Street, in what is now the Barbican, and in Great St Helens, further east. He also probably acted at the Theatre and the Curtain Theatre in Curtain Road as well as the better-known Globe, south of the Thames (now rebuilt).

Westminster Abbey to the Tower: roughly west to east

Westminster Abbey, *Broad Sanctuary, SW1*
Almost every English monarch has been crowned in the Abbey and many are buried here, including Henry V whose funeral takes place here at the

beginning of Henry VI Part I. *There is a Shakespeare memorial designed by William Kent in the Abbey's Poets' Corner which misquotes lines from* The Tempest.

House of Commons, *St Margaret Street, SW1*
The opening scene of Henry IV *takes place in Westminster Hall, the only surviving part of the original Palace of Westminster, now the vestibule of the House of Commons.* Henry VI Part III *begins here with York demanding that he and his heirs reign following the king's death.*

Middlesex Guildhall, *Parliament Square, SW1*
In Richard III *Edward IV's widow, Elizabeth, flees into sanctuary here with her six children after Richard, Duke of Gloucester (the eventual Richard III), takes her eldest son, Edward V, to the Tower. Richard then persuades her to let him have another son (Richard, Duke of York) as company for Edward, and then arranges the murder of the so-called Princes in the Tower.*

head along Victoria Embankment to Savoy Street

Site of Savoy Palace, *Strand between Savoy Court and Lancaster Place, WC2*
In Richard II *John of Gaunt and the Duchess of Gloucester meet at the former's thirteenth-century palace which used to occupy a huge site here by the Thames to discuss the forthcoming battle between Bolingbroke and Thomas Mowbray. In* Henry VI Part II *Jack Cade urges his followers to 'go some and pull down the Savoy'.*

head east along Strand

St Clement Dane's Church, *Strand at Aldwych, east end, WC2*
When Falstaff in Henry IV Part II *tells Master Shallow 'We have heard the chimes at midnight', he is referring to St Clement Dane's, rebuilt by Christopher Wren after the Great Fire of London.*

head east along Fleet Street

Inner Temple Garden, *WC2*
In Shakespeare's Henry VI Part I *Richard Plantagenet and the Earls of Somerset, Suffolk and Warwick take a stroll in the Inner Temple Garden, argue about the rights to the throne of the Houses of Lancaster and York, and choose the coloured roses that still identify the counties of Lancashire and Yorkshire (white for Lancaster and red for York). Battle lines are then drawn for the forthcoming War of the Roses which sends 'a thousand souls to death and deadly night'.*

head east past Ludgate Circus and south at Creed Lane

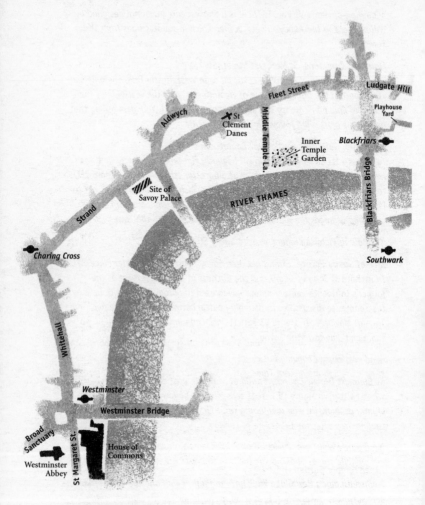

Ireland Yard, *Blackfriars, EC4*
*Shakespeare is believed to have lived in Ireland Yard in a house which he
bought in 1613 for £140 and which was destroyed by the 1666 Fire.*

return to Ludgate Hill and head east

London Stone, *111 Cannon Street, EC4*
*In Henry VI Part II Jack Cade, the Kent rebel who led a band of men to
London in 1450 to try and seize control of the city, stops for a rest by the*

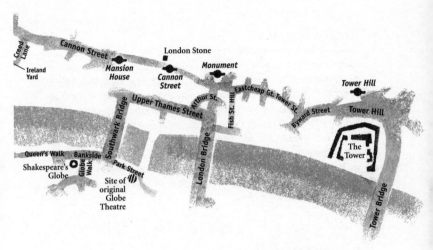

ancient monument of London Stone (which may have been the Roman milestone for all British distances) and orders the 'pissing-conduit [the poor
people's well] run nothing but claret wine this first year of our reign'. Cade
saw off the unpopular Lord Treasurer, James Fiennes, but was routed a few
days later when Londoners tired of the rebellion.

detour south of the river along Southwark Bridge

Shakespeare's Globe (1997–), *Bankside at New Globe Walk, SE1*
The recently built reconstruction of Shakespeare's original Globe in the Elizabethan style stages Shakespeare plays in the open air each summer.

head south along New Globe Walk and turn left at Park Street

Site of the Globe Theatre (1599–1644), *south side Park Street east of
Southwark Bridge Road, SE1*
The original Globe saw the first run of a number of Shakespeare plays –
Henry V (1599), which opened the theatre and the Prologue of which con-
tains a dedication to the place, Julius Caesar (1599) and Cymbeline (1611).
During the premiere of Henry VIII in June 1613 cannons being used as stage
props set the thatched roof ablaze and the theatre burned down.

head back up London Bridge

Fish Street Hill, *EC3*
Jack Cade cries 'Up Fish Street! down Saint Magnus Corner! kill and knock down! throw them into Thames' in Henry VI Part II, *a scene which Shakespeare mistakenly set in Southwark.*

along Eastcheap to the Tower

The Tower, *Tower Hill, EC3*
The Tower features in a number of Shakespeare plays. In Henry VI Part I *Edmund Mortimer, incarcerated in the Tower, tells Richard Plantagenet that he, Mortimer, should have been king and that Richard is his rightful heir. In* Henry VI Part III *Henry hands over the government to Warwick in the Tower and later, while praying, is murdered here by Gloucester (the eventual Richard III). In the play of that name Richard is responsible for several deaths in the Tower: his older brother, Clarence, whose body is dropped into the malmsey (sweet wine); Lord Hastings, who had refused to help Richard seize the throne ('Thou art a traitor: off with his head'); and the so-called 'Princes in the Tower' – Edward V and the Duke of York, murdered by Dighton and Forrest on Richard's orders.*

Clerkenwell, EC1

In contrast to the nearby City, Clerkenwell, once London's green belt, is a mainly quiet, leisurely area, full of small shops and offices and well-kept Georgian properties; it even exudes a village charm in parts. A forgotten area for much of the twentieth century, this small territory between the City and Islington has recently undergone a revival of sorts and become part-gentrified, and is now a much-sought-after location.

Clerkenwell grew around the priory, established in 1140 by the Knights of St John, who built a well around which local clerks performed mystery plays; hence the name Clerkenwell. (The well can still be seen through an office window at the south end of Farringdon Lane.) The area began to attract artisans and craftsmen in the late seventeenth century, but industry gave it a grey look and it was a slum when Charles Dickens, upset at reading about corpses in local houses decomposing where people lived and ate, set parts of *Oliver Twist* (1839) here. In his 1926 novel *Riceyman Steps*, Arnold Bennett wrote of the 'great metropolitan industrial district of Clerkenwell' (albeit slightly tongue-in-cheek), but in the following decades Clerkenwell's population and (mostly light) industry began to drift away and it wasn't until the 1980s that the area's fortunes revived when people began looking for relatively cheap pre-Second World War property in central London (Clerkenwell having escaped the worst destruction of the Blitz).

Many of Clerkenwell's empty warehouses have since been converted into luxury apartment blocks, media outlets have set up base near Clerkenwell Green (the *Guardian* was already based nearby in Farringdon Road), smart restaurants have opened, and local outlets have put much effort into creating a community feel, with many shops proudly displaying historic maps of the area in their windows.

Exploring Clerkenwell

Clerkenwell's boundaries are City Road (to the north-east and east), the City (south) and roughly Gray's Inn Road (west).

* Landmarks can be reached from Farringdon tube, except where stated.

Sadler's Wells to Bunhill Fields: anti-clockwise around Clerkenwell Green

Rosebery Avenue

Sadler's Wells, Rosebery Avenue at Arlington Way, Angel tube
London's premier dance venue was named after Dick Sadler, who in 1683 discovered a well with supposed medicinal qualities by the City end of the recently constructed New River. Sadler designed a garden by the well and built a concert hall known as Miles's Musick-house or Sadler's Wells at which Wordsworth, as recorded in *The Prelude* (begun 1798), saw 'Singers, Rope-dancers, Giants and Dwarfs, Clowns, Conjurors, Posture Masters, Harlequins'. By the beginning of the nineteenth century Sadler's Wells was hosting Charles Dibdin's aquatic plays in a water tank under the stage and the manager around that time was Joe Grimaldi, the clown whose memoirs were edited by Charles Dickens. Sadler's Wells was derelict by the early years of the twentieth century but was revived by Lilian Baylis and reopened in 1931 with a performance of *Twelfth Night* starring John Gielgud and Ralph Richardson. The latest building on the site was constructed as recently as 1997.

head south-west along Rosebery Avenue and turn right at Farringdon Road

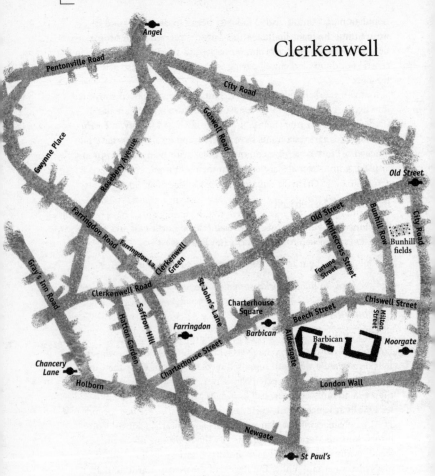

Clerkenwell

Farringdon Road

In his 1889 novel *The Nether World* George Gissing cries 'What terrible barracks, those Farringdon Road buildings . . . the weltering mass of human weariness, of bestiality, of unmerited dolour, of hopeless hope, of crushed surrender'. Things improved when the authorities decamped the poor to new, less crowded slums in outer London in the middle decades of the twentieth century, and Farringdon Road is now a busy traffic route lined with small shops, low blocks of offices and no discernible community. Iain Sinclair used to be a book dealer, trading with the second-hand stalls around the junction of Farringdon Road and Exmouth Market, and in his 1987 *White Chappell Scarlet Tracings* he writes of dealers who 'comb the stalls . . . diving at Hegel, Schopenhauer, Nietzsche, Stein's *World History in the Light of the Holy Grail . . .'*

head north

Gwynne Place

Arnold Bennett's Riceyman Steps, WC1, King's Cross tube
Riceyman Steps, as in the 1923 novel of the same name, are the 21 steps leading from Gwynne Place, a tiny passage on the eastern side of King's Cross Road, to Granville Square, the book's Riceyman Square. The novel is based around events which take place in a second-hand bookshop and features much of local interest, including an account of how London's first tube line was constructed through the area (it runs underneath the steps). In the book Mrs Arb castigates King's Cross Road for having no theatre, music hall, dance hall, picture theatre or even 'one nice little restaurant or tea shop where a nice person could go if she'd a mind'. The road and locality haven't changed much since, and are now a prime target for the sort of gentrification which has taken hold of Bloomsbury proper to the west and Clerkenwell half a mile south.

head south and turn right at Clerkenwell Road, which was once known as Liquorpond Street

Saffron Hill

Now a minor road to the east of London's Hatton Garden jewellery trading centre, Saffron Hill was the Italian Quarter in the nineteenth century and features heavily in Charles Dickens's *Oliver Twist* (1839), where it is the setting for Fagin's den of thieves. Dickens talks about a workhouse in the now vanished Little Saffron Hill ('a dirtier or more wretched place he had never seen') and a Mr Fang who is in charge of the 'very notorious Metropolitan Police Office' at 54 Hatton Garden.

return to Farringdon Road, head north and turn right at Vine Street, the bridge across the railway

Farringdon Lane

Peter Ackroyd's 'House of Dr Dee' site, nos. 14–16
In Peter Ackroyd's *The House of Dr Dee* (1993) Matthew Palmer moves into the Clerkenwell house inherited from his father in which the

Elizabethan mystic John Dee had once lived. Ackroyd sites the house in Cloak Lane which is 'difficult to find . . . some thirty yards north-west of [Clerkenwell] Green' but which in reality doesn't exist and was contrived for the book; the spot Ackroyd describes is that of the original clerks' well which gave the area its name and which can just about still be seen through the window of the office at this address.

Clerkenwell Green

> *'Last Sunday evening I spent on Clerkenwell Green – a great assembly place for radical meetings'* George Gissing, letter to his sister, 1887

Long a setting for demonstrations, Clerkenwell Green was where William Cobbett, author of *Rural Rides* (1830), spoke against the Corn Laws in 1826 and from where, sixty years later, George Bernard Shaw, William Morris and hundreds of others set off on the march that ended in Trafalgar Square in the battle that became known as Bloody Sunday. In Charles Dickens's *Oliver Twist* (1839) kindly Mr Brownlow is robbed by Fagin's posse of pickpockets outside a shop by Clerkenwell Green as Oliver looks on in horror. Oliver takes no part in the robbery, but he is the only one of the gang left at the scene of the crime when Mr Brownlow turns round, and is chased through the surrounding streets and captured. Clerkenwell Green, though no longer green, still has an old-fashioned drinking fountain and cattle trough and looks more like a continental piazza than a London square.

Marx Memorial Library, no. 37a, tel. 020 7253-1485. Open Mon. 1–6; Tue.–Thu. 1–8; Sat. 10–1

The library, which opened to the public in 1933 on the fiftieth anniversary of Marx's death, houses a large collection of socialist tracts and publications and is based in a former school which, from 1872, was home to the London Patriotic Club, a radical organization co-founded by John Stuart Mill which, unusually for the time, was open to women. When the club closed, some twenty years later, the premises were bought by William Morris, who founded the Twentieth Century Press, one of Britain's first socialist print works, here. Lenin used the presses in 1902 and 1903 to produce issues of his communist paper, *Iskra*. The building was saved from demolition in the 1960s after a campaign involving John Betjeman.

head east, cutting through Jerusalem Passage and across Clerkenwell Road to St John's Lane

St John's Lane

St John's Gate
Dr Johnson had his own office in this gatehouse in the 1730s and 1740s, writing essays, reviews and poems for *The Gentleman's Magazine* which was printed here. The gatehouse, which dates back to 1504, was built for the now demolished Priory of St John of Jerusalem and was where the St John Ambulance Brigade was founded in 1877.

continue along St John's Lane, which soon reaches St John's Street, once the last leg of the journey for cattle and sheep from Middlesex into London, and turn left at Charterhouse Street

Charterhouse Square

Former Charterhouse School, Barbican tube
Charterhouse opened as the Carthusian Priory in the fourteenth century and became a school for poor boys in 1611, moving to Surrey in 1872. Past pupils at this site include Joseph Addison (later founder of *The Spectator*) who came here in the 1680s, John Wesley (1710s) and Thackeray (1820s) who derided it as the Slaughterhouse in *Vanity Fair* (1848) and Greyfriars in *The Newcomes* (1855). Most of the original buildings were destroyed in the Second World War but the site was sympathetically restored and is now used mainly by St Bartholomew's Hospital.

turn left at Aldersgate Street and right at Fann Street

Fortune Street

Site of Fortune Theatre (1600–1621, 1623–49), Fortune Street at
Whitecross Street, north-west junction, Moorgate tube
Where the Globe Theatre in Bankside (see p. 330) was circular, the Fortune, opened by Privy Council decree in 1600, was square. It was run by Edward Alleyn after he left the Rose and out of the profits he founded Dulwich College (see p. 339) and art gallery. The Fortune burned down in 1621, reopened two years later, and was ordered to close by the Puritans in 1642, although performances continued in defiance of the law until soldiers raided the building in 1649.

head south along Whitecross Street and turn left at Silk Street

Milton Street

Former Grub Street

Traditionally associated with hack writing, Grub Street was the name of a real turning (now Milton Street) which Samuel Johnson in his *Dictionary* describes as 'originally the name of a street in Moorfields much inhabited by writers of small histories, dictionaries and temporary poems'. In *The Dunciad* (1728) Alexander Pope wrote about Grub Street writers in the memorable couplet 'While pensive poets painful vigil keep/Sleepless themselves, to give their readers sleep'. Grub Street was renamed Milton Street in the 1830s, not after the poet, John, but after the landlord who owned most of the properties. George Gissing's *New Grub Street* (1891) is about a writer finding his way in London at that time. Much of the street was demolished when the Barbican was built in the 1960s.

head north-east to Bunhill Row

Bunhill Row

Site of John Milton's address (1663–74), no. 125, Moorgate tube

Milton finished *Paradise Lost* (1667) and wrote its follow-up, *Paradise Regained* (1671), and *Samson Agonistes* (1671) in a long-demolished house in what is now Bunhill Row and was then Artillery Row. John Dryden visited in February 1674, looking for permission to rewrite *Paradise Lost* as a heroic opera in rhyming couplets. Milton consented but had to suffer the embarrassment of Dryden's version outselling his. Milton died here that year.

Bunhill Fields, Old Street tube

John Bunyan, Daniel Defoe and William Blake are among those buried in this ancient graveyard, disused since 1854, and just about the only green space in this heavily built-up part of London. Bunhill Fields, originally called Bone Hill Fields on account of the huge quantity of bones piled in it, was opened as a burial ground for plague victims in the 1660s, but the land was never consecrated and was later taken up for use by Dissenters (Southey described it as the Campo Santo of Nonconformity).

John Bunyan's presence is surprising as he spent most of his time in Bedford, where he wrote *The Pilgrim's Progress* (1684). He died on a rare visit to London from a fever caught during a heavy downpour of rain in 1688. When Daniel Defoe died in 1731, he was in hiding from creditors and other enemies and his simple tombstone was marked Mr

Dubow. Nearly 150 years later an obelisk was erected after an appeal in *The Christian World* newspaper, but it disappeared, was discovered many years later in Southampton, and can now be found in Stoke Newington Library (see p. 282). Defoe had explained in *A Journal of the Plague Year* (1722) how Bunhill Fields had become a plague pit: 'many who were infected and near their end ran wrapped in blankets or rags and threw themselves in and expired there, before any earth could be thrown upon them'. The third famous grave (regularly adorned with fresh flowers, such is his present-day popularity) is that of William Blake, who died in 1827.

All three graves can be found in the central paved area of the Fields. In J. B. Priestley's *Angel Pavement* (1930) Mr Smeeth goes to Bunhill Fields where he 'stared through the iron railings of the old graves' and is told by a passer-by that Defoe, Bunyan and Blake 'lie in the sooty earth while their dreams and ecstasies still light the world'.

From Dickens House to Fagin's Den
– a walk through the heart of Dickensian London

There is little of London that isn't Dickensian, so intensely did the author walk its streets and use both its major landmarks and its more obscure sites in his stories. A convenient starting (and finishing) point for a walk through Dickens's London would be the Doughty Street house that is now home to the Dickens Fellowship and Dickens Museum where he wrote many of his novels.

Charles Dickens's address (1837–9)/The Dickens House, *48 Doughty Street, WC1, tel. 020 7405-2127. Open Mon.–Sat. 10–5. Admission £3.50 (£2.50, £1.50).*
Dickens moved to this plain four-storey Georgian house in March 1837 when he was 25 and just beginning to make his name as a novelist. In two years here his output was prodigious. He finished the final pages of The Pickwick Papers *(1837), wrote* Oliver Twist *(1839), most of* Nicholas Nickleby *(1839), the opening of* Barnaby Rudge *(1841), and edited the memoirs of the clown Grimaldi. Dickens's wife Catherine, whom he had married shortly before moving in, gave birth to two children at Doughty Street, but the author was closer to her sister, Mary, who lived with them but soon died from heart failure, aged only 17. Her death moved Dickens so much that he wrote: 'I solemnly believed that so perfect a creature never breathed,' and he used her to symbolize innocence and an almost implausible purity in the guise of Rose Maylie in* Oliver Twist *(1839), Little Nell in* The Old Curiosity Shop

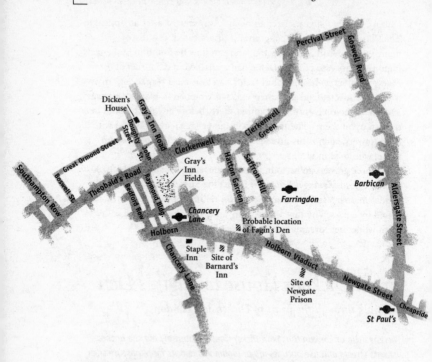

(1841), *whose death is modelled on Mary's demise, and Florence in* Dombey and Son *(1848). The museum contains first editions, original manuscripts, signed letters, personal papers, books the author used for his dramatic productions and which contain his own hand-written stage directions, the velvet-covered desk Dickens designed and took with him on his travels, and the grille from the Marshalsea prison where his father was imprisoned for debt.*

head south along Doughty Street and its continuation, John Street, and turn left at Theobald's Road, continuing east

Hatton Garden, *EC1*
Mr Fang is in charge of the 'very notorious Metropolitan Police Office' at 54 Hatton Garden (now a shop in the heart of London's jewellery trade) where Oliver Twist is sent after being accused of picking Mr Brownlow's pocket.

Saffron Hill, *EC1*
This was the Italian Quarter in the nineteenth century and features heavily in Oliver Twist, *where it is the setting for Bill Sikes's local, the Three Cripples pub. In* Bleak House *Phil Squod has a tinker's beat 'round Saffron Hill, Hatton Garden, Clerkenwell and Smiffield'.*

at the junction with Farringdon Road detour up Vine Street towards Clerkenwell Green

Clerkenwell Green, EC1
Kindly Mr Brownlow in Oliver Twist, 'a respectable-looking personage, with a powdered head and gold spectacles', is robbed by Fagin's gang of pickpockets outside a Clerkenwell Green shop as Oliver looks on in horror. The latter takes no part in the robbery but is the only one of the gang left at the scene of the crime when Mr Brownlow turns round, and he is chased through the surrounding streets and captured. Clerkenwell, Dickens's 'venerable suburb', is where Gabriel Varden, the locksmith in Barnaby Rudge, lives, 'a great wooden emblem of a key' dangling from the house-front. Our Mutual Friend's Mr Venus, in contrast, lives in a 'narrow and dirty street' in Clerkenwell.

cut through the back streets east to Goswell Road

Goswell Road (formerly Goswell Street), EC1
When Mr Pickwick opens his chamber window and 'looked out upon the world beneath Goswell Street was at his feet, Goswell Street was on his right hand – as far as the eye could reach, Goswell Street extended on his left; and the opposite side of Goswell Street was over the way'.

head south and along Aldersgate Street past the site of the Albion Hotel (roughly where Thomas More House stands) where Dickens and friends celebrated the completion of Nicholas Nickleby. *Aldersgate Street becomes St Martin's-le-Grand south of the Barbican and meets Cheapside by St Paul's tube.*

Cheapside, EC2
There are several mentions of Cheapside in Dickens's novels. Mr Jaggers meets Pip here in Great Expectations and invites him to dinner. In Sketches by Boz: The Bloomsbury Christening 'everybody that passed up Cheapside, and down Cheapside, looked wet, cold and dirty'. Mr Mould, the undertaker, lives 'deep in the City, and within the ward of Cheap' in Martin Chuzzlewit.

head west along Newgate Street

Site of Newgate Prison, Newgate Street at Old Bailey, south-east junction, EC4
The former prison, which stood where the Central Criminal Court (better known as Old Bailey) can now be found and which was demolished in 1902, features in much of Dickens's work. He saw it as a symbol of the 'guilt and misery of London' and there is a detailed account of the place in Sketches by Boz. In Oliver Twist Fagin is tried, sentenced and executed here. In Barnaby

Rudge *Dickens tells how prisoners who had escaped during the Gordon Riots returned the next day 'drawn back to their old place of captivity by some indescribable attraction' and were flung back into their cells. Rudge, the simpleton hero of the novel, is imprisoned in Newgate for taking part in the Riots and is set free by the mob. Kit Nubbles is wrongly imprisoned here in* The Old Curiosity Shop. *Magwitch in* Great Expectations *is saved from a trial at the prison courts by dying.*

Holborn Viaduct, EC1
In building the viaduct in the 1860s, the 'covered ways and yards . . . where drunken men and women were positively wallowing in filth', as described in Oliver Twist, *were swept away. It was in one of these yards, by the now vanished Field Lane near the north-west corner of Holborn Viaduct, that Fagin has his den. In Dickens's day there was no viaduct and the road was known as Holborn Hill, as featured in the amusing opening to* Bleak House *in which Dickens imagines meeting a 'megalosaurus, forty feet long or so, waddling like an elephantine lizard up Holborn Hill'.*

St Andrew's Church, EC4
On walking past Holborn Circus with Bill Sikes, Oliver Twist looks up at the St Andrews church clock and notices it is 'hard upon seven!'

Site of Thavies Inn, *Shoe Lane, south of St Andrew's Church, EC4*
Mr Guppy describes how to get to this Inn of Chancery (destroyed in Second World War bombing) in Chapter IV of Bleak House: *'We just twist up Chancery Lane, and cut along Holborn, and there we are in four minutes' time, as near as a toucher.'*

Site of the Bull Inn, *Holborn at Hatton Garden, north-west junction, EC1*
Where Mrs Gamp and Betsey Prig nurse Mr Lewsome in Martin Chuzzlewit. *The Inn, known as the Black Bull at the beginning of the nineteenth century, was demolished in the 1870s and replaced by the Gamage's department store, itself demolished in the 1970s.*

Site of Barnard's Inn, *Holborn at Fetter Lane, south-west junction, EC1*
In Great Expectations *Pip, on first arriving in London, stays with Mr Pocket in what was then an Inn of Chancery and is now occupied by Gresham College. But Pip is disappointed when he gets to Barnard's Inn. He had naïvely imagined it to be an inn run by a Mr Barnard and, when he finds out the truth, realizes that he has found 'the dingiest collection of shabby buildings ever squeezed together in a rank corner at a club for Tom-cats'.*

Site of Furnival's Inn, *Holborn at Brook Street, north-east junction, EC1*
Alfred Waterhouse's gory red-brick Prudential Assurance Company building

stands on the site of the former Inn of Chancery where Dickens had chambers from 1834 to 1837 and where he wrote The Pickwick Papers. *The latter's success enabled him to move to larger premises within the complex, and in 1837 he left for Doughty Street (see above). He later put* Martin Chuzzlewit's *John Westlock in chambers here.*

Staple Inn, *Holborn opposite Grays' Inn Road, EC1*
This former Inn of Chancery's sixteenth-century black-and-white timber-framed frontage which overhangs the road perilously was described by Dickens in his last novel, the unfinished Mystery of Edwin Drood, *as 'a little nook composed of two irregular quadrangles . . . one of those nooks where a few smoky sparrows twitter in smoky trees'. Took's Court, a well-hidden courtyard just south of Staple Inn, was the model for Cook's Court in* Bleak House *where law stationer Mr Snagsby 'pursues his lawful calling'.*

Chancery Lane, *WC2*
  'Yes,' said Mr Bucket. 'Do you know this turning?'
  'It looks like Chancery Lane.'
  'And was christened so, my dear,' said Mr Bucket.
Much of Bleak House *is set around the road that links High Holborn and Fleet Street. Tom Jarndyce 'in despair blew his brains out at a coffee-house in Chancery Lane' in the same novel. In his first day working as a solicitor's clerk in nearby Gray's Inn in 1827, Charles Dickens went for lunch along Chancery Lane wearing a new cap and was accosted by a 'big blackguard fellow' who greeted the young aspiring writer, 'Halloa, sojer.' Dickens was so annoyed he struck out at his tormentor and was dealt a black eye in return.*

turn right at Warwick Court and head north to Gray's Inn

Gray's Inn, *WC1*
  'Gray's Inn, gentlemen. Curious little nooks in a great place, like
  London, these old Inns are' Mr Pickwick from *The Pickwick Papers*
When he was 15 in 1827, Dickens worked as a solicitor's clerk for the firm of Ellis and Blackmore in Gray's Inn, one of the four Inns of Court, which dates back to the fourteenth century. Originally he was based at 1 South Square (at the south-east corner of the complex) and then at 6 Raymond Buildings and, disliking the place and the work, took his revenge in Uncommercial Traveller: Chambers, *in which he described it as 'one of the most depressing institutions in brick and mortar known to the children of men'.*

head west

Bedford Row, *WC1*
In Uncommercial Traveller: Chambers, *this elegant stretch is described as 'replete with the accommodation of Solitude, Closeness and Darkness, where you might be as easily murdered, with the placid reputation of having merely gone down to the sea side'.*

turn left at Theobald's Road. Bloomsbury Square is just north-west of Theobald's Road's junction with Southampton Row

Site of Lord Mansfield's address (1780s), *29 Bloomsbury Square, WC1*
Barnaby Rudge *deals with the story of the Gordon Riots, a violent uprising against Catholics that took place in London in the summer of 1780, following government plans to repeal anti-Catholic legislation. In the novel (as in real life) a group of Protestant militants, after besieging Newgate Gaol in the City (see above), charge almost a mile west into Bloomsbury Square to wreck the home of Lord Mansfield, the Lord Chief Justice. Finding him not at home they burn down the house and destroy his renowned law library. Rudge, the half-witted hero, is due to be hanged in the square for his part in the riots but wins a last-minute reprieve and instead two crippled boys are hanged and made to face the house as the noose is tightened.*

head north along Southampton Row and turn right at Cosmo Place

Hospital for Sick Children, *Great Ormond Street opposite Barbon Close, WC1*
Dickens *raised money for this famous hospital in 1858 and later gave a public reading of* A Christmas Carol *here. Little Johnny dies 'with a kiss for the Boofer lady' here in* Our Mutual Friend.

turn left at Millman Street and right at Guilford Street. Doughty Street, where Dickens House is situated, is only a few yards further east

Covent Garden (including Holborn and Strand), WC2

'Better a seedy Soho than a tarted-up tourist attraction like Covent Garden'
from *Soho in the '50s*, Daniel Farson, 1987

Covent Garden, as Farson intimated, represents the worst of chocolate-box 'heritage' London – a sanitized, modern-day distortion of the Victorian city. In medieval times it was Westminster Abbey's walled garden – the *Convent* Garden – which grew into the flower and vegetable market for which the area was best known until the 1970s.

Covent Garden

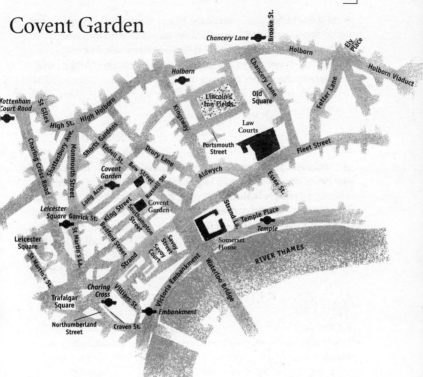

The market fascinated many writers. Tobias Smollett in *Humphry Clinker* (1771) described a 'dirty barrow-bunter in the street, cleaning her dusty fruit with her own spittle'; Charles Lamb, who lived nearby in the early nineteenth century, wrote to Dorothy Wordsworth about 'Covent Garden, where we are morally sure of the earliest peas and 'sparagus'; and in Charles Dickens's *Oliver Twist* (1839) Bill Sikes refers to a 'common garden' where he can take his pick from fifty or so boys a night to join his gang of thieves.

Meanwhile Covent Garden became a centre for theatre and opera, following Charles II's decision to license two Theatre Royals in 1660, rescinding the Puritans' ban on drama. In the eighteenth century the area began to fill with coffee houses as patronized by Pope, Sheridan, Boswell and Fielding, who edited a local publication, *The Covent Garden Journal*, under the pseudonym Sir Alexander Drawcansir. The coffee houses died out during the nineteenth century but the opera houses and theatres remain, particularly along Charing Cross Road and Strand.

In the 1970s the area suffered the loss of the market moving to Nine Elms, Battersea. Covent Garden's buildings were threatened with demolition but the Environment Secretary stepped in and spot-listed almost everything in sight. The main market building was converted to an indoor flea market and Covent Garden re-emerged as a crowd-drawing shopping area, albeit one wrapped up in ersatz Victoriana.

Exploring Covent Garden

All landmarks within the WC2 postcode have been included in this section, the boundaries being High Holborn (to the north), roughly Chancery Lane/Holborn Circus (east), the Thames (south) and Charing Cross Road/Leicester Square (west). For easy exploring, in this book Covent Garden has been divided into four sections: Charing Cross Road and Leicester Square; Seven Dials; Holborn; and Strand to the river.

CHARING CROSS ROAD AND LEICESTER SQUARE

- Landmarks can be reached from Tottenham Court Road or Leicester Square tubes.

Bookshops

> 'I went first of all to Charing Cross Road; but couldn't find any book I really wanted to buy' from Arnold Bennett's *Journal*, 1926

London's best concentration of bookshops can be found in Charing Cross Road and a few alleys to the east. On the west side of the road is the massive but confusing Foyle's and its younger rival, Waterstones; on the east side the specialists such as Silver Moon, and the second-hand stores with their chaotic bargain basements. 84 Charing Cross Road, made famous in Helene Hanff's story about a transatlantic literary friendship, is now a pizza parlour.

New

There are four main bookshops in Charing Cross Road for new works and books in print.

north to south

Foyle's, no. 119, tel. 020 7437-5660, is still perhaps the most famous bookshop in Britain and is fabulously stocked with difficult volumes that seem to have disappeared from other stores. But it also suffers from a strange purchasing system whereby customers must wait in one queue to have the book priced and then in another to pay.

Borders, no. 120, tel. 020 7379-6838, is rivalling Waterstone's and Co. by having its own coffee shop and bargain racks.

Blackwell's, no. 108, tel. 020 7292-5100, is another addition to the new books outlets, specializing in textbooks.

Second-hand

The east side of Charing Cross Road, especially the section south of Shaftesbury Avenue, is dominated by second-hand bookshops.

north to south

Any Amount of Books, no. 56, tel. 020 7240-8140, vies with the Charing Cross Road Bookshop as the area's best second-hand store.

Henry Pordes, nos. 58–60, tel. 020 7836-9031, contains rather too many over-priced titles and is illogically laid out upstairs. A better bet is to head downstairs where the more interesting stock is kept.

Quinto's, no. 48a, tel. 020 7379-7669, has the best range of subject titles in Charing Cross Road and a superb arts section through an opening in one wall.

Specialist

east side:

Shipley, no. 70, tel. 020 7836-7906, has art books galore, but is not the sort of place for idle browsing.

west side

Murder One, 71–73 Charing Cross Road, tel. 020 7734-3483, is a huge store devoted to crime.

Cecil Court

There are about ten small shops selling antiquarian books and old pictures in this tiny alleyway east of Charing Cross Road just to the south of Leicester Square tube. In Hanif Kureishi's *Buddha of Suburbia* (1990) Haroon Amir buys the books on 'Buddhism, Sufism, Confucianism and Zen' in Cecil Court which propel him towards becoming the 'Buddha of suburbia'. Christopher Petit's *Robinson* (1993) also features the Cecil Court bookshops.

north side: west to east

Nigel Williams, nos. 22 & 25, tel. 020 7836-7757, has lots of excellent first editions.

T. Alena Brett, no. 24, tel. 020 7836-8222. Situated in a building that was a tearoom where the poets Edward Thomas, Walter de la Mare and Rupert Brooke sat in the early decades of the twentieth century.

Red Snapper, no. 22, tel. 020 7240-2075, Beat Generation and counter-culture literature and ephemera.

Martin Murray, Colin Narbeth, no. 20, tel. 020 7379-6975.

Peter Ellis, no. 18, tel. 020 7836-8880. Good for first editions.

Marchpane, no. 16, tel. 020 7836-8661, has a hard-to-beat children's selection.

P. J. Hilton, no. 12, tel. 020 7379-9825. Antiquarian and general books, especially English literature, first editions and bibles..

Tindley and Chapman, no. 4, tel. 020 7240-2161, twenty-first-century first editions and architecture.

south side: east to west

The Italian Bookshop, no. 7, tel. 020 7240-1634, is devoted to books on and from that country.

Goldsboro Books, no. 1, tel. 020 7497-9228 billed as 'the book collec-tor's bookseller'.

David Drummond, no. 11, tel. 020 7836-1142, specialists in children's books pre-1940.

Travis & Emery, no. 17, tel. 020 7240-2129, are specialists in music (non-rock).

Watkins Books, no. 19, tel. 020 7836-2182 has much on the occult and mystery. The theosophists, who denied the existence of any personal God, used to meet here a hundred years ago.

Omega, no. 27, tel. 020 7836-3336. Modern first editions and illustrated books.

Tottenham Court Road end to Leicester Square end: north to south

Charing Cross Road

Centre Point, Charing Cross Road at Andrew Borde Street
No one has ever been able to find a satisfactory use for this 380-foot honeycomb-patterned '60s tower block which has been controversially

listed as a building of architectural importance by the Department of Environment. In his poem *Ode to Centre Point* Alan Brownjohn describes the eyesore as a 'barren phallus of egg-boxes without eggs' and writes about 'crass concrete walls with square/Fingered fountains jetting the Water'. Nowadays the pool can't even manage any water, let alone a fountain.

Molly Mogg's, no. 123
A tourist trap with a typically absurd name, this is where the hero of Colin Wilson's *Adrift in Soho* (1961) ends up after leaving the Midlands looking to find excitement in the capital.

The Circus, Charing Cross Road at Shaftesbury Avenue, south-west junction
In John le Carré's George Smiley books this innocuous-looking block contains the headquarters of a spy ring which runs espionage across Britain. George Smiley has a room on the 5th floor which is decorated with old prints of Oxford.

The Spy Who Went out in the Cold
In John Le Carré's *The Spy Who Came in from the Cold* (1963) Alec Leamas takes a tortuously convoluted route from here to George Smiley's Chelsea house in Bywater Street to ward off followers. From the corner of Charing Cross Road and Old Compton Street a few yards away, he walks south through Charing Cross to Fleet Street where he catches a bus going east towards Ludgate Hill. There he jumps out and, entering Blackfriars station, takes a tube one stop back to Temple before changing direction and going all the way round to Euston Square. Leamas then walks back to Charing Cross where he picks up the Circus van to get to Bywater Street.

T. S. Eliot's address (1920s), Burleigh Mansions, 20 Charing Cross Road
Eliot used a flat in this block as a retreat when he wanted to get away from his mentally disturbed wife, Viv (they lived together near Regent's Park (see p. 160)). Obsessed with secrecy, Eliot told friends who wanted to call on him to ask the porter for a 'Captain Eliot' and then knock three times. When Osbert and Edith Sitwell turned up early for dinner one day, they rumbled an unlikely Eliot secret: the poet was wearing green face powder so as to heighten his natural look of suffering and appear a more authentically doomed-looking literary figure.

Leicester Square

> '. . . now the brute mass of ignorance is urban. The village idiot walks in
> Leicester Square' from *The Unquiet Grave*, Palinurus (Cyril Connolly),
> 1944

Just as non-Parisians head for the Eiffel Tower when in the French capital, and tourists visiting Edinburgh make for Princes Street, so visitors to London, decade after decade, gravitate to Leicester Square. When they get there, they are in for a disappointment: the Square itself has little to offer other than hordes of people looking for something to happen. As long ago as 1908 this was apparent to G. K. Chesterton, who wrote in *The Man Who Was Thursday*: 'it will never be known whether it was the foreign look that attracted the foreigners or the foreigners who gave it the foreign look'.

The square was laid out in the seventeenth century by the second Duke of Leicester, who was required by law to provide trees and footpaths and so enclosed the central grassy area (technically known as Leicester Fields). It was an attractive place in the eighteenth century when residents included Swift, Hogarth and Blake – but not Shelley, who was once found sleepwalking in the square, having somnambulated half a mile from his lodgings in Poland Street. During the nineteenth century it became a setting for public meetings – Winston Churchill made his first public speech here – and in the twentieth century began to attract cinemas and nightclubs.

In Charles Dickens's *Barnaby Rudge* (1841) the Gordon Rioters plot to burn down Sir George Saville's house by the square. In P. G. Wodehouse's *The Code of the Woosters* (1938) Bertie Wooster is arrested for lifting a policeman's helmet in Leicester Square on Boat Race night. Graham Greene's unpublished early novel, *The Episode*, was a historical account of Spanish exiles, the Carlists, conspiring in Leicester Square. Doris Lessing wrote about coming here to find revellers on New Year's Eve 1950, only to find the streets more or less empty – something scarcely believable nowadays.

Site of Joshua Reynolds's studio (1760–92), no. 47

The great English painter entertained Dr Johnson, James Boswell, Oliver Goldsmith and Fanny Burney at his studio on this site (where there is now a bar) in the late eighteenth century. It was at Reynolds's house that Johnson met Laurence Sterne, and when the latter read him a few lines from the dedication of the recently completed *Tristram Shandy* Johnson proclaimed: 'I told him it was not English, Sir.' One unhappy visitor was William Blake, who had denounced Reynolds's *Discourse on Art* lectures for its neo-classicism and was harangued by Reynolds when he dropped by.

St Martin's Street

Site of Fanny Burney's address (1774–*c.* 1790)

Westminster Library stands on the site of the house where in a room at the top of the house the 25-year-old Fanny Burney wrote *Evelina or The History of a Young Lady's Entrance into the World* (1778). Burney felt obliged to write the book under an assumed name as it was not then considered proper for a young woman to write a novel. (She had started the book when she was 15 and was caught by her stepmother, who burned it in disgust.) *Evelina* so obsessed Joshua Reynolds that he used to read it while being spoonfed meals.

SEVEN DIALS

Named after the junction where seven roads, including Earlham and Monmouth streets, meet, Seven Dials is now a fairly characterless sprawl of shops and offices. But before the twentieth century it was one of the capital's worst slums, a maze of courts and alleyways immortalized in Hogarth's *Gin Lane* and remembered by Dickens for its 'dirty, straggling houses . . . as ill-proportioned and deformed as the half-naked children that wallow in the kennels'.

- Landmarks can be reached from Covent Garden tube.

Bookshops

Stanford's, 12–14 Long Acre, tel. 020 7836-1321, is London's best and biggest shop for maps and travel books.

St Giles High Street to Drury Lane: roughly west to east

St Giles High Street

Henry Fielding in 1751 wrote an essay called *An Enquiry into the Causes of the Late Increase of Robbers*, in which he describes the community around St Giles's Church as having a 'great number of houses set apart for the reception of idle persons and vagabonds'.

St Giles-in-the-Fields Church, opposite Earnshaw Street, Tottenham Court Road tube

There is a memorial on the north wall to the poet Andrew Marvell, who was buried here in 1678. The present-day St Giles, dating back to the 1730s, is the third church on the site and, like its namesake a little further south, St Martin-in-the-Fields, is now entirely bereft of the greenery that gave it its name.

head south along Monmouth Street, through Seven Dials

St Martin's Lane

Former *Night and Day* offices, no. 97, Leicester Square tube

Night and Day was a society/literary magazine modelled on *The New Yorker* and founded in 1937 by Graham Greene, among others, with an unusual editorial policy of asking famous writers to contribute on unlikely subjects. So Louis MacNeice came up with a piece on dogs and the art critic Herbert Read one on detective fiction. Graham Greene wrote film reviews but got muddled up when in a review of a Humphrey Bogart film, *Marked Woman*, he described gangster rule of Chicago as 'feudal'. When asked to elaborate, Greene explained that he got the idea from Bogart himself, who at one point in the film supposedly says 'it's feudal'. It was pointed out to Greene that what Bogart had actually said was 'it's futile' – in the American manner. But Greene got into serious trouble when he denigrated Shirley Temple in a review of *Wee Willie Winkie*. Temple sued for libel and won the then stiff sum of £3,500 damages. By then *Night and Day*, with its poor sales, had stopped publishing.

head back up St Martin's Lane to Garrick Street

Garrick Street

Garrick Street is named after the famous eighteenth-century actor, David Garrick, who grew up with Samuel Johnson in Lichfield.

Garrick Club, no. 15

The Garrick was established in 1831 by actors who were being refused membership of the select Pall Mall clubs and began to attract figures from the world of entertainment such as W. S. Gilbert and Arthur Sullivan. Shortly after the death of the latter, Gilbert, walking through the club, was asked by a woman what Sullivan was now doing. 'Nothing,' replied Gilbert. 'But surely he is composing?' the woman inquired. 'On the contrary, madam,' Gilbert retorted, 'he is decomposing.' Scores of

CENTRAL LONDON: Covent Garden *111*

authors have whiled away their time at the Garrick but few more so than Kingsley Amis, who in his later years spent almost all his waking hours here. By the 1990s he found the climb to the first-floor bar too difficult and gave up visiting the club. The Garrick made the news in 1998 when the Disney Corporation paid the club £50 million for the rights to *Winnie the Pooh* which the author A. A. Milne, a Garrick member, had bequeathed.

Rose Street

John Dryden was mugged in this street in December 1679 by a gang in the pay of the Earl of Rochester, who wrongly believed that the then poet laureate was responsible for an essay satirizing him and the king. The essay had been written anonymously by the Earl of Mulgrave.

King Street

Former Communist Party headquarters, no. 16
Doris Lessing came here to join the Communist Party in the early '50s and was interviewed by Sam Aaronovitch (father of *Independent* columnist, David), who asked her why she wanted to join the party at a time when most intellectuals were leaving it. He told her he looked forward to reading her denunciations of the party when she left.

● Coleridge lived at no. 10 in 1801–2 when he was a journalist on the *Morning Post.*

head back to Bedford Street

Bedford Street

St Paul's Church
When the Earl of Bedford told the architect Inigo Jones in the 1620s that he wanted a chapel, but nothing too expensive – 'nothing much better than a barn' – Jones replied, 'You shall have the handsomest barn in England.' St Paul's became the first new Anglican church to be built in London after the Reformation, although little is left of the original, which was considerably damaged in a fire in 1795 and then rebuilt to Jones's designs. It is known as the actors' church: Ellen Terry is buried here and there are memorials to Marie Lloyd and Vivien Leigh. In his 1662 diary, Samuel Pepys records seeing the English version of the Italian Punchinello (Punch and Judy) under the church's Tuscan portico. The funeral of Samuel Butler (the seventeenth-century satirist,

not the nineteenth-century author of *Erewhon*) took place here in 1680, with Aubrey as one of the pall-bearers. Professor Higgins meets Eliza Doolittle outside the church in the opening scenes of George Bernard Shaw's *Pygmalion* (1913).

head south until reaching Henrietta Street

Henrietta Street

Former Left Book Club office, no. 14

Victor Gollancz opened a publishing house here in 1928 – Dorothy L. Sayers was his first big name – and in 1936 founded the Left Book Club, one of the big publishing success stories of the 1930s. Before long, some 57,000 members were receiving a new Left Book Club title every month, as well as frequent newsletters dictated by Gollancz, whose frantic production schedule led to complaints about clattering typewriters from the nearby Covent Garden Opera House. The LBC books, nearly all of which sported ghastly orange covers, were mostly Stalinist propaganda, with the Communist Party line taking precedence over literary quality. So H. N. Brailsford's critiques of the Moscow trials were ruled out because of their Trotskyite tone and Gollancz turned down George Orwell's *Homage to Catalonia* because the author had criticized Russia's role in the Spanish Civil War. (Admittedly he did later commission Orwell to visit Wigan's mining communities for what became *The Road to Wigan Pier*.)

The Club's fortunes declined rapidly after the Hitler–Stalin pact of 1940 but revived briefly prior to the 1945 general election (which returned a huge Labour majority) when the LBC's yellow-backed anti-Tory pamphlets each sold around a quarter of a million copies. Once Labour was elected, however, the Left Book Club fizzled out, the public's ardour now dimmed by the realities of a socialist government, and the club was dissolved in 1948. Gollancz turned away from politics to religion and began spending his days in the Savoy Grill Room. The name Gollancz still survives in the publishing imprint based nearby.

Jane Austen's address (1813, 1814), no. 10

In the summer of 1813 and March 1814, Jane Austen stayed with her brother in the flat above the bank he owned, describing the property as 'all dirt and confusion, but in a very promising way'. While in Covent Garden she saw *Don Juan* at the Lyceum Theatre and *The Merchant of Venice* at Drury Lane's Theatre Royal. The property was later used as a hospital and is now offices.

Former Air Recruitment Office no. 4

T. E. Lawrence, despite his military success in the Arabian desert during the First World War, came unstuck when he came here to join the Royal Air Force under the pseudonym John Hume Ross in 1922. When the officers in charge, Captain W. E. Johns (later the creator of Biggles), and a Sergeant-Major Gee, asked 'Ross' for his papers, Lawrence was unable to produce any. So they sent him away to get some documentation and Gee phoned Somerset House to look up his particulars; there was no entry in the records for the Ross that Lawrence had outlined.

Lawrence then returned with a special messenger from the Air Ministry, who insisted that the recruit be given a medical. During the medical the doctor asked Lawrence 'What are those marks on your back?' He claimed he had been hurt in an accident, but in fact the marks had been inflicted by a friend with whom Lawrence had indulged in a masochistic beating session. When Johns and Gee asked the Ministry why the wretch before them deserved special treatment, they were astonished to be told that they were dealing with Lawrence of Arabia. Eventually the Air Ministry ensured Lawrence was taken on and his experiences formed the basis for his astonishingly frank portrayal of service life, *The Mint* (1936).

Covent Garden

The name Covent Garden applies not just to the area but is also the name of the paved piazza south-east of the tube station, where a huge popular indoor market can be found and which is now one of London's most congested spots, overrun at most times of the day with fire-eaters, jugglers, musicians and skateboarders. The piazza was designed in the 1630s in the Italian style – luxurious stuccoed houses around a colonnaded square facing a church – by Inigo Jones, and was the centre of the Covent Garden flower and vegetable market until the 1970s.

Site of the Great Piazza Coffee House, Covent Garden, north-west corner

Richard Brinsley Sheridan watched the Theatre Royal, which he ran, burn down while sitting in the Great Piazza Coffee House on 24 February 1809. When a fellow customer queried Sheridan's calmness, the playwright replied, 'Can't a fellow enjoy a drink by his own fireside?' Jos Sedley 'dined with nobody' in the Great Piazza in Thackeray's *Vanity Fair* (1848).

head for the south-western corner of Covent Garden piazza

Southampton Street

Former *Strand* magazine office, nos. 7–12

The monthly literary magazine which George Newnes founded in January 1891 out of the profits of his *Tit-bits* publication was selling an astonishing half a million copies within five years, thanks to the Sherlock Holmes stories. When Conan Doyle (temporarily, it turned out) killed off Holmes in 'The Final Problem' (1893) 20,000 people cancelled their subscription. A *Strand* mainstay for 35 years in the early part of the twentieth century was P. G. Wodehouse.

Tavistock Street

Site of Thomas De Quincey's address (1821–5), no. 36

De Quincey wrote *Confessions of an English Opium Eater* (1821), still the most imaginative book on drugs in English literature, while lodging in these premises in the 1820s. He was able to write down his experiences as by this time he had begun cold turkeying from a daily intake of some 320 grains. The *Confessions* first appeared in September 1821 in the *London Magazine*, which ran a banner: 'we cannot neglect the opportunity of calling the attention of our readers to the deep, eloquent and masterly paper which stands first in our present Number. Such Confessions so powerfully uttered cannot fail to do more than interest the reader.' The book was immediately successful and gave De Quincey the money to buy . . . opium. His intake subsequently became greater than before, he began to suffer shooting pains in his limbs, and was seized by bouts of incessant sneezing.

Wellington Street

Charles Dickens's office (1859–70), no. 26

From this house Dickens published his popular magazine *All the Year Round*, whose contributors included Elizabeth Gaskell and Wilkie Collins. When the latter's *The Moonstone* was serialized in the magazine in 1868, it proved so popular that crowds would gather in the street outside, waiting for the latest instalment. Dickens himself lodged above the shop in the late 1860s, shortly before he died, while visiting London to do his public readings. The office at no. 16, a little further south along Wellington Street, where Dickens published *Household Words*, the magazine he ran before *All the Year Round*, was demolished when Aldwych was constructed around 1900.

head north along Wellington Street

Russell Street

Thomas Davies's address (1760s), no. 8

James Boswell met Samuel Johnson for the first time on 16 May 1763, at no. 8 (then Thomas Davies's bookshop, now a café predictably called Boswell's). He recorded the historic meeting in his *London Journal*: 'I drank tea at Davies's in Russell Street, and about seven came in the great Samuel Johnson, whom I have so long wished to see.' Boswell was wary about how Johnson might treat him, given the great man's aversion to Scots, so he tentatively admitted, 'Indeed I come from Scotland but I cannot help it,' to which the latter replied: 'That I find is what a very great many of your countrymen cannot help.'

Site of Will's Coffee House, no. 20

Will's, which opened in 1671, came to be particularly associated with John Dryden, who used the place for about forty years, had his own chair and, according to Pepys, attracted 'all the wits of the town', engaged in 'very witty and pleasant discourse'. Other Will's regulars in the seventeenth century were Aphra Behn, England's first known professional woman writer, the satirist Samuel Butler, described by one doctor as an 'old paralytick claret drinker', and Jonathan Swift, whose *On Poetry: A Rhapsody* urged young poets to publish a poem and then go to Will's the next day to 'lie snug and hear what the Cricticks say'.

- Button's, a Restoration-era coffee house patronized by Joseph Addison, Jonathan Swift and Alexander Pope, stood at No. 10.

Bow Street

This small street, home to the Royal Opera House, is also known for the Bow Street Runners, Britain's first police force, and Bow Street Magistrates Court. The Bow Street Runners were founded by *Tom Jones* author Henry Fielding and his near-blind half-brother, John. Henry had been made a magistrate by George II as a reward for supporting the Hanoverian cause, while John had written an important crime report entitled *Thieving Detected: Being a True and Particular Description of the Various Methods and Artifices Used by Thieves and Sharpers to Take in and Deceive the Public; with Proper Cautions to Guard against Such Destructive Measures*. The two Fieldings fought against the corrupt practices of the day, which saw JPs regularly taking bribes and anyone who turned in a criminal being rewarded.

Bow Street Magistrates Court, nos. 19–20

Oscar Wilde was charged with gross indecency at these courts in April 1895 and thrown into a cell where he was allowed the rare luxury of a rug. When Wilde woke after a fretful night he ordered a breakfast of tea, toast and eggs from the nearby Tavistock Hotel, which was brought across on a tray. In 1913 Tommy Earp (who became a well-known art critic) was up before the court for being drunk and disorderly, having been discovered the worse for wear in a huge basket of strawberries in Covent Garden. When the magistrate asked him why he'd climbed into the basket, Earp, in an exaggerated upper-class accent, replied, 'For valetudinarian reasons, purely valetudinarian reasons.' The astonished magistrate exclaimed: 'Don't address me as if you were president of the Oxford Union,' to which Earp replied, 'But I am' – and he was.

Two years later, Bow Street magistrates found D. H. Lawrence's *The Rainbow* (1915) obscene. As well as the alleged obscenity, the authorities were concerned with the novel's anti-war content, for at that time British Forces were having problems on the western front and army recruitment was low. In November 1928 the obscenity trial for Radclyffe Hall's *The Well of Loneliness*, published that year, took place at Bow Street. Hall arrived in court in a leather driving coat and Spanish riding hat but was not allowed to take the witness stand as the libel laws of the time were directed against the publisher and distributors, not the author. Around forty defence witnesses were called, including Virginia Woolf; nevertheless *The Well of Loneliness* was banned after being found to contain 'acts of the most horrible, unnatural and disgusting obscenity'. It wasn't published in Britain until 1949, by which time the author was dead.

In Dickens's *Oliver Twist* (1839) the Artful Dodger is brought to Bow Street after being caught stealing a handkerchief from a gentleman's pocket. Dickens also used the cells in *Barnaby Rudge* (1841), the hero being taken prisoner for his involvement in the Gordon Riots and sent here before being jailed in Newgate Prison (see p. 73). In the Sherlock Holmes story 'The Man with the Twisted Lip' (1891) Hugh Boone, the outrageous-looking beggar and hero of the story, is brought here on suspicion of the murder of Neville St Clair. Holmes arrives with a wet flannel, which he takes to Boone's face while the beggar is asleep, washing off his make-up and revealing him to be none other than St Clair in disguise.

(Covent Garden) Royal Opera House, Bow Street at Floral Street

The Opera House dates back to 1732 and was soon showing the plays of the day such as Oliver Goldsmith's *She Stoops to Conquer* (1773) which was premiered here, the playwright having brought along friends from the Literary Club to lead the applause. Thomas De Quincey wrote in *Confessions of an English Opium Eater* (1821) how the Opera House was 'by much the most pleasant place of public resort in London for passing an evening'. In Iris Murdoch's *The Black Prince* (1973) Bradley Pearson, not wishing to 'be sick within the precincts of the Royal Opera House', finds relief over a grille in one of the nearby side streets.

head east towards Drury Lane

Drury Lane

In his 1665 diary, written at the height of the Plague, Samuel Pepys notices two or three houses on Drury Lane marked with a red cross (signifying that infection was raging inside) and 'Lord have mercy upon us' written on the door in the regulation one-foot-high letters. Houses so marked were usually boarded up for forty days . . . with the victims inside. Feeling guilty, Pepys buys some tobacco to smell and chew, 'which took away the apprehension', for tobacco was seen as a kind of palliative, and supposedly no tobacconist died during the Plague. Daniel Defoe noted in his *A Journal of the Plague Year* (1722) how London began to take the Plague seriously when 'two men, said to be Frenchmen, died of the plague . . . at the upper end of Drury Lane'. The street later became another Grub Street, attracting hack poets, and by Victorian times was a wretched area, as Dickens recounted in 'A Gin Shop' from *Sketches by Boz* (1837): 'The filthy and miserable appearance of this part of London can hardly be imagined by those who have not witnessed it.' Nowadays such a description is hard to appreciate as the filth and squalor have gone and the streets around Drury Lane have an easy-going feel.

Theatre Royal, Drury Lane at Russell Street
John Dryden, Colly Cibber and Richard Brinsley Sheridan were all involved at various times in running this theatre, which opened in May 1663, burned down in January 1672, and was then rebuilt by Christopher Wren two years later. Colly Cibber, who became the theatre's actor-playwright-manager at the end of the seventeenth century, joined Thomas Betterton's company but fluffed his first line on the opening night. Betterton wanted Cibber fined and, when he found that Cibber wasn't being paid, demanded that the actor receive ten shillings a week and be immediately docked five shillings for the mistake. Garrick made his name here between 1747 and 1775.

Sheridan began producing his plays at the theatre after gaining a share in the place in 1776. Like Cibber, his career didn't get off to too good a start. His play *The Rivals* (1775) was panned on the opening night after a bad performance by John Lee, one of the leading members of the cast, who was accidentally hit on the head by an apple. A Frank Reynolds play, *The Caravan*, did better. On the opening night, when Sheridan saw the scene in which a dog jumps into a pool to save a drowning child, he knew he had a hit. Backstage he rushed in shouting, 'Where is my saviour?' An elated Reynolds rose to be thanked but Sheridan rushed past him and picked up the dog.

In February 1809 the theatre burned down again and Sheridan, who was in the House of Commons, rushed to Covent Garden but, instead of coming to the theatre, went to the Piazza Coffee House (see above) to get a better view of the blaze. These days the theatre is best known for staging musicals. In the late 1950s *My Fair Lady* ran for over 2,200 performances.

HOLBORN

Now mostly offices, many of which are associated with the legal profession (Lincoln's Inn, Gray's Inn and the Royal Courts of Justice are nearby), Holborn takes its name from the Holebourne stream, now culverted. West of Kingsway, the traffic route which was driven through the old slums in 1905, there are a number of quiet streets with small shops and firms. East of Kingsway the area is dominated by Lincoln's Inn Fields, a rare slice of greenery in a hugely built-up part of central London.

- Landmarks can be reached from Holborn tube.

Kingsway to Holborn Circus: west to east

Kingsway

Site of Charles and Mary Lamb's address (1795–96), Kingsway at Parker Street

While living in a house on this site Mary Lamb accidentally stabbed her mother to death during a row with a servant. Having previously suffered fits of insanity, she was sent to an asylum in Hoxton. She was eventually released but was prone to violent spells and so Charles would take a strait-jacket when they went on holiday – just in case. Both the house, no. 7, and the road it was in, Little Queen Street, have been demolished. The disused Holy Trinity Church stands on the site.

head south and turn left at Sardinia Street

Portsmouth Street

The Old Curiosity Shop, no. 13

Despite the misleading claim above the awning, this was not the model for Charles Dickens's Old Curiosity Shop (that stood either at 24 Fetter Lane or at 10 Orange Street, by Leicester Square), for at the end of the novel Dickens explains that the shop had long ago been pulled down. Moreover, 13 Portsmouth Street was renamed the Old Curiosity Shop in 1868, nearly thirty years after the book was published. As a shop, however, it dates back to 1567 and used to be a dairy. It is also the only remaining building from Clare Market, which was swept away at the end of the nineteenth century when Kingsway and Aldwych were created.

head back north

Lincoln's Inn Fields

Lincoln's Inn Fields is the name of both the large square grassed area, a couple of hundred yards south-east of Holborn tube station, and the road surrounding the fields. The green was laid out by Inigo Jones in 1618 and was later described by Macaulay as 'an open space where [in the late seventeenth century] the rabble congregated every evening . . . to hear mountebanks harangue, to see bears dance, and to set dogs at oxen'. At the eastern end of the square is Lincoln's Inn, one of four surviving Inns of Court (along with Gray's Inn and the Inner and Middle Temple), past members of which include Thomas More (who became a junior barrister in record time), John Donne, Benjamin Disraeli, H. Rider Haggard, John Galsworthy and Arnold Bennett.

Alfred, Lord Tennyson's address (1854), no. 60

Tennyson stayed here briefly.

Dante Gabriel Rossetti's address (1860s), no. 59

Rossetti came to live here after a spell in nearby Red Lion Square and soon afterwards his wife, Elizabeth Siddal, gave birth to a still-born child, went into depression, and began taking laudanum. One day while Rossetti was out she took an overdose. She died soon afterwards, and some years later in a notorious incident Rossetti dug up her grave in Highgate Cemetery (see p. 275).

John Forster's address (1850s), 58 Lincoln's Inn Fields
Forster, Dickens's biographer, gave up a legal career to write biography
– on Goldsmith and Swift as well as Dickens. Dickens, in *Bleak House*
(1853), used this address as the home of the ill-fated Mr Tulkinghorn,
where lawyers 'lie like maggots in nuts'.

Sir John Soane's Museum, no. 13, tel. 020 7405-2107. Open: 10–5 Tue.–
Sat. and 6–9 p.m. first Tuesday in month. Admission: free.
Described by many as the best museum in London, the house was the
address of Sir John Soane, architect of the Bank of England and an
obsessive collector of arcana. Much remains as Soane left it and the
complex layout with trick mirrors and countless alcoves ensures that
there are surprises at every turn. Highlights are the original Hogarth
works, *The Rake's Progress* and *The Election*, and a huge library on
architecture.

Lincoln's Inn Hall, south-east corner Lincoln's Inn Fields
At a dinner for soldiers who had helped quash the 1780 Gordon Riots,
Edward Gibbon, author of *Decline and Fall of the Roman Empire* (1788),
waxed forth on the political debates of the day, finished his soliloquy,
and sat back to take in the applause. Most of the guests clapped but
one turned on him and denounced his arguments one by one, humiliating the author. The speaker was William Pitt the Younger, and when
the future prime minister finished Gibbon made his excuses and left.
Until the Law Courts were built in the Strand in 1874 the hall, which
dates back to the 1420s and is the oldest building in the area, was used
as the High Court of Chancery, as Dickens recounts in *Bleak House*
(1853), in which it is the seat of the Lord High Chancellor and the setting for the interminable case of Jarndyce vs. Jarndyce.

head east through the Inn

Old Square

Lincoln's Inn Chapel
The chapel was founded by John Donne, who was divinity reader here
in 1616, and it was probably the chapel bell that Donne had in mind
when he wrote in *Devotions* '. . . for whom the bell tolls; it tolls for
thee'. The bell is still tolled around lunchtime the day after a member
dies.

head east to Chancery Lane

Chancery Lane

In his first day working as a solicitor's clerk in nearby Gray's Inn in 1827, Charles Dickens went for lunch along Chancery Lane and was accosted by a 'big blackguard fellow', who greeted the young aspiring writer, 'Halloa, sojer.' This annoyed Dickens so much he gave the lad a whack and was dealt a black eye in return.

north to south

Site of 'Orthotex', no. 87
In Graham Greene's *Ministry of Fear* (1943), Orthotex, 'the Longest Established Private Inquiry Bureau in the Metropolis, still managed to survive at the unravaged end of Chancery Lane'. When Arthur Rowe arrives looking for Mr Rennit, the office is empty and a half-eaten sausage-roll lies, looking as if it might have 'lain there for weeks'. No. 87 was then home of Shedlock & Stammers, shorthand writers.

Former *Academy* magazine offices, no. 27
When the 21-year-old James Joyce came to these offices to deliver a book review, the magazine's editor, C. Lewis Hind, was unimpressed with the unfavourable line Joyce had taken and handed it back, stating, 'This won't do, Mr Joyce.' Joyce took his review, mumbled, 'Sorry,' and began to leave the room, but was stopped by Hind, who exclaimed: 'Oh come, Mr Joyce, I'm only anxious to help you. Why don't you meet my wishes.' The argument continued and Hind pointed out that he simply wanted a positive comment from the reviewer. 'I only have to lift the window and put my head out and I can get a hundred critics to review it,' he concluded. 'Review what? Your head?' Joyce replied fatuously. Thus ended the London book-reviewing career of the twentieth century's most celebrated novelist.

Former *Poetry Review* office, no. 93
Harold Monro ran *The Poetry Review* from this address in 1911.

head back up Chancery Lane and turn right at the main road, High Holborn

Holborn

Staple Inn
Best known for its black-and-white timber-framed frontage which perilously overhangs the road (for years the image famously featured on the Old Holborn tobacco packets), Staple Inn is London's only existing

sixteenth-century domestic architecture (although much of it was heavily bombed in the Second World War) and a former legal Inn of Chancery. Dr Johnson lived at no. 2 (now rebuilt) from 1759 to 1760 and probably wrote *Rasselas* (1759) here in one week to pay for his mother's funeral. Charles Dickens described it in his last novel, the unfinished *Mystery of Edwin Drood* (1870), as 'a little nook composed of two irregular quadrangles . . . one of those nooks where a few smoky sparrows twitter in smoky trees'.

Brooke Street

Site of Thomas Chatterton's address (1770) and deathplace, no. 4
Few writers who have died so young (Chatterton took a fatal dose of arsenic when only 17) have left as deep a mark as this mysterious poet. Living in London, penniless and surviving off a halfpenny roll and water, he offered the publisher Robert Dodsley some poems but they were rejected and, in a fit of depression, he supposedly poisoned himself with a large dose of arsenic on 24 August 1770. (There is no proof that he did commit suicide; some believe he was taking arsenic to alleviate a dose of VD.)

It was only after Chatterton died that he earned a reputation as a poet of genius. Found among his papers were poems which he had claimed were written by Thomas Rowley, a fifteenth-century monk. The Rowley poems (including the ones Dodsley had rejected) were published in 1777 and hailed as masterpieces. But critics were torn over their authenticity. Was Rowley the author or Chatterton? Eventually the scholar Thomas Tyrwhitt 'proved' that the poems could not have been written by the monk, citing the line 'Life and its good I scorn': the possessive pronoun 'its' didn't come into use until the seventeenth century. Tyrwhitt immediately published a new edition of the poems which included 'An Appendix to Prove that They Were Written by Chatterton'.

Chatterton became a hero to the romantic movement, especially once the story of his demise emerged; the tale of how, a few days before his death, Chatterton had fallen into an open grave while out walking with a friend and had seen this as a premonition of his impending death added to the myth. John Keats dedicated *Endymion* (1818) to him, describing Chatterton as 'the purest writer in the English language' as he had used almost no French idioms; but Thomas De Quincey was less impressed and dismissed the Chatterton controversy as 'the very midsummer madness of affectation'. The poet's death inspired Vigny's play, *Chatterton* (1835), the hero seen as a symbol of how society mistreats poets. In 1856 Richard Wallis painted *The Death of Chatterton* in the room where the poet died, the novelist and poet George Meredith posing as Chatterton. A year later, Meredith's wife left him for Wallis.

About a hundred years after his untimely death Chatterton supposedly saved the life of the poet Francis Thompson, who was on the point of committing suicide until Chatterton appeared to him in a vision and warned him not to do so. Peter Ackroyd's 1987 novel, also entitled simply *Chatterton*, interweaves Chatterton's life with that of a modern-day aspiring writer, Charles Wychwood. The house in which Chatterton died was demolished in 1880. Barclays Bank now stands on the site.

continue east along Holborn (also see the Charles Dickens walk, p. 100)

Holborn Viaduct

St Andrew's, Holborn Viaduct at Shoe Lane
Benjamin Disraeli, despite his Jewish background, was baptized in this Wren church in July 1817 after his father, the writer Isaac D'Israeli, fell out with the elders of Bevis Marks Synagogue. Disraeli lost his religion but gained the chance to have a political career, Jews at that time being excluded from Parliament. The essayist William Hazlitt married here, Charles Lamb acting as best man. In *Oliver Twist* (1839) Oliver and Bill Sikes pass by the church on their way to Hyde Park Corner and look up at the clock which is 'hard upon seven'.

Ely Place

In Shakespeare's *Richard II* (1596) John of Gaunt makes his famous 'scepter'd isle' speech in Ely House, the London palace of the Bishops of Ely (long demolished) where he stayed after his Savoy Palace was wrecked in the Peasants' Revolt. Ely Palace also features in *Richard III* (1593), the pre-regal Richard (then Duke of Gloucester) reminding the Bishop, 'When I was last in Holborn, I saw good strawberries in your garden there; I do beseech you, send for some of them.' St Ethelreda's, Ely Place's church, is the oldest Catholic church in England. Until recently this exclusive terrace was guarded by men in top hats and frock coats. It now has just commissionaires.

STRAND TO THE RIVER

'I should have mentioned last night that I met a monstrous big whore in the Strand' from *Boswell's London Journal*, James Boswell, 1763

Originally the shore of the river linking Westminster and London, until modern times Strand was the main road link between Westminster and the City. John Evelyn in his seventeenth-century diary recorded the triumphant return to England of Charles II, who disembarked from his boat and paraded along here 'after a sad & long exile'. The young Samuel Taylor Coleridge tried to pick a gentleman's pocket while walking down the Strand in the 1780s. The man turned round to accost the would-be thief and exclaimed: 'What! so young and so wicked?' Coleridge quickly explained that he wasn't picking the man's pocket but was trying to impersonate Leander swimming the Hellespont. The would-be victim was impressed and gave Coleridge a subscription to the library in King Street.

By the eighteenth-century Strand had become one of the most fashionable streets in London, and during Victorian times this status was maintained by the arrival of theatres, hotels, restaurants and the Royal Courts of Justice; but in recent years Strand has become shabby, despite the continuing presence of the Savoy Hotel and the plush Simpson's. Most of the shops are disappointing, the street is lined with tramps, and there are few decent bars or restaurants. There are however plans to revamp the sadly neglected Somerset House (former Public Records Office) at the south-eastern end by linking it with the South Bank complex on the other side of the Thames.

Before Victoria Embankment was built (1864–70), the streets south of Strand led directly to the river and the area was full of coal wharves and dingy warehouses such as Warren's Blacking Factory where Charles Dickens worked, covering pots of blacking paste, when he was twelve. There were numerous dark alleyways and passages, and Dickens in *David Copperfield* (1850) wrote of 'wandering about . . . because it was a mysterious place with those dark arches'. Some of these 'dark arches' remain: try Lower Robert Street, which runs round a blind alley through the bowels of a building, and the alleys leading south of the Strand around Savoy Hill.

The Strand has many literary associations. T. E. Lawrence in the 1920s walked down it in flowing white Arabian robes and carrying a jewel-encrusted sword. In the early 1960s Anthony Burgess could be seen staggering along carrying suitcases filled with review copies of books which he was about to sell at second-hand shops. Dickens mentioned the Strand in a number of works, including *Sketches by Boz* (1837), *Nicholas Nickleby* (1839), *Barnaby Rudge* (1841) and *Our Mutual Friend* (1865). In the former he tells of following a group of people 'who furnished food for our amusement the whole way'. Graham Greene, in his poem *1930*, wrote about 'The sick swim of faces/Huddled beneath umbrellas in the Strand', and in *Brighton Rock* (1938) he gave Ida Arnold a job in Henekey's, a fictitious bar in the Strand. In Somerset Maugham's *Cakes and Ale* (1930) Rosie picks up an old actor friend for the night in the Strand despite having just buried her only child.

- Landmarks to the west can be reached from Charing Cross and Embankment tubes. Those further east are accessible from Temple tube.

Trafalgar Square to Temple Bar: west to east

Trafalgar Square

William Morris and George Bernard Shaw were among those who tried to lead the 200,000-strong demonstration into the square on Sunday, 13 November 1887, an event which became known as Bloody Sunday on account of the violence that ensued. In one incident, the short-story writer R. B. Cunninghame-Graham led a charge across the street, was struck by a policeman, and was stepped on by a police horse which wrenched off the nail of his big toe. In his future-set *News from Nowhere* (1890) Morris beautified the square by filling it with apricot trees. George Orwell slept rough in Trafalgar Square in his tramping period in the 1920s, bedding down under newspapers and washing in the fountains before spending the days in the not typically itinerant pursuit of reading Balzac in the original French. Aiming to get arrested so that he could experience the inside of a cell, Orwell contemplated lighting a bonfire in the square, until it was pointed out to him that the authorities would probably treat such behaviour as an ex-public schoolboy's prank. Orwell later set his Joycean dialogue-only scene in *A Clergyman's Daughter* (1935) in Trafalgar Square, and he revisited the place in *1984* as the setting for the Victory Square rallies where traitors and prisoners-of-war were executed. Orwell took the idea for the Victory rallies from the real-life Victory Loan rallies held here in 1918 to mark the ending of the First World War.

National Gallery

> *'There is no rule against carrying binoculars in the National Gallery'* from
> *Metroland*, Julian Barnes, 1980

Barnes's first work, which won the Somerset Maugham prize, opens in the gallery with the two smug protagonists, Chris Lloyd and Toni, using long-distance glasses not to study the paintings in more detail but to examine and mock the mannerisms and expressions of other visitors. Joseph Conrad proposed to his typist, Jessie George, by the entrance to the National Gallery while taking refuge from the rain. Never the most romantic of souls, Conrad announced, 'We had better get married and out of this. Look at the weather,' and later wrote to a cousin back in his native Poland, 'She is a small, not at all striking-looking person (to tell the truth, alas – rather plain!).' During the First World War E. M. Forster worked here cataloguing pictures. Novelists who have used the place as a convenient location where characters can meet include Iris Murdoch in *The Bell* (1958) and Antonia White in *The Lost Traveller* (1950), in which Nicole and Clara plan to meet here or in the British Museum like 'guilty characters in Henry James'.

St Martin's Place

St Martin-in-the-Fields
Francis Thompson, the opium-addicted poet, described this church by Trafalgar Square as 'Jacob's ladder/Pitched between Heaven and Charing Cross' as a way of thanking one of the wardens for helping him when he was destitute in the 1880s. In *Uncommercial Traveller: Night Walks* (1860) Charles Dickens tells of coming to the 'great steps of St Martin's Church as the clock was striking three' and stumbling upon a 'beetle-browed, hare-lipped youth of twenty' clothed in a bundle of rags. The author is about to give the wretch some money, but when he lays his hand on a shoulder the rags come off and the vagrant makes off, naked. Ted Hughes gave the memorial address to Henry Williamson here when the author (best known for *Tarka the Otter*) died in 1977. Williamson had remained a staunch supporter of the Fascist leader Oswald Mosley till the end, which led the literary establishment and the public to ignore his 15-volume masterpiece, *A Chronicle of Ancient Sunlight*. In his address Hughes rhetorically asked the congregation, 'Who is to say that the ideas in themselves were wrong?'

head south to the Strand and turn left

Northumberland Street

Ben Jonson is believed to have been born in this street in June 1572.

The Sherlock Holmes, Northumberland Street at Craven Passage
Sherlock Holmes memorabilia fill the walls of this cosy, hard-to-find
pub, the side of which in Craven Passage stands opposite the now-
closed Turkish baths which Holmes and Watson used in 'The Illustrious Client' (1925). The pub's Holmesian artefacts include the contrived
(brier pipes and bent poker sticks based on the stories) and the genuine (superb cuttings, such as the one depicting a group of American
men in the semaphoric positions of the characters in 'The Dancing
Men' welcoming Conan Doyle to a stateside town). Upstairs, next to
the restaurant, is a life-size reconstruction of Holmes and Watson's
221B Baker Street sitting-room, complete with Holmes mannequin (as
used in 'The Empty House'), violin, books, period furniture and
shelves laden with foul-looking bottled chemicals. The collection dates
from the 1951 Festival of Britain exhibition of Holmes memorabilia displayed at Abbey House in Baker Street, the modern-day 221B.

Craven Street

Herman Melville's address (1849), no. 25
Early in his career Melville came to London and, when paid £200 for a
first edition of his new book, *White Jacket*, left for Paris, Brussels and
Cologne. He returned briefly to London but, homesick for the USA,
left for New York to start work on *The Whale*, the story that became
Moby Dick. A skyscraper office block now stands in the garden of
no. 25.

head north to Adelaide Street

Adelaide Street

Oscar Wilde statue
Wilde is commemorated with a statue in the form of a seat inscribed
with one of the writer's best-known quips: 'We are all in the gutter but
some of us are looking at the stars.'

Strand

Charing Cross station, Strand at Villiers Street
Phileas Fogg leaves this terminus to go around the world in eighty days
in the Jules Verne adventure story of the same name. The Victorian
poet Francis Thompson used to sleep rough under the arches. H. G.
Wells wrote in *Kipps* (1905) how London 'presented itself as a place of

great grey spaces . . . centring about Charing Cross Station'. The station features several times in the Sherlock Holmes stories (see the Sherlock Holmes walk, p. 176). In *Fulbright Scholars*, the opening poem of Ted Hughes's *Birthday Letters* (1998), Hughes buys a peach from the stall that stands outside the station.

Site of Francis Bacon's birthplace, Strand at Villiers Street, south-east junction
The Elizabethan statesman, philosopher and essayist was born on 22 January 1561 in York House, which belonged to the archbishops of York and then stood here.

Villiers Street

Rudyard Kipling's address (1889–91), no. 43
While living in rooms on the third floor of this block opposite Charing Cross station, Kipling, then in his twenties, wrote the partly autobiographical novel *The Light That Failed* (1891), in which Dick Heldar takes rooms overlooking the Thames near Charing Cross. Below the flat, Harris, the so-called 'Sausage King', sold his suppers; and in his autobiography, *Something of Myself* (1937), Kipling wrote how Harris would give him as much sausage and mash for tuppence as he could carry upstairs. Across the street, which Kipling described as 'primitive and passionate in its habits and population', stood Gatti's music hall (where the Players' Theatre now stands) from which he derived the atmosphere of *Barrack-Room Ballads* (1892). Kipling wrote the latter at no. 43 with a fez on his head and a note on the door which read: 'To publishers: a classic while you wait.'

Site of Warren's Blacking Factory, Villiers Street at Embankment Place
So poor was Charles Dickens's family in 1824 that even though he was only 12 he was sent to work in Warren's Blacking Factory which stood by the Thames at no. 30 Hungerford Stairs (from which Mr Micawber emigrates to Australia in *David Copperfield*). At Warren's, Dickens covered pots of paste with paper and string, but to alleviate the boredom he began developing stories to entertain workmates, one of whom was called Bob Fagin. A few weeks after he started working at Warren's, Dickens's father, John, was arrested for debt and locked up in Marshalsea gaol. This meant that after work the young Dickens would have had to join his father and the rest of the family for dinner in Marshalsea before going back to his own lodgings. Dickens was so pained by these events that he revealed them to nobody throughout his life

other than to his biographer, John Forster, but the factory's pitiful appearance continued to haunt his imagination and was re-created as Fagin's lair in *Oliver Twist* (1839), as 'a crazy building undermined by the rats' in *The Old Curiosity Shop* (1841) and, most sharply of all, in the semi-autobiographical *David Copperfield* (1850), where it is Murdstone and Grinby's, 'a crazy, tumbledown old house abutting the river and literally overrun with rats'. At the end of 1824 the factory removed to Chandos Street, a little further north.

take the steps down to Victoria Embankment

Victoria Embankment

> 'The embankment juts out in angles here and there, like pulpits' from *The Voyage Out*, Virginia Woolf, 1912

The Embankment was built in 1870 as part of a sophisticated land-reclamation and road-building project.

Victoria Embankment Gardens

A section of the Thames was filled in to create these gardens which – for no apparent reason – contain a statue of Robert Burns, a Scottish poet who never came to London.

Cleopatra's Needle, Victoria Embankment, between Hungerford Railway Bridge and Waterloo Bridge

Probably the oldest exposed artefact in London, Cleopatra's Needle was cut from granite quarries in Aswan, Egypt, around 1475 BC, carved with dedications to various gods and rulers, and erected in Alexandria. It eventually fell into the sand and in 1819 was presented to the British by Mohammed Ali, Viceroy of Egypt, before being brought to London amid much difficulty in 1878. Its arrival led Alfred, Lord Tennyson, then poet laureate, to write the poem *Cleopatra's Needle* in which he imagines the Egyptian queen recalling, 'I have seen the four great empires disappear. I was when London was not. I am here.' Cleopatra's Needle was the first London monument to be hit by enemy air attack – during the First World War in 1917.

head back to Embankment tube and cut through Villiers Street and Watergate Walk until reaching Buckingham Street

Buckingham Street

Before the Embankment was built in the nineteenth century, the Thames flowed at the foot of this street (where steps lead through an arch down to Watergate Walk and Embankment Gardens). Past residents include Samuel Pepys, Henry Fielding, Samuel Taylor Coleridge and Charles Dickens. John Betjeman's mother, Mabel, ran a milliner's and dressmaking business from no. 19 under the name Betty Burton around the turn of the nineteenth century.

Samuel Pepys's address (1679–84), no. 12

After being released from the Tower, where he had been imprisoned for alleged involvement in a plot to put a Catholic on the throne (the Popish Plot), Pepys came to Buckingham Street to stay with a friend, William Hewer. In 1684 Pepys was reinstated as secretary to the Admiralty but had to move from no. 12 when a nearby wooden water tower caught fire. He then suffered another blow: his belongings were stolen when neighbouring houses were demolished in order to stop the fire spreading. Pepys later moved to the rebuilt no. 14 (demolished 1791), which soon after became the meeting place for the Saturday Academists, a group whose number included fellow diarist John Evelyn. When Pepys fell ill in 1701 he left Buckingham Street and moved in with Hewer, who by then was living in the countryside in Clapham (see p. 378). No. 12's original staircase is still in place.

Site of Charles Dickens's address (1833), no. 15

Dickens came to Buckingham Street when working as a reporter and he later put David Copperfield in a 'set of chambers' at no. 15 in the novel of the same name. Prior to Dickens, residents at no. 15 included Russian Tsar Peter the Great (in 1698) and Henry Fielding (1753).

turn right at John Adam Street

Durham House Street

Site of Durham House/Walter Ralegh's address (1583–1603)

Walter Ralegh wrote most of his best poetry, including *A Report of the Fight about the Isles of the Azores* (1591), while living in the palace that stood here and which Elizabeth I had granted him at the height of his court popularity. When she discovered that he had seduced and secretly married one of her maids of honour, Elizabeth Throckmorton, the queen flew into a rage and sent both Ralegh and his wife to the Tower. (A different theory has it that Ralegh was arrested for sedition after getting involved with a body of independent thinkers known as the School of Atheisme and the School of Night.) By 1593 Ralegh was free, back in favour, and once again living in Durham House, and he soon became a leading figure in the Society of Antiquaries, one of the first great literary clubs, whose number included John Donne, Edmund Spenser and Christopher Marlowe and which met here and at the Mermaid Tavern in the City (see p. 59). When Elizabeth died in 1603, Ralegh tried unsuccessfully to thwart James VI of Scotland's succession to the throne. So when the latter became James I of England, Ralegh found himself back in the court's bad books, and he was arrested for treason, forced to leave Durham House, again, and sent back to the Tower.

Robert Street

No. 1

The Song of the Shirt poet, Thomas Hood, lived here (1828–30), as later did *Peter Pan* playwright J. M. Barrie (1911–37) and *Forstye Saga* author John Galsworthy (1917–18). Barrie came to Robert Street after his divorce, and one night during the First World War he, Thomas Hardy, H. G. Wells, Arnold Bennett and George Bernard Shaw naïvely sheltered here – they weren't really safe – while German bombs fell nearby. Galsworthy moved into his flat shortly after returning to England from the Alps where he had been a volunteer in a hospital for wounded French soldiers.

head along Robert Street towards the river

Adelphi Terrace

The Adelphi

Next to nothing is left of the grand colonnaded Classical development which the Adam brothers built between 1778 and 1785 (in what was then an excellent riverside location) in a style evoking the ruined palace of Diocletian at Spalato (Split). (They called it Adelphi because *Adelphoi* is the Greek for brothers.) The Gilbert & Sullivan impresario and Savoy Hotel/Theatre founder, Richard D'Oyly Carte, lived at no. 4 between 1888 and 1901 and hired Whistler to decorate the library walls with a tint of yellow so that they appeared warm with sunshine even during winter. Dr Johnson used to visit Garrick, the actor-manager, at no. 6, where he lived from 1772 to 1779. From 1862 to 1867 Thomas Hardy worked at no. 8 for the architect, Arthur Blomfield, who specialized in restoring Gothic churches. The novel Hardy wrote at that time, *The Poor Man and the Lady*, about an architect who falls in love with the squire's daughter, was rejected on the advice of the publisher's reader, the novelist George Meredith, and was never published in that form. George Bernard Shaw lived at no. 10 from 1899 to 1927, mainly with Charlotte Payne-Townshend, with whom he shared an unconsummated marriage, and there he wrote *Man and Superman* (1903) and *Major Barbara* (1905). The Adelphi was pulled down, despite much opposition, in 1936 and replaced with Colcutt and Hemp's rather totalitarian-looking block.

head back to the Strand along Adam Street

Strand

Adelphi Theatre, Strand opposite Adam Street
Oscar Wilde pulled the production of his first play, *Vera*, due to be premiered here in 1881, when the Russian Tsar, Alexander II, was assassinated. The Tsar was married to the Prince of Wales's sister-in-law and Wilde insisted on withdrawing the play out of consideration for the Prince's feelings.

turn right

Ivybridge Lane

Site of Oscar Wilde's address (1879–81)
After achieving a double first at Oxford, Wilde, unable to get an academic post on account of his flamboyant reputation, came to London and set himself up as 'art critic and professor of aesthetics'. He and fellow housemate, the colour-blind painter Frank Miles, moved into a house (no. 13) in Salisbury Street, which then stood here, and renamed the place Thames House. They began hosting daily at-homes at half past five in the afternoon, and these attracted society beauties such as Ellen Terry and Lillie Langtry, who wanted to be painted by Miles. Salisbury Street was later demolished and the site is now covered by Shell-Mex House.

Savoy Court

Savoy Theatre
Built by Richard D'Oyly Carte in 1881 to stage his productions of Gilbert & Sullivan's light operas, the theatre opened with the latter's *Patience* in which George Grossmith, later co-author of *The Diary of a Nobody* (1892), played Reginald Bunthorne, an Aesthetic Movement poet based partly on Oscar Wilde and partly on the painter James Whistler.

Savoy Hotel
D'Oyly Carte built this hotel in 1889 out of the profits made from his Gilbert & Sullivan light operas, which were being performed at the nearby Savoy Theatre. The hotel opened with César Ritz (who went on

to found the Ritz Hotel) as manager and Auguste Escoffier as chef; and it had seventy bathrooms at a time when even the largest hotels had only four or five. In the early 1890s Oscar Wilde conducted his affair with Lord Alfred Douglas in Room 346. Arnold Bennett's last and longest novel, *Imperial Palace* (1930), is based on the running of the hotel. To protect himself from accusations of libel, Bennett claimed his hotel was set in St James's rather than Strand, but he got most of his ideas from a series of meetings with Savoy managers and he stayed here extensively in the late 1920s while preparing the book. A lavish 70th birthday party for H. G. Wells was thrown at the Savoy in October 1936, attended by J. B. Priestley, J. M. Barrie, John Galsworthy, John Maynard Keynes, A. A. Milne and Somerset Maugham, who described George Bernard Shaw, another of the guests, as 'a magnificent figure with white beard and white hair, clear skin and bright eyes'.

The Savoy

> '*Now go some and pull down the Savoy*' Jack Cade from *Henry VI Part II*,
> William Shakespeare, 1591

The tiny lanes and blind alleyways between Charing Cross station and the approach to Waterloo Bridge are dominated by the name Savoy: Savoy Buildings, Savoy Court, Savoy Hill, Savoy Place, Savoy Row, Savoy Steps, Savoy Street and Savoy Way as well as the Savoy Hotel, the Savoy Theatre and the lesser-known Savoy Chapel. All these are named in honour of the long-demolished Savoy Palace which in the thirteenth century Henry III donated to his wife's uncle for an annual rent of three barbed arrows. It later became the property of Chaucer's patron, John of Gaunt, but burned down during the 1381 Peasants' Revolt when 32 men trapped in the wine cellar starved while drinking themselves to death. The palace was rebuilt as a hospital in 1505 but was demolished in the 1820s when Waterloo Bridge was built; only the chapel in Savoy Street remains.

Strand

Site of William Blake's address (1821–7) and deathplace, 3 Fountain Court, 103–4 Strand

On 12 August 1827, William Blake died in a house which stood on this site, six years after moving into what Henry Crabb Robinson described as a 'squalid place of but two chairs and a bed'. Ironically, by the end of his life Blake was at last gaining respect (as opposed to mockery), particularly as a painter.

Savoy Street

Savoy Chapel
The original Savoy Chapel, part of the Savoy Palace which then stood here (see above), was destroyed during the 1381 Peasants' Revolt, but it was rebuilt in 1510 when the palace was converted into a hospital and it still stands despite several fires and much alteration. The chapel features stained-glass memorials of Chaucer, his patron, John of Gaunt, and John Wycliffe, the religious reformer and first translator of the Bible into English. Samuel Pepys complained about the quality of the sermons.

Strand

Site of George Eliot's address (1851–3), no. 142
Publisher John Chapman lived above his office in a ménage-à-trois with his wife and mistress and, when George Eliot (then Mary Ann Evans) came to London and needed a roof, he put her up too. (She marked the move to London by changing the spelling of her name from Mary Ann Evans to Marian Evans.) Soon after, she began editing *The Westminster Review* which Chapman had bought.

Somerset House, Strand, east of Lancaster Place
This monumental eighteenth-century riverside complex was home of the General Register of Births, Deaths and Marriages until 1973 and now houses the Courtauld Institute galleries. It also features in various detective stories, including Dorothy L. Sayers's *The Unpleasantness at the Bellona Club* (1928) and P. D. James's *An Unsuitable Job for a Woman* (1972).

Bush House, Strand at Montreal Place
Towards the end of the Second World War Muriel Spark was interviewed here for a Foreign Office job by Sefton Delmer, former European correspondent for the *Daily Express*, who had met several Nazi leaders before the war. Delmer told her that before being taken on by the Foreign Office she would have to be vetted, which meant that her past life would have to be examined. Spark explained that vetting would be difficult, given that she had recently spent a few years in Africa, and when Delmer asked her if she had come to England in a convoy she replied that she didn't know. It was the right answer: British citizens had been warned 'not to know' about the movement of ships and troops, and so she got the job. Bush House is now home of the BBC World Service and houses a number of civil service departments.

St Mary-le-Strand

This James Gibbs church, situated a couple of hundred yards west of St Clement Dane's, dates back to 1717 and is the church that was featured on the front cover of *Strand* magazine for many years. St Mary's was saved in the mid-1980s after a campaign led by John Betjeman, who wrote a poem in its honour which ran 'There's nothing quite so grand/as the Baroque of your Chapel/of St Mary in the Strand'.

King's College, Strand opposite St Mary-le-Strand
John Ruskin attended King's in the 1830s, reading logic, English literature and translation.

Strand Lane

'Roman' Bath, access from Surrey Street
There is no evidence that the bath dates back to Roman times. It is more likely to be Tudor and was once part of Arundel House, the medieval town house of the bishop of Bath and Wells which stood here until the seventeenth century. Charles Dickens used to take a regular plunge in the ice-cold waters and has David Copperfield do likewise in the novel of the same name. The bath, situated in the basement of a King's College building, is now closed to the public but part of it is visible through a window. It is however extremely hard to find. Strand Lane is blocked off from the Strand end and the entrance is through an alleyway from Surrey Street which is open only during daylight hours.

Strand

St Clement Dane's Church, Strand at Aldwych, east end
Although this Wren church is cited as the St Clement's featured in the nursery rhyme 'Oranges and Lemons', the St Clement's in question is more likely to be St Clement's, Eastcheap, which was near the docks where oranges and lemons used to be unloaded. John Gay wrote lovingly about the Strand church and the area in *Trivia, or, The Art of Walking the Streets of London* (1716). Dr Johnson, who worshipped here, is remembered by a statue behind the building. In Shakespeare's *Henry IV Part II* (1600) Falstaff's line 'We have heard the chimes at midnight, Master Shallow' refers to the chimes of this church and gave Orson Welles the title of his film based on Falstaff – *Chimes at Midnight*. In George Orwell's *1984* St Clement Dane's serves as the model for the 'oval building with rectangular windows near the Palace of Justice' [the Law Courts on the Strand], which Winston Smith remembers

when shown the picture by Charrington. When Charrington reveals himself to be in league with the secret police, he scarily recites the 'Oranges and Lemons' nursery rhyme. The church was bombed in the Second World War, when the bells were broken, and it was still unrepaired when Orwell wrote the novel in the late 1940s.

Site of Clement's Inn, Strand at Royal Courts of Justice
Nothing remains of this old Inn of Chancery which was demolished in the 1890s apart from the name given to a street by the Courts of Justice. Clement's Inn is mentioned by Falstaff in Shakespeare's *Henry IV Part II* (1600). It is also where Psmith, P. G. Wodehouse's city slicker, has a flat.

Essex Street

This street, just east of Temple tube by the City boundary, is named after Essex House, the Tudor mansion owned by the Earls of Essex, where Edmund Spenser, a member of the Earl's household, began working on *The Faerie Queene* in 1578. The only remnants of that building are the brick arch and steps at the bottom end of the street that used to be part of one of the gates. In Dickens's *Great Expectations* (1861) Pip finds a respectable lodging house for Magwitch in Essex Street when the latter arrives in England, risking death as a returned convict.

The Edgar Wallace, no. 40
On the outside wall of this pub, named in honour of the thriller writer, is a board proclaiming Wallace as 'soldier, reporter, foreign correspondent, author and playwright'.

head towards the river and west to Temple tube

Temple Place

Temple Underground Station
While waiting here for a train in 1901, Baroness Orczy thought up much of the outline of *The Scarlet Pimpernel*, published four years later.

Walking Through James Boswell's London

Boswell fled Scotland for London in 1760 with the intention of joining the Catholic Church but decided instead to join the capital's literary society and was soon fraternizing with Laurence Sterne (whose Tristram Shandy had made him a celebrity) and an endless retinue of whores, whom he often picked up in the Strand. In 1763 Boswell famously met Samuel Johnson in a Covent Garden bookshop and thus one of the most celebrated partnerships in literary history began. Boswell's London is confined mainly to the City, the Covent Garden area and Westminster, in those days the only heavily built-up parts of the metropolis.

Buckingham Palace to the Tower: roughly west to east

Site of Buckingham House, The Mall at Queen's Gardens
Boswell stops at the royal palace (since rebuilt as Buckingham Palace) on 22 December 1762 and manages to engage the sentries in conversation (something almost impossible today). Even more surprisingly, the sentries ask Boswell for a pint of beer, which he brings for them.

head along Birdcage Walk to the Houses of Parliament

House of Lords, St Margaret Street, Westminster
Boswell hears George III open Parliament on 25 November 1762. 'It was a very noble thing . . . His Majesty spoke better than any man I ever heard.'

Westminster Bridge
Picking up a 'strong, jolly young damsel' in Haymarket on 10 May 1763, Boswell takes her to Westminster Bridge, where 'in amour complete did I engage her upon this noble edifice'. He instantly despises himself 'for being so closely united with such a low wretch'.

head up Whitehall

Downing Street, Westminster
Boswell's first proper London address was 'up two pairs of stairs with the use of a handsome parlour' opposite the no. 10 address where prime ministers have lived for the past 200 years. There Boswell wrote much of what became the London Journal. The property has since been demolished.

continue north to Trafalgar Square

Strand

Boswell's favourite rendezvous for engaging prostitutes was along the Strand, the main road linking Westminster with the City. For his 14 December 1762 entry, he tells how he is particularly fond of a 'civil nymph with white-thread stockings who tramps along the Strand and will resign her engaging person for a pint of wine and a shilling'. Later, on 12 April 1763, he goes to a tavern with another Strand whore who 'displayed to me all the parts of her enormous carcass'.

take the Strand east

Southampton Street

Shortly after arriving in London in November 1762, Boswell makes for Southampton Street to see his 'first love', Miss Sally Forrester. When he knocks he finds the people of the house 'broke and dead, and could hear nothing of her'.

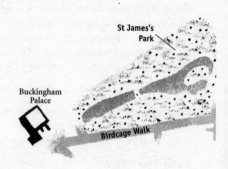

head up Southampton Street and turn right at the top

Boswell's (formerly Thomas Davies's bookshop), *8 Russell Street*

Boswell meets Samuel Johnson, the man with whom he came to be indelibly associated, for the first time at Thomas Davies's bookshop on 16 May 1763. Wary of the Doctor's well-known aversion to Scots, Boswell tentatively approaches and apologetically announces, 'I come from Scotland but I cannot help it,' to which the latter replies, 'That I find is what a very great many of your countrymen cannot help.' The building is now Boswell's Café.

head up Bow Street

Royal Opera House (Covent Garden), *Bow Street at Floral Street*

On his first night in London, 19 November 1762, Boswell takes in a perform-

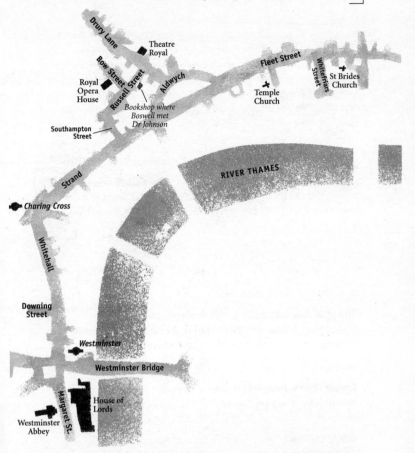

ance of Ben Jonson's Every Man in his Humour *in which 'Woodward played Bobadil finely'.*

head south-east

Theatre Royal, *Drury Lane at Russell Street*
Boswell sees David Garrick play Scrub in George Farquhar's The Beaux' Stratagem *in November 1762. At a later visit he catches Garrick playing Henry IV. The scene between the king and his son 'drew tears from my eyes'.*

take Drury Lane south and turn left at Aldwych

Fleet Street
Boswell patrols up and down on 13 January 1763, 'seeming to myself as one of the wits in King Charles the Second's time' (a hundred years previously).

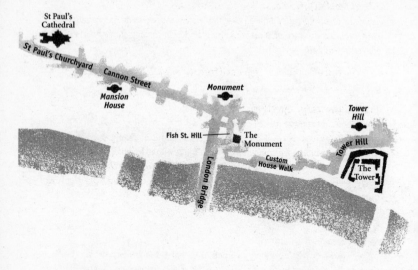

turn right at Inner Temple Lane

Site of Dr Johnson's address, *1 Inner Temple Lane*
Boswell visits Johnson here for the first time on 24 May 1763, noting that 'Johnson lives in literary state, very solemn and very slovenly'.

continue east

Temple Church, *Inner Temple Lane*
Boswell hears 'a very good sermon on "Set thy house in order, for thou shalt shortly die",' on Sunday 10 April 1763 at the Temple chapel.

Site of the Black Lion, *Whitefriars Street at Hanging Sword Alley*
On first arriving in London on Friday 19 November 1762, Boswell heads for the Black Lion in Water Lane, having been given a list of 'the best houses on the road'. The following January he takes a Covent Garden actress, Louisa, back to the inn and seduces her as 'the bells of St Bride's church rung their merry chimes hard by'. Boswell is pleased with his courtship: 'The whole expense was just eighteen shillings.'

St Bride's Church, *Fleet Street at St Bride's Avenue*
On Sunday 17 April 1763, Boswell and his friend Temple have to leave before the sermon as the parson is 'so heavy and drawling'.

continue east along Ludgate Hill

Site of Child's Coffee House, St Paul's Churchyard
Boswell's favourite coffee house, which he visited every Saturday, was by the Cathedral, but no trace of it remains. He included in the Journal snatches of conversations held here.

continue east along Cannon Street and its continuation, Eastcheap, and turn right at Fish Street Hill

The Monument, Fish Street Hill
Boswell goes to the top of Christopher Wren's Fire memorial on 2 April 1763. 'This is a most amazing building . . . When I was about half-way up, I grew frightened. I would have come down again, but thought I would despise myself for my timidity.' Nevertheless Boswell was so worried he thought that 'every heavy wagon [passing] down Gracechurch Street . . . would make the tremendous pile tumble to the foundations'.

head south to London Bridge

London Bridge
While walking across in January 1763, Boswell notices 'enormous shoals of floating ice which often crashed against each other'. Because of the heavy foundation of the bridge and the slightly different course of the river, in those days the Thames froze regularly at this point.

head east along the river walk

The Tower, Tower Hill
Boswell and Temple go to see 'the landing of the Venetian ambassadors' on 18 April 1763. 'It was very elegant to see the fine barges.'

Fitzrovia, w1

A densely packed area of narrow streets and alleyways, small fashion houses, media offices and tiny art galleries, Fitzrovia, despite its easy-going charm and accessibility, is an area ignored by most Londoners and tourists, sporting a name that appears on few maps. The word 'Fitzrovia' was coined as recently as the 1930s and, according to conflicting sources, was either taken from Fitzroy Square or Fitzroy Street to the north of the district (the Fitzroys were local eighteenth-century landowners) or from the Fitzroy Tavern, the area's best-known pub.

For much of the twentieth century the latter was the centre of a *louche* Bohemian scene, involving Dylan Thomas, the artist Augustus John, the dilettante writer Julian Maclaren-Ross (whose unfinished

Memoirs of the Forties is the definitive work on the area), J. M. Tambi-muttu (editor of *Poetry (London)*) and the critic/novelist Rayner Heppenstall, a one-time flatmate of George Orwell; the atmosphere contrasted sharply with the humourless stiffness of the nearby Bloomsbury Group and reached its peak during the Second World War when the pub and its many neighbours (see box, below) offered escape from the dangerous world beyond Fitzrovia (which for local non-combatant writers meant the BBC). Unable to move around easily on account of the war, the Fitzroy set stayed put and warred with each other for the few scraps of available writing work.

In the 1950s the scene slowly died, the camaraderie disappeared, and the new generation of beats moved south to Soho. Fitzrovia became a largely forgotten area of sweat shops and Italian cafés (captured by Iris Murdoch in 1954's *Under The Net*, in which Mrs Tinckham keeps a 'dusty, dirty, nasty-looking corner shop' in the area), but trendification set in during the 1980s and Fitzrovia now attracts media agencies, TV companies and magazines that can't afford the rents in Soho.

Exploring Fitzrovia

Fitzrovia's boundaries are Euston Road (to the north), Tottenham Court Road (east), Oxford Street (south) and Regent Street–Langham Place–Portland Place (west). For easy exploring, in this book Fitzrovia has been divided into two sections: Around the BBC and Around Telecom Tower.

'I wander thro' each charter'd street' – William Blake's Fitzrovia

Blake, a vigorous and tireless walker, often strode through these streets, leaving his house in Broad (now Broadwick) Street, Soho (see p. 199), heading along Oxford Street towards Tottenham Court Road and turning left at St Giles High Street (New Oxford Street did not then exist) past the almshouses and the boundary stone where the parish charity boys were whipped. Along Tottenham Court Road Blake would pass the Blue Posts pub (not the current building), a timber yard on the east (where the hi-fi stores can now be found), and the fields that then covered most of the area. At the junction of Tottenham Court Road and New Road (now Euston Road) stood a turnpike and two pubs – the Adam and Eve, which features in Hogarth's *The March to Finchley*, and the Farthing Pie House, mentioned by Defoe and Dickens. From here Blake would walk up Green Lane (the modern-day Hampstead Road) towards Highgate and Hampstead and Old Wylde's farm (see p. 296).

AROUND THE BBC

- Landmarks can be reached from Great Portland Street or Oxford Circus tubes.

Portland Place

Broadcasting House, Portland Place at Langham Street

With two minutes remaining before going on air to do a live poetry reading of Dryden in the 1940s, Dylan Thomas, having had too much whisky, was fast asleep and snoring in front of the mike. The producer gave him a shake and frightened him into near-sobriety just in time to announce that he would be reading 'Shaint Sheshelia's Day'. He then made a miraculous recovery and delivered a near-perfect rendition, apart from one Latin phrase which had to be attempted three times. On another occasion Thomas stopped during his own radio broadcast and announced, 'Somebody's boring me. I think it's me.' Over the last few years the Corporation has moved many of its studios to White City in west London.

head south

Langham Place

Langham Place, the short stretch between Portland Place and Regent Street, takes on a sharp curve because local landowners refused to allow John Nash to continue Regent Street in a straight line north. At the opening of John Buchan's *The Thirty-Nine Steps* (1915) the hero, Richard Hannay, describes how he lives in a first-floor flat 'in a new block behind Langham Place'. Buchan lived at 76 Portland Place around the time of the First World War, the house having since been demolished and replaced by the Institute of Physics.

All Souls Church, Langham Place at All Souls Place
Dombey marries Edith Skewton in this John Nash church in Charles Dickens's *Dombey and Son* (1848). Dante Gabriel Rossetti was christened here in 1828.

Oxford Street

For introduction, see Soho.

George Orwell's Ministry of Truth canteen, no. 200
George Orwell based the canteen in *1984*'s Ministry of Truth on the one he used while broadcasting Allied war propaganda to the Far East in the makeshift BBC studios that were based here during the Second World War. The surroundings were dismal – there were no windows and the canteen served 'metallic stew' – shifts were long, and staff often slept in the office after an 18-hour day. Meanwhile the offices were drowning in endless memos about the mirrors in the ladies' loos and the quality of carpets in the recording booths. The only relief from the drudgery was the dinner ladies, wheeling round trolleys laden with Victory coffee – a scene relived in *1984*. William Empson, the critic best known for *Seven Types of Ambiguity* (1930) who also worked here at the time, recalled Orwell's paranoia – claiming that his microphone was not wired up and that someone pretending to be George Orwell was broadcasting false propaganda overseas from a different part of the building. But Orwell began to see the funny side of things when Malcolm Muggeridge pointed out that the signal was so weak no one in the Far East could hear a word anyone was saying. Orwell left the BBC in November 1943 to work for the Labour Party weekly, *Tribune*.

head east along Oxford Street

Corner Oxford Street/Great Titchfield Street

Thomas De Quincey recalled in *Confessions of an English Opium Eater* (1822) how he parted company with his young prostitute friend, Ann, at the corner of Oxford Street and Great Titchfield Street, intending to rendezvous a week later. He returned to the spot day after day in the hope of seeing her, but she never turned up and they never saw each other again. Nor could he ask anyone for her whereabouts: he had foolishly failed to learn her surname.

Berners Street

Four major writers lived in this street during the nineteenth century: George Du Maurier stayed at no. 8 in 1860 after returning to London from Paris; George Eliot wrote *Silas Marner* (1861) at no. 16, where she lived from 1860 to 1863; Samuel Taylor Coleridge had lived with the Morgans, friends who tried to rid him of his opium addiction, at the adjacent no. 17 from 1812 to 1813 and there wrote *Remorse*; and Wilkie Collins lived with his mother and brother in the 1850s at no. 38, where he wrote *Antonina* (1850). All the houses have long since been demolished.

turn left at Newman Street

Newman Passage

In his 1991 short story, *Newman Arms*, Christopher Petit explains how on first arriving in London in the early '70s he sought solace in the lonely city by familiarizing himself with London film locations such as the Charlton park where Antonioni shot *Blow Up* and the Covent Garden pub Alfred Hitchcock used in *Frenzy*. But his favourite site was the location of the murder depicted at the opening of Michael Powell's film, *Peeping Tom* – Newman Passage, off Newman Street – which Petit describes as a 'partly roofed, narrow alley-way with a hidden dog-leg, out of sight at either end'. Fitzrovian chronicler Julian Maclaren-Ross claimed it was known as Jekyll and Hyde Alley, where 'one sometimes guided girls in order to become better acquainted'.

continue along Newman Street, turning left at Mortimer Street

Great Portland Street

Griffin, the invisible man in H. G. Wells's novel of the same name, makes himself disappear for the first time in a 'large unfurnished room in a big ill-managed lodging house in a slum near Great Portland

Street'. There he sets up his equipment – understandably Wells doesn't go into too much detail, but it includes two little dynamos and a cheap gas engine – and succeeds in making some white wool fabric 'flicker in the ashes . . . and fade like a wreath of smoke and vanish'. He then turns his attention to the cat and has trouble with the claws and the pigment at the back of its eyes, but, after succeeding in removing all trace of the animal, lets it out. Four days later Griffin notices that it is alive 'down a grating in [nearby] Great Titchfield Street' but that a crowd can't understand where the miaowing is coming from. Griffin returns to the house and, satisfied with his procedures, sets to work on making himself vanish, motoring his dynamos, taking drugs to decolourize his blood, and then enduring a 'night of racking anguish' which finally makes all his visible flesh disappear. In his torment he sets fire to the house and flees along Great Portland Street, where he crashes into a man with a basket of soda-water siphons.

Mash, no. 19

William Boyd threw a party in this hi-tech restaurant in April 1998 to celebrate the release of his biography of Nat Tate, the fictitious American artist whose existence he and Davie Bowie had fabricated to hoodwink the art world. The idea for the Tate wheeze had been germinating in Boyd's mind for some time. In 1987 he had published a novel, *The New Confessions*, which took the form of a fictional autobiography, and a few years later David Hockney asked Boyd to contribute to a series of essays accompanying the painter's depictions of the letters of the alphabet. Boyd chose 'N' and concocted the identity of a supposed Laotian/French writer, Nguyen N, throwing a launch party for a new N book, at which one guest claimed he knew of the author and had begun a search for one of his works.

Boyd probably chose the name Nat Tate for his new creation in mock honour of Nahum Tate, the little-known but genuine seventeenth-century poet laureate whose most significant contribution to Restoration era literature was rewriting *King Lear* so that Cordelia marries Edgar and lives happily ever after. Tate also wrote the Christmas carol which includes the well-known line 'While shepherds watch'd their flocks by night'. By the time the party took place at Mash, the Tate scam had been exposed in New York, where the local art world – having fallen for the hoax – had been thoroughly humiliated.

heading north

Site of Leigh Hunt's address (1812–13), no. 35

While living here, Hunt was imprisoned in Horsemonger Lane Gaol, Southwark (see p. 335) for libelling the Prince Regent (the future George IV). He had described the Prince as 'a man who had just closed half a century without one single claim on the gratitude of his country or the respect of posterity', after reading an article in the *Morning Post* newspaper which lavishly praised the despotic royal as the 'Protector of the Arts', the 'Maecenas of the Age' and 'the Adonis of Loveliness'. Hunt was jailed for two years and fined £500. A restaurant now stands on the site of the house where Hunt lived.

The George, no. 55

Until the recent exodus of much of the BBC to the wastelands of White City, hopeful scriptwriters would hang around this ornate Victorian pub, hoping to bump into producers and editors, as a chance meeting could be worth a score of phone calls or begging letters. One who made full use of this procedure was Dylan Thomas (or perhaps he just liked the beer). To the conductor Sir Thomas Beecham the pub was known as the Gluepot because he claimed his musicians kept on getting stuck here.

Langham Street

Doris Lessing's address (1959–63), Holbein Mansions, no. 25

Millionaire socialist Howard Samuels, who once bankrolled *Tribune*, the soft-left Labour Party newspaper, arranged for Lessing to stay cheaply in a flat in this block. Her most unlikely visitor was Henry Kissinger, who wanted to meet activists from the Campaign for Nuclear Disarmament and find out more about their views on the nuclear question.

Site of Edward Malone's address (1779–1812), no. 40

Malone, a member of Dr Johnson's Club and a friend of Boswell, spent much time at this address working on his biography of Johnson and editing a volume of Shakespeare's works.

Ezra Pound's address (1909), no. 48

After being ejected from his rooms in nearby Duchess Street, Pound moved here, next to the Yorkshire Grey pub. He tried writing prose but it didn't work out, or, as he later put it, 'burnt m/s of damn bad novel'. He also wrote the poem *The Ballad of the Goodly Fere* in his head while walking from here to the British Library.

return to Great Portland Street

Great Portland Street

Site of James Boswell's address (1788–95), no. 122

By the time the biographer was living here, all the people he had written about in his *London Journal* were dead, as was his wife, and he was feeling rather lonely. One night in 1790 Boswell was thrown into a cell for persistently crying out the time late at night while drunk. In his defence he claimed he was teaching the watchman how to shout the time. He died here in 1795.

head west to Hallam Street

Hallam Street

Site of Christina Rossetti's address (1830–36) and birthplace, nos. 106–110

Rossetti House now occupies the site where Christina Rossetti was born. Six years later she and her family moved to 50 Charlotte Street, half a mile east.

AROUND TELECOM TOWER

- Landmarks can be reached from Goodge Street or Tottenham Court Road tubes.

Bookshops

French's Theatre Bookshop, 52 Fitzroy Street, tel. 020 7255-4300, has copies of almost every play currently in print, as well as a full range of books on other aspects of the theatre.

Cleveland Street to Percy Street: roughly north to south

Cleveland Street

Charles Dickens's address (1816–17, 1829–31), no. 22

Dickens's parents moved here – Charles was nearly four at the time – when his father became a clerk at Somerset House in the Strand. The family stayed here for two years and then moved back for another two years in 1829. The ground floor is now occupied by a café.

Fitzroy Square

Although most of the square is spoiled by excessive and ugly pedestrianization, the east side was designed by the Adam brothers (the south is a pastiche, having been destroyed in the Blitz). Charles Dickens railed against the 'dowager barrenness and frigidity of Fitzroy Square' in *Nicholas Nickleby* (1839).

George Bernard Shaw's address (1887–98)/Virginia Woolf's address (1907–11), no. 29

When he wasn't annoying his mother by mis-playing selections from Wagner's *Ring* on the piano, Shaw began writing for the theatre following some unsuccessful novels. His first play, *Widowers' Houses* (1892), an attack on slum landlords, was badly received, and the second, *Mrs Warren's Profession* (1893), was banned by the Lord Chamberlain for containing suggestions of incest; but *Arms and the Man*, which opened in 1894, fared better.

A bizarre incident involving Shaw, a policeman, and several tradesmen took place in the square in February 1890 after the playwright came home ecstatic from a performance of Vincenti's dancing at the Alhambra Theatre in Leicester Square. Finding the square deserted, Shaw decided to try out his Vincenti-style pirouettes in the circular roadway which encircles the green and, after his umpteenth fall, was approached by a policeman who said he'd been watching him for five minutes and wondered what he was doing. When Shaw explained, the policeman asked him to hold his helmet so that he could have a go. The policeman then fell into the gutter and suffered a bloodied nose, but the two of them were determined to pirouette around Fitzroy Square at least once. Before long they were joined by a postman and a milkman who broke his leg having his turn and had to be taken to hospital by the other three. Shaw moved out in 1898 when he married Charlotte Payne-Townshend, his 'green-eyed Irish millionairess', who was originally his nurse. When she asked him to move in with her, Shaw realized that their living together would raise moral questions so he insisted that they get married.

Nearly ten years after Shaw moved out, Virginia Woolf (then Stephen) and her brother Adrian moved into the same five-storey cream-coloured Georgian house. On Thursday nights they entertained friends, reviving the soirées which their late brother, Thoby, had started at their previous address in Gordon Square, Bloomsbury (see p. 8). They also held Friday night readings of Restoration plays, Shakespeare and favourite Victorian poets. In 1911, shortly after

Rakes & Ale – Fitzrovia's literary pubs

' *"Where are those pubs," I asked him. "In Fitzrovia. The other side of*
Oxford Street." ' from *Memoirs of the Forties*, Julian Maclaren-Ross

In its mid-twentieth-century hey-day Fitzrovia's colourful literary scene
revolved around a number of pubs, mainly situated near the junction of Charlotte, Percy and Rathbone Streets.

roughly north to south

Fitzroy Tavern, 16 Charlotte Street

This garish, over-decorated Victorian pub was London's most celebrated Bohemian meeting place in the middle decades of the twentieth century, once artists and
writers had vacated the Plough in Bloomsbury to gather round the Fitzroy's honky-
tonk piano. Mainstays were Dylan Thomas, the painters Augustus John and Nina
Hamnett (the latter used to approach strange men and cajole them into buying her
a drink by rattling a money box in their face), the poet John Singer and Gerald
Wilde (the model for Gully Jimson in Joyce Cary's *The Horse's Mouth* (1944)).
Another regular crowd included aspiring politicians Hugh Gaitskell (later Labour
Party leader), Tom Driberg (a future party chairman and peer) and the hangman
Albert Pierrepoint. By the time the Second World War broke out, the Fitzroy had
become too touristy for the arty drinking crowd, who moved to the nearby Wheat-
sheaf (p. 151). Nowadays there's little of a literary nature to recommend the Fitzroy.

head through Percy Passage to Rathbone Street

Duke of York, 47 Rathbone Street

Anthony Burgess was having a drink here with his wife, Lynne, in 1943 when a
razor gang marched in, ordered several pints of beer, and poured the contents on
the floor. They then threw their glasses at the wall and brandished the jagged edges
at the terrified customers. When Lynne Burgess proclaimed, 'What a waste of
good beer,' the gang's leader went behind the bar and pulled pint after pint, which
he ordered her to drink. Anthony Burgess tried to intervene and was warned off,
but Lynne downed the lot. The gang was so impressed, they handed over the
money for all the beer they had drunk and offered her protection from other local
gangs. She later told Burgess that she found herself unable to take the roughs seriously as they reminded her of Pinkie's gang in Graham Greene's *Brighton Rock*.

The Newman Arms, 23 Rathbone Street

For many years this pub had no spirits licence, which is probably why the beer
snob George Orwell twice modelled pub scenes in his novels on the place. Orwell
had the Newman in mind for the scene in *Keep the Aspidistra Flying* (1936) in
which Gordon Comstock and Ravelston row about socialism – 'four hours a day
in a model factory tightening up bolt number 6003'. In *1984* (1949) the pub in
which Winston unsuccessfully tries to find out from a prole about life before the
revolution is based on the Newman. Delightfully positioned over an alleyway

and renowned for its pies, the Newman is now full of advertising workers at lunchtimes, an irony that would have amused Orwell, given Comstock's [i.e. Orwell's] loathing of the advertising industry.

Marquess of Granby, Rathbone Street at Percy Street
The Marquess was always considered to be a little too violent for most of Fitzrovia's '40s crowd, which is why Dylan Thomas liked coming here to pick fights with guardsmen who themselves had dropped by to pick on homosexuals. However, as it was in a different licensing area, it stayed open half an hour later than its neighbours and attracted the Fitzroy/Wheatsheaf crowd after half past ten.

The Wheafsheaf, 25 Rathbone Place
Sick of being gawped at in the Fitzroy Tavern, the 1930s Fitzrovians moved to the Wheatsheaf, which served the hard-to-find Younger's Scotch Ale, stronger than most London beers; and it was here in 1936 that Augustus John introduced Dylan Thomas to his eventual wife, Caitlin Macnamara. Despite the competition, the pub's most colourful character in those days was the dilettante Julian Maclaren-Ross, who wore a teddy-bear overcoat, carried a silver-knobbed cane, and was court-martialled in 1943. Anthony Powell cast him as the incorrigible X. Trapnell in his *A Dance to the Music of Time* series, and *A Buyer's Market* (1952), an early novel from the series, featured a fictitious Fitzrovia pub, The French-Polisher's Arms (probably based on this) which Trapnell clears of customers when he promises to buy them all drinks at a rival hostelry. Rayner Heppenstall in his 1953 novel, *The Lesser Infortune*, cast Maclaren-Ross as the writer Dorian Scott-Crichton, who wears a jacket of 'mustard-coloured velvet, chocolate-coloured trousers, with sueded shoes to match'. In the novel the narrator (Heppenstall) looks at Scott-Crichton's notebooks and notices long-term plans for books yet to be written, complete with publisher and price. This was based on Maclaren-Ross's own actions, but his plans came to nought. By the 1960s, drunk and debt-ridden, he was being paid for his memoirs chapter by chapter and died of a heart attack in 1964 with the work unfinished. George Orwell picked up the idea of Winston's rat phobia in *1984* in the Wheatsheaf from listening to a conversation with set designer Gilbert Wood, who was working on a film entitled *Death of a Rat*.

Bricklayers Arms, Gresse Street
When the '40s arty/literary crowd wanted more privacy than the Wheatsheaf or Fitzroy Tavern allowed, they would come to this pub, which was known as the Burglars' Rest after a gang broke in, drank themselves stupid, and fell asleep on the premises.

Black Horse, 6 Rathbone Place
A dark and uninviting place, the Black Horse used to have a ladies-only bar where, according to Julian Maclaren-Ross, 'old dears in dusty black toasted departed husbands with port and lemon from black leather settees'. One of the landlords around that time drank himself to death in a three-day binge.

Virginia called off her engagement to Lytton Strachey, she and Adrian moved to 38 Brunswick Square, Bloomsbury.

The premises now house offices for chartered accountants, and a plaque on the front of the house reads somewhat fulsomely: 'From the coffers of his genius he [Shaw] enriched the world'.

● Shaw, surprisingly for a modern writer, was also active politically, serving between 1897 and 1903 on St Pancras Council, which he claimed was 'cheerfully corrupt politically'.

Roger Fry's Omega Studios (1913–19), no. 33

Omega, opened to produce 'well-designed articles of daily use', was run by Bloomsbury Group acolyte Roger Fry, who padded the walls with seaweed to keep out the noise. Wyndham Lewis also used the place but left after a row in 1915 and set up the Vorticists. In his ire he described the place as 'Mr Fry's curtain and pin-cushion factory'. In Evelyn Waugh's *Brideshead Revisited* (1945), Charles Ryder buys a screen at its closing-down sale in 1919. The building is now occupied by the London Foot Hospital.

Fitzroy Street

George Bernard Shaw's address (1881–6), no. 37

Shaw moved here with his mother when he was 25 and began writing a novel, *Cashel Byron's Profession*, which sold badly. He also contracted smallpox. In 1886 Shaw moved a little further north to 36 Osnaburgh Street, before going to Fitzroy Square the following year.

Charlotte Street

In Anthony Powell's *A Buyer's Market* (1952), part of his *Dance to the Music of Time* series, Charlotte Street is described as retaining 'a certain unprincipled integrity of character'. It is now Fitzrovia's main street.

north to south

Site of Rupert Brooke's address (1912–14), no. 76

Brooke lived here while researching at the British Museum.

L'Etoile, no. 30

This darkly lit, romantic restaurant was T. S. Eliot's favourite. In 1914 Ezra Pound and Wyndham Lewis celebrated the launch of their magazine, *Blast*, here.

Bertorelli's, no. 19

In the 1950s Bertorelli's was the home of the Wednesday Club, founded by the reviewer and minor novelist, Philip Toynbee, and named in honour of Richard Hannay's Thursday Club in John Buchan's *The Three Hostages*. The Wednesday Club attracted scores of writers, including Rex Warner, John Berger and Christopher Isherwood, and conversation was usually of the highest intellectual order; on one occasion it was revealed that Ezra Pound's name in Japanese meant 'this picture of a phallus costs ten yen'. At one lunch T. S. Eliot was asked to cite his all-time favourite piece of prose. The audience hushed, wondering which masterpiece the great poet would deliver. Would it be a passage from *Moby Dick*, *Barnaby Rudge*, or perhaps *Heart of Darkness*? No. Eliot stood up and recited: ' "Well," cried Boss McGinty at last, "is he here? Is Birdy Edwards here?" "Yes," McMurdo answered slowly, "Birdy Edwards is here. I am Birdy Edwards." ' No one recognized the source – the Sherlock Holmes novella, *The Valley of Fear*. Kingsley Amis, once he had made his name with his first novel, *Lucky Jim*, began lunching here once a week in the late '50s with Anthony Powell.

Fitzroy Tavern, no. 16

See Rakes & Ale box, above.

Percy Street

west to east

Former Eiffel Tower Hotel, no. 1

The Poets' Club began meeting at this hotel/restaurant in 1909, its driving force being Ezra Pound who was dissatisfied with the poetry of the day (it was a great period for prose, but not for verse) and suggested replacing the then fashionable poetic styles with Japanese *tanka* and *haikai*. By 1914 the Vorticists, the avant-garde art and literature group led by Wyndham Lewis, were meeting here to thrash out the contents of *Blast*, their short-lived publication which was printed on yellow paper with grotesque pink covers, its avowed purpose being to 'blast away' Victorian attitudes. (At one Vorticists' meeting Pound read out his *Sestina Altaforte* poem so passionately that the manager placed a screen round the table.)

After the First World War regular lunchers included Aldous Huxley and (separately) Evelyn Waugh, who used the Eiffel as model for Lottie Crump's hotel in *Vile Bodies* (1930). The place at that time was run by an Austrian, Rudolf Stulik, who had reputedly been chef to Emperor Franz Josef. Stulik would usher upstairs customers who wanted to use a private room, and one couple who prospered from this arrangement was Dylan Thomas and Caitlin Macnamara, whose affair in the late '30s was bankrolled involuntarily by Augustus John. The artist discovered this only when Stulik presented him with a bill for £43, then a tidy sum. 'I know you cheat me outrageously, Stulik, but £43 for lunch for two is a bit steep,' John declared. Stulik replied in broken English: 'Is not for lunch only. Little Welshman with curly hair [Dylan Thomas]. He stay two weeks and eat. He says you pay.'

In 1938 the place became the White Tower Restaurant, and is now the No. 1 Restaurant.

The Elysée, no. 13

During the 1940s George Orwell, Arthur Koestler and Malcolm Muggeridge used to eat at this restaurant two or three times a week, and after the war Orwell returned with Graham Greene, going out of his way, as at the Akropolis (see below), to annoy the owner by taking off his jacket and being thrown out.

Coventry Patmore's address (1863–4), no. 14

Patmore, the Pre-Raphaelite poet and critic, wrote to a friend after moving here: 'I am very comfortable in my new place but I have had to call a policeman many times to the organ boys who prevent me from reading and writing and thinking.'

Site of the Akropolis Restaurant, no. 24

George Orwell was regularly thrown out of this restaurant in the 1940s for the heinous crime of taking off his jacket – behaviour which in those days was frowned on, almost always being punishable by ejection. Lunching here one day with Malcolm Muggeridge, Orwell asked if he could swap places with the journalist. When Muggeridge asked why, Orwell told him that he had spotted *New Statesman* editor Kingsley Martin eating nearby and couldn't bear looking at Martin's 'corrupt face'. (Martin had riled Orwell by taking a Stalinist stance during the Spanish Civil War and Orwell later described him in his private notebook on Communist fellow-travellers as a 'decayed Liberal, very dishonest'.)

Julia and Winston's Room, no. 18

The upstairs room in which Julia and Winston conduct their dangerous affair in George Orwell's *1984* is modelled on the flat where Sonia Brownell (who later became Orwell's second wife) used to live in the mid-1940s. Since Orwell had not at that stage won her over, using the place as the inspiration for Julia and Winston's affair was probably wish-fulfilment on his part.

A Tour Through George Orwell's 1984

George Orwell's 1984 is set in a London pock-marked with bomb sites and overseen by busybody officials who want to know everyone's business. Orwell was not so much predicting the future as satirizing the recent past – he initially planned to call the book 1948. Many places referred to in the novel are based on real London locations.

Trafalgar Square to Bethnal Green: roughly west to east

Victory Square, *Trafalgar Square, WC2*
Winston and Julia begin their ill-fated affair in Trafalgar Square, cast in the novel as Victory Square in memory of the 'Victory' rallies which were held

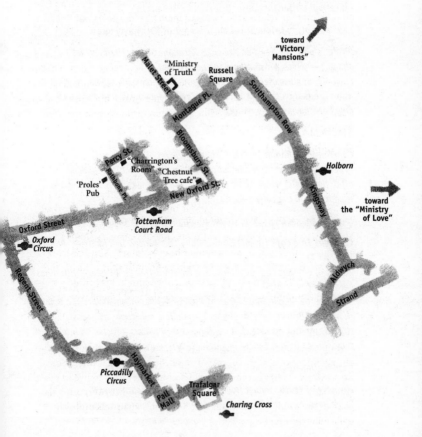

here after the First World War. In the book, Big Brother, rather than Horatio Nelson, 'gazed southward from the top of a column towards the skies where he had vanquished the Eurasian aeroplanes'.

head north (up Regent Street) to Oxford Circus

Ministry of Truth Canteen, *former BBC Canteen, 200 Oxford Street, Oxford Circus, W1*
Orwell based the canteen in the Ministry of Truth (Minitrue) on the one he used while working here during the war for the BBC, broadcasting Allied propaganda overseas. Many basic foods had been replaced with processed alternatives, such as margarine for butter and saccharine for sugar (as in the novel), and the dinner ladies used to wheel round mugs of Victory Coffee (another 1984 touch). The rest of the Ministry was based not on these BBC offices but on Senate House, Bloomsbury (see below).

head east along Oxford Street and turn left at Rathbone Place

'Prole' 's pub, *the Newman Arms, 23 Rathbone Street, Fitzrovia, W1*
The pub in which Winston buys the prole a pint of beer before trying, unsuccessfully, to elicit useful information from him about life before the revolution is based on the Newman, which Orwell regularly visited and which sold only beer, having no spirits licence.

head further east

Charrington's Room, *18 Percy Street, Fitzrovia, W1*
Orwell based the room where Julia and Winston conduct their dangerous affair on the flat where Sonia Brownell, who later became his second wife, used to live in the early 1940s.

take Tottenham Court Road south, turning left at New Oxford Street

Chestnut Tree Café *(former Express Dairy Co., 40 New Oxford Street, Bloomsbury, WC1)*
'Haunt of painters and musicians', the Chestnut Tree Café where Winston has become a fixture after his 'conversion' at the end of the novel was loosely based on the Bloomsbury branch of the Express Dairy Company chain. Being so near the British Museum and its surrounding bookshops and artists' studios, the Express attracted a fair number of writers, artists and intellectuals. Orwell used the place regularly. It is now a branch of McDonalds.

head north up Bloomsbury Street

Ministry of Truth, *Senate House, Malet Street, Bloomsbury, WC1*
Winston works in the Records Department of the 'enormous pyramidal structure of glittering white concrete', a building modelled on Senate House (the

University of London's administrative headquarters), then just about the only tower block in London. During the war, Senate House was requisitioned by the government for use as the Ministry of Information, which gave Orwell his idea.

head south through Holborn to the Strand

'Oval building with rectangular windows', *St Clement Dane's, Strand at Clement's Inn, WC2*
Looking at a picture in Charrington's upstairs room, Winston recognizes the 'oval building with rectangular windows and a small tower in front . . . a ruin now' as being 'in the middle of the street outside the Palace of Justice [the Royal Courts of Justice on the Strand]'. The building is St Clement Dane's Church which, having been bombed during the Second World War, was in ruins when 1984 was being written.

head two miles north

Victory Mansions, *27B Canonbury Square, Canonbury, N1*
Winston Smith's seedy block of flats which smells of 'boiled cabbage and old rag mats' is based partly on the Canonbury Square address where Orwell lived from 1944 to 1947 and where he wrote much of 1984. At that time the property was in a bad state of disrepair, hence the disparaging descriptions of the place, but it has since been renovated into a luxury terrace.

head two miles south-east

Ministry of Love, *the former Bethnal Green Police Station, 458 Bethnal Green Road, E2*
The cells in 1984's Ministry of Love are based on the inside of this former police station where George Orwell spent a few hours in 1931 after his arrest in the Mile End Road for being drunk and disorderly. Orwell was perversely hoping to be mistreated, as it would make for better copy; but even he had to admit that he was fed well for a prisoner: bread, marge, tea and the ser-geant's wife's meat and potatoes. He spent the night counting the porcelain bricks on the walls – as Winston does in the novel.

Marylebone, mostly W1

Lying to the north of Oxford Street and to the west of Portland Place, Marylebone is an elegant but largely featureless district of Georgian streets and terraces, and the setting for London's best-known literary address, 221B Baker Street, home of Sherlock Holmes and, occasionally,

Dr Watson. Where exactly 221B is, though, is a matter for Holmesian conjecture (see below). The name Marylebone is a corruption of St Mary's [church] by the [river] Tyburn, the Tyburn being a long-culverted stream that runs underneath the narrow, twisting Marylebone Lane. The area developed around the estates by the manor house opposite the parish church and began to take its modern form from a 1719 plan drawn up by the architect James Gibbs (best known for St Martin-in-the-Fields church by Trafalgar Square). The street pattern that has developed has a rigidity that is unusual for London – Disraeli moaned about the 'flat, dull, spiritless streets' – but is relieved by squares and mews alleyways and the obvious signs of opulence in Harley Street, home of private clinics, and Wimpole Street.

Exploring Marylebone

Marylebone stretches north of central London's main northern boundary, Marylebone Road, but the bulk of the area lies between Marylebone Road (to the north), Portland Place (east), Oxford Street (south) and Edgware Road (west). For easy exploring, in this book Marylebone has been divided into three sections: Around Marylebone station; Around Baker Street; and Around Wigmore Street.

AROUND MARYLEBONE STATION

While the streets around Marylebone station are unmemorable by London standards, the cream-coloured stucco villas by Regent's Park rank as some of the most prestigious addresses in the capital. Edith Sitwell described this small area as 'moon coloured crescents [overlooking] large gardens full of huge purring leaves and great bright flowers' in her 1937 novel, *I Live under a Black Sun*.

- Landmarks can be reached from Marylebone or Baker Street tubes.

Bookshops

Stephen Foster, 95 Bell Street, tel. 020 7724-0876, has lots of paperbacks at dirt-cheap prices.

The Archive Bookstore, 83 Bell Street, tel. 020 7402-8212, also has a huge selection of cheap paperbacks. It is worth descending into the basement music section, which looks as if it has been untouched for years but is a wonderful place to pass an hour or so.

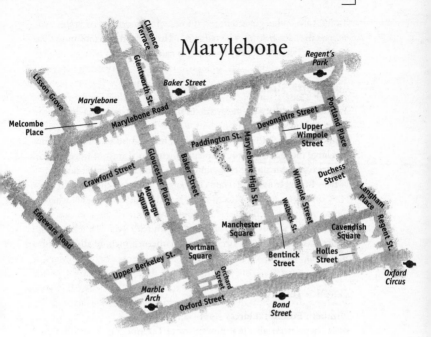

Lisson Grove to Regent's Park: west to east

Lisson Grove

Benjamin Haydon's address (1817–22), no. 116
On 28 December 1817, Keats met Wordsworth for the first time at a dinner party in this house, which then belonged to the painter Benjamin Haydon. After dinner, Wordsworth began speaking but, when Keats opened his mouth to agree, Wordsworth's wife touched him on the arm and warned, 'Mr Wordsworth is never interrupted.'

Melcombe Place

Site of E. M. Forster's birthplace and address (1879–80), no. 6
Although given the first names Edward Morgan, Forster should have been called Henry Morgan, under which he was originally registered. When the verger at the christening asked his father, Edward, for the boy's name, Forster Senior mistakenly gave his own, which the verger wrote down and used. A year later his father died of TB, and E. M. was

brought up by his grandmother, on whom he modelled Mrs Honey-church in *A Room with a View* (1908). The Melcombe Place house has long since been demolished.

Glentworth Street

T. S. Eliot's addresses (1920–32), Clarence Gate Gardens, Glentworth Street at Melcombe Street

Unhappy living with his wife Viv, Eliot, feeling restless, moved within this large red-brick art-nouveau apartment block west of Regent's Park several times during the 1920s and 1930s. The Eliots were at no. 9 (where he wrote some of *The Waste Land*) from 1920 to 1926; no. 98 in 1928; off after a few months to no. 177; and then on to no. 68, where their marriage fizzled out. He left, but Vivien stayed on, and two years later she sent an advert to *The Times* which read 'will T. S. Eliot please return to his home, 68 Clarence Gate Gardens, which he abandoned Sept. 17th, 1932'.

Clarence Terrace

Elizabeth Bowen's address (1935–52), no. 2

It was here, ironically, that Bowen wrote *The House in Paris* (1935), as well as two London-based novels, *The Death of the Heart* (1938) and *The Heat of the Day* (1949). Bowen wrote to Virginia Woolf in 1935 telling her that she had fallen in love with the place.

Hanover Terrace

This outstanding cream terrace, designed by John Nash, is part of an unfinished scheme planned by the Prince Regent.

Harold Pinter's address (1968–78), no. 7

Long before Pinter, the address had been the home of Wallis Simpson, who later married Edward VIII, probably causing his abdication in 1936.

H. G. Wells's address (1937–46) and deathplace, no. 13

When buying this house, Wells told the owner, the poet Alfred Noyes, that he was looking for a place where he could die, but he still man-aged to last out for nine years in what he described somewhat disin-genuously as 'an old tumble-down house on the borders of Regent's Park'. Soon after H. G. Wells moved in, Orson Welles in America recorded his now infamous radio broadcast of the former's sci-fi story, *The War of the Worlds* (1898), which had much of America believing that the Martians had landed. Wells thought about suing his American near-namesake but eventually saw the funny side of it. H. G. then went on a lecture tour to New York but gave a series of barely audible talks which saw visitors leaving in droves. By the end of the Second World War Wells was disillusioned and painted a mural in one of the rooms depicting man's evolution, writing beneath the section portraying modern times the words 'Time to go (for man)'. Yet despite wartime bombing he refused to move out, even when the house next door was destroyed.

● For a few months during the war George Orwell and his wife stayed in the flat above Wells's garage at the back of Hanover Terrace. One day Wells, in a fit of paranoia, came to the conclusion that the Orwells had been gossiping about him and kicked them out, despite Orwell's protestations.

Wilkie Collins's address (1850–59), Edmund Gosse's address (*c.* 1901), no. 17
While living here, Collins was often visited by Charles Dickens, whose daughter, Kate, married Collins's brother, Charles. Collins began contributing to Dickens's magazine, *Household Words*, in the 1850s and joined the staff in 1856. In the early years of the twentieth century the house was occupied by Edmund Gosse, a major critic whose best-known work, the autobiographical *Father and Son* about his austere childhood with his widowed father, was published anonymously in 1907.

AROUND BAKER STREET

Bookshops

Daunt's, 83 Marylebone High Street, tel. 020 7224-2295, based in a long galleried room, has one of the best travel sections in London.

● Landmarks can be reached from Baker Street tube.

Crawford Street to Devonshire Street: roughly west to east

Crawford Street

T. S. Eliot's address (1916–20), 18 Crawford Mansions, Crawford Street at Homer Row

While living here, Eliot, who had a mania about the slightest sound when working, used to complain incessantly about the noise from the raucous pub that stood on the corner and from two sisters in the same block who would continually shout down to the street to talk to friends. Seeking sympathy from the landlord, he was told, 'Well you see, sir, it's their artistic temperament. We ordinary folk must learn to make allowances for artists.' During the First World War Eliot on one occasion was warned by the authorities about leaving his curtains open too wide at night and showing too much light.

Montagu Square

Anthony Trollope's address (1871–80), no. 39

Because he had a job at the Post Office in the City, Trollope would get up at 5.30 a.m. and before breakfast write to a rigid pattern: 250 words every quarter of an hour in the 'little backroom on the ground floor behind the dining room'. Trollope revealed his mechanistic method in an autobiography which also detailed wordage rates, word-counts, delivery dates and every last penny of his income.

• John Forster, Dickens's great friend and major biographer, lived at no. 46 in the 1850s.

Gloucester Place

west side: north to south

Elizabeth Barrett's address (1835–8), no. 99

Barrett complained about being 'walled up like a transgressing nun and out of hearing of that sea' after her father insisted on moving from Devon into what was her first London address when he became short of money. To relieve the boredom and the gloom of the grimy city, she took a nightly dose of opium, but grew to love the area. In April 1838 the family moved to Wimpole Street (see below).

Wilkie Collins's address (1868–76, 1883–8), no. 65

Collins wrote *The Moonstone* (1868), which T. S. Eliot called 'the first, the longest, and the best of modern English detective novels', while living at no. 65. Incapacitated most of the time from taking too much laudanum – his excuse was that he had gout in the eyes, a medical impossibility – Collins dictated much of the book.

Charles Dickens's address (1863), no. 57
Dickens stayed here briefly while writing *Our Mutual Friend* (1865).

Mrs Humphry Ward's address (1891–1919), no. 25
After moving in, Ward wrote to her father: 'Of course Grosvenor Place is terribly smart and I dread the extra society it might bring.'

east side

Thomas Monkhouse's address (1823), no. 34
Samuel Taylor Coleridge, William Wordsworth and Charles and Mary Lamb used to come here to visit Monkhouse, an MP, not a writer.

head north

Dorset Street

Elizabeth Barrett and Robert Browning's address (1855–6), no. 13
Barrett was visited by Alfred, Lord Tennyson and Dante Gabriel Rossetti at what became her last English residence. (Rossetti based his sketch of Tennyson reading *Maud* aloud on a scene that took place here.) In Dorset Street, Barrett wrote the poems *Aurora Leigh* and *Fog*, which tells how 'the great tawny weltering fog' strangles the city and draws it off 'into the void'. The appalling London fogs, the so-called 'pea-soupers', which feature in much Victorian and early twentieth-century literature, faded after the 1960s Clean Air Act.

Algernon Charles Swinburne's address (1865–70), no. 22
Swinburne was attacked by critics for the 'feverish carnality' in his *Poems and Ballads* (1866), which were written in this grand terraced house. The book was withdrawn.

Baker Street

> '*I went to look at Baker Street, but I came back terribly disappointed. There is not the slightest trace of Sherlock Holmes there*' from *Letters from England*, Karel Capek, 1925

The 'Empty House', no. 118
In the Sherlock Holmes story of the same name, published in 1903, Holmes and Watson wait in a deserted Baker Street building, Camden

House, opposite their rooms at 221B, to pounce on a villain. Camden House was then a prep school at 13 York Place (now 118 Baker Street) and is now occupied by a beauty school. The story marked the resurrection of Holmes, who at the end of 'The Final Problem' (1893) was presumed dead after grappling with Professor Moriarty, his arch enemy, and supposedly falling into the Reichenbach Falls in Switzerland. After much public clamour, Conan Doyle relented and resuscitated Holmes.

heading north

Baker Street station

In his 1954 poem, *The Metropolitan Railway*, John Betjeman sits in the station buffet admiring the electric lampholders, the woodwork and the smell of dinner, and he gazes at the Underground company's nostalgic pictures of semi-rural Middlesex, designed to entice claustrophobic City workers to suburban 'Metroland', further along the line, at a time when 'Youth and Progress were in partnership'. The poem relates a sad tale of shattered hopes in which a couple buy the Metroland dream and meet each night 'at six-fifteen/Beneath the hearts of this electrolier' at the station after he has finished work in the City and she has finished shopping in Oxford Street, before going home to their villa and 'autumn-scented Middlesex'. Decades later, the Metroland idyll has been compromised, the county spoiled, and the couple have passed away, he from cancer, she from heart disease, their home replaced by an Odeon cinema. Some of the station platforms have murals of scenes taken from the Sherlock Holmes stories and in 1999 a statue of the detective was put up outside the Marylebone Road entrance.

Chiltern Court

Arnold Bennett and H. G. Wells had flats in this smart apartment block above Baker Street station in the 1930s. From 1929 to 1937 Wells lived at no. 47 (a luxurious flat without character, according to visitors such as Charlie Chaplin), where he wrote *The Shape of Things to Come* (1933). Arnold Bennett moved into no. 97 in 1930 and died here of typhoid a year later. During his death throes, the council spread straw on the road to reduce the noise, but it rained overnight and was so slippery by morning that a milk cart overturned and scores of bottles were smashed.

Sherlock Holmes's address, no. 221B, NW1

Probably the most famous address in literature, 221B Baker Street becomes Sherlock Holmes and Dr Watson's address in the first Holmes story, *A Study in Scarlet* (1887), after Watson, at a loose end in London, meets an old hospital colleague who reveals that someone at work 'was bemoaning himself this morning because he could not get someone to go halves with him in some nice rooms which he had found'. The latter turns out to be Holmes; he and Watson move to 221B, which consists of 'a couple of comfortable bedrooms and a single large airy sitting room, cheerfully furnished and illuminated by two broad windows'.

But where did Conan Doyle set 221B? When Holmes first appeared, Baker Street's numbers went up to 85 and the street ran only as far north as Crawford Street/Paddington Street. Doyle himself gave no clues about the inspiration for 221B (except in the use of the 'B', which meant that the rooms were above a shop), nevertheless Holmes scholars have zealously attempted to locate the model. The recently demolished no. 31 (then no. 72) has some support because the property had a back yard large enough to accommodate a 'solitary plane tree' (as in 'The Problem of Thor Bridge'), while other Holmesologists stipulate that 221B can be found by looking opposite Camden House, the 'Empty House' in the story of the same name (see above). Most Scotland Yard detectives, let alone someone with Holmes's powers of detection, would spot a flaw in these arguments: when Doyle moved Holmes and Watson into Baker Street he had not even considered writing 'The Empty House' (1905) or 'The Problem of Thor Bridge' (1927), so clues offered in those stories can't be cited.

In 1930 the council extended Baker Street north and made a Georgian house no. 221 (it would have been 41 Upper Baker Street in 1887, home of a dentist, John Faulkner, so no clues there). Soon afterwards the house was demolished and replaced by Abbey House (nos. 215–229), headquarters of the Abbey National Bank and Building Society, which during the 1951 Festival of Britain staged a Holmes exhibition with a reconstruction of the 221B sitting-room that now can be found in the Sherlock Holmes pub off the Strand (see p. 127) and which still receives around forty letters a month addressed to Holmes and Watson.

head back to Marylebone Road and turn left

Marylebone Road

St Marylebone Church, Marylebone Road opposite York Gate
Elizabeth Barrett and Robert Browning were married in secret – her father disapproved of their relationship – in this church on 12 September 1846, the first time they had ever met outside her Wimpole Street home. On the morning of the wedding Barrett slipped out of the house with her maid but fainted *en route* to the church and had to be revived with *sal volatile*. After the wedding they parted temporarily,

Barrett returning home as if nothing had happened, and a week later they eloped to Italy with her maid and dog, Flush. To the south-east of the church is the garden of the former church, demolished in 1813, where Richard Brinsley Sheridan was married and Byron baptized.

Site of Charles Dickens's address (1839–51), Marylebone Road at Marylebone High Street
Ferguson House marks the site of No. 1 Devonshire Terrace (demolished 1962), where Charles Dickens wrote most of *The Old Curiosity Shop* (1841), *American Notes* (1842), *A Christmas Carol* (1843), *Martin Chuzzlewit* (1844), *Dombey and Son* (1848) and began *David Copperfield* (1850). Here Dickens kept a raven which became the model for Grip in *Barnaby Rudge* (1841). There is a bas-relief of Dickensian characters on the Ferguson House wall.

turn right at Devonshire Place

Upper Wimpole Street

Arthur Conan Doyle's consultancy (1891), no. 2
Conan Doyle wrote two of the most memorable Sherlock Holmes short stories, 'A Scandal in Bohemia' and 'The Red-Headed League', here while waiting for clients to turn up to his consulting oculist practice. Having introduced Holmes in the novellas *A Study in Scarlet* (1887) and *The Sign of Four* (1890), he now turned to shorter episodes so that the continuity of writing wouldn't be interrupted too much if any patients turned up. None did, but the phenomenal success of the Sherlock Holmes stories more than made up for the shortcomings of Doyle's medical career and he soon gave up being an eye specialist to write full time, moving to Norwood, south-east London (see p. 347).

Devonshire Street

In John Betjeman's 1954 poem *Devonshire Street W.1.* a man who has X-rays taken at one of the street's private consultancies discovers that he has some dreadful disease and faces a 'long and . . . painful death-bed'. The grim news, symbolized by the cold austere street and the shutting of the heavy door of the practice, reduces him and his wife to talking mundanities – whether to catch the 19 or the 22 bus – when leaving the clinic for home.

Elizabeth Barrett and Robert Browning's address (1850), no. 26
Barrett and Browning returned to England four years after they had married in secret at Marylebone Church (see above) and eloped to

Italy; soon after moving here, Barrett published the collection of poems that included *Sonnets from the Portuguese* (Browning used to call her 'my little Portuguese'). The house is now part of Langham's Bistro.

Wilfred Owen's address (1915), no. 21
Owen, the First World War poet who was killed crossing the Sambre Canal a week before the armistice, lived here shortly before enlisting in the army.

AROUND WIGMORE STREET

Bookshops

The Talking Bookshop, 11 Wigmore Street, tel. 020 7491-4117, has a large stock of books on cassette, with gems such as T. S. Eliot reading *The Waste Land*.

- Landmarks to the west can be reached from Marble Arch tube; those further east from Bond Street or Oxford Circus tubes.

Edgware Road end to Regent Street: west to east

Upper Berkeley Street

Max Beerbohm's address (*c.* 1890–1910), no. 48
Beerbohm completed *The Works of Max Beerbohm* (1896), *The Happy Hypocrite* (1897) and his best-known novel, *Zuleika Dobson* (1911), here before going off to live in Italy.

- L. E. L. (the poet Letitia Elizabeth Landon) lived at no. 28 in the 1830s before going to Africa, where she was poisoned.

Portman Square

Site of Elizabeth Montagu's address (1780s), no. 22
Montagu, a society hostess, held literary salons attended by Boswell, Johnson and Walpole at her mansion, which stood approximately at the north-west corner of the square. She also threw annual dinners for London's chimney sweeps, for whom she acted as a sort of unofficial patron. Montagu Square is named after her – it was designed by a former chimney sweep.

Rebecca West's address (1930s), 15 Orchard Court, east side Portman Square

West moved in with husband Henry Andrews in 1930, shortly after producing her study of D. H. Lawrence.

Former _Poetry Review_ headquarters, no. 33

Muriel Spark became editor of _The Poetry Review_ in 1947 on condition that she be allowed to live in a Poetry Society-owned flat above the office. But the Society's officers dithered over her request, Spark's ex-husband refused to allow their son to leave Edinburgh, and she never got the property. Nevertheless she took the editor's chair and in her first editorial urged members to stop 'railing against the moderns'; not only had the _Review_'s readers refused to accept Eliot and Pound, many of them flinched from anything more demanding than _Hiawatha_. Spark soon found the strangest things going on in the name of poetry. One American would-be poet had sent some appalling stuff and a cheque for $25 made out personally to Spark. She sent back the money, and the piece, but the American woman wrote again, saying that the previous editor had always welcomed her money. It turned out that some contributors were paying the magazine to print their verse and that of their friends, instead of the other way round. Spark lasted a year, the victim of intense office in-fighting, and, after being dismissed, founded an alternative magazine, _Forum_. She used her experiences working here for her 1981 novel, _Loitering with Intent_.

Orchard Street

Site of Richard Brinsley Sheridan's address (1770s), no. 22

After marrying Elizabeth Linley at the now-demolished St Marylebone Parish Church in 1773, Sheridan moved to Orchard Street, where he wrote _The Rivals_ (1775), the play which features Mrs Malaprop, whose habit of finding the wrong word at important moments led to the term malapropism.

• From 1806 to 1809 Sydney Smith lived at no. 18, where he wrote _The Letters of Peter Plymley_.

head north-east to Manchester Square

Manchester Square

The Wallace Collection

> 'The Wallace Collection – Do you know it? Off Baker Street. It's always sooth-
> ing, I find' Guy Clinch, from *London Fields*, Martin Amis, 1989

Anthony Powell took the title for his twelve-part series, *A Dance to the
Music of Time*, from Nicolas Poussin's painting of the same name
which can be found here, and in the opening chapter of the series' first
book, *A Question of Upbringing* (1951), likens the 'physical attitudes' of
a group of workmen to Poussin's scene in which the Seasons 'Hand in
hand and facing outward tread in rhythm to the notes of the lyre that
the winged and naked greybeard plays'.

head east along Hinde Street

Bentinck Street

Charles Dickens lived at no. 18 (now gone) with his parents in 1833
when he was 21, working as a parliamentary reporter, and had just had
his first story, 'A Dinner at Poplar Walk', published. Sherlock Holmes
is nearly run down, deliberately, by a van driven by Moriarty's men at
the corner of Bentinck Street and Welbeck Street in 'The Final Problem' (1893).

Edward Gibbon's address (1773–84), no. 7

Gibbon wrote most of *Decline and Fall of the Roman Empire* (1776) at
no. 7 (since rebuilt), which he called 'the best house in the world' and
which he shared with his housekeeper, butler, cook, four maids, parrot
and dog.

Welbeck Street

Anthony Trollope died in a nursing home at no. 33 (now replaced by
Welbeck Mansions) following a stroke in 1882.

Elizabeth Barrett and Robert Browning's address (1852), no. 58

Barrett and Browning briefly moved here (now a hotel) after returning
to England from Italy.

Wimpole Street

Wimpole Street is best known for the clandestine romance between Elizabeth Barrett and Robert Browning which took place at no. 50 in the 1840s. Wimpole Street was also the setting for Tennyson's *In Memoriam* (1850), in which he stands in the 'long unlovely street' following the death of a friend, Arthur Hallam, who lived in Wimpole Street. Virginia Woolf did not agree with Tennyson's description of Wimpole, claiming it to be 'the most august of London streets'.

Site of Elizabeth Barrett's address (1838–46), no. 50

One of the best-known romances in literature, that of Elizabeth Barrett and Robert Browning, began in this now-rebuilt house, despite much opposition from Barrett's tyrannical father, who even discouraged friends from visiting his 32-year-old daughter. Browning met Barrett in 1843 after favourably reviewing a collection of her poems and writing to her: 'I love your verses with all my heart, Miss Barrett.' He soon became more daring, told her that he loved her, and by 1845 was visiting twice a week. Their marriage took place in secret at St Marylebone Parish Church in September 1846 and she returned to Wimpole Street as if nothing had happened, eloping with Browning (and Flush, her dog) a week later. Her father never forgave her. Barrett's and Browning's romance was sentimentally portrayed by Rudolph Besier in his 1930 play, *The Barretts of Wimpole Street*.

- Hilaire Belloc lived at no. 17 for a few months after his birth in 1870. Wilkie Collins died at no. 82 in 1889. In George Bernard Shaw's *Pygmalion* (1913) Professor Higgins lives at 27A. In P. G. Wodehouse's Bertie Wooster comedies, Sir Roderick Glossop is a nerve specialist at 6B.

head south to Oxford Street and turn left

Holles Street

Site of Lord Byron's birthplace (1788), no. 16

Byron was born George Gordon Byron in this street on 22 January 1788, and when he was six months old his mother took him to Aberdeen, returning to London when he was 11 and had recently assumed the peerage on the death of the incumbent Lord Byron. The buildings in Holles Street were destroyed in the Blitz.

head north

Duchess Street

Site of Ezra Pound's address (1906, 1908), no. 8
Pound's first London address was a (now demolished) boarding house, which he liked so much – 'the acme of comfort while it lasted' – that he came back to it a couple of years later when he returned to 'Dear Old Lunnon'. In those days Pound spent much of his time in the capital in the British Museum Reading Room, looking up 'Latin lyricists of the Renaissance'. When he could no longer pay his rent, the landlady ejected him and he took new rooms in Langham Street, Fitzrovia (see p. 147).

Portland Place

For entries on the east side of Portland Place, see Fitzrovia.

Edgar Wallace's address (1928), no. 31
Wallace was earning so much money by this time that he installed a soundproof glass cabinet from which he dictated stories to a secretary in another room. He was soon off to Hollywood where he died while working on the script of *King Kong*. The building is now the Chinese Consulate.

Langham Place

Langham Hotel, Langham Place at Portland Place
Ouida (Marie Louise de la Ramée) lived in the Langham in the 1860s, keeping her black velvet curtains fully closed to keep out of the sunlight; and she held a number of literary evenings, the visitors including Robert Browning. Others who have stayed in the hotel at various times include Mark Twain and Longfellow. The careers of Oscar Wilde and Arthur Conan Doyle took an upward turn after being invited to the Langham in August 1889 to meet Joseph Stoddart, an agent working for the American magazine publishers Lippincott, who were looking to hire writers. Wilde, then a well-known literary figure but not yet at the height of his powers, was commissioned to write what became his only novel, *The Picture of Dorian Gray* (1890). Conan Doyle, who had successfully published one Sherlock Holmes story, *A Study in Scarlet* (1887), considered himself a writer of historical romances rather than detective stories but, after a good lunch, agreed to take on his first Holmes commission, and this became the novella *The Sign of Four* (1890).

Regent Street

The Polytechnic, Regent Street, opposite Little Portland Street
Ezra Pound walked into this college in January 1909 and, when asked if
he wished to enrol, replied that he wanted to give a course himself.
That winter he held a series of classes in the Development of Literature
in Southern Europe and the following year ran one on Medieval
Literature.

From Bart's to Baker Street
– *a walk through Sherlock Holmes's London*

*The London of Sherlock Holmes and Dr Watson is a city at the height of its
powers, the capital of the world's most powerful empire and the setting for
the most bizarre crimes, mysteries and puzzles. It is also one seemingly
shrouded for ever in a yellow fog through which only Holmes can see any
light. The detective is first introduced to Dr Watson at St Bartholomew's Hospital in the City. They then move into 221B Baker Street, Marylebone, three
miles west; but significant events in their cases take place in the area
between the two locations, particularly around Charing Cross and the Strand,
as Arthur Conan Doyle, not completely confident about his London geography, made things easy for himself by regularly using places in one area.*

St Bartholomew's Hospital (Bart's), *Giltspur Street, Smithfield, EC1*
*Sherlock Holmes meets Dr Watson for the first time in the chemical laboratory
of Bart's Hospital early on in the first Sherlock Holmes story,* A Study in Scarlet. *A plaque on the wall of the curator's room adjoining the hospital's patho-
logical lab claims that Holmes's first words to Watson are 'How are you? . . .
You have been in Afghanistan, I perceive', but in fact Holmes has already
said to Watson (and to Stamford, the hospital dresser who introduces them)
'I've found it! I've found it. I have found a re-agent which is precipitated by
haemoglobin, and by nothing else.' Despite Holmes's excitement at dis-
covering this infallible test for bloodstains, the finding is never referred to
again in the stories.*

head south towards the river

Site of the 'Bar of Gold', *former Paul's Wharf, off Upper Thames Street south
of St Benet's Church, EC4*
*In 'The Man with the Twisted Lip' Watson is shocked to come across Holmes in
an opium den, the Bar of Gold (by Paul's Wharf south of St Benet's Church in*

the City) while looking to rescue an old friend. Holmes is himself looking for Neville St Clair, a City businessman who has disappeared but has been spotted at a window above the den by his wife. It transpires that St Clair has been using the den to change from his respectable City clothes into beggar's garb, in which he makes more money than he ever did in business. Paul's Wharf and the surrounding 'vile' alleyways depicted in the story were demolished in the 1960s.

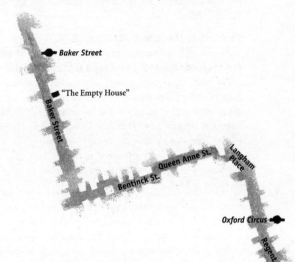

head west

Pope's Court, *Poppin's Court, off Fleet Street, EC4*

In 'The Red-Headed League' ginger-haired pawnbroker Jabez Wilson sits in an office in Pope's Court (probably based on Poppin's Court at the north-eastern end of Fleet Street), copying out the Encyclopaedia Britannica for the then grand sum of £4 a week. Wilson has been hired by the so-called Red-Headed League, in reality a bunch of crooks who have lured him out of his business in Saxe-Coburg Square (based on Charterhouse Square, a few yards west of Barbican tube) so that they can rob the adjacent bank. After a few weeks of copying, during which Wilson becomes excessively acquainted with 'Abbotts and Archery and Armour and Architecture and Attica', the League is dissolved. A distraught Wilson turns to Holmes, who eventually foils the bank raid, of course.

Waterloo Bridge, *WC2*

John Openshaw drowns in the water near this Thames bridge, probably murdered by the Ku Klux Klan, in 'The Five Orange Pips'. The tragedy is arguably Holmes's single greatest failure.

Lyceum, *Wellington Street, WC2*

Mary Morstan meets an agent acting for the Sholtos, who have been sending her jewels from her late father's treasure, outside this ballroom in The Sign of Four. *Conan Doyle carelessly mixes up the dates in setting the appointment and then bizarrely sends the four-wheeler containing Morstan, Holmes and Watson from Wellington Street to Sholto's Brixton villa through Rochester Row and Vincent Square, Westminster (see p. 236), instead of straight over Waterloo Bridge.*

Simpson's-in-the-Strand, *100 Strand, WC2*

At the end of 'The Adventure of the Dying Detective' in which Holmes hoodwinks everyone into thinking he has a fatal oriental fever so that the villain will be lured into a false sense of security, Holmes announces, 'When we have finished at the police station I think that something nutritious at Simpson's would not be out of place.' In 'The Illustrious Client' Watson arranges to meet Holmes at Simpson's and finds him 'sitting at a small table in the front window, and looking down on the rushing stream of life in the Strand'. Simpson's, now a sumptuous restaurant, opened in 1818 as a 'home of chess', with players lounging on divans, and began catering when a John Simpson took over in 1848.

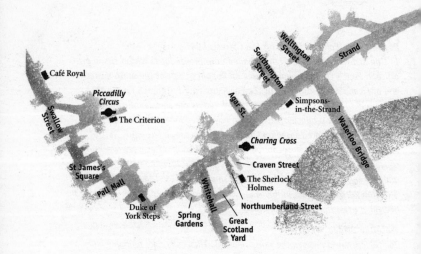

Former **Strand** ***magazine office**, 7–12 Southampton Street, WC2*
Nearly all the Holmes stories were first published in Strand *magazine, a literary monthly founded in January 1891 and based at this address for many years. The cover of the magazine featured a scene depicting a bustling Strand around the corner from this address. The* Strand *closed in 1950.*

***Site of Charing Cross Hospital**, Agar Street at Chandos Place, WC2*
Dr Mortimer's walking-stick, which he absent-mindedly leaves at 221B Baker Street at the start of The Hound of the Baskervilles, *is inscribed 'from his friends of the CCH' – Charing Cross Hospital. Holmes is taken here after being attacked outside the Café Royal in 'The Illustrious Client'.*

***Site of Lowther Arcade**, Strand opposite Charing Cross station, WC2*
Watson dashes out of a cab, through Lowther shopping arcade, and into

another cab on the other side as part of an elaborate getaway route during Holmes's escape from Moriarty's gang in 'The Final Problem', originally intended to be the final Holmes story. Lowther's, with its myriad of toyshops, was demolished in 1904, and a branch of Coutt's Bank has since been built on the site.

***Charing Cross Hotel**, Strand at Charing Cross station, WC2*
Holmes sets a trap in the hotel's smoking-room for Oberstein, the spy in 'The

Bruce-Partington Plans', and thus prevents top-secret submarine documents falling into enemy hands.

Charing Cross station, Strand at Villiers Street, WC2
Readers of the Holmes canon never discover why Mathews 'knocks out the detective's left canine in the waiting-room at Charing Cross', as the incident is referred to only in passing while Holmes is looking up his collection of villains whose names begin with an 'M' in 'The Empty House'. Irene Adler sets off from here on the 5.15 train bound for the continent after outwitting both the King of Bohemia and Sherlock Holmes in 'A Scandal in Bohemia'. In 'The Second Stain' a woman 'answering to the description' of the Creole Mme Fournaye 'attracted much attention at Charing Cross station by the wildness of her appearance and the violence of her gestures'. Holmes and Watson take a Charing Cross train for Marsham in 'The Abbey Grange' and for Chatham in 'The Golden Pince-Nez'.

Site of the American Exchange, Strand by Charing Cross station, WC2
In A Study in Scarlet the police find two letters from the Guion Steamship Co., 'one addressed to E. J. Drebber and one to Joseph Stangerson', address 'American Exchange, Strand', on the body of the murderer Drebber. The American Exchange was a kiosk outside Charing Cross station which Americans in London could use as a postal address and where a wide range of US newspapers could be bought. It is outside the station by the Exchange in 'The Illustrious Client' that Watson catches a glimpse of the shocking headline on the newspaper being displayed by the one-legged news-vendor – 'Murderous Attack on Sherlock Holmes'.

Site of the Mexborough Private Hotel, 43–46 Craven Street, WC2
In The Hound of the Baskervilles Stapleton keeps his wife a prisoner at the Mexborough Private Hotel while engaging in his war of attrition against Sir Henry Baskerville. The Mexborough was probably based on the Craven Family Hotel which then stood here.

Site of Charing Cross Post Office, 457 Strand, WC2
In the opening of 'Wisteria Lodge' John Scott Eccles makes himself known to Holmes by sending a telegram from this Post Office. Inspector Gregson finds Eccles by 'picking up the scent at Charing Cross Post Office'.

Former Neville's Turkish Baths, 23 Northumberland Avenue, WC2
Holmes and Watson visit the baths at the start of 'The Illustrious Client', the date given as 3 September 1902, which Conan Doyle probably chose because it was Oliver Cromwell's 'lucky day'. The baths have long since closed down, but the building remains and the old entrance can be spotted in Craven Passage at the side of the Sherlock Holmes pub.

The Sherlock Holmes, *Northumberland Street at Craven Passage, WC2*
Sherlock Holmes memorabilia fill the walls of this pub, artefacts including the contrived (brier pipes and bent poker sticks based on the stories) and the genuine (superb cuttings such as the one depicting a group of American men in the semaphoric positions of the characters in 'The Dancing Men' welcoming Conan Doyle to a stateside town). Upstairs, next to the restaurant, is a life-size reconstruction of Holmes and Watson's 221B Baker Street sitting-room, complete with Holmes mannequin (as used in 'The Empty House'), violin, books, period furniture and shelves laden with foul-looking bottled chemicals. The collection dates from the 1951 Festival of Britain exhibition of Holmes memorabilia, displayed at Abbey House in Baker Street, the modern-day 221B. Some sources cite the pub, formerly the Northumberland Arms, as the (fictitious) Northumberland Hotel in which Sir Henry Baskerville stays in The Hound of the Baskervilles.

Charing Cross, *SW1*
Charing Cross refers, not to the monument in front of Charing Cross station, but to the junction where the north end of Whitehall meets the Strand, the site of the original cross that Edward I erected in memory of his late wife, Eleanor, in 1290, and which was pulled down in 1647. At the end of 'The Man with the Twisted Lip' Holmes declares that he deserves to be kicked 'from here [Neville St Clair's home at Lee in Kent] to Charing Cross' for his slowness in solving the case.

Former Cox and Co., *16 Whitehall, SW1*
'Somewhere in the vaults of the bank of Cox and Co., at Charing Cross, there is a travel-worn and battered tin dispatch-box with my name, John H. Watson . . . painted upon the lid,' Watson reveals in 'Thor Bridge'. More importantly, Watson also keeps the papers which record Sherlock Holmes's case in the box. Cox's stood at this address, then 16 Charing Cross, until it was destroyed in the Second World War. It has since been rebuilt.

Former Scotland Yard, *4 Great Scotland Yard, SW1*
The headquarters of the Metropolitan Police were based in the alleyway, Great Scotland Yard, off the north-east end of Whitehall from 1829 to 1890, i.e. when first mentioned in the Holmes canon. The police moved to New Scotland Yard, at the southern end of Whitehall by Westminster Bridge, in 1890 and are now based near St James's Park.

The Admiralty, *Spring Gardens, SW1*
The Admiralty is 'buzzing like an over-turned beehive' after the theft of the top-secret submarine documents, the Bruce-Partington Plans, in the story of the same name.

head along the Mall and turn right past the ICA

Duke of York Steps, *Waterloo Place at the Mall, SW1*
In 'His Last Bow', Baron Von Herling and Von Bork discuss getting a signal-book 'through the little door on the Duke of York's Steps'. The steps connect Waterloo Place and the Mall and are overlooked by the statue of Frederick, Duke of York, brother of George IV and William IV, on top of a tall column. The door led to the German Embassy, which stood at 7–9 Carlton House Terrace until the First World War, and now leads to an underground car park.

Diogenes Club, *The Athenaeum, 107 Pall Mall, SW1*
In 'The Greek Interpreter', Holmes drops into the Diogenes, 'the Queerest club in London', probably based on the Athenaeum, to meet his brother, Mycroft, 'one of the queerest men', whose deductive powers – but not his energy – outstrip Sherlock's.

The London Library, *14 St James's Square, SW1*
Needing a 'goodly volume' on Chinese pottery to help Holmes trap Baron Gruner in 'The Illustrious Client', Watson comes to this revered library.

head north to Piccadilly

Site of St James's Hall, *Piccadilly, between Swallow Street and Air Street, W1*
Holmes and Watson go to watch Sarasate (a real-life Spanish violinist) at the concert hall that then stood here (demolished 1905), during a break from their investigations in 'The Red-Headed League'.

The Criterion, *224 Piccadilly, W1*
In the first Sherlock Holmes story, A Study in Scarlet, Watson is having a drink in this plush bar at Piccadilly Circus when he bumps into Stamford, his former hospital dresser, who reveals that a colleague, one Sherlock Holmes, is looking for someone to share a room.

head north along Regent Street

Regent Street, W1
In The Hound of the Baskervilles Holmes notices that a cab is following Sir Henry Baskerville along Regent Street. When he later catches up with the cabman, the latter reveals that Sir Henry's mystery pursuer gave his name on leaving the cab as 'Mr Sherlock Holmes'.

Café Royal, *68 Regent Street, W1*
In 'The Illustrious Client', Sherlock Holmes is nearly murdered outside the Café Royal by 'two men armed with sticks', who escape by making their way through the establishment.

Langham Hotel, *Langham Place at Portland Place, W1*
Captain Morstan in The Sign of Four *stays in this lavish hotel where Conan Doyle had earlier received the commission for writing the story. Other characters who stay here include the King of Bohemia in 'A Scandal in Bohemia' and the Hon. Philip Green in 'The Disappearance of Lady Frances Carfax'.*

head west

Queen Anne Street, *W1*
Watson takes rooms here after moving out of 221B Baker Street, as he reveals in 'The Illustrious Client'.

turn left at Welbeck Street

Bentinck Street, *W1*
Holmes is nearly run down by a van driven by Moriarty's men at the corner of Bentinck Street and Welbeck Street in 'The Final Problem'.

continue west through Manchester Square

The 'Empty House', *118 Baker Street, W1*
In the story of the same name Holmes and Watson wait in a deserted Baker Street building, Camden House, opposite their rooms at 221B, to pounce on Colonel Sebastian Moran. Camden House was then a prep school at 13 York Place (now 118 Baker Street) and is now occupied by a beauty school.

head north

Sherlock Holmes's address, *221B Baker Street, NW1*
221B Baker Street becomes Sherlock Holmes and Dr Watson's address in the first Holmes story, A Study in Scarlet, *and consists of 'a couple of comfortable bedrooms and a single large airy sitting room, cheerfully furnished and illuminated by two broad windows'. Holmes scholars have been unable to agree where Conan Doyle sited 221B for, when Holmes first appeared, Baker Street's numbers went up to 85 and the street ran only as far north as Crawford Street/Paddington Street. Conan Doyle himself gave no clues as to where 221B may have been, but Holmes experts have since made many suggestions. Some claim it must be the recently demolished no. 31 (then no. 72) as it had a back yard large enough to accommodate a 'solitary plane tree' (as revealed in 'Thor Bridge'), while others stipulate that 221B can be found by looking opposite Camden House, the 'Empty House' in the story of the same name (see above). Of course there's a serious flaw in these arguments: when Doyle moved Holmes and Watson into Baker Street in 1887 he had not even considered writing 'The Empty House' (1905) or 'The Problem of Thor Bridge' (1927).*

In 1930 the council extended Baker Street north and made a Georgian

*house no. 221 (it would have been 41 Upper Baker Street in 1887). Soon
afterwards the house was demolished and replaced by Abbey House (nos.
215–229), headquarters of the Abbey National Bank and Building Society,
which during the 1951 Festival of Britain staged a Holmes exhibition with a
reconstruction of the 221B sitting-room that now can be found in the Sherlock Holmes pub off the Strand (see above) and which still receives around
forty letters a month addressed to Holmes and Watson.*

Mayfair, W1

The smell of money hangs in the air in what has traditionally been
London's wealthiest area and home of the aristocracy. Mayfair is dominated by elegant Georgian terraces, swish hotels and luxury office blocks;
consequently it has attracted only the wealthiest writers, such as Benjamin Disraeli, Somerset Maugham and Ian Fleming.

Mayfair is named after the annual bawdy May Fair, which was held
near what is now Shepherd Market, off Piccadilly, until the 1730s. As
London grew, luxurious houses were built to the east of what is now
Hyde Park in smart turnings such as Chesterfield Street (which Somerset Maugham moved into at the height of his success as a West End
playwright), and with them came the mews for stables (many of these,
such as Hays Mews, where Ian Fleming lived in the late 1940s, just
before he began writing the Bond books, remain). Much of the land is
owned by the Duke of Westminster, the biggest individual landlord in
the country, whose family name, Grosvenor, is to be found in a
number of local street names. Mayfair's street pattern is haphazard in
general, with long stretches of small streets broken up by three busy
squares – Berkeley, Grosvenor and Hanover.

Fictionally, Mayfair has been depicted as the home of either the
upper-class twit (as in countless P. G. Wodehouse books; Bertie Wooster is described as a 'Mayfair consultant' in 1949's *The Mating Season*)
or the risible toff (as in Evelyn Waugh novels, such as *A Handful of
Dust* (1934), which Cyril Connolly described as 'a savage attack on Mayfair from a Tory angle'. Other novels set or partly set here include Jane
Austen's *Sense and Sensibility* (1811), Thackeray's *Vanity Fair* (1848),
Oscar Wilde's *The Picture of Dorian Gray* (1890), Saki's *The Unbearable
Bassington* (1912) and Michael Arlen's *The Green Hat* (1924), the quin-
tessential Mayfair novel and a bible of sorts for the Bright Young
Things between the two world wars.

Exploring Mayfair

Mayfair's boundaries are Oxford Street (to the north), Regent Street (east), Piccadilly (south) and Park Lane (west). For easy exploring, in this book Mayfair has been divided into two sections: North Mayfair and South Mayfair.

Mayfair

NORTH MAYFAIR

- Landmarks up to Culross Street can be reached from Marble Arch tube; those around Brook Street from Bond Street tube; and those further east from Oxford Circus tube.

Marble Arch to Heddon Street: roughly west to east

Oxford Street

Until the gallows moved to Newgate Prison in 1783, the condemned used to be carried on a cart to the gallows at Tyburn (by what is now Marble Arch) along this, the main east–west route out of London.

- For full Oxford Street introduction, see Soho (p. 197).

Site of Tyburn, Oxford Street at Cumberland Gate
John Nash's Marble Arch stands close to the spot where the Tyburn gallows stood until 1783. Pepys was among those who used to come here to witness the hangings, in which a rope was put round the condemned man's neck as he stood on a cart under the gallows; the cart would then move off, leaving him dangling. As there was no drop, friends and relatives would have to pull on the body to bring on death quickly and alleviate the victim's suffering. In the seventeenth century a custom began whereby authors would approach those about to be hanged, seeking approval to publish already written material which would be publicized as last confessions or memoirs. In return the condemned would advertise the forthcoming work to the crowds. In his own preface to *Barnaby Rudge* (1841) Charles Dickens, referring to the proliferation of hangings in the late eighteenth century, cites the case of teenage mother Mary Jones who was hanged at Tyburn after stealing some linen, even though she put the material back on the shop counter when she saw the proprietor watching her.

head south along Park Lane

Culross Street

John Betjeman's address (1930s), no. 3
Betjeman shared this flat, which he described as 'small, luxurious with limewood walls and pale carpets', with Randolph Churchill, who corrected the galley proofs of Betjeman's first book of poems, *Mount Zion* (1931). *Mount Zion* was originally printed on pink and green paper and was meant to be seen only by a handful of friends and associates, and shortly after its publication hundreds of copies were piled up in the hallway. A first edition is now worth around £500.

head east to Grosvenor Square and the north-east corner

Brook Street

Savile Club, no. 69

V. S. Pritchett watched a very elderly W. B. Yeats meet H. G. Wells here in 1938, settle down for lunch, and begin a conversation full of reminiscences of past friends, all of whom, it turned out, were dead. 'Do you remember that girl we took out boating at Richmond who wore a pink dress and had beautiful long gold hair?' asked Wells. 'Surely she can't be dead? She was much younger than us!' Yeats queried. 'No, she isn't dead,' Wells replied, 'just paralysed all down one side. [To the waiter] I think I'll have the steak.' In Victorian days, Savile's, then based at Trafalgar Square, was one of the capital's most important literary clubs, with Alfred, Lord Tennyson, Matthew Arnold, Robert Browning and Thomas Hardy among its members. It moved here in 1927.

South Molton Street

> '*I write in South Molton Street what I both see and hear/In regions of humanity, in London's opening streets*' from *Jerusalem*, William Blake, 1820

William Blake's address (1803–21), no. 17

After some years in Sussex, where he was unsuccessfully tried for sedition after throwing a soldier off his land, Blake moved to South Molton Street (the house still survives) and spent much of his time painting portraits of biblical and historical figures. Blake would often spend the evening with the artist, John Varley, making sketches of historical figures such as Wat Tyler and various monarchs, and a friend remarked that it was 'strange to think of Blake shut up in dingy, gardenless South Molton Street designing such pastorals!' At that stage Blake's work was not taken seriously by everyone: George III was shown some of his drawings and brushed them aside with a curt 'Take them away'. In 1967 when the council received an application to turn the downstairs into a bookmaker's angry letters appeared in *The Times*. 'Can you imagine the Soviet government allowing the homes of, say, Tolstoy or Dostoevsky to be turned into betting shops?' one person wrote. The campaign didn't succeed, but no. 17 is no longer a bookmaker's.

continue east

St George Street

St George's Church, St George Street at Maddox Street. Oxford Circus tube

Writers married in the church where the composer Handel was once warden include Shelley in 1914 to Harriet Westbrook (who later drowned in the Serpentine) and Benjamin Disraeli in 1839 to the widow, Mary Lewis. The latter marriage was something of a surprise. A few months previously, Disraeli had paid a visit to her Grosvenor Gate home and ordered her to marry him. In the row that followed she threw some money she owed him in his face, called him a 'selfish bully', and insisted that he never see her again. The author-statesman went home and wrote her a thousand-word letter which, he claimed, he wrote as if it was his last night before being executed. It worked.

When George Eliot married John Cross under her real name, Marian Evans, in 1880, soon after the death of her long-term partner, George Lewes, she was 60 and he 40. She died a few months later. In September 1905 John Galsworthy married Ada Cooper Galsworthy, the divorced wife of his first cousin, here. John Buchan married Susan Grosvenor in St George's in July 1907, but her mother forbade a wedding photo on the grounds that people might be bored posing for one. In fiction Lady Clara Pulleyn marries Barnes Newcome here in Thackeray's *The Newcomes* (1855). In the Sherlock Holmes story 'The Noble Bachelor' (1892), Lord Robert St Simon, a descendant of the Plantagenet kings, marries Hatty Doran at St George's.

Savile Row

This street has been the home of British tailoring since the mid-nineteenth century, with world-famous names such as Gieves & Hawkes at no. 1 and Hardy Amies at no. 14.

Richard Brinsley Sheridan's address (1813–16) and deathsite, no. 14 Sheridan died in poverty in the unfurnished rooms of a filthy house that stood on this site after being bed-ridden for a week and lying in his own excrement. Yet he was joking till the end, his last words, 'I won't die, Bridget. I don't like death', being lifted from one of his characters. Even once he had died, Sheridan wasn't free of creditors. A visitor who came to look at the corpse, claiming he was a long-lost relation wanting to look at his dear relative one last time, revealed himself to be a bailiff when the coffin was opened and promptly arrested the dead playwright for non-payment of bills. No funeral was allowed to take place until Sheridan's friends had paid his debts. This prompted his son, Tom, to recall the time that Sheridan had told him that their family was descended from Irish kings and should properly be known as O'Sheridan. Tom replied, 'Yes, that's because we owe everybody money.' Jules Verne gave Phileas Fogg Sheridan's former address in *Around the World in Eighty Days* (1872), mistakenly citing the year of the playwright's death as 1814 and the house as no. 7.

Heddon Street

Cave of the Golden Calf, no. 9
Wyndham Lewis designed the publicity material for the avant-garde nightclub which Strindberg's second wife, Frida, ran from this basement around the time of the First World War. Yeats and Pound were among those who came to the club regularly.

SOUTH MAYFAIR

● Landmarks can be reached from Green Park tube, except where stated.

Bookshops

Waterstone's, 203–206 Piccadilly, tel. 020 7851-2400, is the largest bookshop in Britain and something of a social centre, with its juice bar, café, internet station and sofas.

Hyde Park Corner to Piccadilly Circus: roughly west to east

Piccadilly

> 'Though the Philistines may jostle/You will rank as an apostle/In the high aesthetic band/If you walk down Piccadilly/With a poppy or a lily/In your medieval hand' Reginald Bunthorne from *Patience*, W. S. Gilbert, 1881

The word 'Piccadilly' exudes an air of cosmopolitan excitement and casual opulence that has led many lesser cities to adopt the name for their main streets. London's Piccadilly, the original, was one of the two traditional routes west from central London (the other being Oxford Street), and the name comes from the 'picadil', a stiff collar made by a local tailor, Robert Baker, who in 1612 built himself a mansion, Piccadilly Hall, on the site of the modern-day Great Windmill Street. Other aristocratic mansions followed, of which Burlington House and the

Albany remain, as did hotels, the most famous of which, the Ritz, can be found on the south side of the road near London's most renowned food store, Fortnum & Mason.

Oscar Wilde never actually strolled along Piccadilly with a lily in his hand. That was a Gilbert & Sullivan fabrication, concocted for the light opera, _Patience_ (1881), in which Wilde is caricatured as the aesthetic poet Reginald Bunthorne, played in the original show by _Diary of a Nobody_ author George Grossmith. In Bram Stoker's _Dracula_ (1897), Jonathan Harker, the first person in the book to fall under the Count's diabolic spell, spots Dracula, to his horror, walking along Piccadilly a couple of months after being rescued from the latter's nightmarish Transylvanian castle. It transpires that the blood-sucking Count has bought no. 347 Piccadilly (real numbers don't reach that high).

head east along Piccadilly

Lord Peter Wimsey's address, no. 110A
110A is the fictitious address of Dorothy L. Sayers's hero. Park Lane Hotel now stands on the site.

head north along Down Street

Hertford Street

Richard Brinsley Sheridan's address (1790s), no. 10
One of the playwright's twelve London addresses, 10 Hertford Street was bought by Sheridan when he was manager of the Drury Lane Theatre from the comedy playwright General John Burgoyne, later depicted as Gentlemanly Johnny in George Bernard Shaw's 1900 play, _The Devil's Disciple_.

● Edward Bulwer-Lytton wrote _The Last Days of Pompeii_ in the early 1830s at no. 36, where his son, the poet Owen Meredith, was born in 1831.

take the back streets north to Curzon Street

Curzon Street

Benjamin Disraeli's address (1876–81), no. 19
Disraeli bought this black-brick house with the £10,000 advance he received for his novel _Endymion_ on retiring from active politics (he was twice prime minister) and being ennobled. Disraeli finished the novel just before he died, and on his deathbed rejected Queen Victoria's offer to visit him, remarking that 'she will only ask me to take a message to Albert [the late Prince Consort].'

Heywood Hill, no. 10
Evelyn Waugh claimed that while Nancy Mitford was working as an
assistant at this long-running bookshop during the Second World War,
it was 'a centre for all that was left of fashionable and intellectual
London', customers including society figures such as Chips Channon,
Osbert Sitwell and Cecil Beaton, as well as Waugh. Mitford left following the success of her first novel, *The Pursuit of Love* (1945). These days
Heywood Hill retains its period charm, books being wrapped in parcels
and bills handwritten.

Chesterfield Street

Somerset Maugham's address (1911–19), no. 6
Maugham bought this tall red-brick house shortly after his first run of
success as a playwright which at one stage saw four of his plays running
simultaneously in the West End. Here Maugham wrote much of his
epic semi-autobiographical novel, *Of Human Bondage* (1915), in which
he purged himself of his childhood demons – his nervousness, sexual
confusion and sense of inferiority – and showed critics that he could
deal with weightier formats than drawing-room dramas. When the
First World War started, Maugham began spending much time abroad,
engaged in intelligence work for the British Government (see
10 Downing Street, p. 222) but then caught TB, brought about by over-
work, and had to enter a Scottish sanatorium to recover. Back in Mayfair, he managed to find time to write another exceptional novel, *The
Moon and Sixpence* (1919), the story of a banker who flees his humdrum life and responsibilities to paint in Tahiti, partly based on the life
of Paul Gauguin. Maugham's private life, however, did not fare too
well around this time. His lover, Gerald Haxton, was charged with
gross indecency after an incident at a Covent Garden hotel and was
expelled from Britain, despite Maugham's best efforts.

head west along Charles Street to Hays Mews

Hays Mews

Ian Fleming's address (1947–50), no. 21
Fleming lived in this mews cottage at the back of his mother's Charles
Street house shortly before he began writing the James Bond thrillers,
and he decorated it in his favourite 'masculine' colour, navy.

take the back streets south to Shepherd Market

Shepherd Market

Shepherd Market is named after Edward Shepherd, the architect who in 1735 laid out the market on the site of the May Fair, which had been abolished for being too bawdy. When Anthony Powell moved into Shepherd Market in the 1920s, his neighbours included prostitutes who did the Piccadilly beat, but the locale is now sanitized and is full of expensive food shops, wine bars and antique stores.

Anthony Powell's address (1920s), no. 9

After leaving Oxford, Powell chose to live in Mayfair simply because it was the setting for Michael Arlen's 1924 novel, *The Green Hat*, a rather sexually liberated work for the time which scandalized the older genera-tion but was a big hit with Powell, Evelyn Waugh and other Bright Young Things. Powell later gave Nicholas Jenkins, hero of his 12-part series *A Dance to the Music of Time*, a Shepherd Market address next to an all-night garage and opposite a block of flats inhabited by pros-titutes.

head east to Half Moon Street and south to Piccadilly

Piccadilly

Hugh Walpole's address (1930s, 1940s), 90 Piccadilly at Half Moon Street

One night in 1930 Walpole, the best-selling but critically reviled novel-ist, returned to his flat at the corner of Piccadilly and Half Moon Street and settled down to judge entries for the Book Society's choice of novel of the month. Among his reading was a page-proof copy of *Cakes and Ale*, Somerset Maugham's new work. Walpole read a few pages and began to fume; surely it was him Maugham had portrayed as the risible Alroy Kear, a barely literate novelist with as much talent as 'a heaped-up tablespoon of Bemax'? With this novel Maugham not only got his revenge on Walpole over a personal matter (see Albany, below) but succeeded in exacting retribution on the salon school of literary reputations which had cast him as good second-division material but the social-climbing Walpole, unable to pen a single memorable body of work, as a literary superstar. During the Blitz, the ceiling and most of the walls were blown in. Walpole, who was out when the bomb fell, left to stay at the Dorchester.

Bolton Street

Henry James's address (1876–85), no. 3

While lodging here, James wrote *The Europeans* (1878), *Daisy Miller* (1879), *Washington Square* (1881) and *The Portrait of a Lady* (1881), and picked up ideas for *Princess Casamassima* (1886) while strolling through the local streets. Of Bolton Street James wrote, 'I have excellent lodgings in this excellent quarter, a lodgings whose dusky charms – including a housemaid with a prodigious complexion but a demure expression and the voice of a duchess – are too numerous to repeat.' He also wrote a short story, 'In the Cage', about a Post Office worker confined every day to a small enclosed working area who dreams about relationships hinted at in the telegrams she handles.

- Fanny Burney (Madame D'Arblay) lived at no. 11 from 1818 to 1826.

Berkeley Street

Bertie Wooster lives at the fictitious 3 Berkeley Mansions in Berkeley Street in P. G. Wodehouse's comedies.

take Berkeley Street north to Berkeley Square

Berkeley Square

Immortalized in Eric Maschwitz's Tin Pan Alley song, *A Nightingale Sang in Berkeley Square*, the square was portrayed as Buckley Square in Thackeray's *Yellowplush Papers* (1838) and Gaunt Square in the same author's *Vanity Fair* (1848). Colly Cibber, poet laureate in the 1730s and lampooned by Alexander Pope in *The Dunciad* (1728), died in 1757 in a house which stood at no. 19. Horace Walpole, son of the first prime minister, Robert, and Gothic novelist, died in 1797 at no. 11, where he had lived since 1779. Henry James briefly lodged at no. 3 when visiting London with his parents in 1855. Evelyn Waugh describes the area in *Decline and Fall* (1928).

Bruton Street

Richard Brinsley Sheridan came into some money when he lived in this street (number unknown) in 1784 and so was able to retrieve the family silver from the pawnbrokers and throw a dinner party. Determined to show guests an impressive library, he hired a bookseller for the evening, who lined the walls with bookshelves and volumes and stayed throughout the evening dressed as a waiter to watch over his goods.

head back to Berkeley Square and east along Hay Hill to Dover Street

Dover Street

Former Albemarle Club, no. 37

Oscar Wilde's slide into disgrace and, eventually, jail began in February 1895 when the Marquess of Queensberry, furious about the affair between his son, Lord Alfred Douglas, and Wilde, left a note here for the poet which read 'To Oscar Wilde Posing Somdomite [*sic*]'. Wilde issued libel proceedings and the peer was subsequently arrested for 'unlawfully and maliciously publishing a certain defamatory libel'. Wilde failed to win the case and was eventually prosecuted for gross indecency at the Central Criminal Court (see p. 73). One day during the trial Lord Alfred Douglas's brother, Percy, saw his father walking along the road. Seething with anger over the bad publicity the case had caused, he challenged his father to a fight. The Marquess replied that for £10,000 he would fight his son anywhere but Piccadilly. Percy wasn't placated and, ignoring the Marquess's own code of boxing rules, still in use today, fought with his father in the street.

Brown's Hotel, no. 23

This elegant hotel, opened in the 1830s by a James Brown who had been butler to Lord Byron, soon became popular with visiting writers, particularly with Americans such as Henry James, Mark Twain and Edith Wharton (who depicted the place in several novels). Rudyard Kipling had his honeymoon here and Agatha Christie used it as the model for Bertram's. The first-ever phone call in Britain was made from a room on the ground floor.

Former Institute of Contemporary Arts address (1950s), nos. 17–18

During a poetry recital in the 1950s, when the ICA was based here, Emmanuel Litvinoff chose to read a poem he had written which condemned T. S. Eliot for anti-Semitism. Litvinoff was particularly incensed by the line in Eliot's *Burbank with a Baedeker: Bleistein with a Cigar* which goes 'The rats are underneath the piles/The Jew is underneath the lot'; as he began to read his poem it was pointed out to him that none other than Eliot had just entered the room. Unperturbed, Litvinoff proceeded with his diatribe, which contained the line: 'I am not accepted in your parish . . . and I share the protozoic slime of Shylock.' Eliot sat still throughout and at the end remarked that the poem was 'good, very good'. A few years later, Graham Greene was ejected from an ICA lecture given by Professor Jack Isaacs for making anti-Semitic remarks.

When the critic F. R. Leavis spoke at another 1950s event, he was asked 'In speaking of modern novelists, and of the Great Tradition, Dr Leavis, you overlooked, I believe, Joyce Cary.' Leavis replied, 'I would remind the speaker that we are here to discuss literature and nothing else.' After Colin Wilson had given a lecture on his headline-making first book, *The Outsider* (1956), a woman asked: 'Mr Wilson, I do not consider myself an intellectual. I have a beautiful home and a well-kept garden, a loving husband and two friendly and well-behaved boys. Please tell me in all seriousness I have gone wrong.' Wilson replied, 'You . . . you're the worst of the lot, a mainstream criminal! Your house is garbage, your husband is Gordon Fitzhomo and your children are dung. You're the dregs of the country.'

- The diarist John Evelyn died in a house in Dover Street in 1706. Another Dover Street resident at that time was Dr Arbuthnot, who had been Queen Anne's physician and helped found the Scriblerus Club (1713), members of which included Congreve, Pope and Swift.

Albemarle Street

John Murray's (publishers) address, no. 50
When Murray's published Lord Byron's *Don Juan* in 1819, the street outside the publishers' premises filled with booksellers' agents demanding copies. Before he died, Byron ordered Murray to burn his memoirs and protect his reputation. Murray duly complied, throwing them into the office fire.

Old Bond Street

Site of Laurence Sterne's address (1767–8), no. 41
Sterne lived above a shop belonging to a Mrs Fourmantel who made hair-bags for the king, and he died here in poverty in March 1768 with bailiffs rifling through his possessions. He was buried in a plot near where Marble Arch now stands, but only a few days later the corpse was stolen by an anatomy professor who wanted fresh cadavers for dissection (see Bayswater, p. 395).

- Shelley lived at no. 13 in 1814, just before he and Mary left for Europe; there is a Shelley's pub at no. 8. Alexander Pope stayed at no. 14 in 1710.

head north

Clifford Street

Buck's, no. 18
P. G. Wodehouse based the Drones Club in the Jeeves/Bertie Wooster books on Buck's, where 'to attract a fellow's attention you heave a bit of bread at him'. The Buck's Fizz drink is named after the place.

return south to Piccadilly

Piccadilly

Burlington House, Piccadilly opposite Duke Street, St James's
Suffragette Mary Wood nearly destroyed a portrait of Henry James when, in March 1914 at the height of the suffragettes' campaign for votes for women, she visited these galleries and suddenly attacked the picture. James's head, mouth and shoulder sustained deep cuts; but Wood, when questioned, explained that she had no idea who he was, or that he had satirized feminism in *The Bostonians*; as far as she was concerned, the painting was simply worth a lot of money. James himself was deeply wounded – psychologically. He received hundreds of sympathetic letters and wrote to a female friend that he felt 'scalped and disfigured'.

Albany, Piccadilly at Albany Court Yard
Albany was built at the beginning of the eighteenth century as a West End mansion for George III's son, Frederick, Duke of York and Albany; when he got into debt it was converted into luxury apartments. Traditionally only gentlemen, bachelors and those with no connections to trade were allowed to live here, and until the 1920s house rules stated that no one was allowed to keep a musical instrument – or a wife. One of the first writers to move in was Lord Byron, who took no. 2 in 1814. Another Albany resident from that period was the Gothic novelist, 'Monk' Lewis, who died from fever on a boat returning from Jamaica in 1818. Lord Macaulay lived in F3 from 1841 to 1856. When he counted his library, he found he had '6,100 books and several hundred more novels'.

In the twentieth century Albany attracted Arnold Bennett, J. B. Priestley (B3, B4), Compton Mackenzie (E1, 1912), Aldous Huxley (E2, 1934), Terence Rattigan (K5, 1946) and Graham Greene, who emigrated to Antibes in 1966 rather than pay taxes to a socialist government.

At a dinner party here in the 1950s, Somerset Maugham curtsied, went down on one knee and announced 'Maître!' when Noel Coward arrived; during the course of the evening the real reason for

Maugham's lampooning of Hugh Walpole as the semi-literate hack novelist, Alroy Kear, in *Cakes and Ale* (1930) emerged: Walpole had 'stolen' a boyfriend off Maugham many years previously. When the book was published in 1930, Maugham had vigorously denied that Kear was Walpole. Once Walpole was dead, he admitted the connection. Fictionally, Fledgeby in Charles Dickens's *Our Mutual Friend* (1865) 'lived in chambers in the Albany'. Another fictional Albany man was Raffles.

Hatchards, no. 187

When he was 18, Noel Coward walked into this bookshop and started filling up a suitcase he had just stolen from the adjacent Fortnum & Mason department store with books he wanted to add to his ill-gotten load. When challenged by an assistant, he quickly retorted, 'Really, look how badly this shop is run! I could have made off with a dozen books and no one would have noticed.' He left with no further bother. One day in the 1950s a young Peter Vansittart (now an historian and novelist) spotted the reviewer and novelist, Philip Toynbee, carrying a huge pile of books to a quiet corner. 'You're not buying all those, are you?' Vansittart inquired, to which Toynbee replied, 'No, I'm just looking myself up in the index.'

head north along Sackville Street

Vigo Street

Former *Yellow Book* office, no. 8

The *Yellow Book*, a controversial though fashionable late-Victorian publication, was published from this address, which also housed Elkin Mathews's bookshop. When Oscar Wilde was arrested on charges of gross indecency in 1895, it was noticed that he was carrying a yellow-backed book. Mistaking this for THE *Yellow Book*, a mob descended on the publication's Vigo Street headquarters and smashed the windows. A decade later, Ezra Pound came to Mathews's bookshop to get his *Personae* published. Mathews asked the young poet whether he'd like to contribute to the costs of the publishing. 'I have a shilling in my clothes if that's any use to you,' Pound replied. 'Oh well,' Mathews sighed. 'I want to publish them anyhow.' Allen Lane, founder of Penguin Books, published his first paperback here in 1935.

Soho, W1

> '*And soon I became quite familiar with the devious, vicious, dirtily-pleasant*
> *exoticism of Soho*' George Ponderevo, from *Tono Bungay*, H. G. Wells, 1909

Soho, traditionally one of the liveliest places in London, has attracted
generations of writers over the centuries: William Blake, who was born
and lived locally; Shelley, who came here after being sent down from
Oxford; Arthur Rimbaud and Paul Verlaine, who came to Soho in the
1870s after the Paris commune fell; Evelyn Waugh, Dylan Thomas and
Brendan Behan, attracted to Soho's numerous pubs and bars after the
Second World War; and, more recently, Ian McEwan, Martin Amis
and Will Self, congregating around the pubs and clubs of Dean Street
and Greek Street.

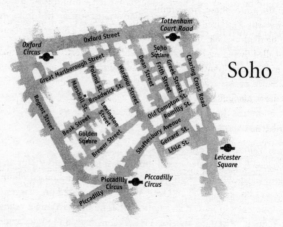

The name Soho dates back to a fourteenth-century hunting cry
when the area was a royal park. In the seventeenth century, property
developer Richard Frith began building on the park land and Henry
Compton, Bishop of London, commissioned St Anne's Church (where
William Hazlitt and Dorothy L. Sayers are buried), turning Soho into a
rich man's playground. At the end of the eighteenth century the
wealthy headed west to Mayfair, and Soho began attracting waves of
immigrants, particularly French Huguenots, Jews and Germans. In the
nineteenth century and early twentieth century, it was a place best
avoided – certainly John Galsworthy thought so in his cutting description of Soho in *The Forsyte Saga* (1922) – and authors often chose the
place when depicting sordid activities, as did Robert Louis Stevenson in

Dr Jekyll and Mr Hyde (1886) and Joseph Conrad in *The Secret Agent* (1907).

During the 1920s and '30s, around 150 nightclubs opened in the area (most of which were visited at one time or another by Noel Coward) but Soho largely escaped the Second World War bombing of the 1940s, and in the 1950s a new feeling of egalitarianism, coupled with the area's tradition for tolerance, gave rise to a Bohemian scene which thrived around its jazz clubs, espresso bars and drinking dens. Colin MacInnes captured this era, with its casual sex, violence and racial tension, in his London trilogy, *City of Spades*, *Absolute Beginners* and *Mr Love and Justice* (1957–60).

But there was also a downside among writers – 'Sohoitis' – which saw Dylan Thomas and hard-drinking associates such as Rayner Heppenstall and Julian Maclaren-Ross traipse from one bar to another, soaking in the atmosphere, but producing little work, and this probably explains why Maclaren-Ross's *Memoirs of the Forties* was unfinished when he died in 1964. In the '60s Soho vied with Chelsea as the centre of so-called Swinging London, a period better reflected in rock music than in literature (Anthony Frewin's *London Blues*, set in the *louche* Soho world of this era, was published in 1997).

In the 1970s Soho lost its way, becoming best known for its porn clubs, and rents dropped. Ironically, this led to the area's renaissance as publishers, advertising agencies and restaurateurs began moving in to take advantage of the attractive property prices. Gay clubs and venues have now replaced most of the porn places, and in the 1980s and '90s scores of designer bars opened to take advantage of the new relaxed licensing laws. This has helped to turn Soho into London's most fashionable quarter, with thousands of tourists, day-trippers and ordinary Londoners drawn to its restaurants, café-bars, clubs and pubs. Meanwhile its reputation as a literary haven continues, centred around writers such as Christopher Petit, whose *Robinson* (1993) is set in the area, as well as the new generation of would-be Julian Maclaren-Rosses getting up just in time to catch the lunchtime crowd at the Groucho and Black's before working the Old Compton Street circuit of venues.

Exploring Soho

Soho's boundaries are Oxford Street (to the north), Charing Cross Road (east) and Regent Street (west). The southern edge of Soho isn't so clear, and lies roughly in a line from Piccadilly Circus through Chinatown to Cambridge Circus. For easy exploring, in this book Soho has been divided into three sections: West Soho; Dean Street to Old Compton Street; and Chinatown.

It was Soho that Conrad had in mind when he set Mr Verloc's seedy back-street shop with its smutty magazines and naughty photos as a cover for more subversive activities in *The Secret Agent* (1907), and since then many writers have come to Soho to sample its sex scene. Graham Greene would discreetly leave the back of his smart St James's flat before furtively descending into the Soho netherworld of vice clubs and drinking dens during the 1950s. Soho prostitutes often appear in his novels, usually pretending to be Belgian or French, as sex in those days was perceived by the British to be a largely continental affair. In *The Human Factor* (1978) 'the names against the flat bells – Lulu, Mimi and the like – were all that indicated the afternoon and evening activities of Old Compton Street'.

A surprising and not particularly willing patron of the porn clubs in the 1960s was Doris Lessing, who would be dragged along by men desperate for a drink at a time when it was difficult to find anywhere that sold alcohol in the late afternoon. Philip Larkin, reminiscing about Soho's porn shops in a letter to Robert Conquest, noted that clubs in Newport Court, a small alleyway to the west of Charing Cross Road, had branched off into 'Dominant Females and Fladge', but that the permissive society 'never permitted me anything as far as I can recall'. Auberon Waugh once revealed in his diaries that he wanted to be a massage parlour inspector if *Private Eye* was closed down.

WEST SOHO

Away from the ever-congested main roads, such as Regent Street and Oxford Street, Soho has a surprisingly easy-going feel, typified by attractive streets such as Beak (home of *The Literary Review* magazine) and Broadwick (where William Blake was born).

- Landmarks to the north can be reached from Oxford Circus tube; those further south from Piccadilly Circus tube.

Bookshops

Grant & Cutler, 55 Great Marlborough Street, tel. 020 7734-2012, is devoted to foreign books and has a huge French section.

Argyll Street to Piccadilly Circus: roughly north to south

Argyll Street

Argyll Arms, no. 18

John Morris, a BBC colleague of George Orwell, got more than he bargained for after going for a drink in this carefully preserved Victorian pub next to Oxford Circus tube one day in the mid-1940s. When asked by Orwell what he was having, Morris said, 'A glass of beer,' rather than the usual 'pint of bitter'. Orwell scornfully retorted: 'You gave yourself away badly; a working-class person would never ask for a glass of beer.' Morris replied, 'I don't happen to be a working-class person,' to which Orwell responded, 'No, but there's no need to boast about it.'

head east along Oxford Street

Oxford Street

A down-at-heel road which has come to be London's high street, Oxford Street is named after Queen Anne's statesman, Robert Harley, first Earl of Oxford, who also gave his name to Harley Street. One day in 1932 Edith Sitwell bumped into T. S. Eliot's first wife, Vivien, in Oxford Street and greeted her by name. Mrs Eliot replied: 'You don't know me. You have mistaken me for that terrible woman who is so like me.' Oxford Street has numerous literary mentions. The diarist Henry Crabb Robinson wrote on 24 July 1811 how he went to a party at Charles Lamb's, where Blake showed Southey 'a perfectly mad poem called *Jerusalem*. Oxford Street is in Jerusalem.'

In *Confessions of an English Opium Eater* (1821) Thomas De Quincey recalled spending his evenings walking up and down Oxford Street with a prostitute, Ann, when he first came to London, penniless. Charles Dickens complained in *Sketches by Boz* (1837) that he could 'discern no speck in the road to encourage the belief that there is a cab or coach to be had' – nowadays Oxford Street is probably the best place in the capital for finding a cab – and in *Nicholas Nickleby* (1839) Charles Cheeryble drags Nicholas 'back into Oxford Street' and bundles him into an omnibus on its way to the City.

Thomas Hardy's 1872 poem, *Coming up Oxford Street: Evening*, makes some attempt to romanticize what has traditionally been a dingy street. In Graham Greene's *The End of the Affair* (1951), Bendrix has a dream in which he describes an Oxford Street where 'all the shops were full of cheap jewellery' (still true today). Virginia Woolf once wrote how the pavement 'seems to sprout horrid tragedies'. Nowadays this usually involves gullible tourists handing over a tenner for 'perfume' which consists mainly of water, something Keith Talent does in Martin Amis's *London Fields* (1989). For Peter Ackroyd's Oscar Wilde (from the 1983 novel, *The Last Testament of Oscar Wilde*) the turning is all street and no Oxford.

Site of Thomas De Quincey's chemist, no. 173

To cure his facial neuralgia, De Quincey bought his first stash of opium – 'dread agent of unimaginable pleasure and pain' – in 1804 at a chemist's which stood where Marks & Spencer's can now be found. By 1816 De Quincey was taking 320 grains a day, his ritual involving breaking up solid opium, boiling it in water, straining it and, after it had been reduced to a sticky gunge, diluting it with brandy before consuming it.

head south

Great Marlborough Street

Great Marlborough Street Magistrates Court, opposite continuation of Carnaby Street

One of the most famous court cases in literary history, the trial of the Marquess of Queensberry for criminally libelling Oscar Wilde, began here on 9 March 1895 with Wilde, wearing a white flower in his lapel, arriving in a carriage and pair with a coachman and a cockaded footman. The case then moved to the Central Criminal Court (see p. 73). In the mid-1960s Anthony Burgess defended Hubert Selby Jr's *Last Exit to Brooklyn* (1964), which was up before the court on charges of being obscene after a censorship campaign led by the then Labour MP, Robert Maxwell. Burgess felt he had to pretend that 'a very mediocre book was good art whose literary qualities were its best defence' when all he wanted to do was defend the right of the author to produce pornography. The book was cleared.

head east

Poland Street

Percy Bysshe Shelley's address (1811–14), no. 15

Shelley chose Poland Street for occasional lodgings simply because he was attracted by the romance of the name. Then 19 and having just been sent down from Oxford for writing a supposedly seditious pamphlet, *The Necessity of Atheism*, Shelley used to stroll around Soho munching a chunk of bread stuffed with raisins.

William Blake's address (1787–93), no. 28

In this narrow house by a timber yard Blake wrote *Songs of Innocence* (1789) and *The Marriage of Heaven and Hell* (1790), which were supposedly revealed to him in a dream by his late brother, Robert. In rare moments of socializing, Blake would visit Dr Johnson, Tom Paine and Mary Wollstonecraft, and the house was also well situated for visiting the King's Arms, a pub frequented by artists and members of a Soho-based druid revival which influenced Blake. In 1793 Blake and his wife moved to Lambeth.

turn right at Broadwick Street

Marshall Street

William Blake's birthplace and address (1757–82), Marshall Street at Broadwick Street

The poet-painter-mystic was born at this address, then 28 Broad Street, where his father ran a hosiery shop. Considered too sensitive to attend school, the young Blake was taught at home by his mother, who introduced him in a rather chaotic way to Latin, Greek, Hebrew, the works of Shakespeare, Milton and Ben Jonson, and the Bible, which was inculcated into Blake's imaginative mind at an early age. When he was nine, Blake claimed he saw his first vision – a tree filled with angels in Peckham Rye – and went home and told his father, who thrashed him until his mother intervened. Blake later said he saw God's face pressed against the window of the Broad Street house. At 15 he became an apprentice engraver and opened up a printer's/engraver's next door at no. 27 in July 1784 when his father died. The shop wasn't successful and three years later he moved to nearby Poland Street. The site of Blake's birthplace is now occupied by one of Soho's few tower blocks – Blake House.

head south

Beak Street

Dickens alludes to Beak Street (then Silver Street) in *Nicholas Nickleby* (1839) – 'In that quarter of London in which Golden Square is situated there is a bygone tumbledown street with two irregular rows of tall meagre houses.' The Crown Inn on the corner of Beak Street and James Street, as recommended by Newman Noggs in the novel, no longer stands. *The Literary Review* is based at no. 51, near where Canaletto had his studio in the 1740s.

head south

Golden Square

Now the haunt of advertising agencies and film companies, Golden Square was in a 'quarter of the town that has gone down in the world', according to Charles Dickens in *Nicholas Nickleby*, in which Ralph Nickleby lives in 'a large spacious house' thought to be at no. 7 (now replaced by a different building). In the middle of the square is a statue of George II which Dickens describes in the same book as 'a mournful statue of Portland stone'. It is near Golden Square in John Wyndham's apocalyptic nightmare, *The Day of the Triffids* (1951), that the hero, William Masen, rescues Josella Playnton from the clutches of a blind molester.

Former Strand Films, no. 1

When Dylan Thomas got a job with Strand Films in 1941 to do his bit for the war effort, he announced that he would not drink during working hours. Instead, as Jonathan Fryer pointed out in his 1983 biography, *The Nine Lives of Dylan Thomas*, he would sit counting down the minutes until the pubs opened. In 1942 Thomas helped produce a series of mini-documentaries for the Ministry of Information, in which he described colleagues as 'queers in striped suits'. When his friend and occasional author, Julian Maclaren-Ross, was taken on, the two began working on scripts for proposed horror pictures they knew would never get past the censor.

head south along Lower John Street, then west towards Regent Street

Regent Street

Café Royal, no. 68

A lavish, ornate venue, originally established by a French wine-merchant in nearby Glasshouse Street in 1865, the Café Royal is probably the closest London has come to a chic Parisian-style café. Oscar Wilde used to lunch here at exactly one o'clock nearly every day, and other Aesthetic Movement followers who were regulars included Aubrey Beardsley and Lord Alfred Douglas (Wilde's lover). By the turn of the century, patrons included George Bernard Shaw, John Buchan (in the opening of *The Thirty-Nine Steps* (1915) Richard Hannay dines here) and T. E. Hulme, the bluff Yorkshire-born Edwardian-era poet, who, during dinner with friends one night, announced that he had a pressing engagement, left the building, and returned twenty minutes later, sweaty and exhausted, to announce that the steel staircase by the emergency exit in Piccadilly Station was 'the most uncomfortable place in which he had ever copulated'.

Other patrons around this time included Ronald Firbank (who wrote largely unreadable novels composed almost entirely of dialogue) and Katherine Mansfield who, on hearing two diners poring over and then mocking a copy of D. H. Lawrence's *Amores* poems, seized the book from them and made off with it. Lawrence himself threw a dinner party at the Café Royal in March 1924 to persuade friends to join him in a pantisocratic commune in New Mexico. The gathering included Samuel Koteliansky, whom Lawrence portrayed as Libidnikov in *Women in Love* (1920) and Ben Cooley in *Kangaroo* (1923) and who later illegally distributed the first, banned, edition of *Lady Chatterley's Lover* (1928). Lawrence got everyone drunk on claret and port but convinced only one person, the Honourable Dorothy Brett, to join him. By the end of the evening the author was so inebriated Koteliansky had to carry him upstairs to bed.

It was in the Café Royal that Enid Bagnold, author of *National Velvet* (1935), claimed she lost her virginity to the lecherous Frank Harris, former editor of *Vanity Fair*: 'He told me sex is the gateway to life, so I went through the gateway in an upper room of the Café Royal.' In the 1930s and '40s John Betjeman, Stephen Spender, Cyril Connolly and Dylan Thomas (temporarily banned in 1935) were regulars. Betjeman, naturally, penned some verse, *On Seeing an Old Poet in the Café Royal* (1940), on the place. In the poem the unnamed hero is still mentally living in the 1890s (like Betjeman) and asks for the whereabouts of Oscar (Wilde), Bosie (Lord Alfred Douglas) and the more obscure Theodore Wratislaw. An impoverished George Orwell's insistence on paying for a meal for him and his friend, the much wealthier Richard Rees, editor of *Adelphi*, inspired the scene in *Keep the Aspidistra Flying* (1936) in which Gordon Comstock embarrasses himself in the Café Imperial. In recent years the Café Royal has attracted a mostly non-literary crowd.

- Sherlock Holmes is nearly murdered by 'two men armed with sticks' outside the Café Royal in 'The Illustrious Client' (1925).

Piccadilly Circus

> ''Ere we are, gents one an' all. Piccabloodydilly Circus. The centre of the
> world. The 'Ub of the Universe. Where all the nobs had their wine, women
> and song' Anon., from *The Day of the Triffids*, John Wyndham, 1951

The centre of London, if foreign students are to be believed, Piccadilly Circus was described by Wyndham Lewis as 'the circus that is

London's Etoile . . . pathetically eloquent of something that just is not there'. George Bernard Shaw disliked the Circus's well-known Eros statue so much he wanted to have the sculptor, Alfred Gilbert, drowned in the fountain.

Piccadilly

The Criterion, no. 222

Dr Watson is standing at the bar of this ornate Piccadilly Circus establishment at the beginning of the first Sherlock Holmes story, *A Study in Scarlet* (1887), when he is spotted by Stamford, his former hospital dresser. When Watson reveals that he is looking for lodgings, Stamford reveals that a colleague of his – Sherlock Holmes – is looking for someone to share rooms he has found. The plaque commemorating this momentous literary event was stolen in the 1960s and no would-be Holmeses have yet unearthed it. John Betjeman cited the Criterion's Grill Room as the kind of place where high-spirited students were likely to make merry, in *The 'Varsity Students' Rag* (1932).

DEAN STREET TO OLD COMPTON STREET

• Landmarks can be reached from Tottenham Court Road tube.

Dean Street

Packed with well-known restaurants and pubs, Dean Street is also the location of Soho's best-known media club, Groucho's.

north to south

Karl Marx's address (1850–56), no. 28

Marx wrote most of *Das Kapital* while living in what he described as 'an old hovel – two evil frightful rooms' at the top of this block during the 1850s. There was no toilet or running water, the rent was £22 a year, and a Prussian friend who came to visit described how 'everything is dirty and covered with dust, so that to sit down becomes a thoroughly dangerous business'. Marx, who lived off the postal orders and crates of wine Friedrich Engels used to send him and who made some extra money by freelancing for the *New York Tribune*, spent most of the day researching what became *Das Kapital* in the British Museum. The 1851 Census has Marx down as Charles Mark, Doctor (Philosophical Author), but makes no mention of the other inhabi-

tants, Marx's wife Jenny and their maid, both of whom were pregnant
. . . by him. When Jenny received an inheritance in 1855, they all moved
upmarket to Primrose Hill.

The downstairs area is now occupied by the huge restaurant Leoni's
Quo Vadis, about whose founder Max Beerbohm once quipped, 'Oh to
be in London now that Leoni's here.' Leoni's is owned by 'superchef',
Marco Pierre White, and pickled sheep artist, Damien Hirst. No one
has yet tried to convert Marx's apartment into a Communist theme
park but customers can ask to look at the rooms with their sagging ceil-
ings and signs of wrenched-off padlocks which date back to the days
when much of Soho was occupied by low-rent tenants.

Crown & Two Chairmen, no. 31

The pub is named after the two sedan chair men who stopped here for
a drink when taking Queen Anne to the studio opposite to have her
portrait painted. It was here that Thackeray met the flamboyant book
illustrator and travel writer, G. A. Sala, and then entertained patrons by
singing *The Mahogany Tree*. George Orwell and Graham Greene were
regulars during the 1940s, occasionally accompanied by Arthur
Koestler.

The Gargoyle, Dean Street at Meard Street

A major drinking club and nightspot for the cream of the literary
world in the middle years of the twentieth century, the Gargoyle was
decorated with Matisse glass murals; regulars included Noel Coward
and Dylan Thomas, who would drop in after the Café Royal closed to
while away the early hours.

Colony Club, no. 41

This poky private drinking den which opened in December 1948 was
run by the foul-mouthed and appropriately named Muriel Belcher who
somehow managed to maintain the right balance between cultivated
seediness and outright sordidness and used to subject customers to her
lashing tongue. One of those she upset was *Room at the Top* author
John Braine, who was greeted with the comment, 'There's plenty of
room at *her* top,' when he entered. (Belcher called all men 'her'.) Domi-
nating the Colony for decades was the artist Francis Bacon, introduced
to the place by society dandy Brian Howard (the model for Anthony
Blanche in Evelyn Waugh's *Brideshead Revisited*) whom Belcher paid
£10 a week to bring in rich customers. Bacon however mainly brought
in his rough trade for casual sex in the gents. Other Colony regulars
of the time included Daniel Farson, whose *Soho in the Fifties* (1987) is
the definitive account of post-war life in the sleazy sector, and Colin

MacInnes, who liked sitting here on sunny days with the curtains drawn, 'gossiping one's life away'. At the Colony, MacInnes met west African seaman Olu Oguntala, whom he portrayed in *City of Spades* (1957), his tale of early black immigration in the capital. When Belcher died in 1979, she was replaced by the even more bad-tempered Ian Board, who had been head barman, and, since his 1994 death, by the more reasonable Michael Wojas. Nowadays the writers are outnumbered by musicians and artists such as Damien Hirst, who owns the nearby Leoni's Quo Vadis restaurant (below the rooms where Karl Marx used to live). Some of Hirst's work is on permanent display around the room, which has barely changed since it first opened.

Groucho Club, no. 45

Taking its name from Groucho Marx's adage about not wanting to join anything that would have him as a member, the Groucho, which opened in May 1985, has become the most exclusive club for the media set in London. The idea for it came from publishers such as Carmen Callil and Liz Calder, who wanted an alternative to the stuffy male-only clubs around Pall Mall; and the place is usually crawling with celebrities – Julie Burchill, Ben Elton, Damien Hirst and Salman Rushdie, who made his second public appearance here in December 1990 after going into hiding following the Ayatollah Komeini's *fatwa*. Formal events that have taken place include meetings of the June 20 Group (a talk-shop comprising John Mortimer, Harold Pinter and Antonia Fraser) and the World One Day Cup in which writers have to pen a novel of 20,000 words in 24 hours. In October 1998 Ted Hughes failed to turn up to collect his Forward Poetry prize for *Birthday Letters*, his poems about life with Sylvia Plath.

The French House, no. 49

A Bohemian haunt for writers and artists throughout the twentieth century, this compact bar opened as the Wine House in 1910 and, after the German who ran it was obliged to leave when the First World War broke out, was taken over by Frenchman Victor Berlemont, at the time one of the few foreign landlords in Britain. Berlemont changed the pub's name to the very English-sounding York Minster – regulars called it the French House – and one day a vicar walked in and announced to the surprised bar staff, 'I'm from the York Minster,' to which the barman replied: 'No, you're *in* the York Minster.' The vicar then explained that he meant he had been sent by the Dean of the Minster in York, who had received the pub's wine by mistake and was now returning it. 'We were so pleased until we looked at the address label and realized that the postman saw the "Dean" bit but not the "Street" bit,' sighed the vicar.

During the Second World War the pub became an important meeting place for the French Resistance – legend has it that De Gaulle himself drew up his Free French call-to-arms after lunch upstairs – and it was also a major drinking den for Dylan Thomas and pals. A few weeks before he went to America in October 1953, Thomas left the only copy of the original hand-written manuscript of *Under Milk Wood* (1952) in the pub. The BBC put up a frantic search, but Thomas had to leave for the States with an inferior typewritten script. It was eventually found by a BBC producer, Douglas Cleverdon, who was spurred on by Thomas's promise that if he found the original he could keep it. Cleverdon later sold it for the then princely sum of £2,000.

Another French House regular of the time was Gerald Hamilton, Christopher Isherwood's model for Mr Norris in *Mr Norris Changes Trains* (1935), who before the war sold forged passports to German Jews and then informed on them to Nazi guards at the border. Hamilton escaped war-time conscription by fleeing to Ireland, dressed as a nun. These days the French House is just another Soho pub with little other than its eventful history to distinguish it from its neighbours.

Golden Lion, no. 51
A long-time gay pub, this was one of the few that Noel Coward used to frequent. The Golden Lion was where mass murderer Dennis Nilsen picked up his victims in the 1980s.

detour west towards Wardour Street

Wardour Street

This street of film company offices and fashionable restaurants acts as an unofficial west–east divide for Soho.

St Ann's Church, Wardour Street at Old Compton Street
Only the tower remains of this late seventeenth-century church, often wrongly attributed to Wren, most of which was destroyed during the Blitz and restored as a community centre in the late 1970s. John Betjeman can be thanked for its conversion, and in tribute he penned the lines, 'Let's make it go again, let London know/That life and heart and hope are in Soho'. Those buried in the churchyard include the essayist, William Hazlitt, and Dorothy L. Sayers, who was a churchwarden. Henry and Hester Thrale, friends of Dr Johnson, were married here in 1763. It was an eventful liaison. When Mrs Thrale wasn't writing her

diaries and letters, she was applying poultices to her husband's pox-ravaged testicles.

head east

Romilly Street

Kettner's, no. 29
Founded by Napoleon III's chef, Auguste Kettner, in 1867, this restaurant became a haunt of Oscar Wilde, who would take his boys to the rooms upstairs. Edward VII and Lillie Langtry also made use of the bedroom facilities.

Frith Street

Bar Italia, no. 22
This authentic Italian café featured in Will Self's *Grey Area* (1994) and the film version of Colin MacInnes's *Absolute Beginners*. Television pioneer John Logie Baird rented out the attic in the 1920s, and it was here in 1926 that he showed members of the Royal Institution flickering pictures on the television he had invented.

head north along Frith Street

Dog and Duck, Frith Street at Bateman Street
Victorian mirrored fittings and mahogany decorate this pub that looks little different from the days when George Orwell was an habitué. Orwell celebrated at the Dog and Duck on hearing that the American Book of the Month Club had chosen *Animal Farm* as its top title for that issue, choosing the pub because the landlord had 'mysteriously acquired a cache of real absinthe', the highly-spiced 135°-proof green liquor which Toulouse Lautrec used to drink from the hollow end of his cane and which Oscar Wilde had described 'as poetic as anything in the world'. For Orwell and friends the barman allowed water to drip slowly through a cube of sugar on to the absinthe, this at a time when sugar was rationed.

Hazlitt's/William Hazlitt's address (1830), no. 6
This exclusive but barely noticeable hotel is named after the essayist who came to live here in September 1830 and died in the property a few months later either from cholera, stomach cancer or drinking too much tea, according to differing stories. Before he died, Hazlitt managed to write *The Sick Chamber* and on his deathbed uttered the words, 'Well I've had a happy life,' which came as something of a surprise to

Charles Lamb, who'd just witnessed the latest in a series of bouts of depression, and amazed Coleridge, who claimed that Hazlitt's manners were '99 in a 100 singularity repulsive'. It was from this hotel some 160 years later that Bill Bryson began the jaunt around England recounted in his best-selling travelogue, *Notes from a Small Island* (1995). Bryson claimed that he chose Hazlitt's because 'it's intentionally obscure'.

Soho Square

> *'But look in Soho Square, the "stately quadrate"'* from *Soho*, Gavin Ewart, 1964

Soho Square is ringed with luxurious offices – the publishers Bloomsbury, 20th Century-Fox and Sir Paul McCartney's company are among the tenants – looking out at well-tended gardens and a rickety mock-Tudor hut that conceals a ventilation shaft for London Underground. The poet T. E. Hulme, whose most famous philosophical essay claimed that 'man is by nature bad or limited' and who was killed in action during the First World War, was urinating in the square one day when he was approached by a policeman and warned about his behaviour. Quick as a flash Hulme retorted: 'Do you realize you are addressing a member [*sic*] of the middle class?' The policeman made off, speechless. On another occasion Hulme dangled Wyndham Lewis upside down over the railings after Lewis had objected to Hulme's seducing his lover, Kate Lechmere.

Greek Street

Samuel Johnson's Club, also known as the Literary Club, was founded in Greek Street in the 1760s and then moved to Gerrard Street (see below). Soho's best-known pub, the Coach and Horses, for decades, until recently, home to 'low life' chronicler Jeffrey Bernard, can be found here.

north to south

House of St Barnabas-in-Soho, no. 1
One of the oldest surviving houses in Soho and the probable setting for Dr Manette's house in Dickens's *A Tale of Two Cities* (1859), the House of St Barnabas is now a women's hostel.

Gay Hussar, no. 2
A 1970s dinner party for W. H. Auden at this Hungarian restaurant, long favoured by Labour politicians and the left-wing end of London's

literati, was enlivened when the poet leant over to Marianne Faithfull and asked her: 'When you're smuggling drugs, do you pack them up your arse?' A few years previously, Rolling Stone Mick Jagger, Marianne Faithfull, journalist Paul Foot and Labour MP Tom Driberg had met here to discuss forming a new socialist party, Logos (Greek for word).

Site of Thomas De Quincey's address (1802), no. 61

De Quincey came to Soho in 1802 when he was 17, having run away from various schools and a reasonably comfortable life. Penniless, he ended up lodging with a solicitor, a Mr Brunell, who lived in and ran his business from a large house that stood on this site. As De Quincey later recalled in *Confessions of an English Opium Eater* (1821), 'the house was large; and, from the want of furniture, the noise of the rats made a prodigious echoing of spacious staircase and hall'. When he could no longer afford his lodgings, De Quincey sought Brunell's help and the latter, who to avoid bailiffs used to stay in a different part of London every night, let him stay here. De Quincey had company – a 10-year-old waif who shared his plight – and they survived by waiting for Brunell to finish his breakfast so that they could gobble up the leftovers. By day De Quincey would tramp the streets of Soho or take refuge in the doorways until being moved on, dreaming of fleeing to the Lake District and meeting Wordsworth, something he eventually achieved.

The Pillars of Hercules, no. 7

A pub has stood here since 1733 and was long established when Dickens came to include it in his 1859 novel, *A Tale of Two Cities*. (The street to the side is named Manette Street in honour of the novel's Dr Manette.) Francis Thompson, the cricket-loving poet, was supposedly rescued while lying in the doorway in a drunken stupor some time in 1888 by Wilfred Meynell, editor of *Merry England*. Meynell subsequently gave Thompson his first chance of being published. In the 1970s the pub was frequented by the new generation of Soho scribes – Martin Amis, Julian Barnes and Ian McEwan – and was used as a home-from-home by the crowd that ran the *New Review*, then based at 11 Greek Street.

Coach and Horses, no. 29

Proprietor Norman Balon has continued the Soho tradition of character-publicans by becoming the so-called 'rudest landlord in London' in presiding over this no-frills pub, long home to the dypso end of the Soho writing classes. The Coach and Horses' best-known regular, until his death in 1997, was *Spectator* columnist and professional alcoholic, Jeffrey Bernard, who could be found perched on a favourite stool, regaling customers with his trenchant wit (as far as fans were concerned) or being the pub bore (as far as everyone else was concerned). Keith Waterhouse even turned his life into a West End show, *Jeffrey Bernard Is Unwell* (1991), the excuse often found on the page where his *Spectator* column, 'Low Life', should have been.

Since the 1960s the pub has been the setting for the fortnightly lunches hosted by the satirical magazine, *Private Eye*, which is based in nearby Carlisle Street. Writers who have attended include Melvyn Bragg, Germaine Greer, Julian Barnes and Salman Rushdie, who scoffed away while Special Branch officers, on the lookout for suspicious characters, posed as ordinary drinkers downstairs. Usually the most dangerous encounter is with Balon himself, who has been known to terrorize lunch guests with a playful 'Oi, where the f— do you think you're going?' as they furtively make their way to the dining-room.

Site of David Archer's bookshop, no. 35

In the 1950s and '60s Archer's bookshop was the most absurdly run in Soho: he often refused to allow customers to buy a volume he wanted to keep himself. At the back of the shop Archer ran a café where writers such as Colin MacInnes and George Barker would congregate until lunchtime, at which point Archer would empty the till and take everyone off to the Coach and Horses. The building is now occupied by a Chinese restaurant.

Old Compton Street

Old Compton Street is the main artery of Soho life, and the centre of the capital's gay scene, full of chic cafés, bistros, bars and restaurants. The French symbolist poets, Paul Verlaine and Arthur Rimbaud, briefly lodged at no. 5 in 1872 after the Paris Commune fell.

CHINATOWN

Shaftesbury Avenue and the streets immediately south have been associated with the Chinese since 1960s' migration from the capital's original Chinatown in Limehouse, east London. According to James Morton's 1992 book, *Gangland*, there was a small but conspicuous Chinese presence in Soho as far back as the 1920s in the shape of drug trafficker Brilliant Chang, who owned a restaurant in Regent Street and dealt in opium as a sideline. Timothy Mo in *Sour Sweet* (1982) wrote about the area's triad gangs and the story of the Chen family's attempts to enter British society.

- Landmarks can be reached from Leicester Square tube.

Shaftesbury Avenue

This traffic-choked route which divides Soho proper from Chinatown was the setting for Alan Ayckbourn's 1961 play, *Standing Room Only*, in which a bus in 1997 is marooned in traffic that is gridlocked from London to Birmingham.

Gerrard Street

> '*Half the blackmail or swindling cases live in Gerrard Street*' Graham Greene, letter to his wife, 1936

The stacks of Chinese vegetables, scores of restaurants and the swarms of tourists who now invade Gerrard Street disguise the fact that this was once a haunt of writers and artists, attracted by the cheap rents. Some of Britain's first foreign restaurants, such as the Mont Blanc, where G. K. Chesterton first met Hilaire Belloc in 1900, were here. In Anthony Powell's *Casanova's Chinese Restaurant* (1960), from his *A Dance to the Music of Time* series, Jenkins and Moreland hear an old opera singer singing 'Pale hands I loved beside the Shalimar' while walking down Gerrard Street.

north side: west to east

Site of James Boswell's address (1775), no. 22

Boswell lodged with a tailor at no. 22 in 1775 ('a very neat first floor at 16 shillings a week') and recalled being woken by the sound of street-sellers and Huguenot hammerers while he tried to sleep off a hangover.

Site of Mont Blanc Restaurant, no. 16

The Mont Blanc (also now a restaurant) was a pre-First World War meeting place for the literary circle that included the poet Edward Thomas (killed in action during the First World War), John Masefield, Joseph Conrad, John Galsworthy, Ford Madox Ford, Hilaire Belloc and G. K. Chesterton.

Mr Jaggers's office, no. 10

Mr Jaggers, the lawyer in Dickens's *Great Expectations* (1861) who informs Pip of his fortune, has his office at no. 10, 'a stately house of its kind but dolefully in want of painting', now occupied by a restaurant, like many of the buildings in this street. Dickens probably chose Gerrard Street because his uncle, Thomas Barrow, had lived there and he had visited the place often. One of the author's first stories was about a barber, William Turner (the father of the painter), who lived in the street.

Site of The Club, no. 9

Samuel Johnson's Literary Club (also known as The Club), which he and Joshua Reynolds founded in the 1760s in Greek Street, moved soon afterwards to the Turk's Head Tavern at no. 9, where it met every Monday at 7 p.m. and where Johnson held court, as recounted by James Boswell in his *Life of Johnson* (1791). Other club regulars included Oliver Goldsmith, the actor David Garrick, and the political philosopher Edmund Burke. No. 9 was used as the headquarters for magistrates during the Gordon Riots, and closed as a pub in 1783. The site is now occupied by a Chinese gift shop.

south side: east to west

Site of John Dryden's address (1687–1700) and The 43 Club (1920s), no. 43

Dryden was probably the first literary great to move into Gerrard Street, taking poky rooms at no. 43 in 1687, a year before England fell to the Glorious Revolution; and he, as a supporter of the departed James II, fell from grace, losing his status as poet laureate. Dryden also had problems with his wife, whom he'd been forced to marry by one of her brothers. She accused him of neglecting her and one day turned to the poet and remarked: 'Lord, Mr Dryden, how can you always be poring over those musty books? I wish I were a book then I should have more of your company.' He is supposed to have replied: 'If you do become a book, let it be an almanac, for then I shall change you every year.'

The 43 Club, another Gerrard Street literary venue, was founded here in the 1920s with Joseph Conrad and J. B. Priestley among its members and the place run by a landlady, Kate Meyrick, who claimed that Dryden's ghost was watching over the place. By the mid '20s it was one of the most fashionable nightspots in the capital, attracting not just the literati but aristocrats and gangsters such as the burglar Ruby Sparks and the Sabini racecourse gang, who would make regular raids on the wealthier members' furs and wallets. The 43 was soon being raided almost nightly by cops, and when Meyrick began ignoring the fines for keeping a rowdy house she was sent to Holloway Prison.

Site of Edmund Burke's address (1787–90), no. 37

Here Burke wrote *Reflections on the Revolution in France*, a major influence on political thinking.

Wardour Street

Former Horseshoe, no. 21

Dylan Thomas was a regular visitor to the Horseshoe, which had a spy hole covered by a sliding panel so that those inside would know who was trying to get in. Thomas loved this as it made him think he was in a Prohibition speakeasy.

Westminster, sw1

The City of Westminster, which grew around the eleventh-century Abbey that Edward the Confessor built on what was then the marshy Thorney Island, is the home of the Crown and British government and contains the nation's great buildings of state: Buckingham Palace, Westminster Abbey and the Houses of Parliament. Its literary history is based mainly around these places, although the gentlemen's clubs of St James's to the north have provided much entertainment and anecdote.

Because of the high concentration of civic, regal and religious buildings and monuments, exploring Westminster tends to be a neck-straining activity. Apart from the well-known sights, there are a few quiet enclaves of dignified houses such as those on Barton Street and Lord North Street, south of the Abbey, and those north of St James's Park around Pall Mall.

Exploring Westminster

Westminster's boundaries (in this book) are roughly Piccadilly–Haymarket–Charing Cross–Northumberland Avenue (to the north), the Thames (east), Vauxhall Bridge Road (south-west) and Grosvenor Place (west). For easy exploring, in this book Westminster has been divided into four sections: St James's; Whitehall; Around Parliament Square; and Victoria to Westminster School.

ST JAMES'S

> *'In St James's they keep their spirits up with wine/they banquet on Silver in*
> *state/the Officers mess at their club/they feed on the highest of game'* from
> *St James's and St Giles's*, anon, nineteenth century

London's exclusive gentlemen's clubs – the Athenaeum, Reform,
Travellers, and so on – can be found in this wealthy enclave named
after St James's Palace which was built by Henry VIII on the site of
St James's Hospital, a quarter-mile south of what is now Piccadilly.

- Landmarks to the west can be reached from Green Park tube; those
further east from Piccadilly Circus tube.

Buckingham Palace to Haymarket: roughly west to east

Buckingham Gate

Buckingham Palace

George III, in 1762, was the first monarch to move into what was then
Buckingham House, a 1705 mansion built for the 1st Duke of Buckingham. A little while later, the king came upon Samuel Johnson in the library, asked the Dictionary compiler whether he was writing anything
and, when Johnson replied that he had done his part as a writer,
responded, 'I should have thought so too, if you had not written so
well.' When Johnson failed to reply, the king asked him if he had any
comment to make. 'No, Sir,' Johnson answered. 'When the king had
said it, it was to be so. It was not for me to bandy civilities with my sov-
ereign . . . Sir, they may talk of the king as they will; but he is the finest
gentleman I have ever seen.' In the 1780s George III contributed to the
Annals of Agriculture under the name Ralph Robinson.

In the 1820s Buckingham House was almost entirely demolished and
redeveloped as Buckingham Palace. Queen Victoria moved in during
the early years of her reign and here was taught landscape drawing by
nonsense poet Edward Lear. She received Charles Dickens at the palace
a few months before his death in 1870 and presented him with an auto-
graphed copy of her *Journal of Our Life in the Highlands*. T. E. Lawrence, fresh from his successful military exploits in the Arabian desert
during the First World War, arrived at the palace in October 1918 to be
decorated by George V, but, as the king took the medal from its velvet
cushion and prepared to hang it from a hook on Lawrence's tunic, the
soldier-writer whispered to the monarch that with all due respect he
could not receive any honour from his Majesty while Britain was about

Walking Henry James's St James's

The great American novelist lived in London for over twenty years, mainly in Kensington and Mayfair, but he spent much of his time walking the streets of the capital, making observations that he used in the essays, *The Suburbs of London* (1877) and *London* (1888). A tour of Henry James's St James's should begin at Hyde Park Corner, which James felt every London lover should apologize for, it being 'so bungled an attempt at a great public place', then head east from this roaring traffic junction along Constitution Hill through the 'convenient, familiar, treeless, or almost treeless expanse of Green Park' towards Buckingham Palace. In *The Suburbs of London* James described the royal palace as 'lamentably ugly'. From here it's a short walk up the Mall, past St James's Palace where Queen Elizabeth I held court and which James thought was 'less shabby only because it is less pretentious', turning left at Marlborough Road, off which is Christopher Wren's Marlborough House or, as James put it, 'is hidden away in a court-yard and presents no face whatever to the world'. The future King George V was born here in 1865 and it is now offices for the Commonwealth.

To the north is King Street (home of the auctioneers Christie's) where the St James's Theatre stood (at roughly no. 23) until 1957. It was here that Henry James's play *Guy Domville* fell flat on its opening night in January 1895. Head back to Pall Mall, where at no. 104 is the Reform Club. James, shortly before the First World War, used to stay here in the winter (summers were spent in Rye, Sussex) and get a member of staff to bore a hole in the door of his room so that his valet could ensure he didn't disturb his writing. Head north along Regent Street to Piccadilly, of which James was so 'fond', he was 'grateful to anyone or anything that does it a service'. Turn right beyond Piccadilly Circus at Haymarket – James went to see Oscar Wilde's *An Ideal Husband* at the Haymarket Theatre the night his *Guy Domville* was booed – towards what James called the 'grimy desert' of Trafalgar Square. From here it's a short walk eastwards to the Charing Cross Hotel by Charing Cross station, where James stayed in 1872, writing to his parents that 'London is the same terrible great murky Babylon as ever'.

to dishonour pledges promised to the Arabs. The king, shocked, put the medal back on the cushion. Lawrence bowed and moved away.

In the 1930s W. H. Auden went to the palace to collect a medal for poetry, also from George V, who said to him: 'Now, Mr Auden, I very much admired that poem you wrote in 1826.' Auden thought to himself, 'Oh Christ, he's really done it now,' but the king quickly corrected himself by saying, 'Ah, I mean 1926.' Then, a few moments later, George asked Auden, 'And how are the boys?' Auden swallowed hard.

Had the King found out about his dalliances with rough trade under Hammersmith Bridge? George noticed Auden's bemused look and explained – to Auden's relief – that he had been told the poet was a prep school teacher.

When Stevie Smith collected the Queen's Gold Medal for Poetry from the palace in 1970, she was so nervous she turned up too early,

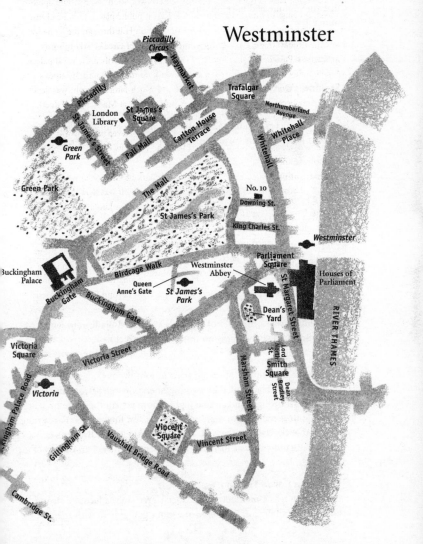

Westminster

went for a walk, watched the changing of the guard and, on deciding it was time to go in, found that the policeman on the gate didn't believe her. So she went for another walk until it started to rain and then found the courage to demand entry. Philip Larkin described getting a CBE in 1975 in *Letters* (1992), 'I bowed and she [the Queen] lassoed me with a pink silk ribbon from which depended a gold cross'. But he felt that the honour had been an 'ordeal, simultaneously boring and unnerving'.

head through Green Park to Piccadilly and turn right until reaching St James's Street

St James's Street

Gentlemen's clubs and long-established shops front this short street which connects Piccadilly and Pall Mall. In T. S. Eliot's *Old Possum's Book of Practical Cats* (1930) Bustopher Jones is the St James's Street cat.

north to south

White's, nos. 37–38

In *The Dunciad* (1728) Alexander Pope describes what is now St James's oldest club (then based at no. 28) as a place where one may 'teach oaths to youngsters and to nobles wit'. Jonathan Swift disapproved of the establishment and used to shake his fist at the building every time he passed. Winston Churchill once declared White's to be the 'centre of London'.

Boodle's, no. 28

Ian Fleming was a member of Boodle's and based Blade's (to which M in the Bond books belongs) on this gentlemen's club.

Brooks's Club, no. 60

When Richard Brinsley Sheridan tried to join Brooks's, he found himself continually blackballed by two members, George Selwyn and the Earl of Bessborough, and so one night before yet another vote he sent Selwyn a note telling him that his house was on fire and the Earl a note stating that his daughter was ill. He was at last elected. Brooks's is where the sandwich was inadvertently invented by the Earl of Sandwich.

Site of the Cocoa Tree, no. 64

Lord Byron was a member of the Cocoa Tree club, a Jacobite stronghold during the 1740s, and he wrote about going there with friends from six in the evening to four the next morning, drinking champagne, claret and a Regency Punch made of Madeira, brandy and green tea. Thackeray mentions the Cocoa Tree in *Vanity Fair* (1848).

William Evans, no. 66
Gunmakers since 1883, Evans's was probably the shop that John Wyndham had in mind when William Masen goes to St James's Street to stock up on weapons in *The Day of the Triffids* (1951).

Site of Lord Byron's address (1808–14), no. 8
Byron was living in a house on this site in March 1812 when the first cantos of *Childe Harold's Pilgrimage* were published. The poet wrote how he 'awoke one morning and found [myself] famous'. The office block which now stands on the site has been named Byron House.

Graham Greene's address (1947–8), no. 5
In Greene's *The Human Factor* (1978) the spymaster, Colonel Daintry, lives in a smart flat above a restaurant at no. 5. Greene modelled Daintry on a real-life secret service officer, Colonel Dansey, who during the Second World War worked here for MI9 (an MI6 offshoot), briefing agents on escaping from enemy territory. After the war Greene, who himself had worked for MI6, moved into Dansey's old flat. Several scenes in his 1951 novel, *The End of the Affair*, the story of novelist Maurice Bendrix's affair with Sarah, the wife of a civil servant, were based on Greene's dalliances with the married Catherine Wolston at St James's Street.

Pall Mall

This once grand street, now spoiled by chaotic development on the north side and a pointless one-way system, takes its unusual name from the croquet-like game, 'Pelemele', which the aristocracy used to play in nearby St James's Park (as Samuel Pepys noted in his diary) and has been home to Daniel Defoe (his Roxanna, heroine of the novel of the same name, lives as a society mistress on Pall Mall), Jonathan Swift, Laurence Sterne, Samuel Taylor Coleridge and Sir Walter Scott. In the seventeenth century Pall Mall began to attract bawdy coffee houses, which were eventually transformed into the gentlemen's clubs for which the area is most famous. The street also attracted expensive shops, as John Gay noted in *Trivia* (1716): 'Oh bear me to the paths of fair Pell mell/Safe are thy pavements, grateful is thy smell.' The Sunday afternoon peace in Pall Mall (in the early 1930s) is described as 'the peace which follows a massacre . . . poverty here had been successfully contested, driven back' in Graham Greene's *It's a Battlefield* (1934).

Reform Club, no. 104

> '... the Reform Club, an imposing edifice in Pall Mall' from Around the
> World in Eighty Days, Jules Verne, 1872

Phileas Fogg bets club members Stuart, Fallentin, Sullivan, Flanagan
and Ralph that he can go around the world in eighty days, in Jules
Verne's novel of the same name. Fogg returns to the Reform as the
clock strikes eight on the eightieth day and wins his bet. After a good
Reform Club lunch at the start of the 1926 General Strike, Arnold Bennett noted in his Journal, 'general opinion that the fight would be short
but violent. Bloodshed anticipated next week.' By then the strike was
over.

When novelist Hugh Walpole discovered in 1930 that Somerset
Maugham had cast him as the venal Alroy Kear in his about-to-be-
published novel, Cakes and Ale, Walpole arranged a lunch here with
Arnold Bennett and J. B. Priestley and asked them to try to obstruct the
novel's publication. Priestley convinced Walpole that Maugham's target
was not him but the poet-playwright, John Drinkwater. (Walpole was
in fact the target, but Maugham never admitted so until Walpole was
dead. See Mayfair, Albany p. 192.)

A violent exchange of words between the poet, Elspeth Barker, and
the reviewer and academic, Professor John Carey, took place here
shortly after the death of the former's husband, the punning poet
George Barker, whose work Carey had rubbished in the Sunday Times.
When Elspeth Barker was asked what she had shouted at Carey, she
replied that 'nothing but the utmost civility passed between myself and
that creep'.

The Travellers, no. 106

Founded in the early nineteenth century to cater for those who had
been on the Grand Tour of Europe, a requirement of the club was that
members must have travelled at least a thousand miles from London.
When J. M. Barrie at a club function asked the African explorer, Joseph
Thompson, what the most dangerous part of his last expedition had
been, Thompson replied, 'Crossing Piccadilly Circus.'

The Athenaeum, no. 107

Founded in 1824 by John Croker (who first coined the term 'Conservative'), the Athenaeum was where Disraeli wrote many of his novels
(despite having once been blackballed) and Trollope penned The Last
Chronicle of Barset (1867). During a break in writing, Trollope wandered through the long drawing-room, overheard two members complaining about one of the characters, Mrs Proudie, and promised them
he would kill her off forthwith. J. M. Barrie, passing through the club

one day, asked a very elderly member whether it was worth dining in the restaurant. The latter immediately burst into tears; it was the first time anyone in the Club had spoken to him since he had become a member. Dickens and Thackeray made up their differences in the Athenaeum after years of animosity, shortly before the latter's death.

Herbert Read, the art critic and author of *The Green Boy* (1945), invited a soldier whose poetry he admired to lunch at the club shortly after the Second World War; he fished out the manuscript, and then told him, 'We have made a very great mistake. Your book is very bad. I can find nothing in its favour. We cannot possibly publish it. You have no talent, no talent at all.' This wasn't out of character for Read, who once dismissed Somerset Maugham with a scornful 'contemptible people who write for money . . . like you'.

Arthur Conan Doyle based the Diogenes Club, 'the Queerest club in London, where no member is permitted to take the least notice of any other one', the setting for the Sherlock Holmes short story, 'The Greek Interpreter' (1893), on the Athenaeum, of which he was a member. In those days the Athenaeum was renowned for its hostility to strangers, who would be ushered into a small room by the entrance where they would have to conduct their conversation in whispers.

detour north

St James's Square

London Library no. 14
Books that the Edwardian poet, T. E. Hulme, borrowed in 1914 from this excellent subscription library (founded by Thomas Carlyle in 1840) were destroyed in Flanders when he was blown to smithereens in the trenches. The Library wasn't very sympathetic and wrote to the poet's estate, expressing its annoyance at his failure to return the volumes (as Ezra Pound noted in *Canto XVI* (1924)). Graham Greene, annoyed that the Library refused to allow his secretary to take out books on his behalf, publicly resigned his membership in protest, making a lot of fuss about it in the papers. The Library then pointed out that the author had never actually been a member – he had been taking out books in his wife's name. When the Library wanted to raise money in 1960, T. S. Eliot, then Library president, prepared a signed copy of *The Waste Land* (1922) and included a new line, 'The ivory men make company between us', inserted in the section 'A Game of Chess'. The manuscript raised £2,800 at Christie's.

return south

Carlton House Terrace

Former Information Research Department, nos. 12–14

Fay Weldon in the 1950s worked for the Foreign Office, a secret department of which was based in this grand, John Nash-designed Regency terrace at the height of the Cold War. She was taken on after a clerk at Soho's Great Marlborough Street employment exchange asked her during an interview what she could do, and when she replied, 'Get things out of my head on to bits of paper,' she was sent to Carlton House Terrace and given a mind-numbing job on the Polish desk writing briefing papers on the Fate of the Boy Scout Movement in the Eastern Bloc. Occasionally a really important paper she had written would be sent to the prime minister, Winston Churchill, and he once returned one of her pieces, on Reconstruction in Communist Poland, inscribed with the letters 'VG', for very good. The Information Research Department was closed down in the late '70s by then Labour foreign secretary, David Owen.

Haymarket

Fyodor Dostoevsky, abroad in London on a Saturday night in 1862 and unable to speak a word of English, was astonished to find people in Haymarket 'celebrating the Sabbath all night long until five o'clock in the morning', as well as prostitutes accompanied by their 'daughters'. Dostoevsky was so upset by the sight of one wretched six-year-old girl, who looked as if she had been severely beaten, he gave her sixpence. She ran off as fast as she could before he changed his mind. The Russian writer was also put out by a leaflet, written in French, which was pressed into his hand. Surprisingly, it was not an advert for *ooh lah lah* but a request to join the Roman Catholic church; Dostoevsky was convinced he had stumbled on a cynical plot whereby the RC church would swamp an area with propaganda and send ministers to inveigle their way into poor people's homes and convert them to Rome. An Anglican minister would never behave that way, the Russian claimed, as 'the poor are not even allowed inside a [Protestant] church because they have not the money to pay for a seat'.

When Oscar Wilde was accosted in this street by a beggar moaning about his lack of work and bread, he replied, 'Work! Why should you want to work? Bread! Why should you want to eat bread? If you had said to me you had work to do but had no intention of doing it, or that you had bread to eat but had no intention of eating it I would have gladly given you two shillings and sixpence.' The beggar was speechless, but the poet handed him half a crown nonetheless. Wilde was also dismissive of a rent boy who stopped him outside the Theatre Royal in Haymarket one day in 1893 and demanded £10 to return the original of a suggestive letter the playwright had written to his lover, Lord Alfred Douglas. 'You have no appreciation of literature,' Wilde claimed, adding, 'If you had asked me for fifty, I might have given it to you.'

WHITEHALL

Synonymous with government for centuries Whitehall, the road that connects Trafalgar Square and Parliament Square, is named after Henry VIII's Whitehall Palace, of which only Banqueting House (junction with Horseguards Avenue) remains. It was there that Charles I was beheaded on 30 January 1649; John Milton, then Latin Secretary for the Council, had the onerous task of telling the world the news of the regicide. The workings of the state machine is not a subject that has gripped many novelists, but it forms the basis of C. P. Snow's eleven-volume *Strangers and Brothers* series, set in the middle of the twentieth century.

- Landmarks to the north can be reached from Charing Cross tube; those nearer Parliament Street from Westminster tube.

Charing Cross to Parliament Square

Whitehall

The Admiralty, north-west end of Whitehall
Raymond Chandler, when he was living in Streatham in 1907, secured what he hoped would be a cushy civil service job – Assistant Store Officer, Naval Stores Branch – which would leave him enough time to write. The work wasn't too demanding – it entailed keeping records of how naval supplies and ammunition were moved from depot to depot – but was bogged down in bureaucracy, and much of the day was spent in petty office politics, such as whether carbon paper, perceived to be a threat to jobs, should be used. Chandler soon decided he'd had enough and left to become a reporter on the *Daily Express*. Ian Fleming put his experiences as personal assistant to the Director of Naval Intelligence in Room 39 to use in the James Bond books. John Betjeman worked here during the Second World War. When asked what he did, he replied, 'God knows.'

Whitehall Place

Former Scotland Yard, no. 4

John Milton lived in a house in Scotland Yard from 1649 to 1651 while working as a civil servant; this is why, when Sir Robert Peel created the Metropolitan Police here (on the site of the palace where visiting Scottish kings had stayed when visiting London) some 170 years later, officers were known not as bobbies or peelers but as miltons. The police moved to a new Norman Shaw-designed building at the junction of Victoria Embankment and Bridge Street in the 1880s and are now based near St James's Park tube.

Downing Street

No. 10

Prime ministers have lived at this address since 1732 when George II presented the house to Sir Robert Walpole, the first modern-style premier, and father of the future Gothic novelist, Horace; only one premier, Benjamin Disraeli, is equally as well known for his writing.

John Buchan was made Director of Intelligence (headquarters at no. 10) during the First World War, recruiting fellow novelists Anthony Hope, Arnold Bennett and Somerset Maugham, but not Thomas Hardy, who declined on the grounds that he was too old. Maugham had the most exciting brief. In the winter of 1917 he was sent to Russia to persuade Alexander Kerensky's provisional government to stay in the war despite the Bolshevik uprising. Kerensky gave Maugham a confidential message to take to prime minister David Lloyd George; Maugham, worried about his stutter, carefully wrote it down. Lloyd George was impressed with the report-back, unimpressed with Kerensky's position, and thanked Maugham, telling him how much he enjoyed his plays.

Mary Wilson, wife of 1960s and 1970s Labour prime minister Harold, fancied herself as something of a poet and was published but to little lasting interest. Wilson himself, bumping into Alan Bennett at a function at no. 10 in the 1970s, refused to believe that the latter was one of the original members of the *Beyond the Fringe* cast. 'You weren't one of the original four, were you,' Wilson remarked. When Bennett insisted that he was, the PM retorted, 'Well I don't remember you, are you sure?' Bennett later said that he appreciated how Trotsky must have felt when he was cut out of the history of the Russian Revolution.

When Margaret Thatcher saw Philip Larkin at a reception here in May 1980, she approached him and exclaimed, 'Oh Dr Larkin, I am a great admirer of your poems,' to which he replied, 'Well quote me a line then.' Thatcher came back with what she thought was a verbatim line from *Deceptions* (1950) – 'All afternoon her mind lay open like a drawer of knives' – but obviously hadn't been briefed well enough. The quote should have been 'All the unhurried day your mind lay open like a drawer of knives'. Later that year Larkin's great friend, Kingsley Amis, was also invited to a Downing Street reception, around the time that his novel, *Russian Hide-and-Seek* (1980), was published. Thatcher wasn't impressed with its story of Britain after fifty years of Soviet rule and told the author to 'get another crystal ball'.

The best-known fictional prime minister is probably Anthony Trollope's Plantagenet Palliser who becomes PM in the fifth Palliser book, *The Prime Minister* (1876). Rebecca West cast 1920s Tory premier Andrew Bonar Law as a Liberal, Hurrell, in her unfinished *Sunflower* (written in the 1920s). Evelyn Waugh imagined 'midnight orgies at no. 10' in *Vile Bodies* (1930). Emmeline Pankhurst in *My Own Story* (1940) described how she and fellow suffragettes took a taxi to Downing Street on Friday 1 March 1910, got out of the vehicle, calmly began throwing stones at the windows, and then stood around, waiting to be arrested, which they were. Harold Nicolson in *Diaries and Letters* (1966) related a now barely believable scene in which he met then prime minister Ramsay MacDonald outside the House one day in the 1920s, joined him on a walk to no. 10, passing by scores of pedestrians who doffed their hats to the prime minister, and casually strolled into Downing Street, where there was little security and no gates (they were put up in the 1980s at Margaret Thatcher's instigation).

- James Boswell wrote much of what became his *London Journal* in a house in Downing Street (opposite no. 10) that has since been demolished.

King Charles Street

Foreign Office

Many were shocked to discover, on reading newly released government papers in 1996, that George Orwell, back in the late '40s at the outset of the Cold War, had collaborated with the Foreign Office to draw up a blacklist of writers thought to be communists or fellow-travellers. (The Foreign Office's Information Research Department had approached Orwell when he was in a sanatorium in Gloucestershire in 1949, shortly before he died of TB.) To some, such as Richard Gott, who had resigned as literary editor of the *Guardian* in 1994 after admitting that he had accepted travel expenses from the KGB, it was no surprise, as Orwell had always been fervently anti-Stalinist, deriding those who took Stalin's line as counter-revolutionaries. During the Second World War a number of writers were found Foreign Office jobs. One unlikely pairing saw Antonia White work alongside Graham Greene in the Political Intelligence Department.

AROUND PARLIAMENT SQUARE

• Landmarks can be reached from Westminster tube.

roughly clockwise around Parliament Square

Little George Street

Middlesex Guildhall

The former Middlesex County Council headquarters marks the site where people sought sanctuary from the authorities in the Middle Ages. In Shakespeare's *Richard III* (1594), Edward IV's widow, Elizabeth, takes refuge here with her six children after Richard, Duke of Gloucester (later Richard III), takes Edward V, her eldest son, to the Tower. Richard then persuades her to let him have another son, Richard, Duke of York, as company for Edward, and then arranges their murder (see the Tower, p. 45).

Parliament Square

James Boswell stopped Lord Thurlow, who was hurrying along this busy road, late for a session in the Lords, and asked him if he had read his *Life of Johnson* (1791). 'Yes, damn you,' Lord Thurlow replied, 'every word of it. I could not help myself.'

Derby Gate

Former New Scotland Yard, Derby Gate at Victoria Embankment
The Metropolitan Police headquarters moved to this Norman Shaw building (featured in countless detective novels) in 1890. In 1929 Scotland Yard officers seized the manuscript of D. H. Lawrence's *Pansies* book of poems after the Director of Public Prosecutions found some of the poems 'nauseous and disgusting'. When Lawrence noticed that some of the poems had been censored, he wrote, 'no doubt there was a rush of detectives, postmen and Home Office clerks to pick out the

most lurid blossoms'. The police moved to a new building by
St James's Park tube station in 1967.

Westminster Bridge

William Wordsworth wrote *Upon Westminster Bridge* (1807), with its
famous opening line, 'Earth has not anything to show more fair', on
the roof of a coach after crossing the bridge with sister Dorothy on
3 September 1802. The sight, 'so touching in its majesty', has changed
considerably since Wordsworth's day. Wordsworth's 'ships, towers,
domes, theatres and temples' have been replaced by Barry and Pugin's
Houses of Parliament, Big Ben, St Thomas's Hospital and New Scotland Yard (although the poet would recognize Westminster Abbey).
James Boswell liked having sex with prostitutes – or, as he put it, meeting Signore Gonorrhoea – on the bridge, which is probably why he contracted VD seventeen times in about the same number of years.

St Margaret Street

House of Commons

From the earliest days of parliament, MPs' numbers have included
writers. Geoffrey Chaucer, Sir Thomas More, Francis Bacon and Walter
Ralegh were among the first writer-MPs, the latter taking his seat in
1593 after being freed from the Tower where Elizabeth I had sent him
for 'treason' (seducing one of her maids). Samuel Pepys, who was secretary to the Navy in the 1670s, felt obliged to represent the body in
parliament and so became member for Castle Rising in Norfolk, followed by Harwich. Joseph Addison, founder of *The Spectator* in 1711
and MP, wasn't much of a public speaker and, after beginning a
speech, 'Mr Speaker, I conceive – I conceive, sire, – sir, I conceive . . .'
was interrupted by a member who exclaimed, 'The honourable
member has conceived thrice and brought forth nothing.' In 1741
Horace Walpole, son of the first prime minister, Robert, and best
known for the Gothic novel, *The Castle of Otranto* (1764), took a
Cornish seat while on the Grand Tour in Italy.

Richard Brinsley Sheridan, who became MP for Stafford in 1780, was
involved in the impeachment of Warren Hastings, the first governor-
general of India. After Sheridan's speech the whole house applauded –
a rare event – and within hours he was offered £1,000 for the copyright. Hastings was eventually acquitted. In February 1809 Sheridan was
in the House when the Theatre Royal in Drury Lane, which he partly
owned, caught fire. Sheridan remained calm enough to declare that he

hoped 'whatsoever might be the extent of the private calamity ... would not interfere with the public business of the country'.

Nineteenth-century writer-MPs included Thomas Macaulay, William Cobbett and Benjamin Disraeli, who twice became prime minister. The historian Macaulay entered parliament as Whig member for Calne in Wiltshire in 1830 and became Secretary for War in Lord Melbourne's government in 1839. William Cobbett, best known for *Rural Rides* (1830), became MP for Oldham from 1832 when he was 69. Benjamin Disraeli, the only prime minister to have been a major novelist, entered the House in 1837 but made a bad start to his parliamentary career when his maiden speech was booed and cat-called. He retorted by warning the House, 'Though I sit down now, the time will come when you will hear me.'

One of few twentieth-century writers to win a seat was Hilaire Belloc (elected for Salford in the 1906 Liberal landslide). During the First World War the House debated whether D. H. Lawrence's *The Rainbow* was obscene. Lawrence was defended by Philip Morrell MP, husband of Lady Ottoline Morrell, whose literary salons in Bloomsbury he frequented. John Buchan was elected to the Scottish Universities seat in 1927 as a Conservative. In 1953 Winston Churchill, then prime minister, won the Nobel Prize for Literature – for his histories rather than the 1900 novel, *Savrola*. In recent years former Tory MP Jeffrey Archer (now Lord Archer) has become one of Britain's most successful blockbuster authors, and spy novelist Nigel West has sat in Parliament as a Tory MP under his real name, Rupert Allason.

- Thomas Love Peacock wrote a novel, *Melincourt or Sir Oran Haut-ton* (1817), about an orang-utan that becomes a Member of Parliament. In the early 1830s Charles Dickens was a parliamentary sketch-writer for the *Morning Chronicle*. 'I have worn my knees by writing on them in the old Gallery of the House of Commons,' he claimed. In *News from Nowhere* (1891) William Morris returns to a London of the future that has become a socialist paradise, the Houses of Parliament converted to a dung market.

Westminster Hall

The only surviving part of the original Palace of Westminster, Westminster Hall is now the vestibule of the House of Commons. In Shakespeare's *Henry VI Part II* (1590), the King sends Southwell, Hume and Bolingbroke to the gallows here. Thomas More was brought to Westminster Hall in 1535 to appear before a special commission for a variety of supposed crimes against Henry VIII's authority, including failure to accept him as head of the English Church. With no defence counsel,

More was tried and convicted of high treason and sentenced to be hung, drawn and quartered. The king himself took pity on More and reduced the sentence to a simple beheading.

House of Lords

The historian Lord (Thomas) Macaulay was ennobled in 1857 but never spoke in the House and died two years later without finishing his *History of England*. On his deathbed he told publishers, 'Let no damn Tory index my history.' Benjamin Disraeli entered the Lords in 1876 as Lord Beaconsfield after two terms as prime minister. Alfred Tennyson was ennobled in 1883 when he was 74. Mark Twain gave a lecture to the Lords on copyright in 1896. When asked what he considered a fair and just time limit, he replied, 'A million years.' Lord Gowrie, arts minister in the Thatcher government in the early '80s, is a poet. The best-known modern-day writer-peer is Jeffrey Archer.

Old Palace Yard

Walter Ralegh was executed here in October 1618, but as his head was placed on the executioner's block he exclaimed: 'What matter how the head lie, so long the heart be right.' In January 1703 the House of Commons failed to spot the satire in Daniel Defoe's tract, *The Shortest Way with the Dissenters*, and resolved that it be burned by the Common Hangman in Palace Yard.

Westminster Abbey

'*Mortality, behold and fear/What a change of flesh is here*' from *On the Tombs in Westminster Abbey*, Anon., 1603

Almost every major English poet is either buried or remembered in the abbey's Poets' Corner, described by Oliver Goldsmith as 'the place of sepulchre for the philosophers, heroes and kings of England'. The abbey, the traditional setting for the coronation of new monarchs (and the burial of the predecessor), was founded by Edward the Confessor in the eleventh century on what was then Thorney Island, a swamp in the Thames.

In medieval times its precincts attracted a large resident population, including Geoffrey Chaucer and William Caxton, who moved into a house at the back of Westminster Abbey in 1476 on returning to England from Belgium, and that year set up England's first printing press in his house. His first work was *The Dictes or Sayengis of the Philosophers* (1477), although a letter printed a year previously still exists. Five years later Caxton moved into nearby Tothill Street (north of Victoria Street) and continued printing in what had been a chapel, which is why to this day journalists' and printers' union branches are known as chapels. Over the next fifteen years Caxton printed 18,000 pages, translated twenty-odd works into English from Latin and French, produced the first edition of *The Canterbury Tales* (a copy of which was sold at Christie's in 1998 for a world record £4.6 million), and edited Sir Thomas Malory's *Morte D'Arthur* (1485). After Caxton died, his press was maintained by Wynkyn de Worde, who moved it to Fleet Street (see p. 74) in 1500.

A gatehouse prison was attached to the abbey in the sixteenth and seventeenth centuries, and it was here that the Cavalier poet, Richard Lovelace, was jailed for seven weeks in 1642 for petitioning the House of Commons in support of Charles I. Inside he wrote *To Althea, from Prison*, which contains the famous lines 'Stone Walls do not a Prison make/Nor Iron bars a Cage'. After the publication of Somerset Maugham's debut novel, *Liza of Lambeth* (1897), Basil Wilberforce made it the subject of his Sunday night sermon, to the delight of Maugham's landlady, Mrs Foreman, who was in the congregation. During the 1985 memorial service to Philip Larkin (who is buried in Cottingham), trad jazz (Sidney Bechet's *Blue Horizon* and Bix Beiderbecke's *Davenport Blues*) was played, as well as the usual religious music. Ted Hughes, who had been made poet laureate when Larkin declined the offer, did the reading.

Shakespeare's *Henry VI Part I* (1590) opens in the abbey with the funeral of the king's father, Henry V (which took place in 1422). Various poems have been dedicated to the abbey. *On the Tombs in Westminster Abbey* was written in 1603 by Francis Beaumont, who is himself buried close to Chaucer and Spenser. Thomas Hood's *An Address to the Very Reverend John Ireland, D.D. The Dean and Chapter of Westminster* (1820) led to the Dean's reducing the entrance charge, although at the end of the twentieth century charges were re-implemented to cut down crowds. John Betjeman's *In Westminster Abbey* was written in 1940 as a tongue-in-cheek 'lady's cry' to 'bomb the Germans' but to 'spare their women for Thy sake'. Adrian Mitchell, in his 1968 work, *To the Statues in Poets' Corner, Westminster Abbey*, addresses the 'stony bunch of pock-skinned whiteys' and warns them that people are buying postcards of them but that they will be freed on William Blake's birthday. Roger Woddis's *Do Not Go Sober* (1981) urges young bards to 'rage, rage against that crabby, Abbey site'. It was written as a parody of Dylan Thomas's *Do Not Go Gentle into that Good Night* after hearing that US president Jimmy Carter was surprised to discover Thomas was not commemorated in Poets' Corner.

Poets' Corner

Geoffrey Chaucer moved into a house in the gardens of the abbey (where the Henry VII Chapel now stands) in 1399 and there finished off *The Canterbury Tales* (*c.* 1400). He died the following year and became the first writer to be buried at the abbey, the position of his tomb dictating the location where scores of authors have since been buried over the centuries in what is now known as Poets' Corner. Admissions to Poets' Corner are decided by the Dean, previous post-holders having rejected Lord Byron (amoral) and George Eliot (agnostic).

Monuments in Poets' Corner

- William Shakespeare (1564–1616) is commemorated with a memorial designed by William Kent, erected in 1740, which Hugh Walpole called 'preposterous', a claim supported by the misquoting of lines from *The Tempest*. Alexander Pope was among those who raised funds for it.
- William D'Avenant (1606–68), possibly Shakespeare's godson, was the second poet laureate, appointed after Cromwell imprisoned Ben Jonson in the Tower (he produced no memorable verse), and lost his nose after an illness.
- John Milton (1608–74) is buried in St Giles Cripplegate in the City (see p. 56) and his memorial here was erected sixty-three years after his death when his puritan views, which had upset Royalists at the time, no longer mattered so much.
- Samuel Butler (1612–80), best known for the burlesque poem, *Hudibras* (1678), is buried in St Paul's, Covent Garden, as his estate couldn't afford to pay the abbey's burial fees.
- John Bunyan (1628–88) has a window in the north transept which portrays four scenes from his *Pilgrim's Progress* (1684).
- Thomas Shadwell (1642–92), poet laureate after Dryden, died in Chelsea of opium poisoning and is buried there.
- John Philips (1676–1709) wrote *Cyder* in praise of the alcoholic apple drink and died of consumption (not alcoholic poisoning) when 33.
- Nicholas Rowe (1674–1718) was Secretary of State for Scotland in the early eighteenth century and poet laureate 1715–18.
- William Congreve (1670–1729), the major comic playwright of the early eighteenth century, died after his carriage overturned in Bath.
- John Gay (1685–1732), best known for *The Beggar's Opera* (1728), is buried under a self-penned epitaph: 'Life is a jest, and all things show it/I thought so once and now I know it.'
- James Thomson (1700–1748), best known for the poem *The Seasons*

(1730), has a monument designed by Robert Adam which was erected in 1762.

- Thomas Gray (1716–71) wrote *Elegy Written in a Country Churchyard* (1751) in Stoke Poges, Buckinghamshire, where he is buried. He has one of the most elaborate monuments in Poets' Corner.

- Oliver Goldsmith (1730–74), buried in the Temple, is remembered with a Nollekens memorial bearing a Latin epitaph by Samuel Johnson.

- Robert Burns (1759–96) has a monument erected ninety years after he died.

- Jane Austen (1775–1817) is buried in Winchester Cathedral and has a surprisingly tiny Westminster Abbey memorial.

- John Keats (1795–1821), like Shelley and Byron, died abroad, in Rome from consumption.

- Percy Bysshe Shelley (1792–1822) drowned in the Gulf of La Spezia and was cremated on a nearby beach. His ashes were then taken to the British Consul building in Rome, where they were stored in the wine cellar for a few months before being buried in the city.

- Lord Byron (1788–1824) died in Greece and was refused an Abbey burial on account of what the Dean called his 'open profligacy . . . an obstacle to his commemoration'. Byron is buried in Nottinghamshire and had to wait until 1969 for this memorial.

- William Blake (1757–1827) has a bust by Jacob Epstein, commissioned in 1957 to mark the 200th anniversary of the poet's birth.

- Walter Scott (1771–1832) was the most prolific novelist of his day but is now considered to be overly melodramatic.

- Samuel Taylor Coleridge (1772–1834) is buried in Highgate (see p. 274) and has a bust by Hamo Thornycroft which was donated by an American doctor in 1855.

- Robert Southey (1774–1843) was poet laureate before Wordsworth and is usually banded together with the Lake poets, although his work was markedly different.

- The Brontë sisters, Emily (1818–48), Anne (1820–49) and Charlotte (1816–55), have a joint tablet which was presented by the Brontë Society in 1947.

- William Wordsworth (1770–1850) is buried at Grasmere in the Lake District and is commemorated here by a seated statue.

- Thomas Macaulay (1800–1859) was an MP for Edinburgh, Secretary of State for War and later a peer, as well as essayist and major historian.

- William Makepeace Thackeray (1811–63) had a bust designed by Marachetti which so annoyed his daughter she had it removed so that another sculptor could hack away at the moustache until she considered it the right length. It was then returned to its original spot.

- John Clare (1793–1864), a farmer and poet, ended up in an asylum in Epping.
- Adam Lindsay Gordon (1833–70) wrote ballads in Australia, where he spent much of his time. His memorial was unveiled in 1934.
- George Eliot (1819–80) is buried in Highgate Cemetery, and an abbey memorial was at first rejected owing to her agnosticism and the fact that she lived, unmarried, with a man.
- Benjamin Disraeli (1804–81) was twice prime minister and a major Victorian novelist.
- Henry Longfellow (1807–82) wrote the schoolroom mainstay, *The Song of Hiawatha* (1855).
- Anthony Trollope (1815–82) was probably the only major Victorian novelist to be born and die in London. His recently erected memorial reads 'novelist, public servant, pioneer of the postal service, the creator of Barsetshire'.
- Matthew Arnold (1822–88) is best known for the poem *Dover Beach* (1867) which compares the sea around England with the 'sea' of spirituality washing against the nation's soul.
- Gerard Manley Hopkins (1844–89), perhaps the greatest of the Victorian poets, is buried in Dublin. This memorial was laid in 1975 on the hundredth anniversary of the sinking of the *Deutschland*, the event that inspired him to write *The Wreck of the Deutschland*, his first major work.
- James Russell Lowell (1819–91), the Harvard professor, poet, and editor of various US publications, has a window dedicated in his honour.
- John Ruskin (1819–1900), the critic and architectural thinker, is commemorated with a bronze medallion.
- Henry James (1843–1916), one of the few non-poets buried in Poets' Corner, was, somewhat prosaically, cremated in Golders Green.
- D. H. Lawrence (1885–1930) was an obviously contentious choice, given the prurience of his novels. His memorial didn't appear until 1985.
- Rudyard Kipling (1865–1936) was the first English writer to receive the Nobel Prize for Literature (in 1907).
- Dylan Thomas (1914–53) has a memorial which was belatedly installed after the then US president, Jimmy Carter, complained that he hadn't been honoured.
- T. S. Eliot (1888–1965), the twentieth century's most influential and celebrated poet, is buried in East Coker, Somerset.

- W. H. Auden (1907–73) is buried in Austria, where he spent his latter years.
- Noel Coward (1899–1973) has a monument which reads 'a talent to amuse'.
- John Betjeman (1906–84) had become a national institution and Britain's best-selling poet by the time he died.
- Laurence Olivier (1907–89) was the last entrant to Poets' Corner, which the authorities deemed to be full in 1989. His ashes were buried here that summer.

Graves

- Geoffrey Chaucer (*c.* 1343–1400), who provided the abbey with its first literary tomb (the origins of Poets' Corner), died in a cottage where the abbey's Henry VII Chapel now stands.
- Edmund Spenser (1553–98), author of *The Faerie Queene* (1606), may have died from starvation in a house near the abbey. At his funeral, various poets threw their own works into the grave alongside his coffin. No one knows exactly where Spenser's grave is situated, and in 1938 the Bacon Society convinced the abbey authorities to dig up the grave nearest Spenser's memorial as part of a general inquiry into the identity of Shakespeare, whose plays, some believe, were written by Francis Bacon. A coffin was found but the evidence was inconclusive.
- Francis Beaumont (1584–1616), the playwright, also wrote the poem *Lines on the Tombs of Westminster Abbey*.
- William Camden (1551–1623), the antiquarian, has a white marble monument with his left hand resting on his most famous work, *Britannia* (1586), which was originally written in Latin.
- Michael Drayton (1563–1631) was known as the English Ovid at the time but is little read these days.
- Ben Jonson (1572–1637), the playwright, died in a house by the abbey and was buried upright after telling the Dean, 'Six foot long by two foot wide is too much for me. Two feet by two is all I want.' His memorial, installed about 100 years after his death, has his name misspelled as Ben Johnson.
- Abraham Cowley (1618–67) was the first subject of Samuel Johnson's *Lives of the Poets* (1781).
- Sir John Denham (1615–69) was an Irish poet, MP and royal surveyor.
- Aphra Behn (1640–89), poet, playwright and novelist, was one of Britain's first professional women writers and is buried in the east cloister, away from Poets' Corner.

- John Dryden (1631–1700) for his funeral at the abbey had almost 100 carriages, but the grave remained unmarked until 1720.
- Joseph Addison (1672–1719), founder of *The Spectator*, is buried in the Henry VII Chapel.
- Matthew Prior (1664–1721), diplomat as well as poet, was plenipotentiary to the Court of Louis XIV in France.
- Samuel Johnson (1709–84), the *Dictionary* compiler, has a bust which Joseph Nollekens crafted while Johnson was still alive. It was donated to the abbey anonymously in 1939.
- Richard Brinsley Sheridan (1751–1816), politician as well as playwright, was one of the most conspicuous literary figures in London in his day and had a share in the Drury Lane theatre (see p. 117).
- Thomas Campbell (1777–1844) was a Scottish poet, little of whose work is read today. He died in Boulogne.
- Charles Dickens (1812–78) in his will left his soul to God and the mercy of Jesus Christ. He wanted to be buried in Rochester.
- Robert Browning (1812–89) died in Venice and the body was brought back here for burial.
- Alfred, Lord Tennyson (1809–92), was poet laureate and is still seen by many as the embodiment of Victorian poetry.
- Thomas Hardy (1840–1928) in his 1924 poem, *A Refusal*, satirized the Dean who had excluded Byron from being buried here and specifically requested that he should not be buried in the abbey but near his family in Dorset. However, when Hardy died his agent arranged a grand funeral at the abbey (Kipling was one of the pallbearers) and after much arguing the writer was buried here – except for his heart, which was taken to Dorset in a biscuit tin and buried in the churchyard of St Michael's, Stinsford.
- John Masefield (1878–1967) was poet laureate during the middle years of the twentieth century.

Parliament Square

St Margaret's Church

William Caxton was buried in 1491 in the previous church on this site. Walter Ralegh was probably buried here in 1618, and soon afterwards Ben Jonson lived in a small cottage that stood between the church and Westminster Abbey. Samuel Pepys married the penniless 15-year-old Elizabeth de Saint-Michel in St Margaret's in 1655. John Milton married his second wife, Katherine Woodcock, here in 1656, but a year later she and their child died and were buried here. Tennyson wrote the inscription for the church's memorial to Caxton and Robert Browning the one for Queen Victoria.

detour west to Queen Anne's Gate

Queen Anne's Gate

Architectural Review offices, no. 9

When John Betjeman worked here in the 1930s, he spent more time working on his verse than on his Classical Orders and Gothic arches, and not always productively. One couplet, 'I sometimes think that I should like/To be the saddle of a bike', was the laborious result of a collaboration between him, W. H. Auden and Louis MacNeice. Labour politician and writer Tom Driberg described it as the 'shortest erotic poem in our language'.

VICTORIA TO WESTMINSTER SCHOOL

- Landmarks from Victoria Square to Bessborough Gardens can be reached from Victoria tube; those from Dean Bradley Street to Little Dean's Yard from Westminster tube.

Bookshops

Politico's, 8 Artillery Row, tel. 020 7828-0010, is a political bookshop aimed at the parliamentary, rather than the revolutionary socialist tract, end of the market.

roughly west to east

Ebury Street

Ian Fleming's address (1936–41), no. 22B

Fleming moved into this elaborately designed converted school (the previous tenant had been British Fascist leader, Oswald Mosley) when life with his mother in Cheyne Walk, Chelsea, proved unbearable. Fleming decked out the pseudo-Gothic interior in the sort of bachelor-pad style that James Bond might have found to his taste – plush sofas, Man Ray photographs, a collection of first editions – but with a bedroom that would have been too small for Bond. One of Fleming's many visitors was the eccentric aristocrat, John Fox-Strangways, whose name Fleming later used for the SIS station chief in *Dr No* (1958) and *Live and Let*

Die (1961) and who won some degree of infamy in 1951 for kicking
Labour politician Nye Bevan on the steps of White's club.

Victoria Square

This small, barely noticeable square just north of Victoria Station is
easily missed by those taking the main traffic routes around the station.

Ian Fleming's address (1953–64), no. 16
Fleming moved here from Carlyle Mansions in Chelsea's Cheyne Walk
(see p. 372) about a month before the first Bond book, *Casino Royale*
(1952), was published, and many of the subsequent titles were written
here. Fleming used to throw editorial lunches here for the stuffy publishing magazine, *Book Collector* (of which he was chairman), charging
participants £9 a head for the privilege. According to Fleming's biographer, Andrew Lycett, the property looks like a doll's house.

Victoria Street

Victoria station
Somerset Maugham stammered so much when trying to buy a ticket
one day in the 1890s, he was pushed to the back of the queue by the
impatient crowd. In Oscar Wilde's *The Importance of Being Earnest*
(1895) a baby is left in a handbag at the station. Dora Chance, the narrator in Angela Carter's *Wise Children* (1991), moans that 'nowhere [in
the modern-day Victoria station] can you get a decent cup of tea, all
they give you is Harvey Wallbangers, filthy capuccino. Stocking shops
and knicker outlets.'

Cambridge Street

George Eliot's address (1853–4), no. 21
Eliot moved in here while working on translations of German literature
and editing the *Westminster Review*. She moved out in July 1854 to live
with George Lewes.

Gillingham Street

Joseph Conrad's address (1893–6), no. 17
After a long voyage as a merchant seaman in the Belgian Congo – he
based much of *Heart of Darkness* (1902) on his experiences – Conrad
took lodgings above a shop in the shadow of Victoria station. But he

was soon stricken with malarial gout and was sent to the German Hospital in Dalston to recuperate. When he had recovered and returned to Gillingham Street, he finished off his first novel, *Almayer's Folly* (1895), sending it to the publishers, Fisher Unwin, in July 1894. Fearing rejection, Conrad enclosed an s.a.e. which he addressed to 'J. Conrad, 17 Gillingham St, S.W., and franked for return by parcel post, by twelve 1d stamps'. Week after week Conrad fretted, anxiously awaiting their reply and making contingency plans to publish it jointly with his aunt under the pen-name, Kamondi (Malay for 'rudder'). By September, sick of waiting, he wrote to the publishers demanding it back. In October they replied that they were planning to publish it. Conrad was at last able to give up seafaring.

Vincent Square

Somerset Maugham's address (1892–5), no. 11

Maugham came to live in Westminster on enrolling as a medical student at Lambeth's St Thomas's Hospital in 1892; but, given that he knew nothing of the locale near the hospital, why did he choose Vincent Square out of all the possible nearby locations? An avid reader of the recently released early Sherlock Holmes stories, Maugham probably remembered that in *The Sign of Four* (1890) Holmes and Watson take an obscure route through Vincent Square to get to Thaddeus Sholto's house in Brixton. Other points in Vincent Square's favour were that the properties were elegant, the setting green and spacious but close to the West End, and the huge square was used by Westminster School as playing fields, thereby giving Maugham the opportunity to leer at the young chaps running around in their tight shorts. At Vincent Square Maugham found time to write some Ibsenesque dramas which he sent to various theatre managers and which were returned, rejected. Years later, in his 1930 novel, *Cakes and Ale*, the narrator, William Ashenden (Maugham's *alter ego*), lives like Maugham in lodgings at this address. In another Holmesian touch Mrs Foreman, Maugham's landlady, is renamed Mrs Hudson.

Bessborough Gardens

Taking a rest in 1889 after more than fifteen years spent sailing round the world as a merchant seaman, Joseph Conrad moved to a now-demolished address in Bessborough Gardens and began considering writing. Despite the fact that English was not his first language (Conrad was a Pole, real name Josef Korzeniowski), he set to work, in English, on what became his first novel, *Almayer's Folly* (1895). But after a while he began pining for the sea, as he recounted in the guise of Marlow in the opening of *Heart of Darkness* (1902). 'I began to look for a ship – I should think the hardest work on earth.' Eventually Conrad's aunt secured him a berth as skipper of a Belgian steamer on the Congo, and so he quickly went to Brussels to meet his new employers, or, as Marlow puts it in the same story: 'I flew around like mad to get ready . . . In a very few hours I arrived in a city that always makes me think of a whited sepulchre [Brussels] . . . They were going to run an over-sea empire, and make no end of coin by trade.' For the next five years Conrad carried the manuscript of *Almayer's Folly* with him on his travels, being fortunate to rescue it from rapids on the Congo.

head north

Dean Bradley Street

Marquis of Granby, Dean Bradley Street at Romney Street
Ian Fleming dreamed up the code name 007 for James Bond after striking up a conversation with a man in the bar who had been given the number DMZ7 when he joined the Bevin Boys (young men chosen to work in coal mines rather than join the forces). The board outside the pub boasts that the Marquis serves the best gin and tonic, as opposed to the more authentically Bondian best vodka martini, in London.

Lord North Street

> 'I stopped the taxi at the corner of Lord North Street' Lewis Eliot from *Corridors of Power*, C. P. Snow, 1964

A small and almost perfectly preserved Georgian street, secreted away south of Westminster Abbey, Lord North Street has been popular with politicians for over 100 years and so was an ideal setting for the home of Tory MP Roger Quaife in C. P. Snow's *Corridors of Power* (1964). Harold Wilson rented a house here in the 1970s, even while he was prime minister and living in 10 Downing Street, and John Major ran his 1995 Tory leadership campaign from the Chief Whip's house at no. 19, once the home of literary salon hostess Lady Sibyl Colefax (see below). Lord North Street was plain North Street (i.e. it led north from Smith Square) until 1936 when the 'Lord' prefix was added, a strange choice, given that Lord North was the prime minister when Britain lost the American War of Independence.

Lady Sibyl Colefax's address (1940s), no. 19

Lady Sybil was a society hostess who had lived in Argyll House in King's Road next to Somerset Maugham but moved here during the Second World War. Times were hard, but she still managed to throw the odd party or two. When an air raid began during one lunchtime gathering, H. G. Wells (who had written a book called *The War in the Air*) refused to take cover and there was a bit of a row, but a compromise was reached whereby the windows were blacked out with screens and lunch was held with the lights on. Wells pontificated for an hour or so on God and the fact that people were no longer reading the Bible; and Maugham, bored to tears, chewed the cord of his monocle for the entire duration of the rant.

Barton Street

Lord Brideshead has his London *pied-à-terre* in Barton Street in Evelyn Waugh's *Brideshead Revisited* (1945).

T. E. Lawrence's address (1922–8), no. 14

Lawrence's wartime exploits for the British cause in the Arabian desert during the First World War made him a national hero – 'Lawrence of Arabia' – yet he was unhappy being in the public eye and felt personal failure when the Near East was arbitrarily carved up by the western powers after the war. Disenchanted, Lawrence decided to adopt a new identity by joining the RAF under a pseudonym (see Covent Garden), and when in London he stayed in the attic at no. 14 above an office belonging to the architect, Sir Herbert Baker. Here he finished off *The Seven Pillars of Wisdom* (1926), his extravagant travelogue-cum-autobiography based on the Arab revolt against their Turk rulers during the First World War, living the life of a recluse, sleeping during the day and eating mostly at railway stations. Work on the book was not made easy by the fact that Lawrence had carelessly lost most of the first draft while changing trains at Reading station a few years previously, so, to relieve the ordeal, he engaged a 19-year-old friend, John Bruce, to come to Barton Street and beat him.

Little Dean's Yard

Westminster School, Little Dean's Yard and Great College Street
Alumni of this famous school, founded in 1560 by Queen Elizabeth, include Ben Jonson (the antiquarian, William Camden, who was headmaster of the school in the late sixteenth century, is believed to

have paid his expenses), John Dryden, William Cowper, Edward Gibbon and Robert Southey, who was expelled for writing an essay against flogging.

RIVER THAMES

London owes its position to the Thames and its prosperity to the trade brought in along the river which, until good roads were built, was also the best means for getting from one end of the capital to the other. In its commercial and industrial hey-day the Thames was a lively place, filled with boats and activity and containing one of the world's great ports. These days, with the port gone and the docks demolished, the Thames is an under-used asset, empty of craft and largely devoid of life, despite the new luxury apartments that have been built alongside. In literature the Thames has usually been depicted either in an idyllic setting, surrounded by picturesque greenery and teeming with congenial wildlife (west of the centre), or as a cesspool, a drain for the capital's morality and a convenient escape route for criminals (east of the centre).

Hampton to the Isle of Dogs: roughly west to east

- In T. S. Eliot's *Old Possum's Book of Practical Cats* (1939) Growltiger, 'the roughest cat that ever roamed at large', rejoices in the title 'The Terror of the Thames'.
- Of the hundreds of novels which have used the Thames as a setting, none epitomizes the bliss of messing about on the river as evocatively as Jerome K. Jerome's *Three Men in a Boat* (1889). Yet this timeless book began not as a comedy travelogue but as a history of the river, until Jerome's editor got involved. In one scene Jerome eulogizes 'the mellow, bright, sweet old wall . . . with fifty shades and tints and hues in every ten yards' by the river at **Hampton**. The protagonists then get caught up in Hampton Court maze.
- The Kenwigs in Charles Dickens's *Nicholas Nickleby* (1839) dine on a 'cold collation, bottled beer, shrub and shrimps' at Eel Pie House, the now-demolished pub on **Eel Pie Island** which is set in the middle of the Thames at Twickenham and is now a haunt of artists.
- Kenneth Grahame created a memorable fantasy Thames world in *The Wind in the Willows* (1908) in which three animals – Rat, Toad and Mole – live in semi-aristocratic Edwardian splendour somewhere around **Richmond**, where Grahame, to his wife's despair, spent much of his time messing about on the river. In the book the animals' river-

ine idyll is spoiled when Toad decides to take up motoring and ends up in gaol for dangerous driving.

- William Morris used to journey up and down the river between his Kelmscott Manor mansion in Oxfordshire and his Kelmscott House villa in **Hammersmith**, as recounted in *News from Nowhere* (1890).

- Mary Wollstonecraft, proto-feminist and mother of Mary Shelley, tried to commit suicide in 1795 by throwing herself off **Putney Bridge** after her partner – she daringly defied convention by refusing to marry – ran off with an actress.

- Jonathan Swift went for a dip in the Thames in **Chelsea** with his land-lady's napkin on his head and, while his servant waited for him to come ashore, swam around for half an hour. When Swift dived below the napkin came off, and when he finally got back to the bank he moaned, 'O faith, the great stones were so sharp, I could hardly set my feet on them as I came out.'

- Graham Greene wrote in *It's a Battlefield* (1934) how 'the trams came screeching like a finger drawn on glass up the curve of **Battersea Bridge** and down into the ill-lighted network of streets beyond'. In John Le Carré's first George Smiley book, *Call for the Dead* (1961), Smiley calls on the murderer, Dieter Frey, who is staying in a house-boat moored near Battersea Bridge. A chase ensues and Smiley corners his foe on the bridge, forcing him over the parapet.

- When in the 1950s the authorities proposed demolishing **Albert Bridge** John Betjeman campaigned in *The Spectator* for its retention. 'Shining with electric lights to show the way to Festival Gardens or grey and airy against the London sky, it is one of the beauties of the London River,' he wrote. The bridge was saved.

- William Wordsworth wrote *Upon **Westminster Bridge***, with its famous opening line, 'Earth has not anything to show more fair', after crossing it with sister Dorothy on 3 September 1802. The sight, 'so touching in its majesty', has changed considerably since Wordsworth's day by the addition of Barry's Houses of Parliament, Big Ben, St Thomas's Hospital and New Scotland Yard, although the poet would recognize Westminster Abbey. James Boswell liked having sex with prostitutes – or, as he put it, meeting Signore Gonorrhoea – on the bridge, which is probably one of the reasons why he contracted VD seventeen times in about the same number of years.

- In Nicholas Royle's *Counterparts* (1993) Gargan, the tightrope walker, crosses the river from **Hungerford Bridge** to **Waterloo Bridge** on the rope despite nearly dropping his pole and having to stay for thirty seconds in the same position until the strength returns to his ankles.

- John Gower, described by many as 'the first English poet' (see South-wark Cathedral, p. 331), was forcibly removed from his boat by Richard II and companions when their two vessels brushed past each other (near where **Waterloo Bridge** now stands) some time in 1385. The king wanted to talk to Gower about poetry.

- In Charles Dickens's *Barnaby Rudge* (1841), Maypole Hugh breaks open the toll-house on **Blackfriars Bridge** during the 1780 Gordon Riots and throws the money on to the street.

- In Joseph Conrad's *Heart of Darkness* (1902), Marlow, the main story-teller, imagines a Roman warrior arriving in London in the first century AD and looking out on either side of the Thames (probably at a spot near where St Paul's now stands, where the Romans first set foot in the area) at a land of 'utter savagery'.

- In Dickens's *Little Dorrit* (1857), John Chivery proposes to the heroine of the novel on **Southwark Bridge** while 'putting his penny on the toll plate'.

- In Dickens's *Our Mutual Friend* (1865), Gaffer Hexham rows from **Southwark Bridge** to **London Bridge**, making a living retrieving corpses from the river.

- Sir Thomas More's head was displayed on **London Bridge** after he was executed at the Tower for treason in 1535, and a scarcely believable story has it that one of his daughters was passing under the bridge one day when she saw the head and cried: 'Oh how many times it has lain on my lap. Oh God if only it could now fall into my lap!', which of course it instantly did. She then safeguarded the skull and sent it to Canterbury Cathedral, where it has remained ever since.

London Bridge, being a favourite haunt of the young Dickens, features in a number of his novels: in *Martin Chuzzlewit* (1844) Jonas Chuzzlewit, after killing Tigg, changes out of his clothes, carries them in a bundle down the steps of London Bridge and lets them sink in the river; in *David Copperfield* (1850) it is Mr Micawber's favourite spot in London; in *Great Expectations* (1861) Pip crosses the bridge in despair after hearing of Estella's betrothal to Drummle. 'Nancy's Steps', where Nancy tells Rose Maylie Oliver's story in *Oliver Twist* (1839), can be found on the southern bank of the river west of London Bridge.

The arches that supported the old London Bridge (and the rubbish strewn in the river) helped the Thames freeze easily in the winter, and fairs were often held on the ice. John Evelyn in his diary for January 1684 wrote of people setting up stalls and even a printing press on the frozen waterway. Virginia Woolf picked up on the theme in *Orlando* (1928) and described the horror of a thaw which left people stranded on lumps of melting ice in the middle of the water.

- The coffin containing the body of Sir Philip Sidney arrived at **Tower Pier** (halfway between London and Tower bridges) in November 1586. The statesman-poet had died, fighting in a war in the Netherlands, after recklessly discarding his leg armour and taking a bullet in the thigh. Sidney then carried on fighting, but the wound became infected and he died a long agonizing death. Over 1,000 soldiers escorted the body back to England on his ship, and he lay in state for three months while the authorities wrangled over his financial affairs. Sidney was eventually buried in St Paul's.

- In the Sherlock Holmes novella, *The Sign of Four* (1890), Holmes, Watson and the police chase the booty plunderer, Jonathan Small, and his poison-dart-blowing accomplice down the Thames from a wharf near the Tower through the **Pool of London** (the stretch between **Tower Bridge** and **Limehouse**), past **West India Docks**, **Deptford Reach**, round the **Isle of Dogs**, and beyond **Greenwich Marshes** (where the Millennium Dome now stands). At **Plumstead Marshes** they draw level and Small, trying to escape, is stumped by his wooden leg, which sticks in the bankside mud. Conan Doyle lifted the idea for this plot climax from Dickens's *Great Expectations* (1861).

- **Mr Baker's Trap**, a dock bridge and suicide spot featured in Dickens's *The Mystery of Edwin Drood* (1870), could be found where Wapping Lane meets the river by Wapping tube. A little to the west was Execution Dock, where pirates were hanged (see p. 255).

- In Iain Sinclair's *Downriver* (1991), Sinclair and Joblard take a trip downriver from the **Isle of Dogs** to the Isle of Sheep (Sheppy) in Kent with a captain who has no charts – 'charts are for wimps' – and asks them 'Which way, boys? Just point me in the right direction.'

- H. G. Wells describes a journey by destroyer down the Thames, an allegory on decay and change in England, in the final chapter of *Tono-Bungay* (1909).

EAST LONDON

The East End/Docklands, E1, E2, E3, E14

'I am made sick by this human hell-hole called the East End' Jack London,
letter to his wife, 1902

Poverty, prostitution, drugs and violence have shaped the East End –
Bethnal Green, Shadwell, Stepney, Wapping, Whitechapel *et al.* –
described by V. S. Pritchett as ugly places with ancient names. The poverty came with successive waves of immigrants, often fleeing per-
secution abroad, arriving by boat near the Tower. With the growth of
the Port of London the number of local prostitutes rose and pubescent
girls were bought on the street like cattle for West End whorehouses, as
Michael Sadler recounted in *Fanny by Gaslight* (1940). For many years
the area was also the centre of the capital's opium smoking, with scores
of dens scattered among the tiny cottages and dismal shops. Charles
Dickens visited one to research *The Mystery of Edwin Drood* (1870), and
Coulson Kernahan visited the same den a few years later for an article
in *Strand* magazine. Arthur Conan Doyle, not inclined to go as far as
to enter one of these places, borrowed liberally from the article for the
description of his infamous den, the Bar of Gold, in the Sherlock
Holmes story, 'The Man with the Twisted Lip' (1891; see p. 50).

Some of the most notorious murders in London's history have taken
place in the East End. The inexplicable and gruesome nature of the 1811
Ratcliff Highway Murders (see below) horrified the nation, led to the
introduction of more sophisticated policing, and provoked scores of
articles, including Thomas De Quincey's essay, *Murder Considered as
One of the Fine Arts* (1827). Seventy-five years later, the Jack the Ripper
murders in Whitechapel reminded a new generation of the evil that
supposedly lurked around every corner, and they continue to inspire
much sensationalist crime literature. In the early decades of the twentieth century the East End became a ferment of political unrest, epitom-
ized by the 1936 Battle of Cable Street (see below); but during the
Second World War much of the area was destroyed by enemy bombers
sent up the nearby Thames. Slum clearance of the 1950s and 1960s was
meant to eradicate the breeding grounds for crime, but instead this was
the period when organized, as opposed to casual, violence took over, in
the shape of the gangland battles involving the Kray twins.

Nowadays attention on the East End centres not on the still-impoverished communities around Commercial Road (the main east–west artery through the area) or on the barren tower-block estates of Poplar but on the riverside developments in what is now known as Docklands, where billions of pounds of investment have turned disused buildings and derelict sites alongside the Thames into hi-tech offices and luxury dwellings. This phenomenon has barely had time to be recorded in literature, although Penelope Lively with *Passing on* (1989) and *City of the Mind* (1991) and P. D. James with *Original Sin* (1994) have addressed the matter. The modern-day writer most closely identified with the East End is Iain Sinclair, who has devoted much of his output to the area, noting how the Romans treated it as a 'necropolis for the Dead' in *Lud Heat* (1975) and visualizing the vanished East End of opium dens, wife-beating and incest in the deserted streets of Shadwell and Stepney Green in *Downriver* (1991).

Exploring the East End

The East End's boundaries are the Regent's Canal/Hertford Union Canal (to the north), the River Lea (east), the River Thames (south) and the City of London (west). For easy exploring, in this book the East End has been divided into seven sections: Bethnal Green; Mile End; Shadwell; Spitalfields; Wapping; Whitechapel and, further east, Limehouse/Isle of Dogs.

BETHNAL GREEN, E2

Wealthy farmland in medieval times, by the eighteenth century Bethnal Green had become the poorest neighbourhood in east London, with families piled up in tenements to sustain the local weaving industry and nearly half the local population living below the poverty level, as John Wesley found to his horror when he visited the area in 1777 and recorded in his *Journal*. Successive governments made the welfare of the area a priority. Slums were cleared, houses demolished and progressive laws passed. The Second World War wiped away much of the squalor, but post-war redevelopment has simply replaced one set of slums with another, and Bethnal Green remains an impoverished and depressing place.

• Landmarks can be reached from Bethnal Green tube, except where stated.

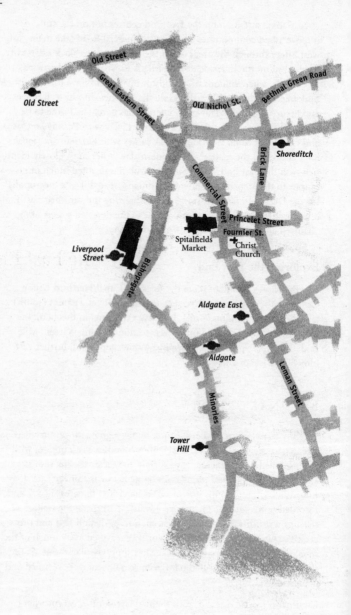

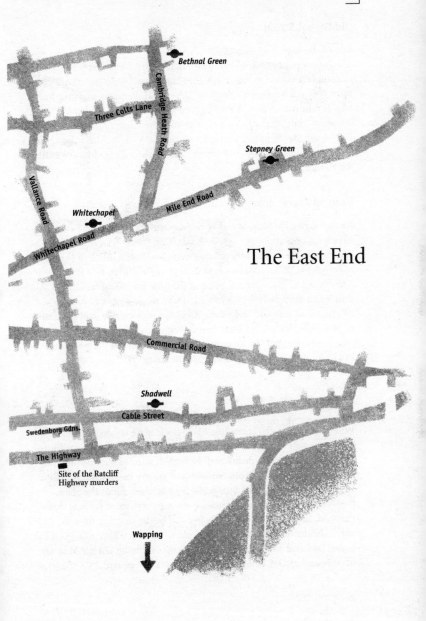

Bethnal Green

Cambridge Heath Road

Three Colts Lane

Stepney Green

Valance Road

Whitechapel

Mile End Road

Whitechapel Road

The East End

Commercial Road

Shadwell

Cable Street

Swedenborg Gdns.

The Highway

Site of the Ratcliff
Highway murders

Wapping

Old Nichol Street

Site of the Jago, Old Street tube

The Jago was a fearsome slum near Shoreditch Church (now rebuilt, but still run-down) in which the East End-born Arthur Morrison set his influential novel, *A Child of the Jago* (1894), the story of a criminal who is reformed – almost – by a priest but who returns to his old ways. Somerset Maugham admitted that he borrowed heavily from Morrison for his 1897 debut novel, *Liza of Lambeth*, and V. S. Pritchett claimed it 'smells of rabid little shops, bloated factories, sub-let workrooms and warehouse floors'.

Bethnal Green Road

George Orwell's 'Ministry of Love' inspiration, the former Bethnal Green Police Station, no. 458, Bethnal Green tube

The cells in *1984*'s Ministry of Love are based on the inside of this now closed-down police station where George Orwell (then Eric Blair) spent a few hours in 1931 after his arrest in the Mile End Road for being drunk and disorderly (see below). Orwell was perversely hoping to be mistreated as it would make for better copy, but even he had to admit he was fed well for a prisoner: bread, marge, tea *and* the sergeant's wife's meat and potatoes. He spent the night counting the porcelain bricks on the walls – as Winston does in the novel.

MILE END, E1

When George Orwell (then Eric Blair) decided he wanted to spend Christmas 1931 in prison, he came to rough Mile End Road on a Saturday night to get blind drunk and, he hoped, arrested. At opening time Orwell went into a pub, poured beer and whisky down his throat into an empty stomach, and a little while later lurched out of the place, barely able to feel his legs. When he saw two policemen coming down the road, he took out a whisky bottle and began swigging from it before falling down. It worked; the officers marched him off to Bethnal Green gaol (see above) and locked him up overnight. On the Monday he appeared at Old Street Magistrates Court (see p. 270).

SHADWELL, E1

A small, much redeveloped, former seafaring community between Commercial Road and The Highway, Shadwell is best known for Cable Street, the turning that runs east–west through the heart of the area, and the setting for an infamous political clash in 1936.

Cable Street

This long, forlorn-looking street, dominated by the Docklands Light Railway viaduct, is best known for the 'Battle of Cable Street', a bloody clash that took place during a British Union of Fascists march through the East End on Sunday 4 October 1936. The march was planned as a welcome home for the Fascist leader, Oswald Mosley, who had been in Spain, but the Fascists also wanted to antagonize the local Jewish population and vanquish local Communists and Socialists at the time of the Spanish Civil War. As Nicholas Mosley, Oswald's novelist son, described in *Beyond the Pale* (1983), when Oswald Mosley's open-top Bentley and motor-cycle escort arrived in Cable Street (then lined with Jewish tailor's shops), his blackshirted troops gave the Fascist salute; opponents tried to charge but they were held back by police, who told Mosley not to start marching until they had cleared the barricades. Fighting in Cable Street raged for two hours as the police tried to push their way through but failed. When Fenner Brockway, secretary of the Independent Labour Party, was injured, he phoned the Home Office, who ordered Mosley to call off the march. Police then escorted the Fascists to the City, where they dispersed. A week later all the windows of the Jewish shops in Mile End Road, half a mile north of Cable Street, were smashed. One of those watching events in Cable Street, but not participating, was Graham Greene, who was so impressed by the anti-Fascists' case he immediately joined the Independent Labour Party, despite having canvassed for the Tories in Oxford and having been a special constable during the General Strike.

SPITALFIELDS, E1

*'Spitalfields meant Architecture, the Prince, Development schemes . . . gay
vicars swishing incense'* from *Downriver*, Iain Sinclair, 1991

Spitalfields, a vibrant area to the east of Liverpool Street station, grew around the influx of Huguenot silk weavers in the late seventeenth century, a phenomenon later noted by William Blake, who wrote about hearing 'the shuttles of death sing in the sky to Islington and Pancras'. In what by the early eighteenth century had become an area rife with non-conformity, the authorities commissioned Nicholas Hawksmoor to build the soaring Christ Church (1714–29), setting for part of Peter Ackroyd's mystery murder novel, *Hawksmoor* (1985), which interweaves the life of an eighteenth-century architect, Nicholas Dyer (based on Hawksmoor), with the investigations by a modern-day detective, Nicholas Hawksmoor, into a series of murders in Dyer's churches. In recent years much money has been spent on renovating Spitalfields' Georgian properties and preserving its covered market, and consequently it has become one of the most fashionable areas in east London.

- Landmarks can be reached from Liverpool Street railway station/tube.

Bookshops

Magpie Bookshop, 53 Brushfield Street, tel. 020 7247-4263, is excellent for comics and sci-fi.

The Bookworm, Spitalfields Market, Brushfield Street, which can be found on the Brushfield Street side of this excellent flea market, has stacks of second-hand paperbacks.

Shoreditch tube to Whitechapel Road end: north to south

Brick Lane

One of London's most fascinating streets, Brick Lane, once a major centre of Jewish immigration to London, is now home to Europe's largest Bangladeshi community, scores of curry houses, a lively Sunday market, and a 24-hour bagel bakery that draws in customers from across the South-East. The downside is that it is also an occasional flash-point for racial violence – National Front attacks on local Asians in the late 1970s and a nail bomb explosion outside a curry restaurant in 1999. In Charles Dickens's *Pickwick Papers* (1837), monthly meetings of the Brick Lane Branch of the United Grand Junction Ebenezer Temperance Association take place in the Mission Hall at no. 160 (since demolished).

Seven Stars, no. 51
In Iain Sinclair's *White Chappell Scarlet Tracings* (1987), Sinclair and Co. hold a seance into the Jack the Ripper murders (which took place locally) at this pub prior to the stripper's coming on stage.

Princelet Street

Former Princelet Street Synagogue, no. 19
In Iain Sinclair's *Downriver* (1991) a bizarre surreal scene takes place in
this former synagogue in which Roland Bowman 'was naked, red, on
all fours; crawling like some obsolete chess piece'. Later Sinclair returns
to retrieve the books abandoned by the former tenant, David Rodinsky,
and finds a 1940s room preserved forty years later as if Rodinsky had
just vacated it. In 1999 *Rodinsky's Room*, a collaboration between Sinclair and the artist Rachel Lichtenstein detailing Rodinsky's strange life,
was published.

Fournier Street

Jamme Masjid Mosque, Fournier Street at Brick Lane
Matthew Halland, the architect hero of Penelope Lively's *City of the
Mind* (1991), is fascinated by this building, which began life as a Huguenot church and then became a synagogue, before being converted to a
mosque as the local demographics changed again.

Former Hebrew Dramatic Club, no. 15
In Iain Sinclair's *Downriver* (1991), Roland Bowman takes over the
Fournier Street premises of the former Hebrew Dramatic Club (where
in 1887 a false fire alarm resulted in seventeen members of the audience
dying in a panic on the stairs) and restores the property with furnishings from Oscar Wilde's Tite Street house.

Christ Church, Spitalfields, Fournier Street at Commercial Street
This towering Hawksmoor church has gripped the imagination of both
Iain Sinclair and Peter Ackroyd. Sinclair in *Lud Heat* (1975) claimed
that the triangle of Wapping lying in between this church and two
other East End Hawksmoor churches – St George-in-the-East (Wapping) and St Anne (Limehouse) – is run by mystic power: 'the frustra-
tion mounts on a current of animal magnetism'. In the book he also
notes 'the curious detail of the windows [of Christ Church] – the pull
that is set up by the sequence of small portholes above tall narrow
lower windows [which] relates to the grail cup above the lance . . . the
cauldron and the sword'. In *Hawksmoor* (1985), Ackroyd sets the first
of a series of murders in the crypt beneath the church.

head south

Jack London in East London

Determined to do some research among the poor but uncertain of the reception a self-styled 'writer' would receive, Jack London passed himself off as an American sailor down on his luck when he arrived in the capital in the winter of 1902–3. The first thing he did on alighting at the docks was to hail a cab. 'Drive me down the East End, cabbie,' London ordered. 'Where to, sir?' the cabbie replied. 'To the East End, anywhere. Go on.' London eventually arrived in the now-vanished Flower and Dean Street, just south of Fashion Street, where the Social Democratic Foundation had found him lodgings, but London was not impressed with the overcrowded squalor in which he found himself, writing how 'everything is grey and drab, hopeless, unrelieved and dirty. Bathtubs are a thing totally unknown. If this is the best civilization can do then give us howling and naked savagery.' His experiences were written up as *The People of the Abyss* (1903).

WAPPING, E1

Until recently an important seafaring community, Wapping, located to the south-east of the Tower in a V-shaped tract of land, grew around the Port of London, and was the first disembarking point in England for many sailors. For centuries Wapping, more so than most London districts, was a hotbed of crime; few murders chill the blood as acutely as the Ratcliff Highway murders of 1811 (see below). In 1969 Wapping was hit by the closure of London Docks, and it became a forlorn and forgotten place, pervaded by what Peter Ackroyd described in *Hawksmoor* as the 'gloom of the secluded wharves and muddy banks'. The area hit the headlines in 1984 for the wrong reasons when Rupert Murdoch moved his News International newspapers from Fleet Street to a new site north of the old docks, and battles raged as pickets tried to stop people entering the buildings. More recently, the old warehouses along Wapping High Street (a rare London high street that is largely free of shops and pubs) have been renovated into luxury apartments, the smell of spices has been obliterated, and the area has emerged as an unlikely magnet for the rich, albeit one devoid of conspicuous life or any semblance of community.

- Landmarks can be reached from Wapping tube.

Cannon Street Road end towards Wapping tube: roughly north to south

Swedenborg Gardens

This small close, north-west of The Highway's junction with Cannon Street Road, is named after the Swedish philosopher, Emmanuel Swedenborg, a major influence on William Blake, who came to Wapping in 1710. Swedenborg was buried in Wellclose Square, a little further west of Swedenborg Gardens; when his body was exhumed in 1908 and returned to Scandinavia, the skull was lost. Iain Sinclair described Swedenborg's time in London in *Radon Daughters* (1994).

head for The Highway and turn left

The Highway (former Ratcliff Highway)

A busy traffic route, bordered on the north side by bleak estates and on the south by imposing office blocks (including the headquarters of the *Times* and *Sun* newspapers), the Highway is one of London's oldest streets and has a peculiar and fascinating history. Until this century it was known as Ratcliff Highway (the Ratcliff coming from 'red cliff', at the eastern end) and in Stone's *Survey of London* (1598) is described as a 'filthy strait passage with alleys of small tenements'. In 1811 the Marr family who lived at no. 29 were suddenly and inexplicably murdered in what were the first of the so-called Ratcliff Highway murders, the most notorious killings of the early nineteenth century.

Site of the Ratcliff Highway murders, The Highway opposite Betts Street
Just before midnight on Saturday 7 December 1811, Timothy Marr, a draper of 29 Ratcliff Highway (since demolished and replaced by a warehouse), sent his maid, Margaret Jewell, to buy oysters. Unable to find any, the maid returned home and, when her knocks went unanswered, left to get help. The party broke in and found Marr and the boy apprentice downstairs, dead, their throats cut. Upstairs, Marr's wife and baby had also been murdered. (According to Peter Ackroyd in *Hawksmoor*, Williams 'smashes their skulls with a mallet and then cuts their throats as they lay dying'.) A few days later on 10 December, a man was seen escaping from an upstairs window of the King's Arms pub at 81 New Gravel Lane, Shadwell (since demolished), crying out, 'They are murdering the people in the house.' There, the publican Williamson, his wife and their maid were found, also with their throats cut.

The ramshackle police force of the day mustered all their strength in their attempts to track down the culprit and advertised for information by offering the highest reward that had ever been promised in a criminal case. Forty arrests were made, and John Williams, a seaman who was believed to have been shipmates with Marr, was charged with the murders. The evidence against him was circumstantial, but he hanged himself before he could be tried. His body was then stolen, a stake driven through his heart (as was the custom in those days to prevent the corpse turning into a vampire) and his body taken through the streets on a cart before being thrown into a hole at the junction of Cable Street and Cannon Street Road, a crossroads being the traditional site for those whose destiny was uncertain. The body was later exhumed and mutilated, the skull removed and secreted at a local pub.

According to Thomas De Quincey in his satirical essay, *Murder Considered as One of the Fine Arts* (1827), Williams 'asserted his supremacy above all the children of Cain' and the Ratcliff Highway murders were 'the most superb of the century by many degrees'. The crime still captivates modern-day writers. Nearly 200 years after the event, P. D. James co-wrote a book about the case, *The Maul and The Pear Tree* (1990), so named because a maul was found at the site of the first murders and Williams had been lodging at the Pear Tree pub (half a mile east of 29 Ratcliff Highway, now demolished) when arrested.

Site of London Docks, south of The Highway, between Thomas More Street and Wapping Lane

Geoffrey Chaucer was Controller of the Customs and Subsidies of Wools, Skins and Hides for the Port of London, based by the river here from 1374 until he became an MP in 1386. The docks opened in 1805 and in the 1870s Joseph Conrad, then a merchant seaman by the name of Josef Korzeniowski, came here to find a berth, having recently disembarked at Lowestoft in Suffolk. Conrad, who spoke little English at that stage, was penniless and wrote to his uncle asking for money, only to receive the reply, 'You write to me as if to some school chum "send me 500 francs which you can deduct from the allowance"; from which allowance, pray? – from the one you give yourself?' In October 1878 Conrad found a place on the *Duke of Sutherland*, a boat bound for Australia, but he had a violent disagreement with the captain (as usual) and ended up having to find several dozens more postings over the next fifteen years before becoming a full-time writer.

Beatrice Webb recorded in *My Apprenticeship* (1926) how she used to get up early and head for the docks to watch the dockers struggle for work at the gates. The dockers smoked 'villainous tobacco and [fought]

continually about the slightest trifle. Dockers work casual shifts – no permanent contract – just when work is there.' In 1949 Doris Lessing arrived at the docks in London from South Africa and wrote in her autobiography how war-damaged London was 'unpainted and cracked and dull and grey'.

London Docks closed in 1969 and the council bizarrely began to fill them in so that they could build more slum houses. Then the government intervened, establishing the Docklands Development Corporation which was charged with administering the area. Subsequent redevelopment has been successful economically, if not socially. Now, with industry gone and the residents of the new expensive apartments barely noticeable, a ghostly calm pervades the area.

Scandrett Street

St John's Churchyard
According to Iain Sinclair in *Downriver*, exotic animals brought back by sailors from long-haul seafaring voyages – 'marmosets, lemurs, genets, tamarins and sugar gliders' – would take refuge in this churchyard after escaping from their owners, until they were hunted down by locals and skinned for their fur. In the same book, Scandrett Street is home of Todd Sileen, an obsessive collector of the works of Joseph Conrad.

Wapping High Street

Site of Execution Dock, Wapping High Street at Captain Kidd pub, no. 108
In medieval times pirates were hanged from the gibbets at Execution Dock which stood by the river at this point, until three tides had washed over them. Captain Kidd was probably the best known of those hanged, which is why the pub has been named after him. In *Downriver* Dr Adam Tenbrücke commits suicide on the shore by the Execution Dock.

WHITECHAPEL, E1

Two of the best-known crime waves in British history are associated with Whitechapel: the Jack the Ripper murders of the late nineteenth century and the gangland violence associated with the Kray twins in the 1960s. The Ripper murders have inspired countless, mostly sensationalist, books, best of which is probably Marie Belloc Lowndes's fictional version, *The Lodger* (1913), and the most ridiculous Ellery Queen's *Sherlock Holmes vs. Jack The Ripper* (1967). The Krays' gangland antics have lost little news value since their 1960s hey-day and have inspired countless more sensationalist books, mainly from the villains involved, hoping to 'put the record straight', although John Pearson's clinical account of the Krays' brutal careers, *The Profession of Violence* (1972), makes excellent reading despite its factual inaccuracies.

In Charles Dickens's *The Pickwick Papers* (1837), Sam Weller notes, as he and Mr Pickwick leave the (now-demolished) Bull Inn, that Whitechapel is not a 'wery nice neighbourhood'. Weller also notices that there is an 'oyster stall to every half-dozen houses' and that 'poverty and oysters always seem to go together'. Whitechapel gave Charles Dickens rich pickings for his characters. He based Fagin in *Oliver Twist* (1839) on Ikey Solomons, a pickpocket known as the Prince of Fences who operated locally in the 1820s and who, when the police raided his house and took away two coachloads of stolen goods, hopefully claimed he was looking after the stuff for his friends.

From the early Victorian period until just after the Second World War Whitechapel had a high concentration of Jewish people, best captured in literature in Israel Zangwill's *Children of the Ghetto* (1892) and the less well-known novels of Simon Blumenfield. More contemporary are Iain Sinclair's *White Chappell Scarlet Tracings* (1987), which weaves tales of modern-day bookdealers searching for East End rarities with seances involving the Jack the Ripper victims, and Paul West's *The Women of Whitechapel* (1991), which explores the relationship between the painter Walter Sickert and one-time heir to the throne, Prince Albert Victor Christian Edward (better known as Prince Eddy).

further east

LIMEHOUSE/ISLE OF DOGS, mostly E14

London's first Chinatown developed in Limehouse at the end of the nineteenth century after the opening of a Strangers Home for Asiatics in West India Dock Road. At a time when few non-whites lived in London, East Enders were fascinated by the sight of Chinese men in pig-tails carrying their wares on long poles around the streets. Equally fascinating were the opium dens, gambling dives and noodle bars that sprang up around Limehouse Causeway and the stories of houses with interconnecting passages that enabled those on the run to hoodwink chasing policemen. The generally perceived view of a Limehouse bedevilled by racketeering and unusual Oriental forms of violence gave the area an edge which appealed to many writers. In Oscar Wilde's *The Picture of Dorian Gray* (1890), the hero visits a Limehouse opium den to 'cure the soul by means of the senses and the senses by means of the soul'. Forty years later, George Orwell came here to rough it among the tramps and out-of-work Lascars. Yet a lot of Limehouse literature was based more on myth than on reality. Thomas Burke's *Limehouse Nights* (1916) stemmed from the author's experiences of talking to a Chinaman outside the embassy when he was six years old, and Sax Rohmer's tales of Limehouse as the centre of the 'Yellow Peril', though more authentic, were still stereotyped.

Non-Chinese Limehouse is also featured in various books. In Dickens's *Dombey and Son* (1848), Walter Gray walks through the area, noticing 'rows of houses with little vane-surrounded masts . . . the air perfumed with chips; and all other trades were swallowed up in mast, oar and block making, and boat building'. Clement Attlee, twenty years before becoming Labour prime minister, wrote a poem laden with social concern called *In Limehouse*. It was published in 1922 (the year in which he became the area's MP) in the *Socialist Review*, more because the editor was Ramsay MacDonald, who in 1924 became Labour's first prime minister, than for any literary merit. One of the best recent books about the area is Daniel Farson's *Limehouse Days* (1991), while Peter Ackroyd's *Dan Leno and the Limehouse Golem* (1995) harks back to the Victorian music-hall era.

Chinatown declined after the 1930s when a new law making it illegal to sign on a Chinese crew in a British port was passed. The area then remained out of the news until the early 1980s when the Social Democratic Party formed here.

- Landmarks can be reached from Limehouse Docklands Light Railway.

Narrow Street to Barking Road: west to east

Narrow Street

A rare surviving early eighteenth-century terrace where Turner and Whistler came to paint, Narrow Street in Iain Sinclair's *Downriver* is the home of Dr Adam Tenbrücke, a book collector who specializes in Judaica and who lives in a house that once belonged to the artist, Francis Bacon.

The Grapes Inn, no. 76
Charles Dickens based the Six Jolly Fellowship Porters Tavern in *Our Mutual Friend* (1865) – 'a crazy wooden veranda impending over the water . . . with a bar to soften the human breast' – on this long, narrow pub. At the back of the pub, by the river, a wooden ladder which leads from the veranda to the shore acts as a reminder of the time when watermen used such means to reach the pub from their boats or to carry drunks to the middle of the river, where they would be drowned so that their bodies could be sold for dissection.

detour north

Three Colt Street

St Anne's, Three Colt Street at Commercial Road
One of six London churches built by Nicholas Hawksmoor, St Anne's was where Iain Sinclair worked as a gardener in the 1970s, as he recalled in *Downriver* in which he and Joblard watch a man wrestle with the church clock and succeed in forcing one of the hands to protrude horizontally from the clock face. The man, John Kay, later turns out to be their pilot on their chaotic journey downriver on the Thames.

return south

Limehouse Causeway

George Orwell began tramping in the capital, as recounted in *Down and Out in Paris and London* (1933), in Limehouse Causeway in 1927, choosing the area probably because he was drawn by its exotic reputation as London's Chinatown. To be accepted by the down-and-outs, Orwell (then Eric Blair) was obliged to dress the part (easy), befriend dockers, beggars 'and possibly criminals' (quite easy), sleep in 'common lodging houses' (slightly more difficult) and disguise his public school accent (much more difficult). His first lodging house was on this small turning at the north-west corner of the Isle of Dogs (now entirely redeveloped and characterless), and on his first night roughing it, Orwell noticed a brawny stevedore reeling towards him. He prepared for what he thought would be the inevitable punch-up, but the docker flung his arms round Orwell's neck and exclaimed: ''Ave a cup of tea, chum, 'ave a cup of tea.' Orwell hoped things would get worse, and they did. His bed was convex-shaped and he had to hold on all night to stop himself falling out. In the early hours, unable to sleep, Orwell lit a match and spotted an old man wearing his trousers around his head. A sailor in the next bed then woke up, began swearing, and lit a cigarette, which prompted another voice to cry out: 'Shut up! Oh for Christ's fucking sake, shut up!'

turn left at Westferry Road

West India Dock Road

Site of The Eastern Hotel, West India Dock Road at East India Dock Road

The sea captain who stays here in Joseph Conrad's *Chance* (1913) describes this locale as an area 'where life goes on unadorned by grace or splendour . . . [the inhabitants] passed us in their shabby garments, with sallow faces, haggard, anxious or weary, or simply without expression'.

head south

Isle of Dogs

> '*So we were fain to stay there, in the unlucky Isle of Doggs, in a chill place,
> the night cold, to our great discomfort*' from Samuel Pepys's diary, 1665

In an area where mystery and unseemliness are never far from the surface, the Isle of Dogs is perhaps the most mysterious and unseemly of all. A U-shaped peninsula rather than an isle, south of East India Dock Road, the origins of its strange name are unknown, but for centuries it was barely populated and was shunned by most Londoners on account of its bad drainage and unhealthy environment. (William Blake associated it with the Dogs of Leutha, whose purpose was to destroy their masters.)

Until quite recently the place was largely cut off from civilization, with no train service, few buses and the only connection to London proper a couple of swing bridges. That all changed in the 1980s when the government's determination to regenerate the former docks area saw development sweep in. Office blocks (Canary Wharf, most famously) were built, filled by media outlets such as the *Daily Telegraph* and the *Independent*, warehouses converted to expensive waterside *pieds-à-terre*, light railway lines and tube links constructed, and now the Isle of Dogs is dominated by swish hi-tech office blocks, although many run-down estates remain.

The Isle of Dogs is also the name of a long-lost play by Thomas Nashe which the Privy Council banned in 1597 after a performance at the Swan Theatre on Bankside for being 'seditious and slanderous'. Many of those involved, including Ben Jonson, one of the actors, were consequently imprisoned at Marshalsea (see p. 333). Iain Sinclair's

Downriver includes a story in which the Isle of Dogs is colonized by the Vatican and renamed the Isle of Doges (Vat City plc).

head east beyond the Isle of Dogs

Barking Road

Bridge House, 23 Barking Road, Canning Town, E16, Canning Town railway station/tube
Daniel Farson wrote in *Limehouse Days* (1991) how he and Anthony Armstrong-Jones (before the latter married Princess Margaret and became Lord Snowdon) dropped into this grim pub by the gas works for a quick drink and joined the dockers leering at the strippers. Armstrong-Jones must have been impressed: he later went back on his own but found to his dismay that the strippers had been replaced by 'elderly fire-eaters'.

Hackney, E5, E8

> '*We never get asked to Mayfair any more – it's always Hackney. Wherever that is*' Anon. from *Downriver*, Iain Sinclair, 1991

Harold Pinter, born locally in 1930, described the locality in *The Dwarfs* (1963) as a 'working class area of big run-down Victorian houses . . . a soap factory with a terrible smell and a lot of railway yards and shops'. In the middle decades of the twentieth century much anti-Semitic activity took place locally and non-Jewish youths often picked fights with Pinter because (as he claimed) he looked Jewish (which he was). The slightly younger Steven Berkoff also grew up here. Both playwrights have used local Jewish idioms in their work.

north to south

Downs Park Road

Former Hackney Downs School, Downs Park Road opposite Bodney Road, E5, Hackney Downs railway station
Both Steven Berkoff and Harold Pinter went to this now-defunct school soon after the Second World War. Pinter's highlight was breaking the school record for the 100 yards. Berkoff, who arrived at the end of the '40s, more or less as Pinter was leaving, was put in the lowest grade but was so shattered by the experience he later wrote how he wept as he walked home across Hackney Downs. Berkoff later

described the place as 'ghastly'. After the departure of their two most famous old boys, the school hit hard times. In March 1963 it burned to the ground after new equipment installed to provide a theatre, ironically, caught fire, and in the 1990s government inspectors closed it down as standards had fallen to irretrievable levels.

Lansdowne Drive

London Fields

> '*But this is London; and there are no fields*' from *London Fields*, Martin Amis, 1989

The first *London Fields* novel was not Martin Amis's 1989 work but John Milne's little-known 1983 work. Amis made a strange choice when he borrowed the name for his last novel of the 1980s, for most of the action takes place miles away in west London and the Fields are hardly referred to, although the narrator reveals, about a quarter of the way through, that he was raised in the area. London Fields itself is a dull patch of greenery in a rarely visited part of Hackney.

Queensbridge Road

Suicide Bridge, Queensbridge Road at Regent's Canal

Iain Sinclair named his 1979 collection *Suicide Bridge* (a 'Book of the Furies, A Mythology of the South & East') in honour of this humpbacked bridge over the Regent's Canal from which gangster Reggie Kray threw his gun and knives into the water after killing Jack 'The Hat' McVitie in a house in Stoke Newington in 1967.

Walthamstow, E17

> '*This morning I scarcely know what I am doing. I am going to Walthamstow*'
> John Keats, letter to Fanny Brawne, 1819

Best known for its dog track and the longest street market in Britain, Walthamstow's literary status is associated solely with William Morris who was born at Elm House in Forest Road in 1834 (demolished *c.* 1900).

Forest Road

William Morris's address (1848–56), Water House, Lloyd Park, Forest Road, tel. 020 8527-3782. Walthamstow tube. Open Tue.–Sat. & first Sun. in month 10–1, 2–5

Morris moved here when he was 14 and his father had just died. The house, named after its moat, later came into the possession of the publisher, Edward Lloyd, whose family donated it to the local council in 1898. Water House now contains a William Morris Gallery which contains copies of all the books published by Morris's Kelmscott Press.

NORTH LONDON

The Angel/Islington, N1

No London district has become more fashionable in recent years than Islington, spiritual homeland of New Labour; Tony Blair lived locally until becoming prime minister and brokered his deal with Gordon Brown to become Labour leader in an Islington restaurant, Granita. The Angel takes its name from the Angel Inn which stood on the corner of Pentonville Road and Islington High Street and which is believed to be the place where Thomas Paine wrote some of his *Rights of Man* in 1790. Until the nineteenth century the area was a rural retreat from the city, one of its most famous residents being Sir Walter Ralegh, who moved here in the 1570s and may have lived at the Old Pie Bull which stood where a modern-day pub can now be found at the corner of Upper Street and Theberton Street. For many years both the Old Pie Bull and the Old Queen's Head (demolished 1829, remembered by Queen's Head Street and Raleigh Street) claimed that the adventurer-poet smoked his first pipe of Virginia tobacco on their premises – which is unlikely, given that at the time when Ralegh lived in Islington he had never been to America.

Islington grew during the massive expansion of London in the late eighteenth and early nineteenth centuries. But it was a slum in Victorian times and for much of the twentieth century. In 1959, the year that Joe Orton moved here, *Punch* magazine published some joke predictions, the most ridiculous of which was thought to be the one suggesting the middle classes would one day move to Islington. They did, in the 1970s, when the opening of the Victoria Line tube cut journey times from northern parts of the borough to the West End and cheap unspoilt property was snapped up. Islington has since become more exclusive, escaping the sort of ill-planned redevelopment that has marred nearby Hackney.

Exploring Islington

For easy exploring, in this book Islington has been divided into three sections: Around Islington Green; Canonbury and Hoxton.

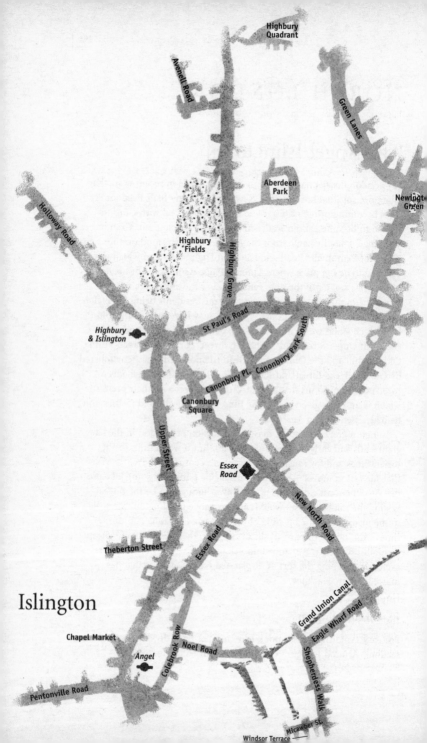

AROUND ISLINGTON GREEN

- Landmarks can be reached from Angel tube.

Bookshops

The Angel Bookshop, 102 Islington High Street, tel. 020 7226-2904, is a compact and welcoming shop featuring an interesting selection of London books.

Chapel Market to Noel Road: west to east

Chapel Market

This side street to the north-west of the Angel is home to a lively cheap market.

Site of Charles and Mary Lamb's address (1797–9), no. 45
Charles Lamb moved here to be near the asylum where his sister, Mary, had been incarcerated after stabbing her mother to death. When Mary was released in 1799, she and Charles moved to no. 36, where they lived until 1801, with Charles always keeping a straitjacket to hand so that he could restrain her if she had a relapse.

Duncan Terrace

Charles and Mary Lamb's address (1823–7), no. 64
Charles Lamb's 'detach'd white house with six good rooms' is a rare surviving building from Islington's rural days, when it was known as Colebrook Cottage on what was then Colebrook Row. The Lambs' visitors included Mary Shelley, Harrison Ainsworth and the short-sighted George Dyer, who left the house one day and walked straight into the nearby New River. Charles Lamb rescued Dyer and wrote about the incident in *Amicus Redivivus* from *Essays of Elia* (1823). In 1827 the Lambs moved to Enfield, Middlesex.

Noel Road

Joe Orton's address (1959–67), Flat 4, no. 25
Playwright Joe Orton and his lover, Kenneth Halliwell, moved into Islington at a time when the area was far from fashionable. Both left eight years later in coffins, Halliwell killing himself after murdering

Orton. In the early '60s the two spent much of their time stealing and defacing books from Islington libraries, before being caught in a manner itself worthy of one of Orton's dramas. Although library staff suspected the pair and took to the police books that had been replaced on the shelves with fake blurbs, they were told they needed to obtain a letter typed on the same machine as the one used on the books before action could be taken.

One obsessive librarian (who, even 35 years later, was threatening legal action should his identity be revealed) took advantage of new legislation allowing councils to remove abandoned vehicles. Sauntering along Noel Road, he found two clapped-out cars near Orton's house (neither of which belonged to Orton or Halliwell) and stuck a deliberately officious notice to the windscreen of one, urging the owner to shift the car within seven days. Halliwell spotted the notice, was most put out by this display of council bumptiousness, and foolishly sent a letter which had been typed on the machine he and Orton had used for the fake blurbs, to the council, complaining about town hall interference. The librarian sent Halliwell's letter to forensics and they matched it with the typeface on the spoiled dust-jackets. A warrant was obtained to search Noel Road, where the police to their amazement found hundreds of stills from Islington library books plastered over the walls. Orton and Halliwell were prosecuted and served six months in Wormwood Scrubs.

After Orton was released, he began writing the plays that made his name, notably *Entertaining Mr Sloane* (1964) and *Loot* (1966). In August 1967 Halliwell beat Orton to death with a hammer in this flat after the last of a number of violent arguments that characterized their fragmenting relationship. Orton's body was discovered after the chauffeur who had come to take him to Twickenham Studios failed to get an answer and called the police. But it was not his body that was found first but Halliwell's – after murdering Orton he killed himself by swallowing twenty-two Nembutal pills. Twenty years after Orton's death, his revealing diaries of life at Noel Road between December 1966 and August 1967 (the period when he was probably the most fêted playwright in Britain) were published. The diary ends nine days before his death at the hands of Halliwell.

CANONBURY

> *'From Canonbury, Dalston and Mildmay Park/The old North London shoots*
> *in a train'* from *The Sandemanian Meeting House in Highbury Quadrant,*
> John Betjeman, 1932

Canonbury is dominated by attractive late-Georgian villas and hand-some black-brick houses, separated from the rather forbidding-looking Marquess council estate by the picturesque and recently cleaned-up New River.

- Landmarks can be reached from Highbury and Islington railway station/tube.

Bookshops

Miles T. & Co., 276 St Paul's Road, tel. 020 7225-3445, is a small but well-stocked shop with an excellent children's selection.

Canonbury Square and eastwards

Canonbury Square

Now one of the most prestigious addresses in the vicinity, Canonbury Square was a decrepit place in the middle decades of the twentieth century when Evelyn Waugh and George Orwell were inhabitants.

Evelyn Waugh's address (1928–30), no. 17a

Having just written his first novel, *Decline and Fall* (1928), and married Evelyn Gardner (dubbed 'she-Evelyn'), Waugh rented a flat in then unfashionable Canonbury. He left after a couple of years, claiming he was tired of having to explain to friends why he was living in so appalling a district. The marriage also broke up not long after.

George Orwell's address (1944–7), no. 27b

It was the very shabbiness of Canonbury Square that attracted George Orwell and made him move there. He and wife Eileen took a top-floor flat when they were bombed out of their St John's Wood address, and for once he was happy. He did some DIY around the flat – the book-shelves were so badly constructed they hung like hammocks – and he and Eileen adopted a son. They became renowned for their traditional English high teas, which comprised various jams and marmalades, gentleman's relish, kippers, toast, scones and very strong tea which he would pour out of a two-handled gallon-sized pot. Within a short

time, however, tragedy struck, when Eileen died. In 1946 Orwell left for
the island of Jura, returned to avoid the Hebridean winter, and then
went off to Jura again for the summer. By this time, after years of
impoverishment, he was a success, thanks to *Animal Farm* (1945). Here
(and in Scotland) Orwell then began working on its follow-up, *1984*,
basing Victory Mansions, home of Winston Smith, (perhaps unfairly)
on Canonbury Square.

Canonbury Place

Weedon Grossmith's address (1891–9), The Old House, Canonbury
Place
The Diary of a Nobody's co-author moved to this imposing property in
a quiet cul-de-sac just before the work was published in book form (it
had originally appeared as a series in *Punch*). The house was later occupied by Ronald Carlton, crossword compiler for *The Times*.

**Oliver Goldsmith's address (1762–4)/Washington Irving's address
(1820s)**, Canonbury Tower/Canonbury Theatre, Canonbury Place
The oldest building in the area, constructed at a point where twenty-
four ley lines meet, Canonbury Tower dates back to 1509 and originally
belonged to the priors of St Bartholomew. It was rebuilt during Elizabeth I's reign, and became the address of the philosopher and essayist,
Sir Francis Bacon, between 1616 and 1625. Oliver Goldsmith, trying to
avoid his creditors in 1762, moved into the tower's Compton Oak
Room, where he wrote *The Traveller*. A surprising nineteenth-century
resident was *Rip Van Winkle* author, Washington Irving. Since 1952 the
building has been the home of Canonbury Theatre. An explanatory
board on a wall at the back in Canonbury Place details the place's
history.

George Orwell's 'Moon Under Water' inspiration, The Canonbury
Tavern, Canonbury Place at St Mary's Grove
Though hard to believe now, the Canonbury Tavern was the inspiration for George Orwell's perfect pub, 'The Moon Under Water', as he
outlined in an *Evening Standard* article on 9 February 1946. Orwell felt
that the décor of such a pub should be 'uncompromisingly Victorian
. . . no sham roof-beams and ingle-nooks; [there should be] a fire burning in the winter; few games (other than darts); no piano or radio;
snacks, rather than main meals; [and] staff [should] know their customers by name'. In his *Letters* Orwell described the Moon Under
Water as a 'kind of gin-palace with cut-glass screens and a big garden
where the proletarians would sit on a summer's evening in whole

families . . . drunks and rowdies never seem to find their way there, even on Saturday nights'. The Canonbury Tavern, in the fifty years since the article was written, has lost much of its character.

HOXTON

Traditionally one of the most violent parts of London, Hoxton's slums were blanket-bombed during the Second World War but rebuilt with low-quality blocks of flats that were little improvement on what had gone before. Recently, parts of the area (near Shoreditch), where artists have renovated old warehouses, have become fashionable.

- Landmarks can be reached from Old Street railway station/tube.

Islington end to Shoreditch end: west to east

Eagle Wharf Road

Site of Hogsden Fields, Eagle Wharf Road at Shepherdess Walk
Ben Jonson killed the actor Gabriel Spenser in a duel in Hogsden (the original name for Hoxton) Fields, which once covered this area, on 22 September 1598. Jonson was imprisoned in Newgate and expected to hang, but a Catholic priest visited the playwright in prison and converted him to Rome; Jonson escaped the gallows on the grounds of 'benefit of clergy' – that he could read the Bible in Latin. After a short gaol term he was released, bereft of his possessions, with an 'M' (for murderer) branded on his left thumb. Jonson remained a Catholic for twelve years.

Windsor Terrace

> ' "My address," said Mr Micawber, "is Windsor Terrace, City Road, I – in short," said Mr Micawber, with the same genteel air, and in another burst of confidence – "I live there." ' Mr Micawber, from *David Copperfield*, Charles Dickens, 1850

Windsor Terrace, home of Mr Micawber, still survives in an area changed out of all recognition since *David Copperfield* was written and now full of 1930s' warehouses and scrapyards. In the novel it is here that Mrs Micawber runs a Boarding Establishment for Young Ladies to which no 'young lady ever came', which results in the Micawbers ending up in the King's Bench debtors' prison. The story line was based on Dickens's own family experiences, his mother having opened a girls' school in St Pancras for which there were no takers and his father getting so deep into debt that he was sent to Marshalsea Prison. A road to the north of Windsor Terrace is now known as Micawber Street.

Old Street

Magistrates Court, Old Street at Hoxton Street
Joe Orton and his lover, Kenneth Halliwell, appeared here before magistrates on 15 May 1962, charged with stealing seventy-two books from Islington Library and defacing them. In court Orton, who gave his occupation as lens-cleaner (he was not then a famous playwright), was sentenced to six months, magistrate Harold Sturge accusing him of 'malice towards fellow library users'. In gaol Orton, bizarrely, was given a library job. (Also see Orton's address near the Angel, p. 265.)

Orton wasn't the first literary figure to be charged at Old Street. George Orwell was convicted of being drunk and disorderly at Christmas 1931 after deliberately setting out to get roaring drunk in Mile End just so that he could be arrested for a trivial offence and experience the inside of a gaol. When he stood before the court, Orwell (then Eric Blair) gave his name as Edward Burton and was fined six shillings. He later borrowed from the incident for *A Clergyman's Daughter* (1935), in which the heroine, Dorothy, waits outside the court while a Black Maria inside which the prisoners are singing 'Adeste Fideles' – just as Orwell and fellow prisoners did – enters the building.

Highbury, N5

'Highbury bore me' from *The Waste Land*, T. S. Eliot, 1922
A beautifully preserved suburb, Highbury has a peaceful, villagey feel that contrasts sharply with the bustle of surrounding parts of north London.

● Landmarks can be reached from Arsenal tube.

Arsenal end to Aberdeen Park: roughly north to south

Avenell Road

Arsenal Football Club
Despite much for writers to admire – the Art Deco stands, the Hector Guimard-style lamps by the main entrance and the quasi-military back-

ground which gave birth to the club as Woolwich Arsenal – London's most successful football team has inspired little literature. Paul Theroux, in his story of south London terrorists, *The Family Arsenal* (1976), employed a running gag in which graffiti about the club are dotted throughout Catford and Deptford (unlikely: few people in south London support Arsenal), but it wasn't until the 1990s that Arsenal were given the full literary treatment when Nick Hornby achieved almost overnight success with his autobiographical rite-of-passage *Fever Pitch* (1992), an often hilarious account of his obsession with Arsenal and the wider neuroses of his personality and perfectly in tune with the spurious PC fashions of the time. *Fever Pitch* achieved rave reviews – Julie Burchill cited it as a new departure in literature – and huge sales, and by the end of the decade scores of imitators had appeared as other sensitive men poured out their souls about the tribulations of supporting Manchester City or playing for Charlton Athletic.

Highbury Quadrant

One of John Betjeman's earliest poems, the intriguingly named *The Sandemanian Meeting House in Highbury Quadrant* (1932), begins with an account of various methods of arriving in Highbury by tram (long gone) or rail (still in use). Strangely, the poem says more about travelling to Highbury than it does about the Sandemanians, a fundamentalist Protestant sect founded in Scotland in 1730 and preserved by the founder's son-in-law, Robert Sandeman, who believed in the essential spirituality of Christianity, or about their Meeting-House in Highbury Quadrant, an awkwardly shaped three-part turning to the west of Clissold Park. The Sandemanians' best-known adherent was the pioneering nineteenth-century scientist, Michael Faraday, who was rejected for burial in Westminster Abbey on account of his beliefs.

Aberdeen Park

St Saviour's

John Betjeman wrote the deeply religious poem, *St Saviour's, Aberdeen Park, Highbury, London, N.* (1948), in honour of this church where his parents had married. In the poem the surrounding area is described as 'weariest, worn-out London', a description that now looks absurd given Highbury's gentility and Aberdeen Park's status as an exclusive private road.

Highgate, N6

Occupying a lofty position over central London and bounded almost entirely by greenery, Highgate is one of the most desirable addresses in London, boasting a superbly positioned hill, a popular village high street, elegant houses and wooded walks. Past residents include Andrew Marvell, Samuel Taylor Coleridge, A. E. Housman (surprisingly, he wrote *A Shropshire Lad* here) and John Betjeman, who nostalgically recalled 1920s Highgate in *Summoned by Bells* (1960), his long narrative poetic tale of his childhood (a lot of which was spent here) which he modelled on Wordsworth's *Prelude*.

- Landmarks can be reached from Highgate tube.

Bookshops

The Highgate Bookshop, 9 Highgate High Street, tel. 020 8348-8202, is a well-stocked neighbourhood store.
Ripping Yarns, 355 Archway Road, tel. 020 8341-6111, has an excellent children's stock.

Hampstead end to Archway end: roughly west to east

Bishopswood Road

Highgate Junior School, no. 3

When John Betjeman (then Betjemann) entered the junior school in 1915 despite an appalling interview in which he failed to answer correctly how many half-crowns there were in a pound (eight), the First World War was raging and Betjemann's German-sounding surname led to his being taunted with chants of 'Betjemann's a German spy. Shoot him down and let him die'. His family dropped the second 'n' soon after. One of Betjeman's teachers was T. S. Eliot, known as 'the American master', who took Latin, French, German and arithmetic, although being from the States he had even more difficulty than Betjeman mastering pounds, shillings and pence. When he was ten, Betjeman presented Eliot with a volume of verse, *The Best Poems of Betjeman* (the volume has not survived), but received little encouragement from the poet, which may explain why, a decade or so later at Oxford, Betjeman eschewed the literary fashion of the day by refusing to write poetry in a sub-Eliot style. Eliot, who had little joy teaching the boys baseball, left at the end of 1916 to join a bank (see p. 65).

The Grove

Coleridge's address and deathsite (1823–34)/J. B. Priestley's address (1935–9), no. 3

The Romantic poet spent the last thirteen years of his life living here with friends Ann and Dr James Gilman (a dentist), trying to cure himself of his opium addiction. Instead, Coleridge's output increased and he rarely left the house except to sit occasionally on Highgate Hill looking down on the smoke of London. One day Coleridge bumped into the essayist, William Hazlitt, in The Grove and, while talking absentmindedly, took hold of the button on the latter's coat. Hazlitt protested that he had to go and, when Coleridge ignored him, took out a penknife and cut off the button to set himself free. J. B. Priestley moved into the same house in the mid-1930s.

West Hill

The pretty road which winds down from Highgate village towards Gospel Oak, now dotted with millionaire pop-star mansions, was where John Betjeman grew up in the early years of the century.

John Betjeman's address (1907–17), no. 31

> 'Deeply I loved thee, 31 West Hill!' from *Summoned by Bells*, John Betjeman, 1960

The three-storey end-of-terrace house where the young Betjeman (then Betjemann) grew up was only a mile or so north of his first address in Gospel Oak but was a significant step upmarket. As Betjeman later explained in his autobiographical poem, *Summoned by Bells* (1960), he grew up 'safe in a world of trains and buttered toast', and when he heard the North London line trains he was glad that he no longer lived in Gospel Oak. But he also had to endure a 'hateful nurse', Maud, who spanked him for being late for dinner and punished him one day, to his horror, by hiding his favourite teddy bear, Archibald Ormsby-Gore. At no. 82, further up West Hill, lived Peggy Purey-Cust, daughter of an admiral and the poet's first love, but a few social classes beyond him. Betjeman was invited to tea – but only once – and every time he subsequently called was told that she was out, ill or away. He took solace in knowing that 'we were slightly richer than my friends/The family next door'.

The family moved to Chelsea when Betjeman was 11, or as he put it in *Summoned By Bells*: 'When I returned from school I found we'd moved – 53 Church St. Yes, the slummy end.' It sounds as if, having left for school that morning, Betjeman came home in the evening to find that the family had left for Chelsea without telling him. In fact he was at boarding school at the time, although it does seem strange that they didn't notify him before the move. In 1975 the house, then owned by former *Spectator* editor Iain Hamilton, was damaged in an arson attack.

North Road

Highgate School, North Road opposite Hampstead Lane
Gerard Manley Hopkins, who attended Highgate from 1854 to 1862, once bet a fellow pupil that he could survive the longer without taking any liquids. He won after a few days, by which time his tongue had gone black. Hopkins won the school poetry prize in 1860 for *The Escorial*.

A. E. Housman's address (1886–1905), Byron College, no. 17
It was in this picturesque Georgian house in the suburbs of north London, rather than in the hills of the Marches, that Housman wrote his best-known work, *A Shropshire Lad* (1896). By day he worked at the Patent Office in Chancery Lane; by night he studied at the British Museum, until 1892, when he became Latin professor at University College, London.

Pond Square

Francis Bacon, the late sixteenth-century essayist and Lord Chancellor, died from pneumonia, which he supposedly caught while stuffing a chicken with snow in the village's Pond Square.

South Grove

St Michael's Church
The tomb of Coleridge, originally buried in Highgate School chapel, was moved here in 1961. A stone on the floor of the nave is inscribed with the epitaph he wrote himself:

> 'Stop Christian passer-by! Stop child of God
> And read with gentle breast. Beneath this sod
> A Poet lies or that which once seemed he.
> O lift one thought in prayer for S-T-C-
> That he who many a year with toil of breath
> Found death in life may here find life in Death!

Mercy for praise to be forgiven for Fame
He ask'd and hoped through Christ
Do then the same!'

Swain's Lane

Highgate Cemetery, Swain's Lane, tel. 020 8340-1834. East Cemetery
open daily 10–5. £1. West Cemetery tours conducted by Friends of
Highgate Cemetery. Admission charge.
There are more than 50,000 graves in Highgate Cemetery, but it is Karl
Marx's that attracts the crowds, one of the first visitors being William
Morris, who came here soon after the political philosopher died in
1883. Others buried at Highgate include George Eliot, Charles Dickens's
parents, Radclyffe Hall, William Foyle (of eponymous bookshop fame),
Sir Leslie Stephen (father of Virginia Woolf and first editor of the *Dic-
tionary of National Biography*) and Christina Rossetti.

Elizabeth Siddal, wife of Dante Gabriel Rossetti, was buried here
after dying of laudanum poisoning in 1862. Rossetti was so grief-
stricken by Siddal's death, he buried a book of new poems in her grave,
but seven years later, poverty-stricken, he realized that the only way he
could make some money would be to publish the poems. So, at dead of
night with permission from the authorities, he made his way to Highgate Cemetery, dug up the coffin, and disentangled the book of poems
from her hair which had continued to grow. Each page had to be
soaked with disinfectant before it was in a fit state to be published –
but it was worth it in the end, for the poems made him a fair sum. The
cemetery is divided into two plots. The East wing contains Marx and
George Eliot. The West is wilder and visually more interesting, with
huge catacombs, vaults overgrown with ivy, and stone angels.

Highgate High Street

Site of Andrew Marvell's address (1670s), opposite no. 112
An obscurely located plaque marks the site of the cottage where the
metaphysical poet died after overdosing on opium, taken to relieve
ague; it reads: 'Four feet below this spot is the stone step, formerly the
entrance to the cottage in which lived Andrew Marvell, poet, wit, satirist, colleague of John Milton in the Foreign or Latin secret service during the Commonwealth and for about 20 years MP for Hull'. Aubrey
later claimed that Marvell may have been poisoned by Jesuits because
of the anonymously written *An Account of the Growth of Popery and
Arbitrary Government in England* which attacked the idea of restoring

the throne with a Catholic absolute monarch. Marvell's poems were published three years after his death by his housekeeper, Mary Palmer, who claimed that she had been married to him and had written the poems. By claiming authorship, Palmer was able to pick up a cheque for £500. It wasn't until around 100 years after his death that Marvell was honoured with writing his own poems.

Holloway, N7, N19

Dickens wrote in *Our Mutual Friend* (1865) how Holloway was a 'tract of suburban Sahara where tiles and bricks were burnt . . . rubbish was shot . . . dogs were fought, and dust was heaped by contractors'. This was at a time when the area was being rapidly developed and colonized by the new hordes of City clerks who could reach work easily on the newly constructed railways, but it was a fictitious clerk, Charles Pooter, the insufferable hero of George and Weedon Grossmith's *Diary of a Nobody* (1892), who gave Holloway its chief place in literary history. In the Grossmiths' book, Pooter, an assistant in a 'mercantile' business, lives at 'the Laurels, Brickfield Terrace, Holloway', a typical suburban villa, and with his bumptiousness and pomposity infuriates everybody with whom he comes into contact. The success of the book, which was initially serialized in *Punch*, and its elevation to cult status, gave Holloway a reputation as the archetypal humdrum north London suburb until the change in demographic patterns around the time of the Second World War saw suburbia move further away from central London. Nowadays Holloway is more inner city than suburbia, and a modern-day Pooter would be more likely to be found in Hillingdon, Hatch End or Havering-atte-Bower than Holloway.

- Landmarks can be reached from Holloway Road tube.

Archway end to Barnsbury end: roughly north to south

Pemberton Gardens

Possible Inspiration for Charles Pooter's 'Laurels, Brickfield Terrace', no. 1

George and Weedon Grossmith set their enduring satire of lower-middle-class respectability, *The Diary of a Nobody* (1892), in Holloway, with the pompous hero, Charles Pooter, and his beleaguered family living in a fictitious villa, the Laurels, Brickfield Terrace. As illustrated in the book, the Laurels is a basic square-shaped house with a dash of baroque features – heavy stone facings on the windows, stucco base, cornice with parapet, porticoed front door (which the Pooters never use) and main living area slightly raised above street level in the Italian *piano nobile* style. Many such properties can still be found in Holloway, but the *Diary* stipulates that a railway line lies at the bottom of the Potters' garden. This limits Brickfield Terrace to Pemberton Gardens in which only no. 1 has the Pooterish look. No. 1 has since been converted into flats, like so many houses of its size and style in north London.

• Kate Greenaway lived at no. 11 from 1878 to 1885.

Parkhurst Road

Holloway Prison, Parkhurst Road at Camden Road
Diana Mosley, wife of the wartime British Fascist leader, Oswald, and sister of the writers Jessica and Nancy Mitford, was incarcerated in this prison as a security risk during the Second World War, later writing up the experience in *A Life of Contrasts* (1977). When Mosley moaned about the intolerable conditions – 'the lavatories became frightful. Floors awash with urine' – the governor asked if she knew anyone in the government who could help. Mosley replied that she knew *all* the Tories, beginning with Churchill, but ruined her case by adding, 'The whole lot deserve to be shot.' One day after exercise there was a rush to use the outside toilets – apart from one cubicle, which everybody except Mosley avoided. When she came out, a horrified prisoner told her that the cubicle had a 'V' on the door. 'Oh, V for Victory?' remarked Mosley. 'No,' the inmate replied. 'V for venereal disease.'

Oscar Wilde spent a couple of weeks here on remand while awaiting trial for gross indecency in 1895, his flamboyant clothes taken from him and replaced with prison clothes embellished with arrows.

Holloway Road

Joe Orton liked to cruise looking for casual sex along Holloway Road in the 1960s, probably because then, as now, it was one of the nastiest main roads in London and any encounters were likely to offer the thrill of danger. In March 1967, shortly after a pederastic excursion to Libya, Orton recalled in his diary (which, in a nod to the Grossmiths' locally set *Diary of a Nobody*, he called *The Diary of a Somebody*) how he entered a 'little pissoir' under the railway bridge in Holloway Road (now boarded up), where he took part in an orgy in the dark with seven other men. 'The pissoir had become the scene of a frenzied homosexual saturnalia. No more than two feet away the citizens of Holloway moved about their ordinary business.' When Orton returned home, he told his lover, Kenneth Halliwell, who retorted that 'eightpence and a bus down the Holloway Road was more interesting than £200 and a plane to Tripoli'.

Islington Library, Holloway Road at Fieldway Crescent
Joe Orton and his lover, Kenneth Halliwell, stole seventy-two books, mainly from this branch, in the late 1950s and early 1960s prior to Orton's success as a playwright. A favourite pastime was to paste their own illustrations over book photos for humorous effect, such as super-imposing a monkey's head on to a rose on the cover of *Collins's Guide to Roses* or drawing a picture of a pot-bellied, tattooed old man next to John Betjeman's name in a critical work on the poet. They also stuck alternative synopses, typed to look authentic, on dust-jackets. For instance, the blurb on a Dorothy L. Sayers mystery was replaced with one claiming the book to be a sado-masochistic tale of a lesbian policewoman who discovers a seven-inch dildo in the police station, while the contents of Emlyn Williams's *Collected Plays* were comple-mented by titles such as *Olivia Prude, Fucked by Monty and Knickers Must Fall* (evidently based on the playwright's best-known work, *Night Must Fall*). Another book featured a paste-up of the actress, Dame Sybil Thorndike, locked in a cell, staring at a huge phallus super-imposed on a Greek statue with a new caption which read: 'During the Second World War I was working from dawn to dusk to serve the many thousands of sailors, soldiers and airmen. American GIs came in shoals to my surgery and some had very peculiar orders for me.'

After placing the books back on the shelves, Orton and Halliwell used to stand around in the library waiting for unsuspecting users to read their handiwork. When the library authorities discovered what was happening, they began the task of finding the culprits. Plain-clothes librarians cruised the shelves, looking for the dust-jacket dood-lers; when Orton and Halliwell were suspected, the library authorities approached the police and an elaborate plan went into action (see Angel/Islington, p. 265). Despite successfully prosecuting Orton, the lib-rary now has an Orton archive which includes some of the defaced books but is heavily guarded against present-day Orton disciples.

head west along Madras Place and through the back streets to Caledonian Road

Caledonian Road

Pentonville Prison, Caledonian Road at Wheelwright Street
When Oscar Wilde spent a short time inside in 1895 after being convicted of gross indecency, friends tried to bribe the governor, J. B. Manning, by offering him £100,000 to help Wilde escape. If Manning
agreed to help, he had to place an advert in the personal column of the
New York World, but he was also warned that if he wasn't interested he
should keep quiet. The plans came to nothing, but Manning stayed
silent; word of the scam didn't get out until 1962. While in Pentonville,
Wilde, unused to the harsh conditions, fell ill. The authorities thought
he must be malingering and threatened severe punishment. Forced to
get up, he then fainted in chapel and was taken to the infirmary.
Friends petitioned the government to protect Wilde, but when doctors
went to check on him they found him sitting up in bed, regaling an
audience with jokes. Soon afterwards Wilde was transferred to Reading,
where conditions were more tolerable, but he was sent back to Pentonville on the day before being finally released, and at dawn on the morning of 19 May 1897, escorted by two friends, he was led away from
prison for the last time.

Hornsey, N8

Better known these days as Crouch End or Crouch Hill, this genteel section of suburbia has become a popular residential area since the 1970s,
despite the appalling transport connections and lack of cultural ameni-
ties. Hornsey has little history of note, but Crouch End earned a rare literary mention with its inclusion in Will Self's *North London Book of
the Dead* (1992) in which the narrator meets his mother in Crouch Hill,
a few months *after* she has died, carrying a bag of groceries from Wait-
rose. The narrator's first question is: 'Mother, what are you doing in
Crouch End? You never come to Crouch End except to take the cat to
the vet, you don't even like Crouch End.'

Bookshops

Prospero's, 32 The Broadway, Crouch End, N8, tel. 020 8348-8900, is a
lavishly stocked shop in the centre of Crouch End.
Muswell Hill Bookshop, 72 Fortis Green Road, N10, tel. 020 8444-7588,
is an attractive community bookshop.

Lower Edmonton, N9

> *'I once gave a concert . . . at Lower Edmonton . . . I had a unique touch'*
> Stanley from *The Birthday Party*, Harold Pinter, 1958

Carol Birch, living in a glum Edmonton tower block, saw it described
as a 'slum' and 'hellhole' in a newspaper article and wrote *Life in the
Palace* (1988) in revenge.

● Landmarks can be reached from Lower Edmonton railway station.

Church Street

Site of John Keats's address (1810), no. 3

Keats came to this (then remote) village in 1810 after his mother died,
and was apprenticed to a surgeon, Dr Thomas Hammond, but after a
row he left to study at Guy's Hospital in Southwark.

Charles and Mary Lamb's address (1833–4)/Lambs' Cottage, Church Street at Lion Road

The Lambs moved to this cottage, which somehow still survives, when
Mary was suffering from severe depression, more than thirty years
after killing her mother during a row. Charles Lamb died here on
27 December 1834 after a fall which brought on erysipelas, and is buried
in the nearby churchyard next to Mary, who died thirteen years later.

Palmers Green, N13

Stevie Smith is probably the only writer ever to have visited this non-
descript tract of suburbia, let alone lived here.

● Landmarks can be reached from Palmers Green railway station.

Avondale Road

Stevie Smith's address (1907–71), no. 1

Smith moved here from Hull with her parents when she was three and
stayed in Palmers Green till the end of her life, despite the area's over-
powering tediousness. Jonathan Miller remembered meeting the poet
when he was a child at one of his parents' literary gatherings in their
St John's Wood home and recalled that to him Palmers Green then

seemed 'a mysterious place of infinitely extended greenery'. Smith had different recollections of those events and wrote a poem describing Miller as a 'spoilt and horrible child'. She wrote her best-known work, *Novel on Yellow Paper* (1936), here in the mid-1930s.

Stoke Newington, N16

On face value, Stoke Newington, with its fancy stores, second-hand bookshops and chic restaurants, looks like the perfect London village; on closer inspection it's a bit of a disappointment, with the Bohemian pretensions outweighed by a pervading shabbiness. Stoke Newington has been colonized over the centuries by successive waves of immigration – Greeks, Turks, Hasidic Jews and West Indians – and Alexander Baron captured some of this melting-pot society in his 1963 novel, *The Lowlife*. Better known is Ernest Raymond's *We the Accused* (1935), which John Betjeman cited as the 'greatest London novel' and claimed that it gave the whole district 'a sense of doom and intending murder and autumn mists in Clissold Park'.

Defoe Road to the east of the park commemorates the period that the author/journalist/government agent spent locally. Defoe was schooled at a Presbyterian academy in Newington Green in the 1670s and lived in Stoke Newington Church Street in the early eighteenth century, a time when there were only about 150 houses in the area. A few decades later, the proto feminist, Mary Wollstonecraft, also spent time in the Newington Green area with the North London Rational Dissenters.

Bookshops

Vortex, 139 Stoke Newington Church Street, tel. 020 7254-6516, set in a huge barn of a building, has plenty of first editions.

- Landmarks can be reached from Stoke Newington railway station.

Stoke Newington Church Street

In Irvine Welsh's *Trainspotting* (1993), Mark, wanting to ascertain whether he really is homosexual, goes back with Giovanni, an Italian waiter, to a basement flat 'somewhair oafay Church Street' and as he lies on the bed wonders whether he has been picked up by another

Dennis Nilsen (the civil servant who butchered a dozen or so homo-sexuals in Muswell Hill in the early '80s and 'biled thir heids in a big pan'). Mark becomes even more worried when he realizes that Nilsen's victims would have suspected little prior to being murdered, but things go off pretty uneventfully in the end.

Site of Daniel Defoe's address (1708–30), no. 95

Despite being in his late fifties, Defoe took to writing novels while liv-ing in Stoke Newington, producing some of his best-known works here, including *Robinson Crusoe* (1719) and *Moll Flanders* (1722). In the latter year he also wrote *A Journal of the Plague Year* (not from per-sonal experience – he was only five when plague broke out). In 1730, when he was nearly seventy, Defoe fled Stoke Newington to get away from his enemies, and went into hiding in the City in Ropemaker Alley (now Ropemaker Street), where he died in 1731. Although Defoe is buried in Bunhill Fields (see Clerkenwell and around, p. 97), his tomb-stone was later lost, then was found by chance in 1940 forming part of the fence of a house in Southampton, and now resides in Stoke Newing-ton Library (Stoke Newington Church Street at Edward's Lane).

Dynevor Road

Joseph Conrad's address (1881–6), no. 6

Conrad lived here during one of his various breaks from being a mer-chant seaman, and he later based Mr and Mrs Verloc in *The Secret Agent* (1907) on the landlord, Adolf Krieger, and his wife.

FURTHER NORTH

Enfield

North of Palmers Green the suburbia around the A105 (Green Lanes) loses its urban edge and segues into the railway dormitory town of Enfield. There's a plaque at Enfield Town station marking the site of John Keats's first school, which became the station house in 1849 and was demolished in 1872.

Chase Side

Charles and Mary Lamb's addresses (1827–33), nos. 87 and 89, Gordon Hill railway station

The Lambs moved to Enfield from Islington and first settled at no. 87, where Charles wanted to stay for good. When, by 1829, the housework began proving too much for Mary, they moved in with a retired haberdasher and his wife next door at Westwood Cottage, no. 89. Despite occasional visits from Hazlitt and Leigh Hunt, the Lambs were lonely and Charles wrote little, other than the *Last Essays of Elia* (1833).

NORTH-WEST LONDON

Camden Town, NW1

Although probably the best place in London for monitoring new waves in rock music or shopping for unusual clothes, Camden Town has little literary history. Charles Dickens lived here when he first came to London as a young boy and the area was still quite rural, and in *Dombey and Son* (1848) he railed against the arrival of the railways which, he realized, would mean the end of the Camden he knew. The modern-day authors most associated with the place are the York-shiremen David Storey (whose 1960 novel, *Flight into Camden*, is set locally) and Alan Bennett, who can often be seen cycling round Camden. The increasingly fashionable Primrose Hill to the west of Camden Town is now home to Martin Amis and Ian McEwan.

Fight into Camden

In his 1983 historical romance, *In Camden Town*, David Thomson dealt with the 1846 Camden Town Riots, a battle for territorial supremacy that took place between Irish and English navvies on the east side of what is now Chalk Farm Road (opposite the Roundhouse). Fighting began when a group of Irish navvies attacked some English railway workmen who, they claimed, had provoked them. The brawl raged for about an hour and hundreds were injured, but the police found themselves powerless to stop the violence and it ended only when most of the protagonists were too exhausted to continue. Some, however, didn't know when they'd had enough. Twenty Irishmen were carried to Albany Street police station but, as Thomson reports, 'so desperately did they fight it took seven constables to carry one of them'. Nor did spirits dampen overnight. The court next day was surrounded by Irish navvies and some witnesses were stoned on the way in. Court proceedings turned to farce when Ellis, a foreman who was presumed to be dead, appeared as a witness to his own murder. Another supposedly murdered man sent news of his recovery from hospital. In the end only one man died; he had only gone to see what the fuss was about but was beaten to death amid cries of 'Kill the fucking Protestant'.

AROUND CAMDEN TOWN STATION

Bookshops

Abbey Books, Market Hall, Camden Lock, tel. 020 8740-0713, is a sprawling stall in the heart of Camden Lock market.

Compendium Bookshop, 234 Camden High Street, tel. 020 7267-1525, is particularly well stocked in political books and pamphlets.

Offstage Theatre and Film Bookshop, Chalk Farm Road, tel. 020 7485-4996, specializes in drama and film.

Walden Books, 38 Harmood Street, tel. 020 7267-8146, named after the Thoreau book, is one of the most useful second-hand bookshops in London but is open only a few days a week.

● Landmarks can be reached from Camden Town or Mornington Crescent tubes.

roughly east to west

Bayham Street

Site of Charles Dickens's address (1822–3), no. 141
When Charles Dickens's father returned to his job at Somerset House in the Strand, he and his wife moved into a poky two-storey black-brick tenement (then no. 16) in what was then one of the few turnings in a poor but largely rural suburb. After a few months the 10-year-old Charles joined the family, which came as something of a shock to him after genteel Chatham in Kent. Dickens, in his later recollections, played down Camden Town's rustic activities (haymaking went on in the meadow at the back) and played up the meanness of the environment – a 'shabby, dingy, damp and mean neighbourhood'. In 1823 the Dickenses moved half a mile south to Gower Street (see p. 3) and Charles later depicted the house in various stories, it being where the Cratchits celebrate the season (in *A Christmas Carol*, 1843) and Mr Micawber's house in *David Copperfield* (1850). A children's clinic stands on the site.

Mornington Crescent

Alfred, Lord Tennyson's address (1850), no. 25
When the poet moved out, he accidentally left the manuscript for *In Memoriam* behind. Coventry Patmore, the pre-Raphaelite poet, went back and retrieved it for him.

Delancey Street

Dylan Thomas's address (1951–2), no. 54

Thomas described this three-storey terrace house, owned by Margaret Taylor, wife of historian A.J.P., as his 'London house of horror'. He and wife Caitlin moved in during the winter of 1951, parking their caravan in the garden. The neighbours were soon coming out of their houses to hear the Thomases' rows. In January 1952 Thomas left England for America.

Parkway

Palmer's Pet Store, nos. 35–37

Graham Greene based his 'zoological shop' in *It's a Battlefield* (1934), which is situated below the lodgings of the Communist leader, Bennett, on this long-running store. In 1969 Palmer's made the headlines after letting a boa constrictor and its twenty offspring loose in the shop at night to deter burglars. In the opening of Alan Bennett's short story, *The Lady in the Van* (1989), Miss Shepherd runs into a 'long, grey snake – a boa constrictor possibly' in Parkway the day after a break-in at Palmer's.

Outer Circle

London Zoo

Dante Gabriel Rossetti went with a friend to the zoo one day in 1860 and suggested they hire an elephant and bring it back to his Chelsea address (see p. 376) to clean the windows. When the friend asserted that such an idea was preposterous, Rossetti agreed but pointed out that when the public saw an elephant in Cheyne Walk trying to clean his windows, they'd come to the house to find out what was happening and could then be cajoled into buying one of his paintings. It was Leonard Woolf (Virginia Woolf's husband) who later claimed that 'London Zoo is an animal microcosm of London . . . even the lions behave as if they have been born in South Kensington'.

PRIMROSE HILL

'The fields from Islington to Marylebone,/To Primrose Hill and Saint John's Wood,/Were builded over with pillars of gold . . .' from *Jerusalem*, William Blake, 1804–20

Thanks to its proximity to Camden Town, Primrose Hill has become an increasingly fashionable place to live, and can count Martin Amis, Alan Bennett, Michael Frayn and Ian McEwan among its inhabitants. The hill which gives the area its name has long been popular with writers. In H. G. Wells's *The Invisible Man* (1897), the hero Griffin contemplates his success in making a cat disappear while 'sitting in the sunshine and feeling very ill and strange on the summit of Primrose Hill', before going back to his Great Portland Street lodgings and making himself disappear. In Wells's *War of the Worlds* (1898), the Martians who are attacking London try to make their headquarters on Primrose Hill.

Edmund Gosse recounted in *Father and Son* (1907) how he and his father arrived at Primrose Hill and 'sat down on a bench at its inglorious summit whereupon [he] burst into tears and in a heart-rending whisper sobbed "Oh Papa, let us go home"'. Louis MacNeice wrote in his 1938 *Autumn Journal* about the trees being cut down on Primrose Hill so that anti-aircraft guns could be installed, but by the time of Aldous Huxley's *Time Must Have a Stop* (1944) an air raid is taking place and on the hill 'the guns were banging away in a kind of frenzy'. In Dodie Smith's *101 Dalmatians* (1956), the dogs run to the 'open space called Primrose Hill' after escaping from Regent's Park. When they get to the top of the hill, Pongo and Missis stand 'side by side and barked to the north, barked to the south, barked to the east and west'. Helen Falconer's 1999 novel, entitled simply *Primrose Hill*, deals with late twentieth-century adolescents chilling out on the hill during summer.

- Landmarks can be reached from Camden Town tube.

Bookshops

Primrose Hill Books, 134 Regent's Park Road, tel. 020 7586-2022, has a tremendous basement second-hand section with a good selection of old Everymans. There's a convenient café next door.

Chalk Farm end to Regent's Park end: roughly north to south

Regent's Park Road

The road which runs through the heart of Primrose Hill is lined with cafés, delis and bijou shops. It was also Kingsley Amis's territory in his later years.

Chalk Farm Bridge, Regent's Park Road at Bridge Approach
In the poem *Epiphany* from *Birthday Letters* (1998), Ted Hughes walks
over this railway bridge on his way to Chalk Farm tube station and is
astonished to meet a man carrying a fox cub in his coat.

Kingsley Amis's address (1985–95), no. 194
This spacious, rambling house by the railway bridge was the third and
final address for Amis and the strange ménage which accompanied him
– his former wife, Hilly Bardwell, and her husband, Lord Kilmarnock.
The set-up and the area inspired his 1990 novel, *The Folks that Live on
the Hill*.

The Queen's, Regent's Park Road at St George's Terrace
The pub opposite the house where Friedrich Engels used to live was
Kingsley Amis's weekend local when he lived in Primrose Hill (during
the week, his copious drinking took place at the Garrick). Amis's
favourite tipple was a large Macallan malt at lunchtime around half-
past twelve. By 1990 Amis was so run down from the effects of a lifetime's drinking that he needed a taxi for the short journey between his
Regent's Park Road home and the pub.

Site of Henry Handel Richardson's address (1910–34), no. 90
Henry Handel Richardson was the unusual pen-name of the Australian
female author, Ethel Florence Richardson. Here she wrote the trilogy,
The Fortunes of Richard Mahoney (1930).

Fitzroy Road

W. B. Yeats's address (1867–72)/Sylvia Plath's address (1962–3),
no. 23
Yeats, who moved here as a baby, never liked the area and longed for
the school holidays which were spent in Sligo, Ireland. Nearly 100 years
later, in December 1962, Sylvia Plath moved into 23 Fitzroy Road
because of the Yeats links, taking the top two rooms and writing about
Yeats's plaque in one of her letters. Plath had recently split up from
Ted Hughes, who had left her for another woman, and, depressed from
this and the unusually cold winter, gassed herself to death before the
children woke, early on the morning of 11 February 1963, helpfully
leaving a note containing her doctor's phone number and asking whoever found it to call him. Plath's last poem, *Edge*, written here on
5 February, told how a woman is found dead, 'wearing the smile
of accomplishment'. After her death Hughes destroyed Plath's
Journals.

• From 1888 to 1889 H. G. Wells, then in his twenties and an assistant master at Kilburn's Henley House School, lived at no. 12 with his aunts. He then moved to the larger no. 46 until 1891.

SOMERS TOWN, NW1 except where stated

Dominated by three great railway termini – King's Cross, St Pancras and Euston – Somers Town is a harsh landscape of train lines, gas stations and canals, not that this stopped George Bernard Shaw becoming a local borough councillor, where he had a 'grand time ... worrying about drains, dust destructors and instituting women's lavatories'. In 1997 the British Library moved to a new site by St Pancras station.

• Landmarks can be reached from King's Cross St Pancras tube.

Bookshops

Porcupine Bookcellar, 5 Caledonian Road, tel. 020 7837-4473, is strong on politics, with lots of second-hand works.

Euston to King's Cross: west to east

Euston Road

British Library, Euston Road at Ossulston Street
Few public projects have been as beset by disaster as the moving of the British Library from the British Museum in Bloomsbury to this St Pancras site in the 1990s. During construction the sprinklers went off by accident, there was a flood from the chief executive's shower, and when the building was unveiled critics fought each other to find the most damning epithet, Prince Charles famously lambasting it as looking like an 'academy for secret police' although it looks more like several suburban supermarkets squashed together.

Despite going £350 million over budget, the completed library has only 1,192 seats – just 11 per cent more than the British Museum Reading Room and well down from the original quota of seats: 3,440. But the Library's biggest embarrassment came in 1998, six months after it opened, when, during a weekend to promote the opening of the public viewing galleries, a slide show beamed on to the building's façade the slogan, 'The British Library. For the nation's written heretage'.

Inside, things are not all bad. The interior has generally been praised for its bold use of space, the creamy Portland stone walls rising the full height of the building; and for users there is the advantage that the catalogue has been computerized and bureaucracy reduced, which has made the ordering of a book less of a chore. For those without a reader's card, the Library is also worth a brief visit for the permanent exhibitions on the history of the book.

Former Midland Hotel, Euston Road at St Pancras station
When Oscar Wilde stayed in this lavishly designed Gothic hotel (now empty, awaiting restoration) during his trial on charges of gross indecency in 1895, heavies sent by his tormentor, the Marquess of Queensberry, threatened the hotel management, who responded by throwing Wilde out.

King's Cross station, Euston Road at York Way, N1
Philip Larkin got the idea for his poem, *The Whitsun Weddings* (1958), while travelling on a train from Hull, where he was university librarian, to King's Cross on Whit Saturday 1955. The train was a slow one and, each time it stopped, married couples boarded on their way to London for their honeymoons, 'all doing the same things, and sort of feeling the same things. Everytime you stopped fresh emotion climbed aboard.' As the train hurtled towards King's Cross on the last stretch, 'you felt the whole thing was being aimed like a bullet – at the heart of things'.

north of King's Cross station

Camley Street

St Pancras graveyard
When Thomas Hardy in his twenties, during the 1860s worked in an architect's office in the Adelphi, off the Strand, one of his first jobs was to survey St Pancras graveyard, where the builders of the new Midland Railway were planning to direct the line over the Grand Union Canal. Hardy had to supervise the removal of the corpses, and one of his more gruesome finds was a coffin containing a man supposedly with two heads. The graveyard work made Hardy ill, and he quit the job and London to recuperate in Dorset.

Hampstead, NW3

'With farmy fields in front and sloping green,/Dear Hampstead, is thy
southern face serene' from *Hampstead in 1815*, Leigh Hunt, 1815

London's most picturesque and exclusive village (although Richmond
comes close), Hampstead can also claim to be the literary and intellectual centre of the capital, having been home over the years to John
Keats, D. H. Lawrence, Aldous Huxley, George Orwell, Agatha Christie,
Kingsley Amis, John Le Carré, Margaret Drabble and others attracted
by the romantic pull of the windswept Heath, the twisting winding hills
and the quaint narrow streets.

Hampstead's lofty position – it is set 440 feet above London – meant
in early industrial times it could boast better air and water than the
centre of the metropolis and so attracted those with sensitive dispo-
sitions, such as Keats (who lived in Well Walk when ill with TB in the
early years of the nineteenth century), or those recuperating (Charles
Dickens and his wife, Catherine, after the death of her sister, Mary, in
1832). As London grew, so Hampstead, protected by the Heath and the
hills, became a sought-after refuge from the sprawling city, attracting
the more Bohemian artists and writers who were quick to wax lyrical
about its charms. E. M. Forster in *A Passage to India* (1924) described it
as 'an artistic and thoughtful little suburb of London', and for Kingsley
Amis Hampstead was 'not so much a village as a small country town
fetched perhaps from somewhere in the west of England and enclosed
by suburbia on three sides and grassland on the fourth'.

But the place has not been to everyone's taste. Dickens recorded in
Barnaby Rudge (1841) that in the late eighteenth century robbers were
so violent, few people would venture into Hampstead at night
'unarmed and unattended'. William Blake said, 'a journey to Hampstead without due consideration would be a mental rebellion against
the holy spirit and only for a soldier of Satan to perform', and D. H.
Lawrence, who had countless temporary addresses in the area, thanks
to hospitable friends, claimed he found the 'eighteenth-century charm
of Hampstead depressing and void'. Ezra Pound wrote in 1913 of Hampstead's being 'a more hideous form of Boston, with its particles of information and gossip', and then cut some laudatory remarks about the
place when he was editing T. S. Eliot's *The Waste Land* (1922). Virginia
Woolf, referring to the conflict between Hampstead's literary set and
the Bloomsbury Group, described Hampstead as 'the heart of the
enemies' camp' in her diary from 1922.

Since the Second World War Hampstead has been the home of the

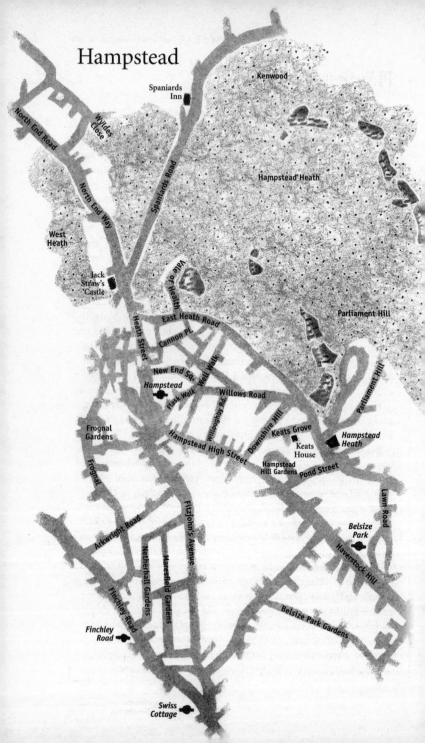

Hampstead Heath

> '*It was an hour before dawn on Hampstead Heath, a dripping, musty, no man's hour . . .*' from *Smiley's People*, John Le Carré, 1979

London's wildest open space has been a favourite haunt of John Keats, Karl Marx, Charles Dickens, George Bernard Shaw and D. H. Lawrence. Marx used to bring his large family up here every weekend to escape from the drudgery of the city. Shaw would come here with fellow Fabians the Webbs (Sydney and Beatrice) to stretch his legs and talk about anarchy after the fortnightly meetings of the Hampstead Historic Society in Hampstead Garden Suburb. While lying on the Heath during the First World War, D. H. Lawrence and Frieda von Richtofen saw a German Zeppelin pass over during one of the first air raids over London. Frieda ironically was a cousin of Manfred von Richtofen, the German air ace known as the Red Baron, but this display of technologically advanced military action convinced them to flee London for the safety of Cornwall. It also inspired the scene in Lawrence's *Kangaroo* (1923) in which Harriet (based on Frieda) looks up as the Zeppelins pass over and says, 'Some of the boys I played with when I was a child are probably on it.'

In the 1950s, Colin Wilson, when he was describing himself as a 'socialist supporter of world government' and before he made his name with *The Outsider* (1956), used to sleep rough on the Heath. Nowadays the celebrity-spotter might chance upon Dannie Abse, the doctor-poet whose mother once told a shop assistant that her son was the Welsh (*sic*) Dylan Thomas, author-broadcaster Lord (Melvyn) Bragg, or ex-Labour Party leader Michael Foot (a former Left Book Club author).

The Heath has also enjoyed numerous mentions in literature. One of the earliest was by Daniel Defoe in *A Tour Through the Whole Island of Great Britain* (1727) in which he writes how 'on the top of the hill indeed, there is a very pleasant plain, called the Heath'. In Chapter I of Dickens's *The Pickwick Papers* (1837), the Pickwick Club reports 'That this association has heard, read with feelings of unmingled satisfaction and unqualified approval the paper communicated by Samuel Pickwick, esq., G.C.M.P.C., entitled "Speculations on the Source of the Hampstead Ponds, with Some Observations on the Theory of Tittlebats".' (Hampstead Ponds can be found at the southern end of the Heath, between East Heath Road and South Hill Park.) In Bram Stoker's *Dracula* (1897) children are found on the Heath with 'tiny wounds in the throat'. In the Sherlock Holmes story, 'The Adventure of Charles Augustus Milverton' (1904), Holmes and Watson flee across the Heath after the murder of Milverton. Later mystery writers have also made use of the Heath, often as a setting where something dangerous may happen, as in Dorothy L. Sayers's *Unnatural Death*, in which the lawyer, Tripp, tells Inspector Charles Parker a story about being lured to a deserted house on Hampstead Heath to write a will for a woman . . . who tries to murder him.

moneyed Left, what Doris Lessing in *The Golden Notebook* (1962) described as a world of 'political intellectuals, reformers, therapists and feminists', and in recent decades mention of the place in polite conversation is usually followed by derogatory phrases such as 'champagne socialist' and 'trendy lefty', a situation wonderfully reinforced in 1992 when Oscar-winning actress, Glenda Jackson, was returned as the area's MP.

Exploring Hampstead

For easy exploring, Hampstead has been divided into seven sections in this book, partly based on the area's traditional 'ends': North End/ Hampstead Garden Suburb; Vale of Health; Main Roads of Hampstead; New End; South End; West End; and Belsize Park.

NORTH END/HAMPSTEAD GARDEN SUBURB, NW11

The land to the north-west of Hampstead Heath was developed in 1906 as London's biggest garden village – a self-sufficient community with a countryside flavour, lots of space, and easily accessible to the city. The initial intention was that the estate would lure the poor from their overcrowded slums to live side-by-side with the middle classes but, as with most garden villages across England, Hampstead Garden Suburb soon became exclusive, attracting the ever so slightly eccentric end of the Bohemian Left or, as the American essayist, Logan Pearsall Smith, noted, 'societies for Mothercraft and Handicraft and Child Study . . . lectures on Reincarnation, the Holy Grail and the Teaching of the Holy Zoroaster'. Today it is an attractive place, less Bohemian than the centre of Hampstead, but with its lack of pubs and shops eerily quiet, especially around Central Square.

- Landmarks can be reached from Golders Green tube or Hampstead tube.

Finchley end to the Spaniards Inn: roughly north to south

Oakwood Road

No. 1B
George Orwell, in the 1920s, often used this address, home of Francis and Mabel Fierz, whom he knew from his home town of Southwold, to

change from his everyday clothes into tramping gear before heading off through the leafy 'burb and north London for the grotty East End. It was here that Orwell typed the first draft of *Down and Out in Paris and London* in August 1931, and when he came to live in London, three years later, the Fierzes put him up until he found a flat above his new workplace in Booklovers' Corner (see p. 308). In those days Hampstead Garden Suburb was full of the kind of cranky socialists that Orwell later attacked with much venom in *The Road to Wigan Pier* (1937), not that that stopped him accepting hospitality from the Fierzes. Orwell also didn't mind taking favours from a neighbour, Max Plowman, between-the-wars editor of the *Adelphi*, a literary quarterly, to which Orwell contributed. Orwell would often visit Plowman and his wife to play badminton, spending much of the game irritating everyone by apologizing constantly for what he believed was his incorrect dress: braces instead of a belt to hold up his trousers.

head through the heart of the garden village

North End Road

Evelyn Waugh's address (1916–28), Underhill, no. 145
The teenage Waugh was so embarrassed when the house's postal address was changed from Hampstead to Golders Green, he would walk back into Hampstead to post his letters so that they bore the post-mark of that area. On his way to school in the mornings, Waugh would leave coins at various points on the road and then return the same way in the evening just so that he could count how many were left. At school, Waugh was the leader of a gang of bullies who tor-mented the young Cecil Beaton (later a leading society photographer). Though shorter than other members of the gang and wearing green knickerbockers, Waugh would approach Beaton and bring his face closer and closer, staring hard at him for several minutes, until Beaton was thoroughly humiliated. Another Waugh trick was to bend Beaton's arms back to front. The author showed no remorse for any of this in later years. Instead, he disputed some of the details and exculpated him-self on the grounds that Beaton was a 'tender and very pretty little boy'.

In 1924, after leaving university, Waugh came home to write a novel, *The Temple at Thatch*, about an undergraduate who inherits land which contains an eighteenth-century folly. After penning a few dozen pages, he showed it to a friend, Harold Acton (who later became a well-known art critic), but when Acton criticized it as being 'too Eng-lish' Waugh destroyed it. A little while later, Waugh invited Anthony

Powell to dinner and read him the first ten thousand words of what became *Decline and Fall*. Powell was impressed and soon after asked Waugh how the book was shaping up. 'I've burnt it,' Waugh replied. He did, however, rewrite it soon afterwards to preserve most of the foundations of what became his first published novel.

Wyldes Close

Old Wyldes

William Blake occasionally stayed in this early seventeenth-century farmhouse (best seen from the heath at the back) in the 1820s when it was the home of the landscape painter John Linnell (who commissioned Blake to do illustrations for a new edition of the Book of Job) and a writers' and artists' retreat. Charles Dickens and his wife, Catherine, stayed here after the death of her sister, Mary, in 1837. In the 1880s the radical Hampstead Historic Club met here. Raymond Unwin, the architect who designed Hampstead Garden Suburb, lived here from 1906 to 1940. The Barnet/Camden borough boundary passes through the garden.

North End Road

The Old Bull and Bush, North End Road at North End
In George and Weedon Grossmith's *The Diary of a Nobody* (1892), Charles Pooter and some friends take a Sunday afternoon saunter over the Heath and arrive at a pub called the Cow and Hedge (an obvious play on the Bull and Bush) where, being after hours, only 'bona fide' travellers can get a drink thanks to a bizarre nineteenth-century law. Pooter's companions claim they've come from Blackheath on the other side of London and so gain entrance, but Pooter with typical naïvety admits to coming from Holloway, too short a distance away to allow him 'bona fide traveller' status, and is obliged to wait an hour outside the pub while his friends enjoy their drink. The Bull and Bush, a favourite of Hogarth, David Garrick and Dickens, was immortalized in the 1903 music-hall song, *Down at the Old Bull and Bush*.

North End Way

Jack Straw's Castle, North End Way opposite Spaniards Road
This famous pub was Charles Dickens's 'good 'ouse', where he had a 'red-hot chop for dinner'. He, John Forster (his biographer) and Wilkie Collins used to end up here after strolls on the Heath. The pub

is named after one of the leaders of the 1381 Peasants' Revolt, who is believed to have taken refuge in a building that then stood on the site. The pub was rebuilt in 1964.

head north up Spaniards Road

Spaniards Road

Spaniards Inn, Spaniards Road and Spaniards End
In Dickens's *Barnaby Rudge* (1841), the Gordon Rioters, marching on Lord Mansfield's house in nearby Caen Wood (Ken Wood) but unable to resist a drink, stop off at this pub (since rebuilt) and are waylaid by the landlord, who sends for the army and prevents the raid.

VALE OF HEALTH

Once a malarial swamp known as Hatches Bottom, the area was drained in 1801 by the Hampstead Water Company and given the euphemistic name Vale of Health. Cottages and villas were built and in 1815 Leigh Hunt moved into the area, although nobody is certain exactly where, partly because until around 1850 the houses weren't named, let alone numbered. Even these days the Vale is relatively undeveloped, containing fewer than 100 houses, no shops or pubs, and is barely represented on most street atlases. (There is, however, an indispensable local map on a board at the East Heath Road end of the main Vale of Health road.) Past Vale of Health residents include D. H. Lawrence, Edgar Wallace and Stella Gibbons.

● Landmarks can be reached from Hampstead tube.

roughly north to south

Leigh Hunt's address (1815–21)/Edgar Wallace's address (1920s), Vale Lodge
Hunt, one of the unfortunately named 'Cockney School of Poets', came to the Vale after his release from a two-year gaol sentence, which he received for describing the Prince Regent as a 'corpulent man of fifty . . . a violator of his word, a libertine'. While living locally, Hunt wrote five sonnets in honour of Hampstead, introduced Keats to Shelley, and was visited by Hazlitt and Charles and Mary Lamb. He was later cast as Harold Skimpole in Charles Dickens's *Bleak House* (1853). No one is sure which house Hunt really lived in, for as well as Vale Lodge there is a Hunt Cottage which is so named because Hunt supposedly lived

there. A hundred years later, Edgar Wallace did live, briefly, at Vale Lodge. He claimed it was haunted.

Stella Gibbons's address (1927–30), Vale Cottage
Gibbons lived in this little whitewashed cottage on the main Vale of Health road near the Heath end in the days before she won fame with *Cold Comfort Farm* (1932).

Compton Mackenzie's address (1937–43), Woodbine Cottage
Mackenzie wrote all six volumes of *The Four Winds of Love* (1945) while living here. Unlike D. H. Lawrence (see below), Mackenzie liked the Vale and remarked that the 'village life only half an hour from Piccadilly Circus was a continuous refreshment and stimulus'.

D. H. Lawrence's address (1915), 1 Byron Villas
Lawrence and his wife, Frieda von Richtofen, took the ground-floor flat in this end-of-terrace house in August 1915 when they were planning to set up a commune in America, and here Lawrence first met Aldous Huxley, was visited by E. M. Forster, the painter Dorothy Brett (cast as Jenny in Huxley's *Crome Yellow*, 1921) and the novelist Michael Arlen (real name Dikran Kouyoumdijan) whose *The Green Hat* (1924) became a bible of sorts for the Bright Young Things of 1920s' Mayfair. Another visitor was Bertrand Russell, whom Lawrence upset when he described him as 'false, cruel and evil' over his attitude to the First World War. Russell came to Lawrence for reconciliation, but that didn't stop the author pillorying him a few years later as Sir Joshua Malleson in *Women in Love* (1920).

While in the Vale, Lawrence and John Middleton Murry (later Katherine Mansfield's husband) set up a literary magazine, *The Signature*, to which Mansfield contributed articles under the pseudonym, Matilda Berry. The magazine's pacifist tendencies at the height of the First World War didn't go down well with readers, and it folded after three issues. Around this time Lawrence's novel, *The Rainbow* (1915), was published but was greeted with hostile reviews on account of its stark emotional honesty, anti-war sentiment and erotic content. Unsurprisingly, Lawrence was unhappy living in the Vale and wrote in a letter, 'I am so sick in body and soul that if I don't go away I shall die.' He and Frieda left for Cornwall on 1 December 1915.

Rabindranath Tagore's address (1912), 3 Villas-on-the-Heath
A year after his brief stay in the Vale, the Calcutta-born Tagore won the Nobel Prize for Literature. In 1915 he was knighted, but later renounced the honour in protest against British policy in the Punjab.

MAIN ROADS OF HAMPSTEAD

Heath Street, which runs through the centre of Hampstead down a long hill from Whitestone Pond, splits in two at the tube station. The residential western part remains as Heath Street and then becomes Fitzjohn's Avenue as it heads for Swiss Cottage. The eastern part, Rosslyn Hill, leads towards Camden Town. In between is Belsize Park (see below).

• Landmarks can be reached from Hampstead tube.

Heath end to Rosslyn Hill end: roughly north to south

Heath Street

Site of the Upper Flask Tavern, no. 124
The Queen Mary Maternity Hospital stands on the site of the tavern which hosted the eighteenth-century Kit-Cat Club, described by Dr Johnson as the best club that ever existed. The strange name came courtesy of the pastry cook, Christopher Katt, who at the club's original central London home made mutton pies known as kit-cats. The Kit-Cat Club's members were mainly Whigs (i.e. they supported the 1714 Hanoverian succession to the throne) and included William Congreve, Joseph Addison, Richard Steele and Sir John Vanbrugh. Each had his portrait painted on joining, the results of which are now in the National Portrait Gallery. The inn, which sold the local spa water as well as the usual alcoholic range, features in Samuel Richardson's *Clarissa* (1748), in which it is described as 'a place where second-rate persons are to be found, often in a swinish condition'.

Everyman Cinema, Heath Street at Hollybush Vale
Hampstead's much-loved rep cinema opened as a drill hall in 1888 and then became a theatre, making the headlines in 1922 when it planned a run of a Noel Coward play, *The Vortex*, in which Coward himself was due to perform. The Lord Chamberlain, who had powers to censor plays, remonstrated at what he called 'a wholly frivolous and degenerate set of people' and got particularly worked up about the scene in which the drug-taking son (to be played by Coward) 'upbraids his mother for the immoral conduct of her life [which is] revolting in the last degree'. Coward managed to obtain a licence to stage the play only on the morning of the first show. The Everyman became a cinema in 1933. In Stewart Home's pulp novel, *Red London*, a posse of Stratford

skinheads raid the Everyman and butcher the audience as they watch a
Fellini film.

Hampstead High Street

Waterstone's, no. 68
Salman Rushdie's first public appearance after a *fatwa* was imposed on
him took place in this branch of Waterstone's in 1990, when he signed
copies of his new children's book, *Haroun and the Sea of Stories*.

The Coffee Cup, no. 74
Tim Harnforth in John Braine's *These Golden Days* (1985) extols the
pleasures of stopping at the Coffee Cup, still a popular Hampstead
meeting place.

Crichton Arms (King of Bohemia), no. 10
See George Orwell box, below.

NEW END

Lying between Heath Street and East Heath Road, the New End area
was built up in the eighteenth century and retains a distinctive period
charm.

● Landmarks can be reached from Hampstead tube.

Bookshops

Keith Hawkes, 1–3 Flask Walk, tel. 020 7435-0614, has a massive stock
in a wonderfully dusty old shop full of hidden corners and enticing
piles of books.

Heath Street end to Pond Street end: roughly north to south

East Heath Road

Katherine Mansfield's address (1918–21), 2 Portland Villas, no. 17
Mansfield and John Middleton Murry, whom she had recently married,
came to this whitewashed Gothic block opposite the Heath when she
was suffering from TB and wanted to take Hampstead's healthy air. On
moving in, Mansfield wrote to Ida Constance Baker, her former lover,
how she wanted to redesign the property. 'All the doors are to be grey
and the skirting boards and the shutters'; once this had been done, she

labelled the house 'The Elephant'. A regular visitor was D. H. Lawrence who, she wrote, was 'just his old, merry, rich self, laughing, full of enthusiasm'. Lawrence portrayed Murry and Mansfield as Gerald and Gudrun, respectively, in *Women in Love* (1920), and Aldous Huxley used them for the characters Burlap and Beatrice in *Point Counter Point* (1928). Mansfield and Murry left for Italy in 1921, and two years later she died in France. He had an affair with Lawrence's wife, Frieda, after the novelist died.

cut through Squires Mount

Cannon Place

Daphne Du Maurier's address (1916–35), Cannon Hall, Cannon Place
Du Maurier moved into this sprawling 1730 mansion during the First World War when she was nine and her father, Sir Gerald, was the leading actor-manager of the day (he had been the first stage Captain Hook in J. M. Barrie's *Peter Pan*). In 1934, when Sir Gerald died, she moved to Cornwall and the house was sold. In 1996 the latest owner (who had paid £2.5 million for the place) caused outrage among locals by announcing plans to gut a room that had once been the local court house in order to extend the car park. The Heath and Old Hampstead Society was particularly upset: Sir Gerald had been a committee member and, although he used to host some wild 'tennis' parties in Cannon Hall and use the Courtroom as a gentlemen's changing room, he had never tampered with the architecture.

Elm Row

D. H. Lawrence's address (1923–4), no. 1
During the winter of 1923–4 Lawrence stayed in this well-concealed house, which belonged to his friends Donald Carswell (a barrister who had checked *Women in Love* for libel) and his wife, Catherine, who helped type the manuscript of *Lady Chatterley's Lover* and, after Lawrence's death, became his first biographer. Lawrence wrote his 1924 short story, *The Last Laugh*, in and about the house.

New End Square

Burgh House, New End Square at Flask Walk
Now a small local history museum, Burgh House was home in the 1720s to William Gibbons, the man who 'proved' Hampstead's waters to be medicinal. Two hundred years later the elderly Rudyard Kipling

Of Mice and Admen – George Orwell's Aspidistra-infested Hampstead

Orwell's 1936 novel, *Keep the Aspidistra Flying*, is a biting satire on society's pre-occupation with money and respectability, as seen through the eyes of Gordon Comstock, a waspish would-be poet ('author of *Mice*, a sneaky little foolscap octavo') who quits his safe job in advertising to sink into his own dead-end and, hopefully, money-free world. More conspicuous at times than Comstock is the aspidistra plant, in those days a symbol of petit-bourgeois England. (Graham Greene wrote in the *Evening News* in 1930 about trying to 'discover what lies behind the dark, thick leaf of the aspidistra that guards like an exotic fungus the vulnerable gap between the lace curtains'.) Much of the action in the novel takes place in Hampstead, where Orwell then lived.

roughly clockwise from Willoughby Road

Gordon Comstock's address, 31 Willoughby Road

Comstock, the novel's anti-hero, lives at no. 31, a house which smells of dishwater and cabbage, under the iron rule of a frightful landlady, Mrs Wisbeach. In the front window, below a green card advertising 'apartments', is 'the peeping foliage of an aspidistra'. Orwell cast Willoughby Road as 'dingy depressing' Willowbed Road, which tries to keep up a 'mingy lower middle class decency'.

head north to Willow Road, turn right and take its continuation, South End Road

Keats Grove (Coleridge Grove)

In the novel Coleridge Grove, a 'damp, shadowy secluded road', is where Paul Doring, the art critic who fails to inform Comstock of the cancellation of his literary soirée, lives. Coleridge Grove – 'Coleridge was rumoured to have lived there for six weeks in the summer of 1821' – is evidently based on Keats Grove, just west of the Heath, where Keats did live from 1818 to 1820. Doring is partly based on the critic, Geoffrey Grigson, who edited the poetry magazine, *New Verse*, from no. 4a Keats Grove in the 1930s.

rented it out, primarily to his daughter, Elsie, and her husband, Captain George Bambridge. Kipling's last trip before he died in 1936 was to visit her here.

Flask Walk

Flask Walk is named after the long-gone Flask Tavern (see above) and is where Clarissa Harlowe lodges in Samuel Richardson's *Clarissa* (1748). Alfred, Lord Tennyson's sister lived at no. 75, Rosemount, and he spent some time there. The studded gateway to the left of the house *return to South End Road and head south, turning left at South Hill Park*

77 Parliament Hill
Orwell wrote some of the novel while living here, on the edge of the Heath, in 1935.

return to South End Road and turn left

Inspiration for Mr McKechnie's Bookshop, South End Green at Pond Street
Comstock's menial job, working in Mr McKechnie's bookshop, is based on Orwell's own experiences working at the shop, Booklovers' Corner, that stood here in the 1930s. Despite finding the work reasonably interesting, Orwell hated living in London and relieved his frustrations by exaggerating the shop's worst points in the novel.

The White Horse (Prince of Wales), 154 Fleet Road
Comstock yearns to be able to afford a drink in the White Horse (based on the Prince of Wales), which he can see from Mr McKechnie's bookshop. In the 1980s the local residents' association successfully campaigned for the retention of the pub's clock in honour of its mention in the novel.

head west along Pond Street and turn right at Rosslyn Hill

The Crichton Arms (King of Bohemia), 10 Hampstead High Street
Flaxman, Comstock's jovial flat-mate, spends most of his non-working hours trying to pinch the barmaid's bum in the Crichton (based on the King of Bohemia) but fails to entice Comstock to join him. To Comstock, the pub 'seemed like paradise when he had no money but bored and disgusted him when he could afford to go there'. When Comstock finally summons up the sociability to join Flaxman, he hovers at the entrance, enticed by the 'warm fog of smoke and beer', but his nerve fails him.

is from Newgate Gaol, and was moved here when the prison was demolished in 1902.

Kingsley Amis's address (1976–82), Gardnor House, Flask Walk at Gardnor Road
Amis, who was living in Barnet, further north, moved to this listed Georgian property in order to be nearer the London literary drinking circuit from which he was feeling increasingly isolated. During his Hampstead period, his marriage to Elizabeth Jane Howard broke down; when she moved out, she left on the mantelpiece a note,

explaining her reasons, which he failed to spot for several days. Amis found it hard to cope alone and, after much discussion, Howard agreed to come back, provided that he gave up drinking, reminding him of an incident in which he had had to crawl upstairs on all fours after a few too many had rendered him incapable of standing up. Amis admitted he couldn't do without the booze, so Howard refused to come back. Amis, who couldn't bear living alone, soon formed an odd *ménage-à-trois* with his ex-wife, Hilly Bardwell, and her new husband, Lord Kilmarnock. This arrangement continued when they moved to Kentish Town in 1982, shortly before one of the walls at Gardnor House collapsed.

Well Walk

Hampstead's rural lethargy was disturbed in the eighteenth century when waters with supposed health-giving properties were discovered in a well. A Pump Room was opened (it stood opposite where Gainsborough Gardens meets Well Walk) and the village began marketing itself as a spa to rival Bath and Tunbridge Wells. Alexander Pope and Dr Johnson came here to use the waters, but Fanny Burney's Evelina talks of the horrors of an evening there in the novel of the same name (1778). John Keats, when he was dying of consumption, was spotted by the antiquarian, William Hone, sitting on a bench in Well Walk 'sobbing his dying breath into a handkerchief'.

west side: south to north

John Masefield's address (1914–16), no. 13
The plaque on the wall commemorates not Masefield, who became poet laureate in the 1930s, established poetry festivals and convinced the government to found the King's Medal for poetry, but the residency of Henry Hyndman, one of the founders of English socialism.

J. B. Priestley's address (1929–31), no. 27
Priestley moved into this fearsome-looking red-brick Queen Anne-style house just after the success of *The Good Companions* (1929).

east side: north to south

T. Sturge Moore's address (1929–40), no. 40
Frieda von Richtofen was staying at this address (once home to the painter John Constable) in 1912 when she eloped with D. H. Lawrence. A little while later, the engraver and poet, T. Sturge Moore, moved in. Moore, once described by A. E. Housman as a 'sheep in sheep's cloth-

ing', had been loosely connected with the Aesthetic Movement back in the 1890s and had associated with Yeats and Pound. By the 1930s Moore, with his wizened white beard and skull cap, had become the Grand Old Man of the London poetry scene, and no. 40 was renowned for its Friday night 'at-homes', at which Moore surrounded himself with young literary hopefuls and would manically recite his own verse, which some claimed to be better than Yeats's but others found absurd ('Quit the earth and climb a cloud' was his most-repeated line). George Orwell occasionally attended, even though he hated literary salons, and once took along his mother, who fell asleep.

D. H. Lawrence's address (1917), no. 32
After being evicted from Cornwall, where the authorities thought Lawrence's wife, Frieda, was a German spy, the couple returned to Hampstead to stay here at the home of the poets Dollie and Ernest Radford.

Site of John Keats's address (1817–18), Wells Tavern
Keats and his two brothers lived for a while in the local postman's house and the poet moved out when one of his brothers, Tom, died. The house, which stood by the now culverted River Fleet, was demolished when the Wells Tavern was enlarged in 1817.

Marie Stopes's address (1918), no. 14
Although her marriage to R. R. Gates was a disaster, Stopes used it as the basis for *Married Love*, which she wrote here. Some years later, Stopes had a relationship with Lord Alfred Douglas, Oscar Wilde's one-time boyfriend and downfall.

turn left at Willow Road

Willoughby Road

Both D. H. Lawrence and George Orwell had bad memories of this street with its tightly packed houses. Although a desirable address now, on account of the lack of redevelopment and the influx of money, the street and much of the area was quite shabby between the wars when Lawrence and Orwell knew it.

D. H. Lawrence's address (1926), no. 30
Lawrence stayed here during his last visit to London in 1926 when he was suffering from bronchial haemorrhages.

Gordon Comstock's address, no. 31
See Orwell box, above.

Downshire Hill

Edwin Muir's address (1932–5), no. 7

When Muir and his wife, Willa Anderson, moved in, they found the garden at no. 7 filled with bones and shells. The woman who had previously lived there had been bed-ridden and had thrown meat bones and oyster shells out of her bedroom window into the garden. Muir and Anderson spent much of their time in Downshire Hill translating Kafka into English and having nightmares about the stories. They also threw literary parties, to which they invited George Orwell – who steadfastly refused to attend because Muir was Scottish. Muir wrote in his autobiography that he was 'in love with its [the house's] sweet battered Mozartian grace . . . the house itself was a source of happiness. It was an old dilapidated Strawberry Hill Gothic house which vibrated gently whenever the underground train passed beneath it.' After the Muirs moved out, the tennis champion, Bunny Austin, moved in.

Keats Grove

Originally called Wentworth Place, it was renamed after its most famous resident in the nineteenth century. George Orwell depicted it as Coleridge Grove in *Keep the Aspidistra Flying* (see box, above).

John Keats's address (1818–20), Keats House, tel. 020 7435-2062.

Hampstead tube. Open Mon.–Fri. 10–1, 2–6 p.m., Sun. 2–5 p.m. Apr.–Oct. only. Admission free.

Now a small museum dedicated to the poet, Keats House was originally two properties, one of which belonged to a Charles Armitage Brown, into which Keats moved in 1818 when he was ill with consumption. In the house next door, which has since been joined with this, lived the 18-year-old Fanny Brawne, with whom Keats fell in love. They got engaged but she was told to avoid spending too much time with him in case it made his condition worse. The house and the gardens inspired a number of Keats's poems, including *On Melancholy* and *Ode to a Nightingale*, which he wrote in the bedroom overlooking the garden.

In October 1819 Keats moved to Great College Street, just south of Westminster Abbey, because his obsession with Fanny made it difficult for him to do any work, but he found it impossible to be away from her, and he came back to Wentworth Place a few weeks later. By this time Keats was so ill he had begun coughing up blood which, with his medical training, he knew came from an artery: 'I cannot be deceived in that colour – that drop of blood – it is my death warrant – I must die,' he told people. The Shelleys urged him to go with them to Italy to recuperate, but he died there in February 1821, aged 25.

A hundred years later, in 1920, the local council bought the house after public subscription saved it from demolition and opened it as a museum. One of the first visitors was Thomas Hardy who was inspired to write the poem, *At a House in Hampstead* (1920), which contrasts Keats's Hampstead with that of Hardy's time. Keats House now contains the poet's annotated books, letters, personal possessions, mementoes, manuscripts, lecture notes from Guy's Hospital (where Keats did his medical training), paintings, locks of hair, his writing desk, a bust of Shakespeare and engagement gifts.

Sylvia Lynd's address (1930s), no. 5

Lynd was a poet, novelist and short story writer, and visitors to her regular Friday night sessions here in the 1930s included Rose Macaulay, Max Beerbohm, J. B. Priestley, Humbert Wolfe and the publisher, Victor Gollancz. Wolfe and Gollancz used to do a Yiddish skit at the Friday night events which went:

'What sort of composer was Mozart?'

'Mozart, Mozart, a rotten composer!'

'Why, he wrote Faust.'

'No he didn't.'

'What, he didn't even write Faust? Didn't I say he was a rotten composer.'

James Joyce and Nora Barnacle had their wedding lunch at no. 5 after getting married at Hampstead Town Hall in 1931. Joyce sang and played the piano.

Edith Sitwell's address (1964), Bryher House, no. 20

Just before she died here, Sitwell told a friend, 'I am dying but otherwise quite well.'

Hampstead Hill Gardens

Aldous Huxley's address (1919–20), no. 18

Huxley moved into this grand stucco semi after getting married in Belgium and he put considerable energy into the furnishing and decorating, buying some 'nice pink wallpaper' and a carpet from Heal's. At the time he was working for John Middleton Murry's magazine, *The Athenaeum*, but he also wrote some war poetry while he was here and a collection of short stories, *Limbo*. Hampstead Hill Gardens wasn't too wise a choice for an address: both the Northern Line tube and the North London Railway run underneath.

SOUTH END

Tiny South End Green, the junction of Pond Street and South End Road, features as a setting in John Wyndham's *The Day of the Triffids* (1951) and John Le Carré's *Smiley's People* (1980). The Green's gents' toilet won a lavish refurbishment grant in 1999, helped by the fact that it was Joe Orton's favourite pick-up point.

- Landmarks can be reached from Hampstead Heath railway station.

South End Green to Parliament Hill end: west to east

Pond Street

George Orwell's address (1934–5), 3 Warwick Mansions, east end of Pond Street
For most of the time Orwell worked in Booklovers' Corner (see below), he lived in rooms in this dingy block, where he wrote some of *A Clergyman's Daughter* (1935). After hours Orwell would invite the shop's assistant, Jon Kimche (later literary editor of *Tribune*), up for chats in which he would rail against the British Empire, rich Cambridge graduates and anything else that took his fancy. In February 1935 Orwell moved to Parliament Hill.

George Orwell's workplace (1934–6)/Mr McKechnie's Bookshop, Pond Street at South End Green
George Orwell's experiences in the mid-1930s working in the bookshop, Booklovers' Corner, which then stood at this corner, provided him with the background for Gordon Comstock's job in Mr McKechnie's bookshop in *Keep the Aspidistra Flying* (1936). Orwell recalled that Booklovers' Corner was frequented by 'all types from baronets to bus-conductors' and featured 'an exceptionally interesting stock'. One of those whom Orwell served was the young Peter Vansittart (later a novelist) who wanted P. G. Wodehouse's *A Damsel in Distress* but emerged with Alfred Aloysius Horn's *Trader Horn in Madagascar* after a conversation with the author. Orwell worked here until early 1936, when Victor Gollancz asked him to report on social conditions among Wigan miners, a trip that resulted in *The Road to Wigan Pier* (1937). The bookshop closed in the 1960s, became a chess

café, and is now a pizza parlour. There is a bust of Orwell on the wall above the shop.

Parliament Hill

Anna Wickham's address (1920s), no. 68

Wickham, the Australian poet, held literary salons in this house (nicknamed Bourgeois Towers) that were attended by D. H. Lawrence and Dylan Thomas, who wrote *Adventures in the Skin Trade* (1955) in the bathroom. Malcolm Lowry began frequenting the place regularly in autumn 1932, having been rescued from a drab bed-sit existence in Bloomsbury by Wickham's son, James Hepburn.

George Orwell's address (1935), no. 77

Friends urged Orwell to move here because the Heath-side location was thought to be congenial to his weak lungs. Unfortunately, the room was just as damp as previous addresses. It was also furnished with little more than a 'Bachelor Griller', which allowed only the most basic cooking and no baking. Nevertheless, Orwell threw a dinner party for the poet, T. Sturge Moore (see Well Walk, p. 304), and Cyril Connolly, who was amazed at his old school chum's haggard demeanour. While living here, Orwell wrote some of *Keep the Aspidistra Flying* (1936), although the novel's hideous landlady, Mrs Wisbeach, was far removed from no. 77's kindly owner, Mrs Obermeyer.

WEST END

Full of secret corners and little lanes running off the winding Frognal, this area is quintessential village Hampstead and includes some of outer London's most desirable addresses.

• Landmarks can be reached from Hampstead tube.

Heath end to Swiss Cottage end: roughly north to south

Hampstead Grove

George Du Maurier's address (1874–95), no. 28

Du Maurier, grandfather of Daphne, was a cartoonist for *Punch* but is best known as an author for *Trilby* (1894), the book which introduced the character, Svengali. Du Maurier initially offered the story to Henry James, who was visiting one day, having walked from Mayfair, but the latter, having little feeling for music, declined to take it. This rambling churchy house has since been divided into flats.

head west

Admiral's Walk

John Galsworthy's address (1918–33) and deathsite/Grove Lodge
One of only two houses in Admiral's Walk, whitewashed Grove Lodge, with its green shutters, was once home to the artist, John Constable, and was where Galsworthy wrote the last section of the seemingly interminable *Forsyte Saga* (1922). In 1932 Galsworthy won the Nobel Prize for Literature, but when he announced that he was too ill to collect the award a delegation came here to deliver it. The author died at Grove Lodge soon afterwards.

Admiral's House
This maritime-looking property – the roof resembles the quarterdeck of a ship – was the model for Admiral Boom's house in *Mary Poppins* (1934), the P. L. Travers novel immortalized on film by Julie Andrews. In the nineteenth century Admiral's House was home to Gothic architect, George Gilbert Scott, who designed the hotel in front of St Pancras station (see p. 290).

continue along Admiral's Walk

Windmill Hill

Joanna Baillie's address (*c.* 1791–1851), Bolton House, Windmill Hill at Mount Vernon
Baillie hosted London's first literary salon in this red-brick Georgian house, with Walter Scott and Wordsworth regular visitors. Wordsworth described Baillie as the 'ablest authoress of the day' and used to walk from central London to Hampstead to stroll around the Heath with her.

head up Mount Vernon

Mount Vernon

Robert Louis Stevenson's address (1870s), Abernethy House, no. 7
While staying in this black-brick villa, Stevenson wrote to a friend: 'Hampstead is the most delightful place for air and scenery near London.'

Frognal Gardens

Walter Besant's address (1893–1901), no. 18
Better known nowadays for his histories than for his novels, Besant,
while living in Hampstead, produced a series of potted histories on
areas of London (such as Shoreditch) that had hitherto been largely
ignored. Besant also founded the Authors' Club to protect authors'
rights and was behind the building of the People's Palace entertainments and educational centre in Mile End. After the Second World
War, Labour politician Hugh Gaitskell (whose wife ran off with Ian
Fleming) moved into no. 18, which he liked so much that he stayed
on here even when he had become Chancellor of the Exchequer in
the 1950s.

detour west along Redington Road and Oakhill Avenue

Bracknell Gardens

Aldous Huxley's address (1917–19), no. 16
Huxley in his early twenties was working as a clerk at the Air Board
when he lived in this suburban road with his father and stepmother.
He hated the Air Board job, moaning that everyone wanted to talk
about making money and their 'hideous homes', while the sixty-hour
week meant that he was so tired in the evenings he couldn't even read,
let alone attempt any writing. Huxley lasted in the job only a few
months and then tried to join the forces, but was rejected by the Army
Medical Board and ended up teaching at Eton. He left Bracknell Gardens for Hampstead Hill Gardens when he married in 1919.

return east to Frognal

Church Row

A short, elegant street of handsome Georgian houses connecting Frognal with Heath Street.

St John's, Church Row opposite Frognal Gardens
Gerard Manley Hopkins and the Du Mauriers are among those who
have worshipped in Hampstead's parish church, built in 1745, which
also contains (near the lectern) a marble bust of Keats, erected by a
group of American Keats-lovers in 1894, and a memorial to Joanna
Baillie, the Scottish poet and playwright who lived nearby in Windmill
Hill. William Morris and Anthony Trollope were among those who

campaigned for the retention of the tower in the nineteenth century. George Du Maurier, Hugh Gaitskell (the former Labour leader) and the architect, Norman Shaw, are buried in the churchyard.

H. G. Wells's address (1909–12), no. 17

Despite the spaciousness of these houses, Wells found no. 17 cramped and he longed for a house in the country with a proper country garden. David Garnett, who wrote a biography of the Bloomsbury Group, recalled how, when he turned up at one of the author's Church Row parties, he found the guests chasing each other around the room and knocking over the furniture. Arnold Bennett, in his *Journal*, wrote of another 17 Church Row dinner party at which he and Wells 'talked his scandal from 12.15 to lunch-time'. Soon after moving in, Wells eloped with Amber Reeves, returning to Church Row only inter-mittently.

Lord Alfred Douglas's address (1907–10), no. 26

Lord Alfred Douglas, or 'Bosie', Oscar Wilde's one-time lover and ruin, moved here with his wife (he was by now officially heterosexual) shortly after winning a libel suit against *The Daily News*, which had run an obituary calling him a degenerate, only to find he was still alive. Though not a great writer, the peer was highly rated by the young John Betjeman, who told C. S. Lewis, his tutor at Oxford, that Douglas was a better poet than Shakespeare.

Frognal

This winding hilly road has been home to writers (Dr Johnson, Kate Greenaway and Stephen Spender), musicians (Kathleen Ferrier, Dennis Brain) and two major twentieth-century politicians (Charles de Gaulle and Ramsay MacDonald, the first Labour prime minister, characterized as the odious Hamer Shawcross in Howard Spring's *Fame is the Spur* (1940), who lived at no. 103 from 1925 to 1937).

Site of Priory Lodge, between Frognal Way and University College School

Dr Johnson used to come to Priory Lodge between 1748 and 1752 to stay with his wife, Tetty, who was staying here while recovering from her heavy drinking. At Priory Lodge, Johnson wrote *The Vanity of Human Wishes* (1749). A rare concrete modernist house stands on the site.

Kate Greenaway's address (1885–1901), no. 39
When Greenaway, the children's book writer and illustrator, moved
into this Norman Shaw-designed house, she told the architect, 'If you'd
ever lived in Holloway you'd know what sort of a paradise Hampstead
must seem.' John Ruskin asked her 'not to call your house a villa.
Could you call it Kate's State or Kitty's Green or something of that
sort?'

Stephen Spender's address (1920s), no. 10
Spender, who became one of the 1930s' so-called pylon poets, described
no. 10 as 'an ugly house in the Hampstead style, as if built from the
box of bricks of a nineteenth-century German child'. Spender was edu-
cated at University College School, a few hundred yards to the north,
which is built above the source of the long-culverted River Westbourne.

Netherhall Gardens

Sidney and Beatrice Webb's address (1892–3), no. 10
Fabians and leading thinkers for the burgeoning Labour Party, the
Webbs moved here on marrying and wrote that 'gloomy weather now
finds us settled 300ft above the sea in a cosy little flat in south Hampstead'. Every morning the Webbs began work on their history of trade
unionism about 9.30 a.m. and wrote solidly until 1.30 p.m., when
Sidney left for the London County Council offices. Their report on the
Poor Law Commission in 1909 was instrumental in the creation of the
welfare state, but the Webbs later became Stalin apologists, claiming
that the slaughter of the Ukrainian Kulaks was necessary in the interests of increased agricultural output.

Maresfield Gardens

**Freud Museum, no. 20, tel. 020 7435-2002. Open Wed.–Sun.
noon–5 p.m. Admission £2.50.**
Freud came here in 1938 after fleeing the Nazis and, although he died
soon after from cancer, his daughter, Anna (a child analyst), continued
to live here until her death in 1982. Freud's study and library have been
maintained to look as they did when he lived here, and one of Freud's
psychoanalyst's couches is still in place.

BELSIZE PARK

Taking its name from the French _bel assis_ (beautifully situated), Belsize
Park is beginning to fade as an exclusive area as more houses are converted into student bed-sits.

• Landmarks can be reached from Swiss Cottage or Belsize Park tubes.

Bookshops

Daunt, 193 Haverstock Hill, Belsize Park, tel. 020 7794-4006, are travel
book specialists.

Swiss Cottage end to Belsize Park tube: roughly west to east

Finchley Road

The Woman in White setting, Finchley Road at Swiss Cottage
In Wilkie Collins's _The Woman in White_ (1860), Walter Hartright is
walking by this junction when 'in one moment every drop of blood in
my body was brought to a stop by the touch of a hand laid lightly and
suddenly on my shoulder from behind me . . . There in the middle of
the broad bright high road . . . stood the figure of a solitary woman
dressed from head to foot in white.' The scene is based on a real-life
incident in which Collins, walking along the road with the painter, Millais, met a girl called Caroline Graves who had just fled a lunatic
asylum. Collins later moved in with her.

head north

Fitzjohn's Avenue

Stella Gibbons's address (1930–32), no. 67
Gibbons wrote _Cold Comfort Farm_ (1932), her most famous novel, in
this huge red-brick semi as well as on the Northern Line tube _en route_
to her job with _The Lady_ magazine.

head east through the back streets

Belsize Park Gardens

Lytton Strachey's address (1907–14), no. 67
Strachey wrote _Eminent Victorians_ (1918), his collection of revealing bio-
graphies about leading nineteenth-century figures, including Florence

Nightingale and Thomas Arnold, in a bed-sit in this imposing white-washed villa. In his letters, Strachey referred to the 'ghastly solitude' of the house and described how downstairs 'there is a basement billiard room, the darkest chamber I've ever seen in my life'. Strachey was so depressed at the time, he even proposed to Virginia Woolf. In 1914 the family moved to no. 6.

head east to the main road

Lawn Road

Agatha Christie's address (1940s), Isokon Flats
A still remarkable-looking Bauhaus 1930s building, the first modernist block of flats built in England, Isokon was created as a haven for artists and writers fleeing the Nazis (and for those closer to home looking to break away from English insularity), and early residents included Agatha Christie, Henry Moore, Bauhaus founder Walter Gropius and Nicholas Monsarrat (author of *The Cruel Sea*). As part of the modernist ideology, designer Wells Coates installed a bar, Isobar, in the basement (residents holed up there during the Blitz mistakenly believed they were immune from the bombs); but the building had its detractors, with Cyril Connolly's *Horizon* magazine voting it second in its Ugliest Building competition for 1946. Isokon's popularity declined after the war, and in 1968 a developer sold it to *The New Statesman* magazine, who tore out Isobar to build more flats and then sold the block to Camden council. It is now graffiti'd and boarded up, awaiting restoration.

return to Haverstock Hill and head north

Haverstock Hill

Setting for George R. Sims's little-known *Haverstock Hill Murder* (1897) which, astonishingly for the time, features a female detective, Dorcas Dene.

Hampstead Town Hall, Haverstock Hill at Belsize Avenue
Lytton Strachey, who lived in Belsize Park at the start of the First World War, was obliged to report to the army at the Town Hall in 1917 to explain why he wouldn't sign up to fight. 'What would you do if a German soldier raped your sister?' an officer asked him, to which Strachey gave his infamous reply, 'I would try and come between them.' James Joyce married Nora Barnacle here in July 1931 after thirty-six years together.

Kentish Town, NW5

Despite the rustic name, Kentish Town is a depressing slice of urbania halfway between picturesque Highgate and lively Camden Town.

- Landmarks can be reached from Kentish Town tube.

Bookshops

The Owl Bookshop, 211 Kentish Town Road, tel. 020 7485-7793, is strong on literature, history and children's books.

Gospel Oak station end to Camden Town end: roughly north to south

Lissendsen Gardens

John Betjeman's birthplace and address (1906), 52 Parliament Hill Mansions, Lissendsen Gardens

The much-loved poet was born a Betjemann, as opposed to a Betjeman. His grandfather had added a final 'n' to Betjeman in the mid-nineteenth century when the popularity of Prince Albert led to a fashion for Germania, but the Germanic ending was dropped, appropriately, at the outset of the First World War. Betjeman was always pleased that he'd been born within a few hundred yards of a station – in this case Gospel Oak – on his favourite railway, the North London Line, even though he was never fond of the area, which has since gone even more downhill. The Betjemanns moved a little further north to Highgate soon after John's birth when business picked up at his father's cabinet-making firm.

head down Highgate Road towards Kentish Town station

Leighton Road

Kingsley Amis's address (1982–5), no. 186

Amis moved in with his former wife, Hilly Bardwell, and her new husband, Lord Kilmarnock, but was unhappy because he couldn't find any pubs without piped music. The house was smaller than Amis was used to and, to raise funds to buy a bigger house, he sold some of his archive, which included letters from John Betjeman.

head south

Lawford Road

George Orwell's address (1935–6), no. 50

Orwell's housemates in this typical north-west London semi were Michael Sayers, an aspiring writer, and Rayner Heppenstall, a ballet critic and drinking partner of Dylan Thomas who later wrote some obscure novels and claimed that Orwell's early novels were the type that seemed 'not worth writing'. A routine was soon established in the flat: breakfast consisted of gravy dips – flour paste fried in yesterday's oil – and in the evening Heppenstall would be sent out for a jug of ale from the nearest pub. Once, when Heppenstall came home from a show very late and very drunk, Orwell tore into him for his 'lack of consideration' and stood in the doorway delivering a rant which took the form: '. . . time of night . . . put up with a lot . . . bit of consideration . . . after all.' When Heppenstall objected, Orwell laid him out. The wounded Heppenstall woke up a few minutes later to find his nose bleeding; he cleaned himself up and decided to sleep in Michael Sayers's unoccupied bed, only for Orwell to lock him in the room. When Heppenstall angrily demanded to be released, Orwell reappeared with a shooting stick, which he used to poke Heppenstall in the stomach. The plumber who lived below eventually rescued the hapless ballet critic and revealed how Orwell's typing often kept him up till four in the morning. The next day, when tempers had cooled, Orwell called Heppenstall into his room, lectured him on his behaviour in his best Burmese policeman manner, and turfed him out of the house. Orwell himself left soon after, early in 1936, after being commissioned by Victor Gollancz for the work which became *The Road to Wigan Pier*.

Kentish Town Road

Former South Kentish Town station, Kentish Town Road at Castle Road

In John Betjeman's bizarre short story, 'South Kentish Town' (1951), Basil Green, an 'income tax official' who works in Whitehall and takes the Northern Line tube home after work, mistakenly gets off the train at the recently disused South Kentish Town when the train driver opens the doors to check a fault on the line. Green, engrossed in his newspaper, doesn't realize he's got off at the wrong stop until the train shoots off, leaving him in darkness. Frantically Green tries to flag down passing trains, to no avail. Without matches, and only the occasional passing train to guide him, he finds an opening in the platform and climbs the spiral stairs – until his head hits the floor of one of the

John Betjeman's Courts of Kentish Town

The John Betjeman poem, *Parliament Hill Fields* (1945), charts a tram's journey from Kentish Town up the hill to Highgate, a journey that parallels Betjeman's own childhood social climb from the Gospel Oak block of flats where he was born to the Highgate villa where his family moved when he was young. The poem is named after Parliament Hill, open heathland at the eastern edge of Hampstead Heath, which at 319 feet is one of the highest points in London. As a boy, Betjeman used to sit here with his friend, Bill, and say, 'We will write poetry.' The 'Parliament' prefix arises from an unreliable legend that Guy Fawkes and his followers came here to watch the Houses of Parliament burn down during their unsuccessful attempt at blowing them up.

'Rumbling under blackened girders, Midland, bound for Cricklewood,'

The poem opens with a Midland Line train making its way through Kentish Town and Gospel Oak *en route* for Cricklewood, chosen by Betjeman probably because of its typical suburban connotations. When Betjeman moved to Highgate and heard a train in the distance, he gladdened himself with the thought that 'I did not live in Gospel Oak'.

'train and tram alternate go,'

The rhythmical pattern of the poem reflects the rattling of the wheels on the tram and train lines. The tram was a London County Council horse-drawn Number 7 which were open top and brown coloured.

'Shake the floor and smudge the ledger, Charrington, Sells, Dale and Co.,/ Nuts and nuggets in the window, trucks along the lines below.'

The movement of the vehicles is smudging the clerks' ledgers at the coal merchant's, Charrington, Sells, Dale and Co., which was based at Gospel Oak station. The 'nuts and nuggets in the window, trucks along the lines below' refers to the coal samples that were displayed in miniature railway trucks in the office window.

'Outside Charrington's we waited, by the "STOP HERE IF REQUIRED",'

There was a tram request stop outside Charrington's.

'Launched aboard the shopping basket, sat precipitately down,'

The tram was built to accommodate large numbers of shoppers and, as soon as people boarded, it would quickly set off, causing them to fall into their seats too quickly.

'Rocked past Zwanziger the baker's'

The German baker's, A. Zwanziger, was based at 385 Kentish Town Road. At the outset of the First World War thugs, riding on a wave of anti-Germanic feeling, stove in the windows. The premises are now occupied by a fish-and-chip shop.

'And the curious Anglo-Norman Parish Church of Kentish Town.'
The parish church is St John the Baptist in Highgate Road, opposite Fortress Walk. Its 'curious feature' is its double spire, the northerly one of which is slightly twisted.

'Past municipal lawn tennis'
By now the tram has passed the railway bridges over Highgate Road which act as a border between grimy Kentish Town and genteel Highgate. North of this bridge, gloomy warehouses and run-down pubs gradually give way to tennis courts, a typical Betjemanian symbol of suburbia to which he often returned (as in *The Olympic Girl* and *A Subaltern's Love-song*). The courts referred to in this poem can be found in Highgate Road opposite St Alban's Road on the edge of Parliament Hill Fields.

'ashlar-speckled spire,/Eighteen-sixty Early English,'
The church is St Anne's at the bottom of Highgate West Hill, but it was actually built in 1855, not 1860.

'Either side of Brookfield Mansions'
Brookfield Mansions is an Art Nouveau Edwardian block of flats at the bottom of Highgate West Hill by Swain's Lane.

'Silver music from the bandstand, barking dogs by Highgate Pond;'
There's a bandstand just west of Highgate Ponds which Betjeman mentioned in *Summoned By Bells* (1960).

'Up the hill where stucco houses in Virginia creeper drown'
The journey from Kentish Town to Highgate Village finishes in the long climb of West Hill, where Betjeman lived.

'And my childish wave of pity, seeing children carrying down/Sheaves of drooping dandelions to the courts of Kentish Town.'
The Betjemans, despite moving up the social scale and the hill to Highgate, have come back to Kentish Town to shop. Returning home, the young Betjeman gives the poor children, who have picked pitiful withering flowers, a 'childish wave of pity' as he passes them *en route* back to Highgate.

shops above. Green bangs his umbrella against the floorboards but, being Friday night, no one is there. In desperation he makes his way down the stairs and starts examining the lift shafts. Climbing, he spots a light at the top, but when he gets there, holding on to the ledge with one hand, the light goes out. Down Green climbs again, and this time he lies down on the platform, wondering what his wife must be thinking – which is where the story abruptly ends.

St John's Wood, NW8

Tree-lined streets of rambling, lavishly designed houses abound in this wealthy district between Hampstead and Marylebone, best known as the home of Lord's cricket ground. The area wasn't always as respectable as it is now. In the nineteenth century it was dotted with high-class brothels and houses where politicians and aristocrats kept their mistresses, which explains why John Galsworthy claimed it was an area in which 'no Forsyte liked to be seen'. Rebecca West thought differently, and in *Sunflower*, her unfinished fictionalized account of her love for newspaper magnate Lord Beaverbrook and the breakdown of her relationship with H. G. Wells, which she wrote in the 1920s, the eponymous heroine looks out of the limousine's windows at St John's Wood, 'liking it all. She liked the neat, little stone houses, their whiteness tinted two colours by the evening . . . the young men and girls walking along in light things and carrying tennis rackets'.

• Landmarks can be reached from St John's Wood tube.

Hampstead end to Lord's: roughly north to south

Abbey Road

George Orwell's address (1941–2), 111 Lanford Court, Abbey Road at Langford Place
Orwell and his wife, Eileen, moved to this block of flats after H. G. Wells, mistakenly believing they had been gossiping about him behind his back, kicked them out of a flat above his garage by Regent's Park. A little while later, Orwell tried to patch things up by inviting Wells to dinner. Wells accepted the invitation and, to the Orwells' amazement, wrote back wondering why they had left the flat so suddenly. When he turned up for dinner, Wells warned the Orwells that he had a bad stomach and couldn't eat rich food. Unfortunately Eileen had made a

curry. 'Oh I couldn't eat that,' groaned Wells, 'just give me a little.' He
had two helpings. A few hours later, the critic, William Empson, turned
up and was offered some plum cake. 'Oh goody,' said Wells, and helped
himself to a slice. A week later, the Orwells received a curt letter from
Wells: 'You knew I was ill and on a diet, you deliberately plied me with
food and drink. I never want to see you again.' He never did.

head east along Langford Place

Loudon Road

Mary Baker, the inspiration for Thackeray's Becky Sharp from *Vanity
Fair* (1863), lived in this street in the nineteenth century.

Stephen Spender's address (1950), no. 15
When Ian Fleming met the elderly Raymond Chandler at a dinner
party at Spender's detached home in 1955, Chandler, to Fleming's
delight, praised the recently published Bond book, *Casino Royale*
(1952), and offered to write a few words of praise for the next edition,
something he never normally did. Chandler later sent Fleming some
complimentary lines, adding somewhat sarcastically at the end: 'If these
are any good would you like me to have them engraved on a gold slab?'

continue east

Acacia Road

Katherine Mansfield's address (1915), no. 5
Mansfield moved into this huge, pink-washed semi, 'near, but not too
near, Hampstead', as she put it, with her partner, John Middleton
Murry, editor of *Athenaeum*, when she was starting a magazine, *The
Signature*, with D. H. Lawrence. They moved out when news came in
that her brother had been killed in action at the front only a few days
after he had left England.

head south

Circus Road

Site of Verbena Lodge, no. 7
In the 1860s no. 7 was the setting for a society brothel-cum-whipping
house, much visited by Algernon Charles Swinburne in which, according to Edmund Gosse, 'two golden-haired and rouge-cheeked ladies
received in luxuriously furnished rooms gentlemen who they consented
to chastise for large sums'.

Wellington Road

Lord's, Wellington Road at St John's Wood

> *'Never play lady's game for the Lord's stake'* from *Finnegans Wake*, James Joyce, 1939

The home of English cricket has inspired much writing – mostly senti-mental stuff of little interest to non-cricket fans – but a few memorable poems, including Francis Thompson's *At Lords* (1908), which famously ends, 'O my Hornby and my Barlow long ago', referring to former Eng-land Test cricketers, A. N. Hornby and R. G. Barlow; and Siegfried Sas-soon's *The Blues at Lords* (1926). A number of writers have played at Lord's. In 1902 Arthur Conan Doyle captained an Authors vs. Pub-lishers match in which P. G. Wodehouse appeared for the authors. Conan Doyle also played for the home team, the MCC (Marylebone Cricket Club), in 1909 when he was nearly 50, taking a career-best 7 wickets for 51 runs against Cambridgeshire.

A rare Ian Fleming failure was a magazine which he planned to pro-duce for the 1927 match between his school, Eton, and Harrow. Flem-ing wrote to potential advertisers, promising 500 copies, but nothing came of it. George Orwell, visiting the ground for a game in 1940, paid a visit to the pavilion, the then males-only bastion of the MCC, and recalled in his diary how when he was an Eton scholar in the early '20s he would have felt that 'to go into the pavilion, not being a member of the MCC, was on a par with pissing on the altar and . . . a legal offence for which you could be prosecuted'. In *Downriver* (1991), Iain Sinclair relates the story of the MCC vs. the Aboriginals match of 1868, at the end of which the Aboriginals ran a hundred-yard sprint backwards, throwing boomerangs and spears and dodging cricket balls that the crowd had been urged to throw at them. A current member of the MCC is Harold Pinter.

West Hampstead, NW6

The area's relationship with Hampstead is tenuous. Much of NW6 lies within Kilburn (not a place with a literary history) and the streets near the three West Hampstead stations are now full of bed-sits, although the small enclave around where Evelyn Waugh was born has the sort of easy-going charm associated with Hampstead.

• Landmarks can be reached from West Hampstead railway station/tube.

Cricklewood end to St John's Wood End: north to south

Hillfield Road

Evelyn Waugh's birthplace and address (1903–8), no. 11
'Hillfield Road was not socially a good address,' Waugh later recalled, 'I
have no more memory of the house where this [his birth] occurred
than of the event itself.'

head south

West End Lane

Joe Orton's address (1951–9), 1a Regent Lodge, no. 161
Joe Orton, when he lived in a shabby flat in this villa long before he
became a well-known playwright, sent forth a volley of whingeing letters to companies and institutions under the guise of Edna Welthorpe,
a loony suburban mischief-maker. On one occasion 'Edna' tried unsuccessfully to hire the Heath Street Baptist Church Hall in Hampstead to
present a play called *The Pansy*, 'which pleads for greater tolerance on
the subject of homosexuality'. There was no such play, but Orton
simply liked the idea of people running around on account of his hare-
brained schemes.

After tiring of that scam, Orton/Welthorpe turned his ire on the
mail order firm, Littlewood's. 'Dear Sirs,' Edna Welthorpe wrote, 'I am
puzzled by several letters I have received from you . . . I assure you that
there is no one called Mr Orton living here.' When he started getting
bogged down in the firm's bureaucracy, Orton signed off in dramatic
fashion. Writing as Donald H. Hartley, he informed Littlewood's that
he had just taken over the flat from a 'disgusting black woman who left
the place in utter confusion'. The pranks were occasionally inspired by
self-interest. On one occasion Orton received eight tickets to the Insti-
tutional Trade Fashion Fair (which he did want to attend) after writing
off (as Edna Welthorpe) asking for 78! When the organizers wrote
back, asking why she wanted so many tickets, Orton wrote back as the
bemused Mrs W., claiming that she had merely asked for seven or eight
tickets, but adding that it was a matter of 'supreme indifference'
whether she or her firm went at all. The organizers, by now anxious to
keep in with someone who could become a major customer, sent eight.

Mortimer Crescent

Site of George Orwell's address (1942–4), no. 10a

When a V1 flying-bomb landed in the street in June 1944, causing Orwell's ceiling to collapse, the only manuscript copy of *Animal Farm* ended up lying in the rubble. Orwell and his wife, Eileen, rummaged around and found it. The script was still legible but needed a bit of cleaning up. The house has since been demolished.

FURTHER NORTH-WEST

Metroland

To tempt Londoners choked by city smog into the green suburbs of Wembley and Harrow (newly joined to London by train), the Metropolitan Railway Company came up with the marketing idea of 'Metroland' and produced gaily painted posters featuring happy couples soaking in the sun in idyllic pastoral surroundings. One tempted by the ads – though not into moving here – was John Betjeman, whose affectionate TV programme, also called *Metroland*, proclaimed the romance of generally ignored suburbs such as Rickmansworth and Pinner to add to the myriad of poems he based on other Middlesex villages.

Barnet

Best known for its ancient market and fair, Barnet at the far northern end of the Northern Line, was where Kingsley Amis moved in the late '60s when he fancied the country life.

Hadley Common

Kingsley Amis's address (1968–76), Gladsmuir, Hadley Common, High Barnet tube

Amis and his second wife, the novelist Elizabeth Jane Howard, bought this massive thirty-bedroom mansion on Hadley Common, a wild expanse of land (well, wild for outer London), after returning to England from a 1968 American lecture tour. Unsurprisingly, the house proved to be too big and Amis soon found himself lost in the vast space and nine-acre garden, which compounded his distress at being so far from the London drinking circuit. He used the house as the model for the home of Sir Roy Vandervane in his 1971 novel, *Girl, 20*. The following year the ailing poet laureate, Cecil Day Lewis, came here to stay and died here.

Harrow

In taking a journey through this monotonous part of Middlesex in his 1954 poem, *Harrow-on-the-hill*, John Betjeman is mentally transported to his beloved Cornwall and imagines Harrow-on-the-Hill as a 'rocky island' on the Cornish coast, the sound of the trolley-buses between the hill and Wealdstone reminding him of the surging waves, with the storm clouds gathering over Kenton and a 'line of harbour lights' at Perivale. The poem is also the first recorded example of the by-now-hackneyed rhyming of the words 'Wembley' and 'trembly'.

High Street

Harrow School, Harrow-on-the-Hill railway station/tube
When Sheridan was a pupil at this famous public school (founded 1571) in the 1760s, he carved his name on a panel in the fourth-form room. Byron, when he was a pupil between 1801 and 1805, carved his name on the same panel. In a letter he wrote in 1822, Byron claimed that the churchyard by the school was his favourite place; a marble plaque near the tomb of John Peachey in the graveyard is inscribed with a verse from the poet's *Lines Written Beneath an Elm* (1807). Trollope was a day-boy here in 1827, and Galsworthy and L. P. Hartley were later pupils. H. A. Vachell wrote a novel about the school called *The Hill* (1905).

Church Lane

St John the Baptist, Pinner tube
A monument on the wall of the south aisle is dedicated to the little-known eighteenth-century poet laureate, Henry James Pye, who was considered a bit of a dullard in his day and was one of the least-talented occupiers of the post. Indeed, Pye wrote so many bad verses in praise of George III that George Stevens wrote the lines: 'when the Pye was opened the birds began to sing, wasn't that a dandy dish to set before the king', which were later added to the nursery rhyme 'Sing a Song of Sixpence'.

SOUTH-EAST LONDON

Bankside, SE1

At the turn of the sixteenth century Bankside was one of the liveliest places in London, a centre of bear-baiting arenas, brothels and theatres (including the Globe, in which Shakespeare had an interest). Then the Puritans closed most of the venues, and over the following centuries it became a forgettable area of wharves and warehouses. In recent years Bankside has been brought back to life, thanks to the opening of the Elizabethan-styled Shakespeare's Globe Theatre and the refurbishment of the former Bankside power station into a new Tate Gallery, making the area a serious rival to the South Bank arts centre, a mile west.

- Landmarks can be reached from Southwark tube.

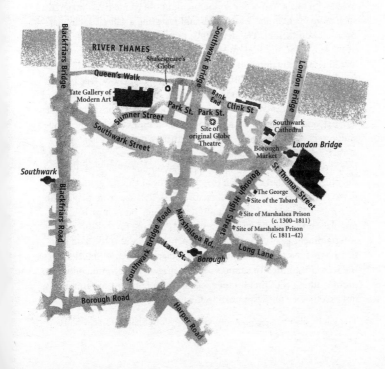

Blackfriars end to London Bridge end: west to east

Hopton Street

Site of Swan Theatre (1595–1640), west side

The largest of the sixteenth-century Bankside theatres, the Swan was built by Francis Langley in 1595 and two years later was caught up in a major row when the authorities deemed a performance of Thomas Nashe's play, *The Isle of Dogs*, to be seditious. Many of those involved, including Ben Jonson, who was one of the actors, were imprisoned in Marshalsea (see p. 333) and all London's theatres were subsequently closed down.

New Globe Walk

Shakespeare's Globe (1997–), New Globe Walk at Bankside, tel. 020 7902-1500

A remarkable addition to London's theatres, Shakespeare's Globe is a quasi-Elizabethan version of Shakespeare's original Globe Theatre, made with black-and-white timbering built out of medieval materials such as goat's hair and water reeds and featuring a galleried, circular open-air auditorium. The new Globe came about thanks to the efforts of the late actor and film director, Sam Wanamaker, but the project was long beset by difficulties. Lambeth council wouldn't sell the land south-east of Southwark Bridge where the original Globe (see below) stood, but, after agreeing to lease this plot, the political complexion of the council changed. Shakespeare was denounced as 'elitist' and the designated land was seized back for council houses. Eventually the Globe's supporters won the argument, and the theatre opened in 1997. It attracts what is for Britain an atypical theatre audience: raucous, restless, irreverent and prone to good-natured booing of villains. Productions, particularly 1997's *Henry V*, have been stunning, mainly through the efforts of artistic director, Mark Rylance (who played the title role in the above). The standing-room-only pit is surprisingly popular and is usually filled with students looking for a cheap night's entertainment, as well as the odd masochist who *wants* to stand for three hours. As the pit and most of the stage are open to the elements, the season is limited to summer. The management recommend waterproof clothing (not that it ever rains much in London) but umbrellas, not exactly very Shakespearean in the first place, are barred.

- The Globe also has permanent exhibitions on 'Shakespeare's World', open all year round.

Bear Gardens

> '*Why do your dogs bark so? be there bears i' the town?*' Abraham Slender
> from *The Merry Wives of Windsor*, William Shakespeare, 1602

Bear-baiting and dog-tossing, introduced to England from Italy during
the reign of King John, were popular activities in this area in medieval
times. A frequent spectator was Samuel Pepys, who wrote in his diary
for 14 August 1666: 'After dinner with my wife and Mercer to the Beare
Garden . . . and saw some good sport of the bull's tossing the dogs.'
Things didn't always go smoothly. One Sunday in January 1583 eight
people were killed when the scaffolding round the bear pit collapsed; the
Puritans claimed it was an act of God. The sport was outlawed in 1835.

Site of the Hope Theatre (1614–56), Bear Gardens at Park Street
The Hope took advantage of the burning-down of the nearby Globe
and opened in 1614 as a theatre-cum-bear-baiting garden, with the first
play a premiere of Ben Jonson's *Bartholomew Fair*. Plays were staged
on Mondays, Wednesdays, Fridays and Saturdays, and bears were
baited on Tuesday and Thursdays when the stage was taken down.
After a couple of years the plays were dropped and bears were baited
daily. The theatre was demolished in 1656.

Rose Alley

Site of the Rose Theatre (1587–1605), Rose Alley at Park Street
The first theatre in the area, the Rose was closely associated with
Christopher Marlowe and the actor, Edward Alleyn, believed to be the
finest of his generation (and later founder of Dulwich College), who
took the lead roles in Rose premieres of Marlowe's *Tamburlaine the
Great* (1587), *The Jew of Malta* (1589) and *Doctor Faustus* (1589). Shakespeare acted at the Rose when he first arrived in London, but the
theatre was not popular with the Corporation of London, who declared
that it was for 'thieves, horse-stealers, whore-mongers, cozeners, conny-
catching persons, practicers of treason and such other like'. The Rose's
foundations, discovered in 1988 beneath the office block that stands on
the site, can now be seen by the public (entrance by 56 Park Street) as
part of an exhibition on the theatre.

Park Street

Dr Johnson occasionally stayed with his friends, Henry and Hester
Thrale, in a grand town house in this street, where he wrote *Lives of the*

English Poets (1781). When Henry Thrale stood for Parliament in 1780, Johnson wrote his speeches. It wasn't until 1942 that Mrs Thrale's diaries were published.

Site of the Globe Theatre (1599–1613, 1614–44), south side of Park Street east of Southwark Bridge Road
The original Globe Theatre, built from the timbers of the Shoreditch theatre in Curtain Road (see p. 52) and owned by Shakespeare's friends, Cuthbert and Richard Burbage, saw the first run of a number of Shakespeare plays, including in 1599 *Henry V* (which opened the Globe and which refers to the theatre as 'this Wooden O' in its Prologue), *Julius Caesar* (1599) and *Cymbeline* (1611). During the premiere of *Henry VIII* in June 1613, cannons being used as stage props set the thatched roof ablaze and the theatre burned down (as witnessed outside by Ben Jonson, who had just returned from Europe). No one was injured, although one man had to be 'doused with pottle ale'. The Globe was rebuilt the next year, but was demolished in 1644 by the Puritans.

Bank End

The Anchor Inn, Bank End opposite Clink Street
Henry and Hester Thrale established a fashionable literary salon in the 1760s in the original Anchor, rebuilt in 1775. Patrons included Oliver Goldsmith, James Boswell and the philosopher, Edmund Burke.

Clink Street

Winchester Palace, Clink Street opposite Pickford's Wharf
The tumbledown remains of this former palace of the Bishops of Winchester stand near the site of the Clink prison which gave its name to the slang word for gaol.

The Borough, SE1

A run-down, decaying district immediately south of London Bridge, The Borough's literary history dates back to the fourteenth century, for it was from the Tabard, a pub that stood on what is now Borough High Street, that Chaucer's pilgrims set forth on their travels, as recounted in *The Canterbury Tales* (*c.* 1400). Due to its riverside location, the area became highly industrialized in the nineteenth century; the historian, George Dodd, wrote about its 'array of tall chimneys, each one a guide post to some large manufacturing establishment beneath' in 1843. Around this time The Borough was also a major location for prisons, which included Marshalsea (where Thomas Malory, Ben Jonson and Walter Ralegh served terms) and the King's Bench Debtor's Prison (where Tobias Smollett and Leigh Hunt were gaoled). Dickens, who first came to The Borough to visit his father in Marshalsea (see below), set much of *Little Dorrit* (1857) in the area. In recent decades, as industry locally has closed, the area has declined and The Borough has become something of a forgotten corner of London which tends to make the news only when one of its decreasing number of historical sites is threatened with demolition (most recently Borough Market).

• Landmarks can be reached from London Bridge tube or Borough tube.

Southwark Cathedral to Newington Causeway: north to south

Cathedral Street

Southwark Cathedral
Memorials to Geoffrey Chaucer, John Bunyan, William Shakespeare and Samuel Johnson can be found in south London's major cathedral (full name: the Church of St Saviour and St Mary Overie), which dates back to the ninth century. Shakespeare, who is believed to have attended services here, is commemorated with a full-size reclining alabaster effigy and there is a stained-glass window depicting scenes from his plays. (Edmund, his younger brother, was buried here on 31 December 1607.) The cathedral features the tomb of the local John Gower (d. 1408) to whom Chaucer dedicated *Troilus and Criseyde* (1390) and who is often described as 'the first English poet', as he wrote in his native language while contemporaries wrote in French or Latin. Others buried here include John Fletcher (d. 1625), who collaborated with Shakespeare on *Henry VIII* (1613) and the contemporary dramatist, Philip Massinger (d. 1640).

Borough High Street

Borough Market, Borough High Street at Bedale Street
Probably the oldest fruit and vegetable market in London and currently threatened by a plan to extend London Bridge station, Borough

Market, with its black brickwork, dark recesses, lively atmosphere and air of uncontrived chaos, is the epitome of what people now describe as 'Dickensian London'. Indeed, it features in Dickens's *Pickwick Papers* (1837), in which Bob Allen takes 'short naps on the steps' of the market office 'under the firm impression that he lived there and had forgotten the key'.

head east

St Thomas Street

Guy's Hospital
Keats read medicine here from 1815 to 1817.

Stainer Street

Site of John Keats's address (1814–17), no. 8
Keats lived over a candle shop in this street (then Dean Street) when he was studying medicine at the local hospital, Guy's. Lonely, he wrote the poem, *O Solitude*, which Leigh Hunt published in the magazine, *The Examiner*, boosting Keats's career. Stainer Street has since been completely rebuilt and is now overshadowed by the vast arches leading to London Bridge station.

return west

Borough High Street

For centuries this road, the approach to London Bridge, was the only route from south London to the City and so attracted many coaching inns, including the Tabard, immortalized by Chaucer. All the inns, apart from the George, have been destroyed.

Site of the White Hart Inn, Borough High Street at White Hart Yard
In Charles Dickens's *The Pickwick Papers* (1837), Mr Pickwick meets Sam Weller for the first time in the White Hart, where the latter is working as the boots, and takes him on as his manservant. In the fifteenth century Jack Cade, the Kentish rebel who features in Shakespeare's *Henry VI Part II* (1591), used the White Hart as his headquarters. Coaching inns such as the White Hart were doomed once the railway came to Southwark, and the pub was demolished in 1889.

The George, 77 Borough High Street at George Inn Yard
A riot of black and white timbering, the George, based in an alley just east of the High Street, is London's only remaining galleried pub, and

dates back to 1676. Dickens mentions the George in *Little Dorrit* (1857) – Tip Dorrit writes a begging letter to Arthur Clennam here. Shakespeare plays are staged in the courtyard in the summer.

Site of the Tabard, Borough High Street at Talbot Yard

'In Southwark at the Tabard as I lay/Redy to wenden on my pilgrimage'
from *The Canterbury Tales*, Geoffrey Chaucer, *c.* 1400

Nothing remains of the Tabard in which Chaucer set the opening of his *Canterbury Tales* and which he chose because it was a popular gathering place for pilgrims *en route* to Thomas à Becket's shrine in Canterbury Cathedral; the Miller in the *Tales* blames any muddled words he may use on 'the ale of Southwerk'. When the pub was rebuilt in 1629 as the Talbot, the landlord hopefully displayed a board outside proclaiming: 'This is the inn where Sir Jeffry [*sic*] Chaucer and the nine and twenty pilgrim's lay, in the journey to Canterbury, anno 1383'. The pub was demolished in 1875.

Site of Marshalsea Prison (*c.* 1300–1811), Borough High Street at Mermaid Court (approximately 100 yards east of the High Street on the north side)

Thomas Malory, author of the school syllabus evergreen, *Morte D'Arthur* (1470), spent several terms in the 1450s in Marshalsea (from which he once escaped). In the sixteenth century Marshalsea was temporary home to Nicholas Udall, headmaster of Eton and dramatist, whose *Ralph Roister Doister* (*c.* 1541) is said to be the first English comedy. Udall, who had been charged with buggery and stealing silver from the college, confessed to the former (not usually thought to be a crime at Eton, even in those days) and served only a short sentence. Walter Ralegh spent a short time in Marshalsea in 1580 after being convicted of a 'fray beside the tennis court in Westminster'. In 1597 the Privy Council deemed a performance of Thomas Nashe's new play, *The Isle of Dogs*, seditious and imprisoned the playwright and some of the actors – Robert Shaw, Gabriel Spencer and Ben Jonson – in Marshalsea. All save Nashe were released after a few months. A year later, Jonson killed Spencer in a duel in Hoxton (see p. 269). Jonson later returned to Marshalsea to serve time for unpaid debts. In 1811 the prison moved a few hundred yards south (see below).

Site of King's Bench Debtor's Prison (1758–1880), Borough High Street, approximately opposite Little Dorrit Court

One of the King's Bench's first inmates, in 1759, was Tobias Smollett, who wrote *Sir Launcelot Greaves* (1761) here. By the nineteenth century the prison had an absurdly lax regime, the courtyard filled with tailors, hatters, piano-makers and oyster-sellers, according to a contemporary description. Dickens put Mr Micawber (modelled on his father) in the prison in *David Copperfield* (1850). The King's Bench was demolished in 1880.

Site of Marshalsea Prison (1811–42), Borough High Street at Angel Place

Only a section of wall remains of the prison where Charles Dickens's father, John, was gaoled for debt from February to May 1824 (when the future author was 12). As was the custom, Dickens Senior was joined in prison by his wife and family, but Charles was spared the ordeal and stayed in lodgings in Little College Street, Camden Town, moving soon afterwards to nearby Lant Street to be near his family. After he had been inside a few months, John Dickens's mother died and he inherited £450, enough to pay off some of his creditors, and was released. Throughout his life Charles Dickens was embarrassed by his father's imprisonment, but he always maintained that the latter's conduct to his family was exemplary and he re-created him affectionately as Wilkins Micawber in the largely autobiographical *David Copperfield* (1850). Dickens also wrote about Marshalsea in *Little Dorrit* (1857), the heroine of which is born here, 'a child of the Marshalsea'. In the preface to the novel Dickens explains: 'Whosoever goes into Marshalsea Place, turning out of Angel Court, leading to Bermondsey will find his feet on the very stones of the extinct Marshalsea Jail.'

Church of St George the Martyr, Borough High Street at Long Lane

Known as the 'Little Dorrit' church, St George's has a window that depicts the kneeling figure of the heroine who, in the book, is baptized and eventually married here. Peter Ackroyd wrote his first novel, *The Great Fire of London* (1982), in the churchyard, inspired by the proximity of the demolished Marshalsea, the exercise yard of which was situated in what are now the church grounds.

Lant Street

> '*There is a repose about Lant Street in the Borough which sheds a gentle melancholy on the soul*' from *The Pickwick Papers*, Charles Dickens, 1837

Dickens lived in a house in this street in 1824 so that he could be near his father, who was in Marshalsea Prison, and he later depicted his kindly landlord and landlady as Mr and Mrs Garland in *The Old Curiosity Shop* (1841). Southwark Council has milked the Dickensian literary links for all they are worth. Not only is there a Charles Dickens School in Lant Street (near where the author lived) but nearby turnings include Copperfield Street, Dickens Square, Pickwick Street and Weller Street.

Harper Road

Site of the Horsemonger Lane Gaol, Harper Road at Newington Recreation Ground

Leigh Hunt was gaoled here in 1813 for calling the Prince Regent a 'fat Adonis of fifty'. In prison, Hunt wasn't too uncomfortable and decorated his cell with wallpaper of trellised roses and with fresh daily flowers. Here Hunt met Byron for the first time. In 1849 Charles Dickens came to Horsemonger Lane to see the hanging of a Mr and Mrs Manning, who had killed a friend for his money. He wrote a mournful article to *The Times* deploring the incident. The prison was closed in 1878.

further east

Jacob Street

Jacob's Island, Bermondsey tube

The small piece of land to the east of Shad Thames was an island in the Thames until the narrow arms of the river that surrounded it were filled in and it was conjoined with Bermondsey. According to Dickens in *Oliver Twist* (1839), Jacob's Island was 'the filthiest, the strangest, the most extraordinary of the many localities that are hidden in London', and home to the novel's villain, Bill Sikes, whose haunts, such as his home in Folly Ditch (now covered by the Dickens Estate on tiny Parker's Row, to the east of Mill Street) and 18 Eckell Street in Metcalf Yard, have all gone. Bill Sikes is hanged on the island at the end of the novel.

Camberwell, SE5 (except where stated)

> *'Camberwell, Peckham, New Cross Gate; places having no recorded past/*
> *Except in the histories of the tram'* from *A 202*, Alan Brownjohn, 1969

One of the oldest communities in south-east London, but now run down and blighted, Camberwell was where Robert Browning was born in 1812. There is a plaque to the poet at 179 Southampton Way, although his birthplace has gone. Camberwell features in a number of Sherlock Holmes stories, most famously in 'The Five Orange Pips'

(1891), which refers to the Camberwell poisoning case of 1887, a story never fleshed out but which, the readers are told, the detective solves by winding a dead man's watch.

- Landmarks can be reached from Denmark Hill railway station.

Camberwell Green end to Herne Hill end: north to south

Camberwell Green

When Dougal and Elaine in Muriel Spark's *The Ballad of Peckham Rye* (1960) reach Camberwell Green, Dougal takes a piece of paper out of his pocket and reads: '"I walked with her to Camberwell Green, and we said good-bye rather sorrowfully at the corner of New Road [now Camberwell New Road]; and that possibility of meek happiness vanished for ever".' Dougal's lines are lifted directly from John Ruskin's memoirs and his affair with Charlotte Wilkes.

Denmark Hill

Site of John Ruskin's address (1843–52, 1854–72), no. 163, opposite Ferndene Road
Ruskin and his parents moved to a large property which boasted 'a stable and a farmyard and a haystack and a pigstye and a porter's lodge where undesirable visitors could be stopped', shortly after he had graduated from Oxford and had written the first volume of *Modern Painters*. In 1848 Ruskin married Effie Gray and moved to Mayfair, but the house was unsuitable – there was a stark brick wall opposite his window – and so in 1852 his father bought him a place in Herne Hill near the house where he'd grown up. When writing, Ruskin came back to his parents' place in Denmark Hill – he produced his massively influential architectural work, *The Stones of Venice*, in the first-floor study in the early 1850s – and at the end of the working day he expected Effie to come to Denmark Hill for dinner, after which they would both drive back to Herne Hill. This lasted for a few years, until the relationship broke down (the marriage was never consummated as he was mortified by the sight of her pubic hair) and Ruskin then returned to 163 Denmark Hill, moving out when his mother died. The house was converted to a hotel, Ruskin Manor, before being demolished in 1947. Opposite the site stands Ruskin Park, where Felix Mendelssohn wrote *Spring Song*, originally entitled *Camberwell Green*.

Herne Hill

Site of John Ruskin's address (1823–43), no. 26, SE24

Ruskin lived in a house on this site (then a rural location) from the age of 4 until his mid-twenties (apart from a spell at Oxford University) and wrote in his autobiography, *Praeterita* (1889), how it commanded 'in those comparatively smokeless days a very notable view'.

Site of John Ruskin's address (1852–4), no. 36, SE24

When Ruskin was in his early thirties, his father bought him a house near the one where he'd grown up. Ruskin was then married, after a fashion (see above), but wasn't too successful in managing the house. Despite being one of the foremost influences on Victorian architecture, he couldn't even organize himself a bookshelf and kept his volumes in a bathtub. He moved out in 1854 when his marriage broke up and his wife, Effie, ran off with the painter, Millais.

Deptford, SE8

> 'When people say they're living in Deptford they mean this, the gasworks, the nasty little shops, these poky houses, the smoke' Lady Arrow, from *The Family Arsenal*, Paul Theroux, 1976

Henry VIII founded the Royal Naval Dockyard in Deptford in 1513, but there were no notable local residents until the diarist, John Evelyn, moved into Sayes Court (remembered by the modern-day Sayes Court Street, off the busy Evelyn Road) in 1652. When Evelyn moved to Surrey in 1694, he rented out Sayes Court, and one of the new tenants was the Russian Tsar, Peter the Great, whom William III invited to work as a shipwright in the local dockyard, paying all his expenses. Unfortunately, Peter wrecked the hedge at Sayes Court by charging at it with a wheelbarrow and, when Christopher Wren in his capacity as surveyor came to check on the damage, he found floors 'damaged by Grease and Inck' and a bedstead 'broake to pieces'. All that is left of Evelyn's gardens, what Pepys called 'this most beautiful place . . . a lovely noble ground', is a patch of grass behind the John Evelyn pub in Grove Street.

These days Deptford is a sorry place, ravaged by thoughtless municipal development. In Paul Theroux's tale of local terrorists, *The Family Arsenal* (1976), Lady Arrow visits the area for the first time, *en route* for the terrorists' cell, and after a quick look around decides that 'she had expected something different. [Deptford] was sadly indescribable . . . characterless, without any colour, a dismal intermediate district, boxed in by little shops and little brown terraces'.

Deptford Green

St Nicholas's Church, Deptford railway station
Christopher Marlowe, who was murdered in Deptford (see below), is buried in an unmarked grave in this church. St Nicholas's stands north of Creek Road, the main road through the area, and it was heavily bombed during the Second World War.

A Dead Man in Deptford

Christopher Marlowe was killed on 30 May 1593 by one of his companions, Ingram Frezer, after a long drinking session in a Deptford tavern. During an argument over the bill, Marlowe attacked Frezer with a dagger, but the latter seized Marlowe's hand and forced the weapon on the playwright, knifing him just above the right eye and killing him instantaneously. Frezer pleaded self-defence at the trial and was acquitted. But was Marlowe murdered or assassinated? Drinking with Marlowe and Frezer were Nicholas Skeres, a servant of the Earl of Essex, and Robert Pooley, a government agent, and Frezer was a business agent for Lady Walsingham, wife of the arch-spy. Marlowe himself may have been a spy, a line developed in Charles Nicholl's _The Reckoning_ (1992) and Anthony Burgess's better-known _A Dead Man in Deptford_ (1993). Another theory is that Marlowe wasn't killed but faked his death so that he could flee charges of atheism which were about to be brought by the Privy Council and which would have led to his execution.

Dulwich, SE21, SE23

What passes for an exclusive area in south-east London is usually described as Brixton borders by those who want to denigrate the area. Dulwich is where Dickens's Mr Pickwick retires to, and he describes it as 'one of the most pleasant spots near London'. Dulwich Village is Valley Fields in P. G. Wodehouse's books. Howard Jacobson's _No More Mr Nice Guy_ (1998) is set in Dulwich and features Frank Ritz, a sex-obsessed middle-aged TV critic who decides that Dulwich isn't the sort of place he wanted to end up in.

Devonshire Road

Raymond Chandler's address (1909–12), no. 148, Forest Hill, SE23.
Forest Hill railway station
Chandler, then a freelance journalist working for several publications
in central London, had a *pied-à-terre* in Bloomsbury but spent much of
his time in the comfort of his mother's Devonshire Road home. Nevertheless, he saw fit to rail against bourgeois conformity in the essay,
Houses to Let, attacking 'the paramount bourgeois spirit . . . those clean
smug bookcases which seem to cry aloud that they have as little as possible to do with literature or learning'. Fed up with London, Chandler
borrowed some money from his uncle to go to America in 1912 when
he was 23.

Dulwich Common

Dulwich College, West Dulwich railway station
This famous school was founded in 1619 by Bankside actor-manager,
Edward Alleyn, who had taken the lead roles in various Christopher
Marlowe plays. Raymond Chandler and P. G. Wodehouse were edu-
cated at Dulwich College around the turn of the nineteenth century.
Chandler showed no literary talent, but Wodehouse had school stories
published in *The Captain*, a boys' magazine in which he introduced
Psmith, his most famous character after Jeeves and Wooster. During
the 1940s, when Wodehouse made broadcasts from Germany to the
then neutral USA, pressure was placed on Dulwich College to remove
the writer's name from the school honours boards. Instead, the school
put the boards into storage. It now has a Wodehouse library and
archive.

Greenwich, SE10

> *'The whole civilized world has heard of Greenwich'* Mr Vladimir, from *The
> Secret Agent*, Joseph Conrad, 1907

Greenwich, home of international time settings (the 0° longitude line
runs through the area), Inigo Jones's Queen's House, the Old Royal
Observatory (where the meridian line can be seen), the National Maritime Museum and the *Cutty Sark* tea-clipper, is one of London's
biggest tourist draws. It is also nearly two miles west of the Millennium

Dome, built at great cost and amid much criticism on a Thames-side peninsula that is also known as Greenwich Marshes.

While neighbouring areas like Deptford and Woolwich grew around shipbuilding and armaments, Greenwich became a royal retreat. It was in a local palace built by Henry V's brother, the Duke of Gloucester, that Henry VIII and Elizabeth I were born, and Shakespeare is believed to have performed in his own plays here before the latter in 1594. The palace fell into disuse during Oliver Cromwell's Commonwealth, was demolished by Charles II, but was eventually rebuilt by Christopher Wren and others as a seamen's hospital, and is now the Royal Naval College. Greenwich has only a small place in literary history. Chaucer and the pilgrims passed by on the way to Canterbury, Johnson and Boswell often came to Greenwich Park, and Dickens occasionally used the place as a setting in his stories. Thackeray wrote about the joys of visiting Greenwich to eat brown bread and butter with whitebait, but the eulogy was published in the *Cornhill* magazine rather than in one of his novels. The area features briefly in Joseph Conrad's *The Secret Agent* (1907; see box, below). Edgar Wallace was found abandoned in a Greenwich street when he was nine days old.

● Landmarks can be reached from Greenwich or Maze Hill railway station.

Bookshops

Greenwich does boast a few decent bookshops among the scores of tacky heritage industry overkill gift-shops.

Halcyon, 1 Greenwich South Street, tel. 020 8305-2675, has a well-rounded stock and room for a good browse.

Market Books, Greenwich Market, is a small shop located on the edge of the covered market but is well stocked with London and travel books.

South London Book Centre, Stockwell Street at Greenwich High Road, tel. 020 8853-2151, housed in a former petrol station, looks enticing, but the stock may disappoint. Go upstairs for comics, sci-fi and a section delightfully entitled 'Small Press/Weird Shit'.

Spread Eagle Antiques, 9 Nevada Street, tel. 020 8305-1666, is situated opposite the back of Greenwich Theatre in an old converted coaching office.

clockwise around Greenwich Park

Greenwich High Road

St Alfege with St Peter

One of Nicholas Hawksmoor's typically eerie churches. St Alfege's was where Henry VIII was baptized and Samuel Pepys worshipped, the diarist writing how he enjoyed 'a good sermon, a fine church and a great company of handsome women'. The church is named after an eleventh-century Archbishop of Canterbury whom the Danes bludgeoned to death with the bones from a feast when he refused to allow a ransom to be paid. A church was built here soon after, and when the nave collapsed in the early eighteenth century it was rebuilt by Nicholas Hawksmoor. During the Second World War the crypt was used as a shelter by George Orwell, who described the stench of live bodies when full as 'almost insupportable'. The church was bombed in 1941 but has since been restored and has recently featured in the books of Iain Sinclair, who believes that it is one of a number of Hawksmoor buildings that make up the points of a 'major pentacle-star' between which lines of influence behave as 'invisible rods of force active in this city'.

King William Walk

Site of the Ship Tavern

Two scenes in Charles Dickens's *Our Mutual Friend* (1865) take place in this long-demolished inn which stood where the *Cutty Sark* tea-clipper can now be found. In the book, Bella Wilfer dines in the Ship with her father 'in the little room overlooking the river', a dinner in which 'everything was delightful, the park was delightful, the punch was delightful, the dishes of fish were delightful, the wine was delightful'. The reception for her marriage to John Rokesmith also takes place here as Bella reminds her father 'that she was his lovely woman no longer'.

Royal Naval College

John Evelyn, diarist, translator and royalist, put up some of the money for Christopher Wren to convert this former Tudor palace by the Thames into a seamen's hospital in the 1690s, and he wrote excitedly in his diary of 30 June 1696 about laying the foundation stone. Wren's work was completed by Vanbrugh and Hawksmoor, and was later described by Johnson as 'too magnificent a place for charity'. The hospital closed in the nineteenth century and the Royal Naval College moved here from Portsmouth. The chapel and ornate Painted Hall are open to the public while the building is being renovated for new use.

Park Row

Trafalgar Inn

The Trafalgar is probably Greenwich's best-known pub and occupies an impressive riverside spot. William Harrison Ainsworth gave a whitebait dinner here in 1851 to mark the release of *Mervyn Clitheroe*.

Maze Hill

Vanbrugh Castle/Sir John Vanbrugh's address (1719–25), no. 121

A riot of turrets, tourelles, false roofs and obscure wings, Vanbrugh Castle was built in the early years of the eighteenth century by the playwright-architect who penned a handful of elegant Restoration comedies, including *The Relapse* (1696) and *The Provok'd Wife* (1697). Uncertainty has long surrounded the nature of Vanbrugh's architectural contribution. Although he is usually credited with designing Castle Howard, Blenheim Palace and this property, many believe his role was that of a patron rather than a practitioner or, as Jonathan Swift quipped, 'Without thought or lecture he [Vanbrugh] hugely turned to architecture.' Vanbrugh originally named the house the Bastille, having spent eighteen months in the Parisian prison for spying.

In Joseph Conrad's *The Secret Agent* (1907) the double-crossing hero, Mr Verloc, persuades his mentally retarded brother-in-law, Stevie, to blow up the Royal Observatory (which stands on a peak in the middle of Greenwich Park) as an anarchist statement against poverty and injustice. Verloc, however, is secretly working as an agent for an unnamed foreign power that wishes to discredit anarchist dissidents exiled in London and hopes that the Observatory bombing will be blamed on the anarchists, who will then be rounded up by the British Government. Unfortunately Stevie, carrying the bomb across the park *en route* to planting it by the Observatory, trips and blows himself up. Conrad based the incident on a real-life event from 1894 when an anarchist, Martial Bourdin, was killed after the bomb he was carrying across the park in a brown paper bag exploded. It is thought he was heading for the Observatory and that he had been duped into carrying the device by his brother-in-law, a police agent posing as an anarchist.

Greenwich Park

This rambling park was an occasional retreat for Samuel Johnson and James Boswell in the late eighteenth century. Boswell wrote in his *London Journal* about how they 'took a sculler at the Temple stairs and set out for Greenwich' one Saturday afternoon (30 July 1763). When Johnson asks Boswell, 'Is not this very fine?' Boswell agrees, but adds, 'Yes sir, but not equal to Fleet Street.' Henry James was also keen on the park and wrote about how the deer 'laze around tame as children'.

Croom's Hill

Cecil Day-Lewis's address (1950s), no. 6
The left-wing Irishman, who became poet laureate in 1968, lived in this winding Georgian lane, just west of Greenwich Park. In his autobio-graphical *The Buried Day* (1960), Day-Lewis described the 'great cargo-liners rounding the Isle of Dogs, the tugs and their strings of lighters, the wharves, warehouses, power stations . . . all the river life here at Greenwich'. He also used the river theme in his guise as Nicholas Blake in the detective novel, *The Worm of Death* (1961).

Lambeth/Waterloo, SE1

Lambeth has two main literary claims: it was home to William Blake from 1793 to 1802 and was a major inspiration for *Jerusalem* (1804–20); nearly 100 years later, the teeming slums by the river were the setting for Somerset Maugham's first novel, *Liza of Lambeth* (1897). Despite the area's proximity to central London, some of the most run-down and blight-ridden parts of the capital can be found here. Alongside the Thames, in contrast, the South Bank arts centre contains the country's greatest conglomeration of cultural buildings – the Hayward Gallery, National Theatre, National Film Theatre, Queen Elizabeth Hall, Purcell Room and Royal Festival Hall – housed in some of London's most exciting post-war buildings.

- Landmarks can be reached from Waterloo railway station/tube, except where stated.

Waterloo to Vauxhall: roughly north to south

Waterloo Road

The Old Vic, Waterloo Road at The Cut, Waterloo railway station/tube
One of London's most famous theatres, the Old Vic opened in 1818 as
the Royal Coburg and for much of the nineteenth century was a music
hall, before being converted into a temperance hall in 1880 by the social
worker, Emma Cons. Eighteen years later, Cons's niece, Lilian Baylis,
began staging opera, but audience figures were low and so during the
First World War Shakespeare plays (with Sybil Thorndike doing male
parts) were added to the bill. By the early '20s the Old Vic was
London's leading Shakespearean theatre and later became the first
home to the National Theatre. Those who have appeared here include
Laurence Olivier, Edith Evans, John Gielgud and Ralph Richardson.

York Road

Waterloo station
In Jerome K. Jerome's *Three Men in a Boat* (1889), the protagonists
arrive at the station to take the 11.05 to Kingston but, after enduring a
nightmare of bureaucratic confusion in which two porters, the station
master and a traffic superintendent cannot agree on the number of the
platform from which the Kingston train will depart, they are obliged to
bribe an engine-driver to take them there.

Lambeth Palace Road

St Thomas's Hospital, Lambeth Palace Road at Westminster Bridge,
Westminster tube
While training at St Thomas's in the 1890s, Somerset Maugham put
more effort into learning how to be a writer than in becoming a doctor, keeping with him at all times a notebook *à la* Oscar Wilde and
recording ideas, snatches of conversations and observations of the
eccentric characters who came here for treatment. Maugham was often
on call for twenty-four hours at a time and would be sent out to help
with births, which occasionally took place in the kind of alleyways from
which he would be the only vaguely official-looking person allowed to
leave in one piece. (He later claimed no policeman would dare visit the
same places and that his only protection was his doctor's bag.) While at
St Thomas's, Maugham had to be treated by colleagues for gonorrhoea.
He seemed quite proud of the fact and tried to pass himself off as a bit

of a lad by telling people that he'd caught it from a prostitute whom he'd engaged for £1. What he didn't say was that the prostitute was male.

Maugham's experiences as an obstetrician in the nearby Lambeth slums provided him with the background for his first novel, *Liza of Lambeth* (1897), ironically subtitled 'A Lambeth Idyll', which was published by Fisher Unwin just as he passed his finals, despite the objections of one of the publisher's readers, who castigated Maugham for his 'revolting' details of the common Lambeth folk. The novel was moderately successful, so when a St Thomas's consultant offered Maugham a job as his assistant he rejected it to concentrate on writing. For many years it seemed as if Maugham had made the wrong choice. He failed to follow up the success of *Liza of Lambeth* and novel after novel, play after play, flopped, until 1907 when *Lady Frederick* took off at the Royal Court Theatre. Within a year Maugham had four plays running in the West End. Maugham later portrayed St Thomas's as St Luke's in *Of Human Bondage* (1915) and *Cakes and Ale* (1930).

detour east

Hercules Road

William Blake's address (1793–1802), 13 Hercules Buildings, Lambeth North tube
Blake was well known for sitting naked in the garden with his wife, reciting passages from Milton's *Paradise Lost*, and when a friend, Thomas Butts, who used to buy one drawing a week from Blake, called one day he was shown into the garden and told 'to come and meet Adam and Eve'. Opposite were the Flora Tea Gardens, where entertainments and fireworks were staged until 1796 when the owner was sent to prison for keeping a disorderly house. The site is now occupied by a gruesome block of flats named after the painter/poet.

Lambeth Road

Former Bethlehem (Bedlam) Asylum, Imperial War Museum, Geraldine Mary Harmsworth Park, Lambeth North tube
After killing his father, Richard Dadd, the obscure Victorian painter and writer, was incarcerated in the Bedlam lunatic asylum, which occupied various sites before moving to Lambeth in 1815. Dadd's madness became apparent during a trip to Rome, when he was overcome by a sudden urge to attack the Pope who, he claimed, was the devil

incarnate. Antonia White in 1922 spent nine months in Bedlam in a padded cell after trying to commit suicide by walking into the Thames. The hospital moved to Surrey in 1930 and the buildings were then incorporated into the Imperial War Museum.

return west to Albert Embankment

Albert Embankment

Site of Mordecai Smith's Boatyard, Albert Embankment at Black Prince Road, Vauxhall railway station/tube
In the Sherlock Holmes novella, *The Sign of Four* (1890), Holmes and Watson with the aid of Toby, the 'queer mongrel', locate the boatyard belonging to Mordecai Smith (where the booty plunderer, Jonathan Small, has hired a vessel to make his getaway on the Thames) at the river end of Broad Street, now Black Prince Road. The area has since been cleared of all boatyards and maritime activity.

Jeffrey Archer's address (1980s–), Alembic House, no. 93, Vauxhall railway station/tube
In an unexpected twist to his bizarre 1997 London travelogue, *Lights Out for the Territory*, Iain Sinclair visits Jeffrey Archer's Thames-side penthouse after asking the Tory politician-cum-blockbuster novelist permission to look over his art collection (said to be worth £10 million). Sinclair, knowing of Archer's obsession with punctuality, rings the bell at the exact moment that nearby Big Ben clangs the hour, only to find that Archer is away, working on a book, but has kept to his side of the bargain: Sinclair can peruse Archer's art collection but will not be able to raise any questions about Archer's past. 'Absent he was immune to ridicule', as Sinclair puts it. Alembic House used to be an MI6 safehouse – the ministry has its headquarters a few hundred yards south by Vauxhall Bridge – and has often featured in TV shows as the kind of place where a self-made go-getter would live. Archer's flat previously belonged to James Bond film-music composer, John Barry, and when the writer bought the place in the early '80s (it cost peanuts then and is worth millions now) colleagues thought him mad to live this side of the river. Archer told them that from his window he could see the Houses of Parliament, the Tate Gallery, St Thomas's Hospital and three Thames bridges, which those who lived by them in Westminster could not.

Norwood, SE19, SE25

A mixed area lying between semi-fashionable Streatham and snooty Dulwich, Norwood was where Arthur Conan Doyle moved after the initial success of his Sherlock Holmes stories.

Tennison Road

Arthur Conan Doyle's address (1891–94), no. 12, SE25, Norwood Junction railway station

Having given up his eye clinic in Marylebone, central London (see p. 166), Conan Doyle moved into this sixteen-room red-brick detached house by what was then open countryside and here wrote scores of Sherlock Holmes stories, including, appropriately enough, 'The Norwood Builder' (1903), the house in which bears many similarities with no. 12. A regular visitor to Tennison Road was E. W. Hornung, creator of the gentleman burglar, Raffles (he and his associate, Bunny, were loosely modelled on Holmes and Watson), who later became Doyle's brother-in-law; but attempts to collaborate on a Holmes-meets-Raffles tale came to nothing. Conan Doyle spent much of his spare time engaged in sporty activities: he loved playing tennis and bowls, was an avid cyclist and appeared in cricket matches with W. G. Grace. (Before he lived in London, Conan Doyle had turned out for then non-League Portsmouth F.C. in goal, under his own name, and as a full back, under the pseudonym A. C. Smith.)

Church Road

Emile Zola's address (1898–9), Queen's Hotel, no. 122, SE19, Crystal Palace railway station

Zola came to Norwood after fleeing France where he had courted public wrath by controversially siding with framed Jewish army captain, Alfred Dreyfus. At the Queen's, Zola registered as M. Richard and wrote *Fécondité* in the mornings, perambulating Norwood after lunch.

Peckham, SE15

'Not many young fellows of your age would be prepared to settle down in a place like Peckham where the scope for any kind of gaiety is so limited' Joyce Willis to Dougal Douglas, from *The Ballad of Peckham Rye*, Muriel Spark, 1960

Daniel Defoe described Peckham in *A Tour Through the Whole Island of Great Britain* (1726) as a 'pleasant village', but industrialization and the growth of London have hit this part of south-east London hard. Peckham is now one of the most depressing areas in the capital, wrecked by cheap council development and tacky shopping precincts,

---

When the salty characters in Muriel Spark's *The Ballad of Peckham Rye* are not squabbling indoors, or trying to skive off work, they can often be found in one of the many local pubs.

The Rye House Hotel, 31 Peckham Rye. At the opening of the book Humphrey Place, refused the opportunity of seeing Dixie Morse, the bride he has recently jilted, drives 'along the Grove' (Grove Lane, the main road connecting Camberwell and Dog Kennel Hill) and 'up to the Common' (Peckham Rye Common) and enters the Rye House Hotel, braving the glares of disapproving locals.

The White Horse, 20 Peckham Rye. After leaving the Rye Hotel, Humphrey walks across to the Tudorbethan-style White Horse and drinks one bitter.

Morning Star, 231 Rye Lane. The Morning Star is the third pub on Humphrey's crawl. The Morning Star is also a favourite of Dougal Douglas, the book's diabolical hero.

Heaton Arms, 249 Rye Lane. After a drink in the Morning Star, Humphrey makes for this still unwelcoming-looking pub.

Site of the Harbinger, 23 Denmark Hill, Camberwell. Humphrey ends his pub-crawl at the former Camberwell Palace of Varieties (which had become the Golden Lion when the book was published) after being refused access to Dixie. When Trevor Lomas, who should have been best man at the wedding, spots Humphrey, he comes over and hits him on the mouth. They are both thrown out. In another fight at the Harbinger, Trevor Lomas smashes a pint glass on the counter so that he can use its jagged edge to attack Dougal. He lunges towards him with the spikes sticking out but misses and rams the spikes into Humphrey's face instead. The building has now been replaced by a shopping centre.

the jaunty area that Muriel Spark brought to life in *The Ballad of Peckham Rye* (1960) a distant memory. The Rye referred to in the title is a large stretch of open land, south of Peckham proper, on which Spark set a number of scenes.

- Landmarks can be reached from Nunhead or East Dulwich railway station.

Memorial to William Blake's 'vision', Goose Green, junction of Ady's Road and Hinckley Road, East Dulwich railway station
There is a memorial here commemorating Blake's first vision – 'a tree filled with angels, bright angelic wings bespangling every bough like stars' – which he saw in the Rye in 1766 when he was nine. Blake claimed that when he went home to Soho and recounted the tale, his father beat him.

FURTHER SOUTH-EAST

Beckenham

Well-to-do suburbia, halfway between Norwood and Bromley, Beckenham occasionally features in novels – H. G. Wells's *Tono-Bungay* (1909) and Hanif Kureishi's *The Buddha of Suburbia* (1990) – as a typical suburban retreat.

Beckenham High Street

Rat and Parrot (former Three Tuns), no. 157, Beckenham junction railway station
Karim Amir and his father stumble in on a Kevin Ayers gig at this pub (now the Rat and Parrot) in Hanif Kureishi's *The Buddha of Suburbia* (1990). Kureishi chose this pub because his great hero, David Bowie, had held his Beckenham Arts Lab (a multi-media avant-garde cabaret night) in the room upstairs in the late '60s. Kureishi bows to Bowie at other points in the book (one of the characters is called Changez, an obvious nod to the Bowie song, *Changes*) and was rewarded by having the singer write the theme-tune to the television version of the novel.

Bexleyheath

An unassuming community on the London to Dover Road, best known for the house Philip Webb built for William Morris.

Red House Lane

William Morris's address (1860–65)/The Red House, Red House Lane, Bexleyheath railway station
While living in this remarkable house, built in what was then Kent countryside alongside the ancient pilgrims' route from London to Canterbury, Morris wrote the unfinished *Scenes from the Fall of Troy* and set up 'The Firm' of Morris, Marshall, Faulkner & Co., decorators with a Pre-Raphaelite touch (Dante Gabriel Rossetti and Ford Madox

Brown were co-directors) who created the template for present-day life-style stores such as Liberty and Habitat. The Firm, which designed the house's stained-glass windows and provided paintings of medieval scenes, had a shop on the premises and Morris, himself, heavily bearded and wearing a blue smock, would often serve customers, some-thing not considered suitable at that time for an Oxford-educated intel-lectual. The house itself is a landmark construction in the history of English architecture, thanks to designer Philip Webb's rejection of Classical and Gothic motifs. By 1865 Morris tired of living this far from London and moved to Bloomsbury.

Bromley

In Hanif Kureishi's *The Buddha of Suburbia* (1990), much of which is set locally, Bromley is full of the 'miserable undead . . . when people in Bromley drowned they saw not their lives but their double-glazing flashing before them'. The book also features insulting references to Chislehurst, an upmarket part of the borough east of Bromley High Street. 'What could be worse than moving to Chislehurst?', Kureishi asks, 'which is inhabited by people obsessed with velvet curtains, Martinis and electric lawnmowers'.

H. G. Wells was born in 1866 at 172 Bromley High Street (since demolished and replaced with a department store); he grew up in the area and was schooled at Morley's Academy (also in the High Street and long demolished). He had a month's trial with a local draper when he left school at 14 and was rejected as unsuitable, but his experiences didn't go to waste and he sent up the trade in his 1910 novel, *The History of Mr Polly*. Wells called Bromley 'Bun Hill' in *The War in the Air* (1908) and 'Bromstead' in *The New Machiavelli* (1911), in which he railed over its suburbanization.

Croydon

A large sprawl of humdrum suburbia at the southern edge of Greater London, Croydon, strangely, has aspirations towards being an impor-tant town in its own right. An unlikely resident at the beginning of the twentieth century was D. H. Lawrence, who taught at a local school.

Norbury Park end to Addiscombe end: roughly north to south

Buckingham Gardens

Kingsley Amis's address (1922–40), no. 16, Norbury railway station
Amis grew up here in net curtain-twitching lower-middle-class
suburbia, and spent much of his life regretting the experience.
Occasionally those regrets appeared in his novels. In *Stanley and the
Women* (1984), for instance, Stanley Duke describes a similar part of
south London as 'cramped, thrown up on the cheap and never finished
off, needing a lick of paint, half-empty and everywhere soiled'. The
Amises moved out in 1940 because, according to Kingsley's mother, the
house was directly underneath the German bombers' flight-path.

head two miles south

Davidson Road

Davidson High School, opposite no. 385, Addiscombe railway station
D. H. Lawrence taught here from 1908 to 1912 and described his pupils
as a 'pack of unruly hounds'.

head half a mile east

Colworth Road

D. H. Lawrence's address (1908–12), no. 12, Addiscombe railway
station
Lawrence lodged in this tiny red-brick terraced house with the Jones
family, who spent most of their time in the kitchen as they couldn't
afford electricity to heat the rest of the property. Lawrence claimed he
sat up all night writing poetry.

SOUTH-WEST LONDON

Battersea, sw11

> *'Battersea, so far off, the roads so execrable, and the rain so incessant'*
> Matthew Arnold, letter to his wife, 1852

Originally Bardic's Island and entirely surrounded by water, Battersea is now best known for its dogs' home and monumental disused power station. Thomas Carlyle in the middle of the nineteenth century wrote about his fear of leaving his Chelsea house in Cheyne Row (now Carlyle House) and crossing Battersea Bridge to Battersea, a 'waste expanse of what attempted to pass for country', with a 'good stick in my hand'. Carlyle came to no harm but was cheered by the sight in the distance of the 'Chelsea lights burnt many-hued'. Arnold Bennett, spending a day in Battersea early in the twentieth century, spotted a *Sunday Express* poster advertising an article by Edmund Gosse on Thomas Hardy and asked in his *Journal* 'how many people in Battersea had heard of Hardy, or of Gosse, or could get up any interest whatever in a . . . novel though it were written by God himself?'

• Landmarks can be reached from Clapham Junction railway station.

head south along the High Street and its continuation, Falcon Road

St John's Hill

Clapham Junction station
Oscar Wilde, handcuffed and dressed in convict's clothes on his way to Reading Gaol to serve part of a two-year sentence for gross indecency, was laughed at and jeered by people when he passed through the station on 13 November 1895. Wilde said that when people realized who he was, they laughed even more. 'For half an hour I stood there in the grey November rain surrounded by a jeering mob.'

Belgravia, sw1

A district of ostentatious wealth, Belgravia, with its Victorian stucco villas, has a uniformity of architecture that makes every street look similar. The area was developed after Lord Grosvenor in the 1820s hired Thomas Cubitt to build on the fields west of Buckingham Palace, and it was named Belgravia as the Grosvenors had an estate in Belgrave, Leicestershire. Being so close to the royal palace, the streets attracted wealthy residents and, before long, embassies, many of which can still be found on the starkly opulent streets.

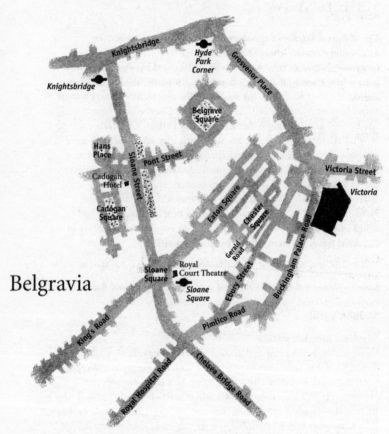

Exploring Belgravia

The area's boundaries are roughly Knightsbridge (to the north), Grosvenor Place (east), the river (south) and the SW7 boundary (west). For easy exploring, in this book Belgravia has been divided into two sections: Sloane Street and West, and East of Sloane Street.

SLOANE STREET AND WEST

- Landmarks can be reached from Sloane Square tube.

Knightsbridge end to Sloane Square: north to south

Hans Place

Site of Jane Austen's address (1814–15), no. 23
Austen stayed at the home of her banker brother, Henry, for nearly two years and wrote that the house was 'delightful . . . the garden is quite a love. I am in the front attic which is the bedchamber to be preferred.'

- Mary Shelley gave birth to a stillborn child when she and Shelley stayed at no. 41 in 1817.

Sloane Street

Sloane Street and Sloane Square are named after Sir Hans Sloane, whose assortment of eighteenth-century curios and treasures formed the basis of the British Museum's collection.

Cadogan Hotel, Sloane Street at Pavilion Street
Oscar Wilde holed up in this hotel in April 1895 while facing charges of gross indecency, knowing that the authorities were giving him a few hours' grace to flee before prosecution. Instead of heading off to the Continent as friends had advised him, Wilde, out of a mixture of laziness and obstinacy, stayed in his room until the police arrived. When they knocked, they found him lounging around, smoking. 'We are police officers,' one of them announced. 'Oh really,' Wilde replied. 'If I must go I will give you the least possible trouble.' John Betjeman imaginatively recast the scene in his 1937 poem, *The Arrest of Oscar Wilde at the Cadogan Hotel*, in which the policeman announces on entering: '"Mr Woilde, we 'ave come for tew take yew/Where felons and criminals dwell/We must ask yew tew leave with us quoietly/For this is the Cadogan Hotel".' But Wilde was not – as Betjeman also claimed and as is generally assumed – reading *The Yellow Book*, but *a* yellow book. Having been snubbed by the publication's founders, he had derided it as 'loathsome, dull', and, really nastily, 'not really yellow at all'. In *Enemies of Promise* (1938), Cyril Connolly claimed that Wilde's arrest put back cultural life in England twenty years.

Cadogan Square

Arnold Bennett's address (1921–30), no. 75
Money from the sales of *Anna of the Five Towns* (1902) and *The Old Wives' Tale* (1908) enabled Bennett to take the lease on this flat. Here he wrote *Riceyman Steps* (1923), which is set in Clerkenwell (see p. 93).

Sloane Street

Holy Trinity, Sloane Street at Sloane Square
John Betjeman led the campaign to save this Arts and Crafts-style church (designed by John Dando Sedding, a friend of William Morris) when it was threatened with closure in the mid-'70s. Thirty years earlier he had dedicated to it the poem *Holy Trinity, Sloane Street*.

Sloane Square

Sloane Square tube station
This Circle/District Line station was, until recently, one of only two in the underground system (the other being Liverpool Street) with a platform bar, as Iris Murdoch noted in *A Word Child* (1975). The bar was known as the Drink Under the River on account of the River Westbourne, the old boundary between Chelsea and Belgravia, which runs above the line and is now a sewer. When the young John Betjeman lived locally he used to get on the tube at Sloane Square, place his beloved teddy bear, Archie, on his lap and talk to it. When people stared, Betjeman would exclaim: 'Everyone's staring at you, Archie. Behave.' The story so impressed Evelyn Waugh, he based Sebastian's relationship with the ursine Aloysius in *Brideshead Revisited* (1945) on Betjeman and Archie. In Henry James's *The Wings of a Dove* (1902), Kate Croy first meets Morton Densher on a tube train as it is leaving Sloane Square.

In Iris Murdoch's *A Word Child* (1975), Hilary Burde takes a train at Sloane Square, rides around the Circle Line ('twenty-seven stations for fivepence . . . each unique'), and notes the 'sinister brightness' of Charing Cross, the 'mysterious gloom' of Regent's Park, the 'dereliction' of Mornington Crescent, the 'futuristic melancholy' of Moorgate, the 'monumental ironwork' of Liverpool Street, the 'twining' art nouveau of Gloucester Road and the Barbican 'sunk in a baroque hole'.

Royal Court Theatre, east side, Sloane Square
Recently reopened after £26m worth of refurbishment, the Royal Court
became London's most innovative theatre in the mid-'50s with the premiere of John Osborne's *Look Back in Anger* (1956). Far from taking the
theatre world by storm, however, things were pretty low-key at the box
office at first, despite some good reviews; but this changed when the
theatre's publicity department answered a journalist's question by
describing Osborne as a 'very angry young man'. The bust of George
Bernard Shaw, which used to stand in the foyer and commemorated
Harley Granville-Barker's productions of more than 700 performances
of eleven Shaw plays here between 1904 and 1907, has gone missing.
Other notable premieres at the Royal Court include Arnold Wesker's
Chips with Everything (1962) and Caryl Churchill's *Serious Money*
(1987).

EAST OF SLOANE STREET

• Landmarks can be reached from Sloane Square tube.

Belgrave Square to Chelsea Bridge, roughly north to south

Belgrave Square

Canning House, no. 2
During a rare trip to London on 9 February 1963 Jorge Luis Borges was
guest speaker here, talking about the Spanish language in South
America. The audience consisted mainly of Argentinians rounded up
from the nearby embassy. Canning House, which is dedicated to South
American culture, also has an excellent Spanish library.

Eaton Square

Raymond Chandler's address (1955), no. 16
Chandler came to London in his late sixties and, after staying for several months in expensive West End hotels (including the Connaught,
from which he was thrown out for the heinous crime of having a
woman in his room), came to Belgravia where he continued drinking
heavily and was amazed to find himself fêted on the London literary
lunch- and dinner-party circuit. (Sonia Orwell, widow of George, told
him that Edith Sitwell used to sit up in bed, looking like Henry IV,
passionately reading his books.) A bemused Chandler told the gathered
assembly that he was just a 'beat-up pulp writer' who in the USA

ranked 'slightly above a mulatto', but finding it hard to refuse invitations he lunched and drank until he could take no more and then just stopped turning up, annoying Somerset Maugham, Noel Coward and J. B. Priestley in the process. When Chandler's resident's permit ran out he returned to America.

Chester Square

Mary Shelley's address (1846–51), no. 24
Nearly twenty-five years after the poet Shelley's death, Mary Shelley, his second wife, moved in here when her half-sister, Claire Clairmont, moved out. She died here in February 1851.

- Matthew Arnold lived at no. 2 from 1858 to 1868 and wrote *New Poems* (1867), which included *Rugby Chapel*, here.

Gerald Road

Noel Coward's address (1930–56) no. 17
Coward was out when this villa was bombed in 1941 and, returning home to find the building and surrounding streets devastated, went to look for casualties. The events inspired him to write the song, *London Pride*. While living here, Coward wrote several plays, including *Cavalcade* (1931) and *This Happy Breed* (1943), and his autobiography. He left Britain in 1955, claiming that 'it is horrid to feel that I should never live there again'.

Eaton Terrace

The Antelope, no. 22
Dylan Thomas set the *Four Lost Souls* chapter of his unfinished novel, *Adventures in the Skin Trade* (1955), in this pub just east of Sloane Square.

Ebury Street

Noel Coward's address (1917–30), no. 111
Coward moved to Ebury Street with his mother when he was 18 and was just starting out in London society. His mother took in lodgers to help pay the rent, but as Coward became more successful he could afford to pay to use the rooms. 'As I rose in the world I went down in the house,' he later remarked.

- Other writers who have lived in Ebury Street include Thomas Wolfe, at no. 75 (now demolished) from 1930 to 1931 while working on *On Time and the River* (1935); Max Beerbohm, who stayed briefly at no. 115 in 1917 after returning from Italy during the First World War; George Moore at no. 121 (1911–33), writing about the area in *Conversations in Ebury Street* (1924) and visited here by Yeats and Shaw; and Vita Sackville-West and Harold Nicolson in the 1920s at no. 182, next door to where, at no. 180, Mozart composed his first symphony in 1764.

Chelsea Bridge Road

Jerome K. Jerome's address (1880s), 104 Chelsea Gardens, Chelsea Bridge Road at Ebury Bridge Road

The palindromic Jerome wrote *Three Men in a Boat* (1889) while living in this flat. He described the 'little circular drawing room' as being 'nearly all windows, suggestive of a lighthouse'.

Brixton, SW2, SW9

When Rebecca West (born Cicily Fairfield) was growing up locally at the end of the nineteenth century the area was a mainly genteel middle-class suburb and West could write in her diary that 'the superiority of the south side of the river is extraordinary – the trees gorgeous, the leaves so perfect, so green'. West grew up at 21 Streatham Place, which she depicted as 21 Lovegrove Place in *The Fountain Overflows* (1957), and described it in her unpublished *Parental Memoirs* as 'one of a line of semi-detached Regency villas which formed one side of a charming street'. West's Streatham Place has since been decimated, her house demolished, and a drive-through take-away restaurant built opposite, while Brixton itself has become a shabby, noisy, cosmopolitan suburb with one of the biggest black communities in Britain.

These days its major literary voices are probably Linton Kwesi Johnson, the Jamaican-born self-styled 'dub poet' who has successfully set his uncompromising radical verse to a reggae soundtrack and used local settings such as Railton Road in his work, and Martin Millar, also born far outside the area, in Glasgow, who peoples his locally set books with the unemployed, squatters and buskers. In Millar's *Milk, Sulphate and Alby Starvation* (1987) the Milk Marketing Board takes out a contract on a local drugs dealer whose allergy to milk has hit sales, while in

Lux the Poet (1988) the hero is chased through Brixton by gangs and the police.

Angela Carter's last novel, *Wise Children* (1991), set in Brixton in the fictitious Bard Road, opens with the question: 'Why is London like Budapest? Because it is two cities divided by a river.' The book's narrator, Dora Chance, then explains, in terms that Rebecca West would doubtless have disapproved, that south London is the 'wrong side of the tracks' and that she and sister Nora have always lived on the 'bastard side of the Thames'.

Chelsea, SW3, SW10

'*Few would venture to Chelsea, unarmed and unattended*' from *Barnaby Rudge*, Charles Dickens, 1841

For much of the nineteenth and twentieth centuries Chelsea was luxurious and Bohemian. Now it is just luxurious, Bohemian elements having long since moved to Hampstead, Islington and Notting Hill, and only the wealthiest writers can afford to live here. Before London's nineteenth-century growth, Chelsea was separated from Westminster by the Five Fields, a marshy expanse of land where highwaymen waited for victims; and when Thomas Carlyle moved to Chelsea in 1834 he wrote to his brother that it is 'unfashionable; also reported unhealthy', but he did note that it was 'literary classical ground' on account of the houses where Smollett wrote 'his *Count Fathom*' and 'More entertained Erasmus'. He could also have mentioned Jonathan Swift, who lived near where Crosby Hall now stands in Cheyne Walk and mentioned various Chelsea sites in *Journal to Stella* (*c.* 1715).

As London grew, so secluded streets like Cheyne Walk, with its delightful position by the Thames, became increasingly popular. During the nineteenth century Cheyne Walk residents included George Eliot, Dante Gabriel Rossetti and Bram Stoker and, a little while later, Henry James and T. S. Eliot. As long as rents were reasonable Chelsea continued to be one of London's most fashionable suburbs (as far back as 1910 E. M. Forster in *Howard's End* was commenting about 'long-haired Chelsea'). Between the wars the liveliest local personality was Dylan Thomas, who mocked the Cheyne Walk set as the Cheyne Gang but was happy to drink himself stupid in the road's Eight Bells pub. In the 1960s Chelsea was the centre of Swinging London, better known for its rock music and fashion than for its literature, and in recent years few writers have bothered about the place, although Anita Brookner has dealt with themes such as the loneliness of people living in its crumbling Georgian terraces in the novels *Brief Lives* (1990) and *Fraud* (1992).

In 1799, when he was 11, Lord Byron was taken to a Chelsea surgeon to have his clubbed right foot treated. It didn't work. When the poet died, his friend John Trelawny uncovered his legs and noticed that both feet were still clubbed and his legs withered to the knee.

Exploring Chelsea

For easy exploring, in this book Chelsea has been divided into three sections: King's Road and North; South of King's Road; and Cheyne Walk.

Bookshops

Books Bought, 357 King's Road, World's End, tel. 020 7352-9376, is packed with cheap second-hand works and is open seven days.
John Sandoe, 10 Blacklands Terrace, tel. 020 7589-9473, is a long-standing shop just west of Sloane Square packed with interesting stock.

KING'S ROAD AND NORTH

- Landmarks to the west can be reached from Fulham Broadway tube; landmarks to the east from Sloane Square tube.

West Brompton end to Sloane Square end: roughly west to east

Redcliffe Street

Dylan Thomas's address (1934–5), no. 5
In a letter to a friend, Thomas wrote how he lived amid 'poems, butter eggs and mashed potatoes' at what was his first London address, which he shared with the artist, Alfred Janes. There is no plaque on no. 5 but the house opposite, no. 10, has one for little-known poet and essayist Austin Dobson.

head south along Redcliffe Gardens and turn left at Fulham Road

Netherton Grove

Site of George Bernard Shaw's address (1876–82), no. 13

Shaw, when he was 20, moved to Chelsea from Dublin (where he had worked as an estate agent) and, unemployed, began attempting to be a novelist. 'I bought supplies of white paper . . . and condemned myself to fill five pages of it a day, rain or shine, dull or inspired. I had so

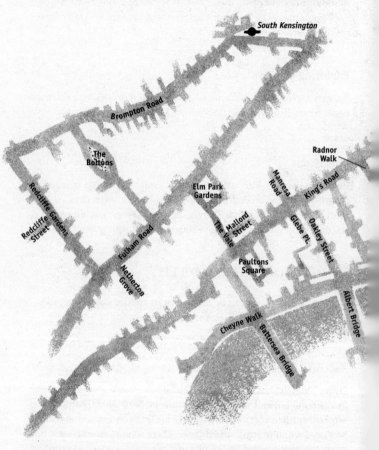

much of the schoolboy and the clerk in me that if my five pages ended in the middle of a sentence I did not finish it until next day.' Shaw produced five novels in five years, none of which gained interest from publishers. The site is now occupied by a nurses' home.

• Arnold Bennett lived at no. 6 from 1891 to 1923.

head north through the back streets

The Boltons

An exclusive oval-shaped enclave of stucco villas, just south of the Old Brompton Road, the Boltons has been home to government ministers and society figures such as Lady Ridsdale, wife of former Tory MP, Sir

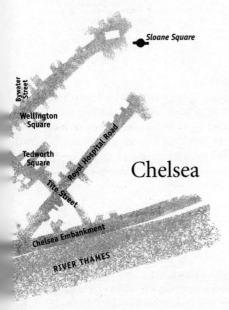

Julian Ridsdale, and model for Ian Fleming's Miss Moneypenny in the James Bond books. During the Second World War Lady Ridsdale worked with Fleming at the Admiralty on special naval operations, and was involved in an ingenious scam in which fake documents were given to a dead civilian and dumped in the sea. The Nazis were fooled into believing the corpse was that of a senior officer bearing invasion plans and they consequently deployed forces in the wrong area.

head east towards Fulham Road

Elm Park Gardens

Laurie Lee's address (1964–84), no. 49

Lee described this U-shaped road as a kind of 'buffer-state Lichtenstein lying in limbo between Chelsea and Fulham. The tall brick-built houses are perhaps not the handsomest in London, somewhat the colour of sulphurous kippers.' When Lee first moved in, Elm Park Gardens had what he called an 'almost Mediterranean life' with families and children running in and out of one another's gardens. The gentrification of the area, with properties renovated into luxury flats, put paid to that.

head south

Mallord Street

A. A. Milne's address (1919–42), no. 13

Milne wrote the children's classics, *When We Were Very Young* (1924), *Winnie the Pooh* (1926) and *Toad of Toad Hall* (1929), his dramatization of Kenneth Grahame's *The Wind In the Willows*, in this ugly three-storey Arts and Crafts house. Milne's son, Christopher Robin, and sister, Alice, used to walk from here to Buckingham Palace to see the changing of the guard, as remembered in the well-known nursery rhyme.

King's Road

London's most fashionable post-war street has a surprisingly small literary history, especially compared with its place in the development of British music and fashion. Dylan Thomas was a King's Road regular in the 1940s and one day Theodora Fitzgibbon, wife of his eventual biographer, Constantine, noticed the poet making his way along the road, carrying a sewing machine – hers. The Fitzgibbons had allowed Thomas to use their Godfrey Street home to work in and gave him a key, but he had responded by attempting to take Theodora's sewing machine to a pawnshop so that he could raise funds for a few drinks.

Cyril Connolly's address (1930s), no. 312A

Connolly arranged a dinner party here in 1935 so that Dylan Thomas could meet Evelyn Waugh and be introduced into London literary society. The evening was not a success. Thomas turned up late, and he bored those present, who included Anthony Powell, with incessant smutty jokes and hysterical laughter at tales of Swinburne's passion for whipping. Evelyn Waugh left, telling Connolly that the Welshman reminded him of his younger self.

head east along King's Road

Manresa Road

Site of Dylan Thomas's address (1942–4), Flat 3, Wentworth Studios, opposite King's College
Thomas lived with wife Caitlin in one room (the kitchen and toilet areas were separated by a curtain) which they fitted with unusual and novel furniture: a table formed out of Dickens and Trollope hardbacks and a 'chair' that was simply a pile of Walter Scotts. One day Thomas asked an old school friend, Dan Jones, to sound out a new wind-up gramophone he'd just bought. The poet put a copy of Verdi's *Il Trovatore* on the machine, but it would only play at twice the required 78 r.p.m., and the music came out several octaves above its normal pitch. Thomas appeared not to realize and sang along enthusiastically, remarking to Jones that 'those Italian tenors wear their testicles in their throats'. The block was demolished after the Second World War.

King's Road

Chelsea Old Town Hall, King's Road at Chelsea Manor Street
Oscar Wilde is still depicted in one of the murals in the hall, but only just. In 1914 a councillor proposed a motion urging that the poet be removed on the grounds that the Town Hall was not built 'for the exhibition of criminals' (see the Central Criminal Court, p. 73). Another councillor pointed out that other figures featured elsewhere in the display, such as George Eliot (adultery) and Henry VIII (reginicide), were none too holy themselves. The motion was carried but was never implemented following the minor interruption of the First World War on council proceedings.

Bywater Street

George Smiley's address, no. 9
In John Le Carré's spy books, his unlikely hero, George Smiley, lives in this charming little terraced house with its shutters and steps. Le Carré chose Bywater Street because a cul-de-sac is 'very hard to keep under surveillance'.

SOUTH OF KING'S ROAD

- Landmarks to the west can be reached from Fulham Broadway tube; landmarks to the east from Sloane Square tube.

Beaufort Street end to Sloane Square end: west to east

Paultons Square

Antonia White's address (1925–30), no. 55
At the time White was head copywriter at an advertising agency and, despite being married for the second time, brought back a number of lovers to Paultons Square, including Bertrand Russell.

Old Church Street

John Betjeman's address (1917–24), no. 53
In *Summoned by Bells* (1960), his long autobiographical poem about his childhood, John Betjeman describes no. 53 as being in Chelsea's 'slummy end'. During the school holidays Betjeman would escape the 'poky, dark and cramped' house as often as he could, exploring deepest Middlesex via the tube's Metropolitan Line.

Katherine Mansfield's address (1917–18), no. 141a
The house has one huge window which occupies a wall from floor to ceiling and which Mansfield called her Thou-God-Seest-Me window. Virginia Woolf, one of Mansfield's callers, described her around this time as 'hard', 'shallow' and 'stinking like a civet cat'.

head south and turn left at Cheyne Walk

Lawrence Street

Henry James's address (1912–13), no. 10
James, American born but a naturalized Briton, loved living in Chelsea and spent much time walking round, talking to locals, shopping and soaking up the atmosphere. He moved from Lawrence Street into a flat in nearby Carlyle Mansions in 1913.

- Tobias Smollett lived at no. 16 from 1750 till 1762 and was visited here by Oliver Goldsmith, Samuel Johnson and Laurence Sterne. At no. 16 Smollett wrote *Peregrine Pickle* (1751), *Ferdinand, Count Fathom* (1753) and *Sir Launcelot Greaves* (1760–62).

Upper Cheyne Row

Leigh Hunt's address (1830s), no. 22

Hunt's marriage was deteriorating while he lived in Chelsea; his wife, Marianne, spent much of her time at the Carlyles' house in Cheyne Row, much to the annoyance of Thomas Carlyle, whom Hunt once described as 'the very miserablest man I ever sat and talked with'.

Glebe Place

Antonia White's address (1921–5), no. 38

Antonia White and her husband, Reggie Green-Wilkinson, moved into the terrace at the southern end of this charming, bending street after getting married. Their union, as one of White's biographers later claimed, was 'disastrous and incomprehensible' for they had little in common: he was into fast cars and drink; she wasn't. But they did enjoy playing toy soldiers together, and the marriage lasted three years before being annulled. White based Archie Hughes-Follett in *The Sugar House* (1952) on Green-Wilkinson.

head back south

Cheyne Row

Carlyle's House/Thomas Carlyle's address (1834–81), no. 24, tel. 020 7352-7087. Open Apr.–Oct. 11–5. Admission charge.

> *'Upon my quoting Thomas Carlyle, he inquired in the naivest way who he might be and what he had done'* John H. Watson on Sherlock Holmes, from *A Study in Scarlet*, Arthur Conan Doyle, 1887

One of a handful of writers' London houses to be preserved as a museum – and probably the most visited of all – this four-storey red-brick Jacobean property was home to the historian for most of his life, even though he originally meant to stay for only a year. When Carlyle and his wife, Jane, moved to Chelsea, the area was rural and unfashionable. There was a clear run from the house and Cheyne Row (which Carlyle described as 'all old-fashioned and tightly done up') to the river, and the rent, at £35 p.a., was £10 cheaper 'than such a house could be had for in Dumfries or Annan', as Carlyle noted in a letter to his brother. But Carlyle hated much about London at first. He spent much of his time wandering around the streets – often with Tennyson – denouncing the government, complaining about the 'acrid putrescence' of the neighbouring houses and the 'black jumble' of the suburbs built on what until recently had been fields.

Carlyle, who was said to suffer from the worst handwriting publishers had ever seen, worked in the attic, which was soundproofed from distracting neighbourhood noise, and had pictures of those about whom he was writing above his desk; he felt that he couldn't write about them if he couldn't visualize them. Jane curtailed her own literary aspirations to support her husband (even though they barely got on) and he made his name with the history of the French Revolution. It was not only a work of great depth and learning, but the first volume of it was written twice. Carlyle loaned the original manuscript to John Stuart Mill, who left it lying around his Kensington Square study and the maid then used it to light the fire. Carlyle was mortified. After years of research and writing he no longer had much interest in the subject; worse still, he had forgotten its structure and destroyed his notes. Mill gave him £200 for the inconvenience and Carlyle grudgingly rewrote it. The incident was satirized by George and Weedon Grossmith in *The Diary of a Nobody* (1892), in which the charwoman, Mrs Birrell, uses Charles Pooter's diary to light the fire, thus destroying six weeks' worth of an even more monumental work.

Things went wrong within the home as well as for the Carlyles: marmalade simmering in a pan boiled over; a servant accidentally poured scalding water over Jane's foot; a workman refurbishing the place fell through a hole in one of the floors; and a dog fell out of a window (Dylan Thomas later claimed that the dog, bored to death by his master, was trying to commit suicide). The Carlyles suffered from a variety of ailments and afflictions, including severe stomach pains, constipation and insomnia. Carlyle died here in 1881, and the house has been a museum since 1896, preserved with many original furnishings and mementoes.

head east along Cheyne Walk

Oakley Street

Graham Greene, bumping into Mervyn Peake's widow at a bus stop in this street in 1975, told her that during a recent flight back to Britain from America the plane's engines had suddenly stopped in what obviously turned out to be a false alarm. Was Greene frightened, she asked. 'I would have been happy to die, very happy to die,' he replied.

'Speranza''s address (1886–96), no. 87

Speranza was the pen-name of Oscar Wilde's mother, Jane, a poet and Irish patriot who took a government pension in 1888. Wilde took refuge here during his trial (see Central Criminal Court, p. 73) when hotels were refusing to put him up.

- Antonia White moved into a room at no. 105 in 1935 after leaving her third husband, Tom.

Chelsea Embankment

In E. M. Forster's *Howard's End* (1910), Margaret Schlegel meets Henry Wilcox again while walking along here and ends up marrying him.

Royal Hospital Road

Chelsea Royal Hospital, Royal Hospital Road at West Road
Diarist John Evelyn was involved in raising finances for this Wren hospital, best known for its red-coat-wearing Chelsea Pensioners, and in the gardens of which the annual Chelsea Flower Show takes place. Thomas Hardy came here in 1896 to use its military museum while researching the Napoleonic Wars for *The Dynasts* (1908).

cut through the back streets north

Radnor Walk

John Betjeman's address (1977–84), no. 29
The by now elderly Betjeman returned to Chelsea when he could no longer bear the noise of lorries in the City, where he was living. This was his last London address, and he died in Cornwall in 1984.

Tedworth Square

Mark Twain's address (1896–7), no. 23
Twain was 61 and badly in debt when he came to London on a worldwide lecture tour – he got the idea from Dickens's successful lecture-tour of the USA – but he and his wife arrived to hear the tragic news that back home their 24-year-old daughter had died of meningitis. One day in June 1897 a reporter from the *New York Journal* knocked on the door, carrying two cablegrams from the paper. One read: 'If Mark Twain dying in poverty, in London, send 500 words.' The other: 'If Mark Twain has died in poverty send 1000 words.' This prompted Twain's now infamous response: 'News of my death has been greatly exaggerated.' Meanwhile Twain's lectures were successful, and the money raised helped pay off debts incurred by his New York

publishing company, Webster's. In Chelsea he also wrote *Following the Equator*, about his travels.

Tite Street

This small street, just west of Wren's Royal Hospital, briefly rivalled Cheyne Walk as the most fashionable address in Chelsea towards the end of the nineteenth century when the artists James Whistler and John Singer Sargent and Oscar Wilde were among its residents. It fell out of favour when the latter was convicted of gross indecency.

Oscar Wilde's address (1881), no. 44

Before Wilde moved in, the Aesthetic Movement architect, Edward Godwin, 'aesthetically' redecorated the brickwork in red and yellow and the roof with green slates. The property was known as Skeates House, the previous owners having been two women called Skeates; but with a flourish of Wildean wit Wilde dropped the initial 'S' and the superfluous 'e' and renamed it Keats House. Wilde shared the house with the artist, Frank Miles, a friend from Oxford whose father was shocked by the erotic nature of some of Wilde's poems. After a row Wilde stormed out, never speaking to Miles again. Years later the latter was revealed to be a child molester.

Oscar Wilde's address (1884–95), no. 34

Wilde bought the plain red-brick house (then no. 16) most associated with him on marrying Constance Lloyd, at a time when he was coming into public recognition as a self-styled 'Professor of Aesthetics', wit and art critic. Wilde asked Whistler to redecorate the property but he refused, saying, 'You have been lecturing to us about the house beautiful, now's your chance to show us one.' Once again Edward Godwin (see above) helped with the redesign, and this time the chosen colour was white: the front door, hall, stairs were painted white and the dining room (as Wilde explained) was decorated in 'different shades of white'. When writing, Wilde worked at a desk that had once belonged to Carlyle, in a room painted not white but primrose, producing the fairytale, *The Happy Prince* (1888), the novel, *The Picture of Dorian Gray* (1890), the plays, *Lady Windermere's Fan* (1892), *A Woman of No Importance* (1893), *An Ideal Husband* (1895) and, most importantly of all, *The Importance of Being Earnest* (1895).

When not at home, Wilde could often be found in the Café Royal or Kettner's, Soho, and he began his affair with Lord Alfred Douglas in a suite of rooms at the Savoy. One day in 1894 Wilde was visited by the Marquess of Queensberry, Lord Alfred Douglas's father. The Marquess was furious and warned Wilde that if he caught him and his son together again, he would thrash the writer. Wilde took the Marquess to meet one of the servants and announced: 'This is the Marquess of Queensberry, the most infamous brute in London. Never allow him to enter my house again.' After Wilde was convicted of gross indecency (ironically, the judge lived only a few doors away), looters broke in and stole his possessions. Once he'd been convicted, the house and its contents, including a valuable library, were sold – for a paltry sum – to help pay off the £600 court costs.

• When the London County Council announced in the 1950s that a plaque was to be erected on the house there was much dissent, a local magistrate denouncing Wilde as a 'common, dirty criminal'.

head north to King's Road and turn right

Wellington Square

Thomas Wolfe's address (1926), no. 32

Wolfe wrote the first of his gargantuan novels, *Look Homeward, Angel*, while lodging in this cream-coloured terraced house off the King's Road in 1926. Every morning at 8.30 Wolfe's landlord would bring him breakfast in bed, the author would then get up, work until lunchtime, and in the afternoon take 'enormous promenades through the East End of London', mentally planning the structure of the book. It was rejected a number of times by publishers but was eventually accepted.

James Bond's address, no. 30

According to Ian Fleming's biographer, John Pearson, this sumptuous cream-coloured stucco terrace was probably the address Fleming had in mind when he wrote in the first James Bond book, *Casino Royale* (1952), that the hero 'lived in a comfortable ground-floor flat in a converted Regency House in a square off the King's Road', his 1930 four-litre supercharged Bentley coupé 'parked under the plane trees'.

CHEYNE WALK

Chelsea's most famous street, apart from King's Road, full of gorgeous Georgian houses and wonderful river views, has probably attracted more major writers than any other in London. George Eliot, Dante Gabriel Rossetti (there is a Ford Madox Brown bust of Rossetti holding quill pen and palette standing on a base in the form of a fountain in Cheyne Walk), Henry James and T. S. Eliot are among its former residents. The Hilberys in Virginia Woolf's *Night and Day* (1919) live in Cheyne Walk in a house with its 'sophisticated drawing room'.

west to east

Ian Fleming's address (1923–36), no. 119

After the death of his father, the teenage Fleming, then at Eton, moved with his mother into this property converted from three small cottages, one of which had been home to the painter, Turner. Mrs Fleming then began having an affair with fellow Chelsea-ite Augustus John, one of the most celebrated painters of the inter-war years. Fleming was still living here in his late twenties, when he had become a stockbroker, as it was a convenient *pied-à-terre* for a man about town. He moved out when he decided he'd had enough of his mother's telling him how to behave.

Hilaire Belloc's address (1900–1905), no. 104

The French-born Belloc became a British citizen two years after moving here and, around the same time, had the area's first telephone installed, the number being KEN(sington) 1724. Belloc left Cheyne Walk after becoming Liberal MP for Salford at the 1906 general election.

Elizabeth Gaskell's birthplace and address (1810), no. 93

Gaskell was born Elizabeth Stevenson and her mother died only a month after giving birth, resulting in her being sent off to an aunt's in Knutsford, Cheshire.

Battersea Bridge

Graham Greene wrote in *It's a Battlefield* (1934) how 'the trams came screeching like a finger drawn on glass up the curve of Battersea Bridge and down into the ill-lighted network of streets beyond'. In John Le Carré's first George Smiley book, *Call for the Dead* (1961), Smiley calls on the murderer, Dieter Frey, who is staying in a houseboat moored near Battersea Bridge. A chase ensues, Smiley corners his foe on the bridge, and forces him backwards over the parapet.

Site of Thomas More's address (1524–34), Cheyne Walk at Danvers Street, west side

Thomas More's manor house, which Erasmus described as a 'commodious house, neither mean nor subject to envy', stood to the west of what is now Chelsea Old Church and occupied a thirty-four-acre site, incorporating gardens, orchard and even a zoo. It became a focus for learning – but also the centre of some bizarre behaviour. More believed that people should see each other naked before marrying, so when Sir

William Roper sought the hand of one of his daughters More invited him over, led him up to the girl's bedroom, where she lay asleep next to her sister, and lifted the bedsheets and the girls' nightdresses. When they stirred and turned on to their stomachs, Roper patted one of them on the buttocks and announced, 'I have seen both sides, thou art mine.' In 1529 More became Lord Chancellor, following the dismissal of Wolsey, who had failed to get Henry VIII a divorce from Catherine of Aragon. More himself resigned three years later and retired here, but in 1534 he was committed to the Tower and his estates confiscated. The following year he was executed. The house was demolished in the eighteenth century.

Crosby Hall, Cheyne Walk at Danvers Street, west side
Recently refurbished according to Tudor specifications, Crosby Hall, built in 1466 and once home to Richard III (when he was Duke of Gloucester) and later to Thomas More, used to stand in the City (see p. 53) but when it was demolished in 1908 the bricks were saved, and in the 1920s it was rebuilt here as part of a hostel for the British Federation of University Women. It was used as their dining room until the 1990s, when the property changed hands.

Chelsea Old Church (All Saints), Cheyne Walk at Old Church Street
'The clock of Chelsea Old Church ground out grudgingly the hour of ten'
from *Murphy*, Samuel Beckett, 1938
A number of writers have had associations with this ancient church, particularly Thomas More, who attended services and sang in the choir in the early sixteenth century. More is commemorated with a huge seated statue outside the building, a Thomas More chapel, and a tomb designed by him, but there is no evidence that he is buried here, even though Aubrey in *Brief Lives* (1692) claimed 'after he was beheaded, his trunke was interred in Chelsey church, neer the middle of the south wall'. John Donne preached here – Izaak Walton was in the audience – in 1625, having come to Chelsea to escape the plague which was then ravaging the City. Jonathan Swift walked from the church to Pall Mall (about three miles) one day in 1711 and measured the distance as being 5,748 steps. Thomas Shadwell, the seventeenth-century poet laureate, is buried in the churchyard in an unknown grave. There is a memorial plaque on the wall to Henry James (whose funeral took place here in 1916) which mentions that he 'renounced a cherished citizenship to give allegiance to England in the first year of the Great War'. The church was heavily bombed in the Second World War; but ironically this helped to preserve its history, for ancient monuments were found in the rubble and restored.

Carlyle Mansions, Cheyne Walk at Lawrence Street, east side
Henry James, T. S. Eliot and Ian Fleming all kept flats in this luxury
block overlooking the river.

- Henry James moved into no. 21 in January 1913 and found 'this Chelsea
  perch . . . just the thing for me'. The hypochondriac author complained regularly of toothache, colds and constipation, which he used
  to compare with terminal cancer, and eventually collapsed with a
  stroke, gasping, 'It's the beast in the jungle, and it's sprung.' Shortly
  before he passed away, James was visited by the biographer, Edmund
  Gosse, who conveyed the news that George V had made James a
  member of the Order of Merit. James was barely able to take in the
  news and, when Gosse left, told the maid to 'take away the candle and
  spare my blushes'. He died a few months later.

- T. S. Eliot and a friend, John Hayward, who had kept Eliot's archives
  and edited some of his poetry, moved in 1946 into no. 19, below the flat
  where Henry James had lived and died. Both Eliot and Hayward shared
  a passion for Sherlock Holmes and Eliot would often recite long passages to Hayward from memory. Hayward suffered from muscular dys-
  trophy and was confined to a wheelchair, and so Eliot would wheel
  him along the Embankment or over Albert Bridge to Battersea Park
  and back most days. On their excursions they would do odd things
  such as watching a football match between the Marylebone dustmen
  and the Chelsea council maintenance staff in the grounds of the Royal
  Hospital Gardens. Eliot, an American and therefore largely unconvers-
  ant with the intricacies of football, stood spellbound as one old man on
  the touchline chanted, 'Come on the Maintenance! Come on the Maintenance!' At around noon on weekdays Eliot would take the no. 19 bus
  to Faber's Bloomsbury office and sit upstairs working on the *Times*
  crossword. Usually his journey was undisturbed, but when an Indian
  student approached him one day and gingerly asked if he was speaking
  to T. S. Eliot the poet became rather perturbed and, after agreeing that
  he was, quickly got off the bus.

- Ian Fleming had a flat two floors above Eliot in the early 1950s but, feeling claustrophobic living in a small space with his new wife and her
  children from previous marriages, went off to Jamaica to write his first
  Bond novel, *Casino Royale* (1952). He came back to Cheyne Walk to
  finish it off but returned home one night to find Cyril Connolly reading page proofs out loud in a mocking, over-dramatic fashion to an
  amused audience. The publishers, Jonathan Cape, were also unimpressed with the book, and with Bond, and agreed only reluctantly to

publish it as a favour to Fleming's brother, Peter, one-time literary editor of the *Spectator*.

The King's Head and Eight Bells, no. 50

Popular in the 1940s with a Bohemian crowd led by Brian Howard, mentor of what biographer Humphrey Carpenter dubbed the Brideshead Generation, this pub was Dylan Thomas's Chelsea favourite. One night in 1934 during a drunken session Thomas explained to Pamela Hansford Johnson that his criteria for being a poet were drinking, being tubercular and being fat. Thomas used to come here to play shove ha'penny and (during the war) taunt tough-looking soldiers into having a fight. George Smiley drinks here in John Le Carré's spy books.

Site of Ruth Pitter's and Richard Rees's address (1920s, 1930s), no. 33

No. 33 was one of the 'safe houses' where George Orwell used to change into his tramping clothes in search of the lowlife experiences later recounted in *Down and Out in Paris and London* (1933). Usually Orwell would head off for Limehouse, some seven miles away, but occasionally he would use the doss-house (now demolished) at nearby 47 Milman's Street, said to be the most luxurious in London. In those days Orwell was very poor but didn't look it, and so he had to go out of his way to wear the shabbiest clothes he could find to compensate for what Pitter called his 'formidable' look. Rees, on whom Orwell loosely based Ravelston in *Keep the Aspidistra Flying* (1936), ran the literary magazine *Adelphi* from here for a while.

Albert Bridge

When the authorities proposed demolishing the bridge in the 1950s, John Betjeman in the *Spectator* campaigned for its retention. 'Shining with electric lights to show the way to Festival Gardens or grey and airy against the London sky, it is one of the beauties of the London River,' he wrote. The bridge was saved.

Bram Stoker's address (1870s), no. 27

After fishing a drowning man out of the nearby Thames, Stoker carried him into no. 27 and laid him on the dining-room table. The unfortunate individual failed to recover; Stoker left the room briefly and a few moments later his wife, oblivious to the drama, entered the room where, to her horror, she found a dead man lying on the table. The Stokers moved out soon afterwards.

Site of Don Saltero's, no. 18

Don Saltero's was a coffee house opened in 1695 by John Salter (valet to British Museum founder Sir Hans Sloane). It was then based further west along Cheyne Walk, but it moved here in 1718 and was patronized by literary figures such as Joseph Addison, Oliver Goldsmith, Laurence Sterne and Fanny Burney, who mentioned it in *Evelina* (1778). When Sloane died, Salter acquired his huge store of antiquities and curios which formed the basis of the British Museum's early stock. Don Saltero's closed in the 1860s.

Dante Gabriel Rossetti's address (1862–82)/George Meredith's address (1862), Algernon Swinburne's address (1862–3), no. 16

In one of the most bizarre set-ups imaginable, Rossetti turned this property, Queen's House, into a haven of poets and exotic animals. Residents included not only his brother, Michael, and fellow poets, George Meredith and Algernon Swinburne, but a raven, jackdaw, owls, lizards, an opossum that came in at night to sleep on Rossetti's table, a racoon that slept in a drawer, a kangaroo, zebra, donkey, armadillo and a wombat which ate a guest's hat and led Rossetti to exclaim: 'Oh poor wombat! It is so indigestible.' There was also a white bull with eyes supposedly like William Morris's wife, and some peculiar dormice which one visitor returned from looking at, holding his nose. 'Wake up little dormice,' Rossetti entreated, prodding them with a pen. 'They can't. They're dead, and I believe they've been dead for some days,' the visitor retorted. Rossetti's peacocks caused the most fuss. They so annoyed everybody that to this day the authorities have banned Cheyne Walk residents from keeping the birds.

Rossetti stayed here for twenty years, but George Meredith's tenure didn't last long. He couldn't cope with seeing Swinburne sliding down the banisters, naked, on his way to his usual breakfast of bacon and six eggs. Swinburne stayed for a while longer and in the downstairs sitting-room wrote the play, *Chastelard*, items for *Poems and Ballads*, and a study of Blake which helped lead to the formation of the Aesthetic Movement. Swinburne, naked, once chased a guest, Simeon Solomon (who was also naked) round the house, and on another occasion pushed William Morris back against a cupboard so aggressively that a piece of Rossetti's precious china fell and smashed, much to the owner's anger. Rossetti ejected Swinburne in 1863 and three years later began suffering from chronic insomnia as well as depression. In 1872 he attempted suicide in Roehampton and died in Kent, a recluse, in 1882.

Pamela Hansford Johnson's address (1930s), no. 6
Hansford Johnson lived here when in her twenties, working on her first
novel, *This Bed Thy Centre* (1935).

George Eliot's address and deathsite (1880), no. 4
Eliot moved into this Queen Anne house with husband, John Cross,
whom she married when she was sixty (he was twenty years her junior)
and mourning the death of her long-term partner, George Lewes. The
couple planned to spend the winter here and the summer by the sea-
side, but three weeks after moving in she was dead from kidney
trouble.

Clapham, sw4

> '*Clapham, like every other city is built on a volcano*' from G. K. Chesterton's
> autobiography, 1936

A mixture of up-market residential neighbourhoods and shabby high
streets, Clapham's modest literary history centres on the ancient
Common, although in the 1980s Angela Carter lived at 107, The Chase.

- Landmarks can be reached from Clapham Common tube.

Clapham Common North Side

Graham Greene's address (1935–40), no. 14
Greene was enthusiastic about moving to Clapham – it was more exclusive in the '30s than now – and discovered to his delight that no. 14, a
Queen Anne house, had been used by the father of the historian
Macaulay as a school. One of his first guests was Soho gadabout, Julian
Maclaren-Ross, who intended writing a screenplay of Greene's *A Gun
for Sale* (1936). Greene invited Maclaren-Ross to lunch but forgot to
inform the housekeeper, who refused to let him in. After much har-
anguing, Maclaren-Ross managed to persuade the servant that he had a
genuine appointment with the author and was shown into the library
to await Greene's return. Maclaren-Ross waited an age and then turned
round to find Greene staring at him, having somehow appeared without making a sound. Over lunch Maclaren-Ross told Greene that he
had done some selling in his time – mainly vacuum-cleaners – which
gave Greene the idea for Wormold's occupation in *Our Man in Havana*
(1958). Greene depicted the house and its destruction by German

bombs during the Second World War in *The End of the Affair* (1951) and also wrote a lesser-known short story, 'The Destructors' (1954), about a gang of boys who pull down a similar house brick by brick. No. 14 was rebuilt after the war and is now divided into flats.

Site of Samuel Pepys's address (1700–1703), no. 29
Pepys retired to the huge black-brick villa (described by diarist John Evelyn as 'very noble & wonderfully well furnished') belonging to William Hewer, his former secretary, after he quit the navy. According to Evelyn, Pepys, by now in his sixties, was 'universally beloved, hospitable, generous, learned in many things, skilled in music', even though he had also become disillusioned. Pepys died here in 1703. The house that stands on the site now was occupied during the nineteenth century by Charles Barry, architect of the Houses of Parliament.

Clapham Common

In P. G. Wodehouse's *Mike* (1909), Psmith and Mike Jackson, invited to the Clapham Common home of the left-winger, Mr Waller, decide that 'the first thing to do . . . is to ascertain that such a place as Clapham Common really exists'. Graham Greene gave the Common a pivotal role in his 1951 novel, *The End of the Affair*.

Clapham Common South Side

Maurice Bendrix, narrator of Graham Greene's *The End of the Affair* (1951), lives in a bed-sit 'at the wrong – the south – side of the Common'.

The Windmill on the Common, Clapham Common South Side at Windmill Drive
Graham Greene depicted this popular pub as the Pontefract Arms in *The End of the Affair* (1951). He used to carry jugs of beer across Clapham Common from the pub to his North Side home when guests came for lunch.

Earls Court, SW5

'Earls Court – a bourgeois slum' from *Earls Court*, Gavin Ewart, 1964
Back-packing students, Australians, cheap hotels, a huge exhibition centre/concert hall, roaring roads and stretches of take-away

restaurants dominate this colourful area, north-west of Chelsea, which Gavin Ewart, in his 1964 poem *Earl's Court*, claimed was full of 'three single girls who share'. Patrick Hamilton's 1941 novel, *Hangover Square*, was sub-titled 'A Story of Darkest Earl's Court'.

Bolton Gardens

Site of Beatrix Potter's address (1866–1913) and birthplace, no. 2, Earl's Court tube

Potter had a very lonely childhood, as her parents didn't allow her to go to school, and so she took solace in the animals that first caught her interest on holiday in the Lake District. Potter began drawing pictures of mice, lizards and rabbits that her governess secretly smuggled into her nursery, and she started visiting the nearby Natural History Museum where she first saw the mouse-tailor's waistcoat depicted in her second book, *The Tailor of Gloucester* (1902). Potter wanted to study the museum's insects but found staff reluctant to spoil the solemnity of the place by answering her questions. She lived in Bolton Gardens until she was 39 then went to the Lake District. A school now occupies the site.

Fulham, sw6

John Osborne described Fulham as a dismal district in his youth (the 1930s) and added that 'even today [he was writing in the early 1980s] the area is gloomy and uninteresting'. By the twenty-first century, on the contrary, Fulham has become one of London's most charming suburbs, with row after row of smart terraced houses and a picturesque riverside aspect.

• Landmarks can be reached from Parson's Green tube.

Bookshops

Books for Children, 97 Wandsworth Bridge Road, tel. 020 7384-1821, actively encourages children of all ages to use the shop. The stock ranges from first reading books to 'classics' aimed at teenagers.

Fulham Palace end to Parson's Green: west to east

Fulham Park Gardens

Arnold Bennett's address (1897–1900), no. 9

Bennett purposely kept his clock a quarter of an hour fast 'as a mark of scorn for most people's attitude to time-keeping'. Another eccentricity was his insistence on having rice pudding with every meal. In Fulham he wrote *The Grand Babylon Hotel* (1902) and the first chapters of *Anna of the Five Towns* (1902).

turn right at Fulham Road

Crookham Road

John Osborne's birthplace and address (1929), no. 2

The Osbornes had half a dozen different addresses in the area in the first few years after John's birth as his mother would regularly row with the landlady and be asked to leave.

head south

New King's Road

Samuel Richardson's address (1754–61), no. 247

Richardson, pioneer of the novel, lived and died in what had been Catherine of Aragon's house.

South Kensington, sw7

South Kensington is dominated by Britain's great museums, whose establishment dates from the profits made out of the Great Exhibition of 1851, based in nearby Hyde Park. William Morris was not particularly enamoured of the Exhibition and fled from it, mortified at the blatant commercialism.

Exploring South Kensington

For easy exploring, in this book South Kensington has been divided into two sections: Hyde Park Gate to Knightsbridge and Around Gloucester Road tube.

HYDE PARK GATE TO KNIGHTSBRIDGE

- Landmarks can be reached from South Kensington tube, except where stated.

Kensington Palace end to Knightsbridge end: roughly west to east

Hyde Park Gate

An impressive street, opposite Hyde Park and lined with grand houses, Hyde Park Gate over the years has attracted Charles Dickens (no. 16, where he stayed briefly in 1862, is gone), Leslie Stephen (father of Virginia Woolf), Robert Baden-Powell, founder of the Boy Scout movement, Enid Bagnold (author of *National Velvet* who lived at No. 29 in the 1930s and 1940s), Winston Churchill and the sculptor, Jacob Epstein.

Virginia Stephen's address (1882–1904) and birthplace (1882), no. 22
Virginia Stephen (later Woolf) grew up in this five-storey whitewashed house and during her teens began her own paper, *The Hyde Park Gate News*, around the time that she had to repel the advances of her half-brother, Gerald Duckworth. Stephen described the first-floor master bedroom as the sexual centre of the house, as she, sister Vanessa, and brothers Adrian and Thoby (all instigators of the Bloomsbury Group in the early years of the twentieth century) were conceived in it. When her father, Sir Leslie Stephen, editor of the *Dictionary of National Biography*, died in 1904 she moved to Bloomsbury.

Winston Churchill's address (1945–65), no. 28
Churchill bought the house as his London base when the Tories' 1945 general election defeat forced him out of the prime-ministerial office; here he began writing his six-volume history of the Second World War which partly led to his winning the 1953 Nobel Prize for Literature. When the house next door, no. 27, came on the market Churchill decided that no. 28 wasn't big enough, and so he bought that and converted the two properties into one. On regaining the premiership in 1951, Churchill let out the house to the Spanish ambassador and, when he was replaced by Anthony Eden in 1955, returned here to write his *History of the English-speaking Peoples* (1956–8). Crowds gathered outside to cheer Churchill on his ninetieth birthday. He died in the house in 1965.

Kensington Gore

The Royal Albert Hall

A week after the death of Sir Arthur Conan Doyle in July 1930, nearly 10,000 people turned up to England's major concert hall, hoping to witness his supposed resurrection. An empty chair, adorned with a reservation card reading 'Sir Arthur Conan Doyle', was placed on the stage between members of his family, tributes were read, hymns were sung and passages from the Bible were recited. Although by the end of the event nobody could verify that they had seen Doyle, the medium in charge assured the crowd that his 'psychic presence' had appeared and had 'sat' in the chair.

Over the next few years the hall witnessed several violent rallies organized by Oswald Mosley's Fascist Party (as later recounted by Evelyn Waugh in 1957's *The Ordeal of Gilbert Pinfold*, in which the hero is pleased not to have worn a black shirt when attending one). But one rally which never took place was that planned by Henry Williamson, author of *Tarka the Otter* (1927). Williamson, more than any other British writer in the '30s, fell under the Fascist spell, never relinquishing support for Mosley, even during and after the Second World War. In 1933 Williamson had the idea of inviting two guests of honour to meet at the hall in front of an audience: his friend T. E. Lawrence (Lawrence of Arabia), a military hero from the First World War, and the former German corporal whom Williamson claimed he'd met on Christmas Day 1914 during the famous break in hostilities between the warring troops – Adolf Hitler, by this time German Chancellor. Such a meeting, Williamson felt, would 'end the old fearful thought of Europe (usury-based) for ever' and prevent war between the two countries. Williamson wrote to Lawrence excitedly and asked if they could meet to discuss his idea. Lawrence invited him to Dorset for lunch but on that day, 13 May 1933, Lawrence crashed his motorbike and fell unconscious, dying of his injuries a week later.

head south

Prince Consort Road

Imperial College, Prince Consort Road at Jay Mews
H. G. Wells attended the college in its earlier guise as the Normal School of Science from 1884 to 1887, but he didn't enjoy a successful career and dropped out. He made some use of what he learned in his sci-fi books and romances, particularly *Love and Mr Lewisham* (1900)

and *Tono-Bungay* (1909), in which the hero, George Ponderevo, enrols here.

head south along Exhibition Road and turn left at Cromwell Road

Brompton Road

Brompton Oratory, Brompton Road at Thurloe Place
In Antonia White's Clara Batchelor trilogy, Clara kneels in prayer in this Italian church (founded by Cardinal Newman) on the night before her marriage to Archie Hughes-Follett.

Montpelier Square

Arthur Koestler's address (1965–83), no. 8, Knightsbridge tube
Koestler and his third wife, Cynthia Jeffries, both members of the voluntary euthanasia society, Exit, committed suicide in a pact here on 3 March 1983. They left all their worldly goods to provide a Chair in Parapsychology at Edinburgh University.

AROUND GLOUCESTER ROAD TUBE

Bookshops

The Gloucester Road Bookshop, 123 Gloucester Road, tel. 020 7370-3503, has an excellent bargain basement.

Kensington end to Fulham Road end: north to south

Cornwall Gardens

Ivy Compton-Burnett's address (1934–69), 5 Braemar Mansions
'You'll recognize the house,' Compton-Burnett told friends, 'it looks like Balmoral.' Braemar Mansions also had a porter and lifts, so it was definitely a step up from her previous addresses. Compton-Burnett wrote some of her best-known novels here – *Daughters and Sons* (1937), *Parents and Children* (1941) and *Mother and Son* (1955), which won the James Tait Black Memorial Prize. During the Second World War she held regular Saturday afternoon parties at which she would harangue latecomers, but in 1942 a bomb fell in the street and the flat was damaged. The building is now occupied by the Paraguayan Embassy.

head south and cross Cromwell Road

The Pope of Gloucester Road

T. S. Eliot, affectionately nicknamed 'the Pope' by those who knew him well, came to live in South Kensington in the 1930s after his marriage broke down. In 1927 he had been confirmed into the Anglo-Catholic wing of the Church of England, insisting on the utmost secrecy, even from close friends, mainly because he didn't want his strange and estranged wife, Vivien, to find out. In South Kensington he began to devote more time to religious duties, although some rare light relief was provided by the area's felines, who inspired him to write _Old Possum's Book of Practical Cats_ (1939).

north to south

St Stephen's, Gloucester Road at Southwell Gardens
Eliot was warden of this church for twenty-five years, from 1940 to 1965, which meant tending to financial matters and supervising the collection. To get to the church on time, Eliot had to get the bus from Chelsea at half-past six in the morning. When at 68 he married his 30-year-old secretary, Valerie Fletcher, the service was held not here but at St Barnabas in Addison Road, West Kensington.

Site of T. S. Eliot's address (1933–40), 9 Grenville Place
Eliot liked living frugally, so drab rooms in the now-demolished church presbytery under which the District Line ran were ideal. Nevertheless, it was so austere that even Virginia Woolf, who came for tea in 1934, flinched. The poet had his washing done by the church nuns, who always managed to forget to replace the cord in his pyjama trousers.

T. S. Eliot's address (1933), 33 Courtfield Road
A Courtfield Road cat, Bubbles, became the inspiration for _Old Possum's Book of Practical Cats_, in which Mungojerrie and Rumpelteazer live in Victoria Grove, half a mile north.

Ashburn Gardens

Antonia White's address (1941–59), no. 13
White wrote her second, third and fourth novels, _The Lost Traveller_ (1950), _The Sugar House_ (1952) and _Beyond the Glass_ (1954), in this flat, sixteen years after her successful debut, _Frost in May_. She also translated most of Colette's canon, often spending 'hours on a single sentence'. Three years after moving out, White returned to have a look at the place and noted sadly how it had become a slum, water having dripped through to leave huge brown stains.

turn right at Courtfield Road

Courtfield Gardens

Antonia White's address (1959–80), no. 42D
This was White's last address, where she lived alone after years of explosive relationships with friends, lovers and family. In her diary White wrote, 'secretly I think it's going to be the most attractive home I've ever had', but revealed that she missed 'shabby, roomy old Ashburn Gardens' (see above).

head back to Gloucester Road

Gloucester Road

J. M. Barrie's address (1895–1902), no. 133
Here in 1896 Barrie wrote *Sentimental Tommy* and *Margaret Ogilvy*, the latter based on his mother, about whom he had something of an Oedipus complex. Around this time Barrie's 'marriage' to Mary Ansell broke down as he was homosexual and had a low sex drive.

head south-east

Onslow Square

William Makepeace Thackeray's address (1853–62), no. 36
Thackeray moved in when he returned from an American lecture tour, and here he wrote *The Newcomes* (1853–5), *The Virginians* (1857–9) and his last complete novel, *The Adventures of Philip* (1861–2). In 1860 he became founding editor of *Cornhill* magazine.

head back west

Selwood Terrace

Charles Dickens's address (1836), no. 11
Dickens briefly took lodgings in this tiny terraced house so that he could qualify to be married at the nearby church of St Luke's. The marriage, to Catherine Hogarth, took place on 2 April, a few days after the publication of the first instalment of *The Pickwick Papers*.

Anglesea Arms, 215 Selwood Terrace at Selwood Place
While wife Caitlin was giving birth to their second child, Aeronwy, Dylan Thomas was in this small glass-fronted pub, just north of the Fulham Road, 'celebrating'. Caitlin's sister, Nicolette Devas, came to take him to the hospital, but once she'd found him she became 'reluctant to leave since Dylan was in one of his brilliant talking moods'.

Putney, SW15

> 'How I found time to haunt Putney, I am sure I don't know; but I contrived,
> by some means or other, to prowl about the neighbourhood pretty often' from
> *David Copperfield*, Charles Dickens, 1850

An easy-going family-orientated slice of suburbia on the south bank of
the Thames opposite Fulham, Putney's main literary connection is the
thirty-year residency of Algernon Charles Swinburne on Putney Hill.

- Landmarks can be reached from East Putney tube.

Roehampton to the river: west to east

Roehampton Lane

Convent of the Sacred Heart, Roehampton Lane at Toland Square
Antonia White was sent here as a boarder in 1908 when she was nine,
despite living only a few miles away in West Kensington. Towards the
end of her spell at the convent, a book she was secretly writing for her
father containing what she called 'unspeakable vices' was discovered in
another pupil's desk. One of the nuns read it and Antonia was obliged
to leave. She thought she had been expelled but discovered many years
later that her father had withdrawn her. Her convent experiences
formed the basis for *Frost in May* (1933), her best-known novel.

Putney Hill

Algernon Charles Swinburne's address (1879–1909), The Pines, no. 11
Swinburne came to Putney so that his friend, Theodore Watts-Dunton,
could make sure he stayed off the drink. He ended up staying thirty
years, churning out heaps of poems and plays and papers – on Shakespeare, Ben Jonson, Dickens and the Brontës – and was visited by the
painter, Ford Madox Brown, William Morris and William Michael Rossetti. The walls of The Pines were covered with pictures, mostly in pen
and ink or chalk, by Dante Gabriel Rossetti who, Swinburne claimed,
had been taught everything he knew by Watts-Dunton. (Swinburne
told the historian, A. C. Benson, that 'Rossetti had no opinions when I
first knew him – and our friend [Watts-Dunton] had merely to say a
thing to him and it was absolutely adopted and fixed in the firma-
ment.') Max Beerbohm wrote a famous essay, *No. 2, The Pines*, about
Swinburne's Putney period and how the poet would cross Putney

Heath with his 'long neck strained so tightly back that he all receded from the waist upwards'. In 1909 Swinburne and several members of The Pines household died after an outbreak of 'flu.

Putney Bridge

Mary Wollstonecraft, proto feminist and mother of Mary Shelley, tried to commit suicide in 1795 by throwing herself off the bridge after her partner – she daringly defied convention by refusing to marry – ran off with an actress.

Tooting, SW17

An increasingly shabby land of bed-sits and dingy terraces, Tooting was once the haunt of Daniel Defoe, who organized a local group of dissenters around the end of the seventeenth century.

Trinity Road

Thomas Hardy's address (1878–81), no. 172, Tooting Bec tube
After making a name for himself as a West Country novelist, Hardy decided he needed a spell in London to boost his career. Strangely, he chose to move to Tooting but managed to force his way into London literary life and even got Matthew Arnold and Tennyson to visit him here. Contracted to write instalments of a new novel, *A Laodicean*, for an American magazine, Hardy became ill with a urinary disease, which was probably exacerbated by the house's exposed position. Because of his illness Hardy had to dictate the text to his wife while lying in a most uncomfortable position with his head lower than his stomach. When he recovered, the couple quit London for Dorset.

Wandsworth, SW18

Traffic-choked and unattractive, Wandsworth has no great literary tradition but was home to George Eliot for a while.

Wimbledon Park Road

George Eliot's address (1859–60), Holly Lodge, no. 31, Southfields tube
Eliot moved into this villa, which she described as 'a tall cake with a
low garnish of holly and laurel', with George Henry Lewes, a couple of
weeks after *Adam Bede* (1859) was published. As Lewes was already married, their association scandalized Victorian society. Here Eliot soon
began work on a new novel which she called *The Tullivers* and then
renamed *St Ogg on the Floss*, before choosing the more agreeable title,
The Mill on the Floss (1860). She and Lewes didn't last long in Wimbledon Park Road. They had too many unwelcome guests, despite making
the spare room uncomfortable enough to deter visitors, and after a
year or so the wagging tongues of the local gossips became too much
for them.

Wimbledon, sw19

Expensive, snooty and culturally moribund, Wimbledon is best known
for the All-England Lawn Tennis Club, which hosts the world-famous
annual championships. Emile Zola, in exile from France in 1898, wrote
approvingly of Wimbledon's shops. In recent years Nigel Williams has
put the place on the literary map with light-hearted novels such as *The
Wimbledon Poisoner* (1990) and *They Came from SW19* (1992).

Wimbledon High Street

Rose and Crown, Wimbledon High Street at Marryat Road, Wimbledon tube
Crowds used to gather in this pub in the late nineteenth century to
watch Swinburne drinking, but the poet was rather shy and would
head off into a different room if approached by a stranger. After his
lunchtime tipple, Swinburne would head back across Wimbledon
Common and Putney Heath to his Putney Hill home for roast mutton
and apple pie.

FURTHER SOUTH-WEST

Richmond

'But Richmond's Fair-ones never spoil their Locks/They use white powder and wear Holland smocks' from *Epigram in a Maid of Honour's Prayer-Book*, Alexander Pope, 1726

Outer London doesn't come any prettier than Richmond, with its sweeping hillside vistas, elegant houses and secluded riverside walks. (Henry James wrote that 'there are few things so picturesque as Richmond Bridge'.) It was in a long-gone Richmond bookshop that an 11-year-old William Cobbett had his literary epiphany after buying a copy of Swift's *Tale of a Tub* (1704). H. G. Wells's *The Time Machine* (1895) is partly set here.

● Landmarks can be reached from Richmond railway station/tube.

Richmond station end to Ham end: north to south

Parkshot

Site of George Eliot's address (1855–9), no. 8
While living in Richmond, Marian Evans first began using the pseudonym George Eliot and started writing *Amos Barton* (1857). The site, just west of the station, is now occupied by a magistrates court.

Paradise Road

Virginia Woolf's address (1915–24), Hogarth House, no. 34
Woolf and husband Leonard moved into a flat in this squat three-storey Georgian house, just south of the main shopping area, when she was recovering from a mental breakdown. In 1917 the Woolfs began publishing on the printing press they had bought in Holborn, Virginia arranging the type and Leonard correcting and operating the machine. Their first work on what they called the Hogarth Press was a 32-page booklet of their stories, but soon the Press was publishing translations of Gorky, Chekhov and Italo Svevo, and new modernist works from Katherine Mansfield, Virginia herself (*Jacob's Room*, 1915) and

T. S. Eliot (*The Waste Land*, 1922). In 1924 the Woolfs, missing the
London social scene, moved back to their spiritual home, Bloomsbury.

Richmond Park

In this huge park, created out of the land that surrounded Henry VII's
palace, Jeanie Deans meets Queen Caroline in Walter Scott's *Heart of
Midlothian* (1818). Bertrand Russell occasionally lived in the park's Pem-
broke Lodge as a child in the 1870s and 1880s.

Sudbrook Lane

Charles Dickens's address (1839), Elm Lodge
Dickens rented what was then Elm Cottage for the summer of 1839 and
here wrote a bit of *Oliver Twist* (1839), which has some local scenes,
and *Nicholas Nickleby* (1839). He also found time for more leisurely pur-
suits, doing athletics in the large garden and swimming in the Thames,
a mile or so downriver to Richmond Bridge. Nearby is a chocolate-box
Dickens Close, full of expensive houses with fancy porticoes and col-
umns, with predictable names such as Gadshill and Copperfield House.

Twickenham

In the late eighteenth century when Horace Walpole lived here,
Twickenham was the most fashionable suburb south-west of London.
Today it is no longer fashionable, but some parts, especially near the
Thames, are as attractive as anywhere in the metropolis.

Richmond end to Teddington end: roughly north to south

Richmond Road

Marble Hill Park, St Margaret's railway station
Alexander Pope advised the owner, Henrietta Howard (George II's mistress), on the design of the gardens; when he met the king, he was
berated by the latter for writing no prose. Pope was in good company:
George II had previously attacked Shakespeare, saying, 'I hear a great
deal of Shakespeare but I cannot read him. He is such a bombast
figure.'

Montpelier Row

Alfred, Lord Tennyson's address (1851–3), Chapel House
Tennyson had just been made poet laureate when he moved to
Twickenham. In the 1990s the house was bought by The Who's Pete
Townshend, an occasional editor at Faber & Faber.

● Walter de la Mare died at South End House in Montpelier Row, in
1956.

Crossdeep

Site of Alexander Pope's address (1719–44), Crossdeep at Grotto
Road, Strawberry Hill railway station
Forced to live this far from London for being a Catholic, Pope, the
most celebrated poet of the mid-eighteenth century and a venomous
critic (known locally as the Wasp of Twickenham), here wrote his most
famous work, *The Dunciad* (1728), which was published anonymously
and attacked leading figures of the day, including Colly Cibber, poet
laureate (1730–57). Pope was visited here by other great writers – John
Gay, William Congreve and even Voltaire who was exiled in London –
and built an elaborate grotto in the garden. Within twenty years of his
death the gardens were in a sorry state, and in 1807 the owner became
so annoyed at the constant stream of visitors she had everything demolished. The mutilated grotto still exists, however, and can be found in
the grounds of St Catherine's Convent in Grotto Road (it is open to
the public on Saturdays).

Pope had an unusually diminutive body (he was only 4ft 6in. tall)
and suffered from curvature of the spine, which meant that he had to
be laced up in a stiff bodice every morning so that he could stand erect.
He also suffered almost daily from severe headaches. Pope died in the
villa in 1744 and is buried in the local parish church, the north wall of
which has a monument explaining his wish not to be buried in Westminster Abbey.

Waldegrave Road

Strawberry Hill/Horace Walpole's address (1747–97), Teddington railway station
Walpole, son of the first prime minister, Robert, moved into the small
coachman's cottage in grounds by the river (where Colly Cibber had

written *The Refusal* in the 1720s) and set about renovating it in an eccentric Gothic manner, with battlements, turrets, churchy windows and a tower – a style pre-dating the Victorians' Gothic Revival by 100 years. Before long the 'cottage' had acquired twenty-two rooms (including a refectory and a library) and nearly fifty acres of gardens, and visitors were charged to look around. By 1757 Walpole set up his own press to publish poetry by friends Thomas Gray and Hannah More and his own blank verse play, *The Mysterious Mother*; while living in Twickenham, he also wrote the Gothic novel, *The Castle of Otranto* (1764), which was inspired by the house and is filled with ghosts and doomed characters. After Walpole died, it took a month to sell off his vast collection of curios. The house is now the arts college of the University of Surrey.

Site of Noel Coward's birthplace and address (1899–1909),
Helmsdale, no. 5, Teddington railway station

Coward, the quintessential English sophisticate, came from a fairly humdrum middle-class background of which he recalled little, if his couplet 'I cannot remember/The house where I was born' is to be believed. Six years before Coward arrived, his mother gave birth to a boy, Russell, and asked R. D. Blackmore, the *Lorna Doone* novelist, who lived locally and whom she knew vaguely, to be godfather. Russell died of meningitis six months before Noel was born and so Blackmore, when asked to be Noel's godfather, refused on the grounds that 'precious young lives must not be subject to the risk I seem to cause them'.

Doone Close

This tiny road, just east of Teddington station, was named after Lorna Doone, heroine of R. D. Blackmore's great pre-adolescent romance of the same name. Blackmore lived locally in the long-demolished Gomer House, and Teddington now has a Blackmore's Grove, Gomer Gardens and a Gomer Place.

WEST LONDON

Bayswater, w2

An area of crumbling stucco houses and seedy hotels to the north and luxurious cream-coloured terraces to the south, near Hyde Park, Bayswater was once one of the most fashionable areas in London but is now a rough, shabby place. In the original version of the Graham Greene short story, 'A Little Place off the Edgware Road', written shortly before the Second World War, Jews with acquisitive faces hang around the area, trying to pick up girls. By the time the story appeared in Greene's *Collected Short Stories* after the war, the reference to Jews had been diplomatically omitted. Hilary Burde in Iris Murdoch's *A Word Child* (1975) has a 'small mean nasty flatlet in Bayswater'.

Exploring Bayswater

For easy exploring, in this book Bayswater has been divided into three sections: Hyde Park, Along Bayswater Road and North of Bayswater Road and Paddington.

HYDE PARK

> 'There are few sights in the world more brilliant than the main avenues of Hyde Park of a fine afternoon in June' from *Lady Barberina*, Henry James, 1883

In the 1820s a man identified solely by the markings 'S. T. Coleridge' on his shirt was found hanging from a tree in the park. The papers reported that the corpse was that of the great poet, Samuel Taylor Coleridge, much to the surprise of the latter, who heard two men discussing his unfortunate death in a London coffee house. It transpired that the shirt did indeed belong to Coleridge, who had lost it several years previously. Ford Madox Ford, in *Return to Yesterday* (1931), wrote about coming upon Emile Zola sitting on a bench in Hyde Park 'gazing gloomily at the ground and poking the sand with the end of his cane'. Zola had recently fled France after siding with framed Jewish army officer, Alfred Dreyfus. In Graham Greene's 1934 novel, *It's a Battle-*

field, Drover, the bus driver, is sentenced to death after stabbing a policeman he thought was about to attack his wife at a Communist rally in Hyde Park. In *The Acceptance World* (1955), from Anthony Powell's *A Dance to the Music of Time*, the series' central figure, Nick Jenkins, comes across a motley crew of old intellectuals who have come to the park for another demo, that for the Jarrow Hunger Marchers.

The Round Pond, Kensington Gardens, south of Queensway tube
It was by the pond that J. M. Barrie, who used to walk his dog here every day, met Jack Llewellyn Davies, inspiration for Peter Pan.

Peter Pan statue, south of Marlborough Gate and Lancaster Gate tube
The sculpture was created in the studio and installed only when complete, as Barrie wanted children to believe it had appeared by magic.

The Serpentine, Hyde Park at Serpentine Road
> '. . . and the Serpentine will look just the same/and the gulls be as neat as the pond/and the sunken garden the same unchanged' from *The Pisan Cantos*, Ezra Pound, 1945

Harriet Westbrook, wife of the poet Shelley, drowned herself in the Serpentine in autumn 1816. In *A Sultry Month* (1965), Althea Hayter wrote how one could catch a lethal fever by taking an evening stroll along the Serpentine's banks during the nineteenth century when raw sewage from newly built houses drained into the water. In the Sherlock Holmes story, 'The Noble Bachelor' (1892), Hatty Doran's wedding clothes are found floating in the lake, which is then dragged for her body.

ALONG BAYSWATER ROAD

- Landmarks at the western end can be reached from Queensway tube; those further east from Lancaster Gate or Marble Arch tubes.

Bayswater Road

J. M. Barrie's address (1902–9), no. 100
Barrie wrote most of *Peter Pan* in the garden summerhouse in 1904.

Lancaster Gate

> *'The tall rich heavy house at Lancaster Gate . . . had figured to her, through*
> *childhood, through girlhood, as the remotest limit of her vague young world'*
> from *The Wings of the Dove*, Henry James, 1902

Henry James *Wings of the Dove* inspiration, no. 56

The house used in James's *The Wings of the Dove* is based on no. 56, home at the end of the nineteenth century of Pearl Craigie, who had written for the Aesthetic Movement's *Yellow Book* and was part of the family that owned Carter's Little Liver Pills.

Lytton Strachey's address (1884–1907), no. 69

Strachey moved with his family into this grand block when he was 4 and, despite being a potential claimant to the throne of Scotland, had to move out during his twenties when money became tight in the household. No. 69 is now part of the Charles Dickens Hotel.

Muriel Spark's address (1940s)/Former Helena Club, no. 82

Spark came to live in this hostel (now a hotel), founded by Queen Victoria's daughter, Princess Helena, for 'Ladies from Good Families of Modest Means who are Obliged to Pursue an Occupation in London', when she arrived in London from Edinburgh at the end of the Second World War. She later depicted the place as the May of Teck Club in *The Girls of Slender Means* (1963), which is set locally. Thanks to her good taste in reading, Spark wangled a plum job with the Foreign Office during the Second World War. While waiting in the queue to find work at the Employment Exchange, she was reading an Ivy Compton-Burnett book. The interviewing clerk was impressed, engaged Spark in a long conversation about the merits of Compton-Burnett's work and, instead of fobbing her off with a dull clerical job, recommended her for intelligence work at the Foreign Office (see p. 134).

Hyde Park Place

Laurence Sterne's original burial site

Laurence Sterne was buried in a now-disused graveyard behind Hyde Park Place at the eastern end of Bayswater Road soon after his 1768 death, but a few years later bodysnatchers dug up the corpse and sold it for dissection. On the slab it was recognized and sent back. In 1969 the Sterne Trust dug up the bones legitimately and reburied him in Coxwold, Yorkshire.

NORTH OF BAYSWATER ROAD
AND PADDINGTON

- Landmarks can be reached from Bayswater tube, except where stated.

roughly clockwise around Queensway

Ossington Street

Wyndham Lewis's address (1930s), no. 33, Bayswater tube
When Lewis's wife returned home with their newborn daughter, she
was made to wait outside the house while Lewis finished having sex
with another woman. This is probably why in the 1930s Lewis had four
operations for VD and fathered five illegitimate children by three
different women. Ernest Hemingway said Lewis had 'the eyes of an
unsuccessful rapist'.

head north

Leinster Square

Ivy Compton-Burnett's address (1916–29), no. 59, Bayswater tube
Compton-Burnett wrote *Pastors and Masters* (1925) and *Brothers and
Sisters* (1929) in what is now the New Linden Hotel.

continue north, towards the Westway

Westbourne Park Villas

Thomas Hardy's address (1863–74), no. 16, Royal Oak tube
Hardy lived in this pretty three-storey Georgian house while working
for architect Arthur Blomfield. The novel he wrote here, his first, *The
Poor Man and the Lady*, was rejected and was never published.

go under the Westway and head north-east

Warwick Crescent

Site of Robert Browning's address (1862–87), no. 19, Warwick Avenue
tube
Browning moved here away from central London so that he could
mourn the death of his wife, the poet Elizabeth Barrett, in seclusion.
After a while he gradually ventured back into society and took part in
Ouida's literary evenings at the Langham Hotel (see p. 171). In 1866

Browning's sister, Sarianna, moved in with him, by which time he was becoming better known for his socializing than for his writing. The house, by a canal T-junction, has since been demolished and replaced by flats.

head south towards Paddington station

Praed Street

Paddington station, Paddington tube/railway station
Dylan Thomas was so frightened of London during his first visit to the capital in 1932, he kept as close as he could to this station, his lifeline back to Wales. Graham Greene twice buried bodies in Paddington station. In *It's a Battlefield* (1934), the body of a prostitute is found in a trunk here, and in *The Ministry of Fear* (1943) Hilfe's corpse is found in a cubicle in the men's toilets. Laurie Lee arrives in London at Paddington in *As I Walked out One Midsummer Morning* (1969) and, leaving the station, notes that 'the sky was different here, high, wide and still, rosy with smoke and the westering sun'.

head west

Devonshire Terrace

Formerly Dr Richmond's practice, no. 15
Deemed to be suicidal and unbalanced after running away from the school where his father was headmaster, the teenage Graham Greene was sent to see psychiatrist Kenneth Richmond, one of London's first shrinks, who practised here. Every morning for a few weeks Greene would have to turn up at 11 a.m. and relate to Richmond the dream he'd had the night before. If he couldn't remember one he'd make something up, invariably featuring a pig. Devonshire Terrace is no longer the kind of street where one would find a celebrated psychiatrist.

Chiswick, w4

A socially mixed slice of suburbia, surrounding the roaring A4 and leading down to some lovely parts of the Thames, especially by Chiswick Mall, Chiswick was where Rousseau briefly stayed while exiled from France from 1765 to 1766, probably in Church Street.

Exploring Chiswick

For easy exploring, in this book Chiswick has been divided into two sections: Bedford Park and Chiswick Village.

BEDFORD PARK

Said to be the world's first garden village, Bedford Park was designed by Norman Shaw in 1876, blending elements of rural life in an urban setting and made viable by the opening of the nearby railway. According to G. K. Chesterton, who set the opening of *The Man Who Was Thursday* (1908) here, it was built of 'bright brick' and was aimed at 'artistic people of moderate incomes'. This invariably led to lots of dabbling with socialism, which mainly took the form of earnest young men learning the theories of William Morris in the local hall.

● Landmarks can be reached from Turnham Green tube.

The Park That Was Saffron

G. K. Chesterton's fantastical political fable, *The Man Who Was Thursday* (1908), opens in Bedford Park (renamed in the book Saffron Park), described as lying on the 'sunset side of London, as red and ragged as a cloud of sunset . . . its skyline was fantastic, and even its ground plan was wild'. The novel recounts the mysterious workings of a secret group of anarchists, named after the days of the week (hence the title) and intent on world domination, who all turn out to be undercover policemen.

Woodstock Road

W. B. Yeats's address (1879–81), no. 8

Yeats was 14 when his father took a two-year lease on the place; it had a bathroom (a luxury then) as well as original William Morris wallpaper. The Yeatses soon moved back to Ireland because W. B.'s artist father received no commissions.

Blenheim Road

W. B. Yeats's address (1888–95), no. 3

Yeats's father rented this three-storey semi when W.B. was in his early twenties and upset at leaving Dublin just as he was beginning to make a name for himself. Yeats liked Bedford Park because it was 'the least Londonish place hereabouts' and went to Kelmscott House in Hammersmith, a mile or so south-east, to visit the ageing William Morris.

CHISWICK VILLAGE

- Landmarks can be reached from Turnham Green tube, except where stated.

Turnham Green end to the river: north to south

Turnham Green

In Dickens's *A Tale of Two Cities* (1859), the Lord Mayor of London is made to stand and deliver by a highwayman who 'despoiled the illustrious creature in sight of all his retinue' on Turnham Green.

Glebe Street

Anthony Burgess's address (1960s), no. 24
Burgess's one-off amorous encounter with an Italian translator on the couch at Glebe Street, a few days before he and his wife moved into this tiny terraced cottage, resulted in his fathering a son whose existence he knew nothing of until some years later. Living in Chiswick, relatively near BBC Television Centre in White City, Burgess could be called upon in emergencies for literary debates. On one occasion he was put off an impromptu Evelyn Waugh obituary by a yawning cameraman and during a BBC2 arts programme, when a table needed moving, Burgess did it himself and almost precipitated an all-out strike in those days of rigid job-demarcation lines.

Chiswick Mall

Walpole House, opposite Chiswick Eyot, Stamford Brook tube
Thackeray attended a prep school here in the 1820s and in *Vanity Fair* (1848) depicted the place as Miss Pinkerton's Seminary for Young Ladies, the pupils of which include Becky Sharp and Amelia Sedley.

Hammersmith, w6

A small but dynamic area, hemmed in by railway lines, stations, elevated motorways and hi-tech office blocks.

Stamford Brook end to Hammersmith Broadway end: west to east

Ravenscourt Square

Ouida's address (1857–66), Bessborough House, no. 11, Stamford Brook tube
The romantic novelist Ouida (real name Marie Louise de la Ramée) arrived in London from Bury St Edmunds and, after a short stay at 41 Lansdowne Road, Notting Hill, came here to live with her grandmother. Two years later, Harrison Ainsworth, the Manchester historical novelist who was a cousin of her doctor, won her a commission writing short stories for *Bentley's Miscellany*. In 1863 Ouida had her first novel, *Granville de Vigne*, published.

head south, crossing King Street

St Peter's Square

Robert Graves's address (1920s), no. 35a, Stamford Brook tube
Graves moved here at a time when Hammersmith was considered slightly Bohemian and he had just written his autobiographical *Goodbye to All That* (1929). The household was an odd one, consisting of Graves, his (first) wife Nancy, and his lover, the poet Laura Riding, who then badgered Graves to complement the set-up with Geoffrey Phibbs, a young Irish poet – to form a *ménage-à-quatre*. Phibbs didn't come out of this too well. He was forced to hand over all his possessions and clothes, which were burnt; after a month, having had enough, he tried to leave. When Riding threatened to kill herself, he relented – but she jumped out of the window nevertheless, breaking her back, and Graves leapt out after her and broke two ribs. Graves then ran off to Majorca with Riding.

head east, crossing the Great West Road

Upper Mall

A gorgeous riverside stretch, packed with drinkers in the summer and walkers in the winter.

The Dove, no. 19, Ravenscourt Park tube
This cosy pub, which boasts having the smallest snug in Britain, was a
regular haunt of Graham Greene's. It was depicted as the Pigeons in
A. P. Herbert's *The Water Gypsies* (1930).

**William Morris's address (1879–96) and deathplace/William Morris
Society Headquarters**, Kelmscott House, no. 26, tel. 020 8741-3735,
Ravenscourt Park tube. Open: Thu., Sat. 2–5 p.m.
Set in a glorious position by the Thames and now owned by playwright
Christopher Hampton (best known for the screenplay of *Dangerous
Liaisons*), this huge brick villa was home for nearly twenty years to William Morris, who bought it from the poet, George Macdonald. The
house already had a fascinating history, the first electric telegraph, eight
miles long, having been constructed here in 1816 by Sir Francis
Ronalds. On moving in, Morris renamed it Kelmscott House – the
name of his country home in Kelmscott, Oxfordshire – and would journey between the two places by boat along the Thames, a distance of 130
miles. In 1890 Morris set up the Kelmscott Press, with its ornate type-
faces and borders, and published reprints of Chaucer's work and new
books such as his own utopian vision, *News from Nowhere* (1891),
which is partly set in a Kelmscott House depicted as a twenty-first-
century guest-house. Here in the late 1880s the Socialist League held
meetings, at which Morris was joined by W. B. Yeats, then in his early
twenties, George Bernard Shaw and the anarchist, Prince Kropotkin.
Morris died here on 3 October 1896.

detour south of the river

Lonsdale Road

St Paul's School, north-east end of Lonsdale Road, SW13, Hammersmith tube
G. K. Chesterton, a pupil here in the 1880s, was so short-sighted he
couldn't read the blackboard, and when Chesterton's mother came to
check on his progress a master told her that as her son's brain was
unusually large he would be either an idiot or a genius – which was an
improvement on a master at his prep school who told him, 'You know,
Chesterton, if we could open up your head, we should not find any
brain, but only a lump of white fat.' Chesterton's closest friend at
St Paul's was Edmund Clerihew Bentley, the man who invented the
pithy four-line verse-story named after his middle name (as in 'Sir
Christopher Wren/Said I'm going to dine with some men/If anybody

calls/Say I am designing St Paul's'). Chesterton dedicated *The Man Who Was Thursday* (1908) to Bentley.

return to the north side of the river

Iffley Road

Godolphin School, Iffley Road at Glenthorne Road, Hammersmith tube

Yeats described the school he attended between 1877 and 1881 and which was intended for the children of not-so-successful professional types as 'rough and cheap'. Perhaps he was just upset at being teased for being Irish.

head east

Hammersmith Broadway

In Irvine Welsh's *Trainspotting* (1993), the narrator Mark arrives in London and heads for Hammersmith Broadway 'seeming strange and alien . . . soft focus . . . probably lack of sleep and lack of drugs'.

Kensington, w8

A perennially wealthy enclave of west London, Kensington grew around Kensington Palace where Queen Victoria was born in 1819 and where until recently the Prince and Princess of Wales occasionally lived. The siting of the palace attracted wealthy residents; in the early years of the twentieth century, artists and writers such as Ford Madox Ford, Ezra Pound and Wyndham Lewis who thought Chelsea too risqué and Bloomsbury too dull came here. Around this time, Kensington's most conspicuous literary figure was Ford, who described Kensington as a high-class Greenwich Village in which the artists should be 'wealthy, refined, delicate and well-born' and was involved in all the local cliques and sub-cliques, ably assisted by Wyndham Lewis and Ezra Pound.

Kensington has retained its elegance and charm to this day, particularly to the east of Holland Park in Campden Hill, and its High Street is one of London's best shopping areas. The area has been recorded in countless books, including Muriel Spark's 1981 novel, *Loitering with Intent*, which starts with Fleur Talbot sitting in an unnamed graveyard in Kensington, and T. S. Eliot's *Four Quartets* (1943), which he originally wanted to call *Kensington Quartets.*

Exploring Kensington

For easy exploring, in this book Kensington has been divided into two sections: Campden Hill and East of Kensington Church Street.

CAMPDEN HILL

The quiet tree-lined streets of Campden Hill, north of Kensington High Street, had their literary hey-day in the early years of the twentieth century when they were home to the Edwardian literary upstarts: Ford Madox Ford, G. K. Chesterton and Ezra Pound. The latter, being an American, was shown round the area personally by Ford, as Pound later recalled in *Canto LXXX* (1948). In Graham Greene's *Ministry of Fear* (1943), Mrs Bellair's house is described as 'old and unrenovated standing among the To Let boards on the slope of Campden Hill'.

- Northern landmarks can be reached from Holland Park tube; those further south from High Street Kensington tube.

Notting Hill end to Kensington High Street: roughly north to south

Campden Hill Square

Llewelyn Davies's address (1890s)/Siegfried Sassoon's address (1925–32), no. 23

J. M. Barrie's main inspiration for Peter Pan, hero of his 1904 play, was the Llewelyn Davieses' precocious son, Jack. When his mother, Sylvia, scolded him one day for eating too many chocolates, warning that he'd be sick tomorrow, Jack replied, 'I shall be sick tonight,' and carried on scoffing. Barrie was so pleased with this remark, he offered the boy a ha'penny royalty for every performance of the play. When the Llewelyn Davieses were orphaned in 1910, Barrie became their guardian. Siegfried Sassoon moved here after the war and wrote his semi-fictional autobiographies, *Memoirs of a Foxhunting Man* (1928) and *Memoirs of an Infantry Officer* (1930) here.

- Harold Pinter lived at no. 52 in the early 1980s.

head east

Campden Hill Gardens

Ford Madox Ford's address (1919), no. 20A

Ford moved into this single-room studio flat when he came out of the army. He was no longer living with Violet Hunt (see below) but the address was still conveniently nearby.

head east

Campden Hill Road

Ford Madox Ford's address (1913–19)/Violet Hunt's address (c. 1908–42), South Lodge, no. 80

From this rambling house, which Wyndham Lewis had decorated with abstract touches and which belonged to the novelist, Violet Hunt, Ford ran *The English Review*, previously based in Holland Park Avenue (see p. 414). More socializing than work used to take place – big lunches, lavish teas, tennis parties and literary soirées at which the men were forced to wear top hats, carry gloves and a cane. That was until Ezra Pound began to attend, dressed in trousers of green billiard cloth, vermilion socks, a turquoise ear-ring and a huge tie hand-painted by a Japanese futurist poet, and the rules were relaxed. (After this the house parrot would shriek only 'Ezra, Ezra'.) Hunt stayed here until 1942, collecting voluminous notes for her unwritten biography of the Pre-Raphaelite associate, Charles Augustus Howell.

• Cecil Day-Lewis lived at no. 96 from 1953 to 1957.

head south

Sheffield Terrace

G. K. Chesterton's birthplace and address (1874–7), no. 32

The larger-than-life creator of Father Brown was born into a comfortable middle-class family – estate agents Chesterton's still practise in Kensington. The Chestertons moved out when G. K.'s sister, Beatrice, died aged 8.

head south along Hornton Street

Campden Grove

James Joyce's address (1931), no. 28B

This was one of Joyce's few London addresses, and he moved here when he was 49 and mainly concerned with legalizing his marriage to

Nora Barnacle. Joyce disliked the area, claimed it was inhabited by mummies, and described the road as 'Campden Grave'. He left for Paris at the outset of winter.

turn right at Kensington Church Street

Holland Place

Ezra Pound's address (1914–20), 5 Holland Place Chambers
Ezra Pound and Dorothy Shakespear moved into what Peter Ackroyd describes as a 'queer, triangular flat' after marrying in 1914. By the end of the war Pound had become dismissive of English culture and told William Carlos Williams, 'there is no longer any intellectual life in England save what centres in this . . . room'. In his hypercritical state Pound wrote *Hell Cantos* (1919). The Pounds left England in 1920 for Paris, where he told an American bookseller that he had been obliged to leave London as 'the water was creeping up, and they might wake up some morning to find they had web feet'. Pound returned to the city only one more time, for T. S. Eliot's memorial service in 1965.

head west along Holland Street (one street south of Holland Place)

Kensington Church Walk

Ezra Pound's address (1909–14), no. 10
Ezra Pound secured his fearsome reputation among the London literati while renting a first-floor room in a cottage on this hard-to-find, meandering alley. The flat had no toilet or running water but there was a cast-iron fireplace with a hob either side of the bars, as Pound described in the poem, *The Bathtub* (1916). When William Carlos Williams sent Pound some poetry he had written at his home in New Jersey, Pound replied, 'Great art it is not,' and sent back a reading list that included the works of Browning, Rossetti and Yeats and the writings of Margaret Sackville, Rosamund Watson and Ernest Rhys – little of which Williams was able to find in that part of America – so that Williams could 'learn what the people of the second rank can do'.

Lascelles Abercrombie, one of the leading Georgian poets (a polite and only slightly anti-establishment group and therefore to Pound and Co. beyond the pale), fared only slightly better than Williams. When Abercrombie suggested in a magazine article that new poets should abandon realism and take up Wordsworth, Pound wrote and challenged him to a duel. Abercrombie laughed it off until someone told him that Pound was an expert fencer and quite serious. Abercrombie took advantage of the challenged party's right to choose weapons and suggested that he and Pound bombard each other with unsold copies of their books. Richard Aldington based the painter, Mr Upjohn, and the studio featured in his 1929 novel, *Death of a Hero*, on Pound and the Kensington Church Walk room. Pound moved out when he married Dorothy Shakespear in 1914.

head south

Kensington Church Street

St Mary Abbott's, Kensington Church Street at High Street Kensington
G. K. Chesterton married the unfortunately named Frances Blogg in this George Gilbert Scott rebuilt church – it has the tallest spire in London at 278 feet – in June 1901. The newly wed Chestertons immediately left for their honeymoon in East Anglia but arrived so late at their Ipswich hotel that Frances was too tired to do anything. Chesterton went off for a walk but got lost, and when he finally made it back Frances wouldn't let him touch her. It is believed she never changed her mind throughout their marriage. Ezra Pound married Dorothy Shakespear, whom one of his friends described as looking like a 'young Victorian lady out skating', here in 1914. St Mary's was a surprising choice as he used to claim when living nearby that the church bells drove him to distraction and he once visited the vicar to complain about their 'foul nuisance'.

head west along Kensington High Street and turn right at Argyll Road

Phillimore Place

Kenneth Grahame's address (1901–8), no. 16
Despite being secretary of the Bank of England, Grahame found time to write *The Wind in the Willows* (1908) which germinated out of the bedtime stories he made up and read to his son, Alistair (known affectionately as 'Mouse'). Despite the idyllic nature of the stories, Alistair's life took a tragic route. A precocious, pampered and troubled child, he used to lie down in the road in front of cars (which, given their scarcity in those days, would stop for him) and later committed suicide by putting his head on a railway line.

detour west

Holland Park

Holland House

Two wings survive of the seventeenth-century mansion, west of
Campden Hill, in which Joseph Addison, founder of *The Spectator*,
lived from 1716 to 1719. Around that time, Holland House was a great
centre for Whig politics and hosted many literary parties, at one of
which, in 1812, Lord Byron met Lady Caroline Lamb. The Holland line
died out in the twentieth century, one of the last incumbents being a
Lady Ilchester, who may have been the inspiration for Aunt Dahlia in
P. G. Wodehouse's Jeeves stories. Literary parties were still being held
here in the 1930s, but Logan Pearsall Smith told Cyril Connolly that
they were 'terribly dull' and mainly featured people delivering interminable monologues on pet subjects such as the route of Alexander's
Indian expeditions. The property was bombed in the Second World
War, after which it was partly rebuilt into a youth hostel.

EAST OF KENSINGTON CHURCH STREET

Away from the main roads, particularly south of Kensington High
Street, some exquisite cottages and imposing villas can be found in
what used to be known as the 'Old Court Suburb'. The area contains a
number of embassies, particularly near Kensington Gardens.

- Northern landmarks can be reached from Notting Hill Gate tube; those
  further south from High Street Kensington tube.

Notting Hill end to Palace Gate end: roughly north to south

Palace Gardens Terrace

Wyndham Lewis's address (1920s), no. 61
While living here, Lewis used to claim that Bloomsbury Group members
Roger Fry and Clive Bell were stationed on the roof, spying on him.

head south

Palace Green

William Makepeace Thackeray's address (1862–3), no. 2
Soon after Thackeray bought land here on the edge of Kensington Gardens, the rather dilapidated house which stood on the site was declared

unsafe and was demolished. He replaced it with an imitation of Wren's
Marlborough House in the Mall and lived here for a year before dying.
The property is now occupied by the Israeli Embassy.

cross the High Street

Young Street

William Makepeace Thackeray's address (1846–53), no. 6
Thackeray wrote some of his best-known works in this double-fronted
yellow-brick house (now a college) next to the modern-day Barker's
department store, including *Vanity Fair* (1847–8), *Pendennis* (1848–50)
and *The History of Henry Esmond* (1852), which contains descriptions of
nearby Kensington Square during the eighteenth-century Jacobite uprising. When he first saw the house, Thackeray exclaimed: 'It has the air
of a feudal castle. I'll have a flagstaff put over the coping of the wall
and hoist a standard when I'm home.' Charlotte Brontë dedicated *Jane
Eyre* to Thackeray, but her attendance at a dinner party here in 1848
was not a success. She was so shy she barely communicated and, when
she was asked if she liked London, managed to reply only, 'Yes and no.'
Halfway through the evening Thackeray slipped out and headed for his
club. A few years after leaving Young Street, Thackeray and a friend
went for a walk around Kensington and, as they passed the house, the
author roared, 'Down on your knees, you rogue, for this is where
Vanity Fair was penned, and I will go down with you for I have a high
opinion of it myself.'

head east along Thackeray Street

Kensington Court Place

T. S. Eliot's address (1957–65) and deathsite, 3 Kensington Court Gardens, no. 37 Kensington Court Place
Eliot moved into this block of flats after marrying Valerie Fletcher and
for the first time in decades was happy, telling journalists he was planning to take up dancing lessons again, despite having turned 70. Eliot
soon discovered, to his astonishment, that Groucho Marx was a huge
fan of his poetry and, on an imminent visit to London, wanted to meet
him. Eliot wrote and told the comic, 'This has greatly enhanced my
credit line in the neighbourhood, particularly with the greengrocer
across the street.' Marx sent back a thank-you note which ended, 'Best
wishes to you and your lovely wife, whoever she may be.' On arriving
in London, Marx was invited for dinner and in preparation read *Murder in the Cathedral* twice, *The Waste Land* three times and 'just in case

of conversational bottle neck . . . brushed up on *King Lear*', but all
Eliot wanted to talk about was the Marx brothers' films *Animal
Crackers* and *A Night at the Opera*. In his later years, Eliot, unwilling to
go out much, would stay in listening to Bartók and reading to Valerie
from Boswell's *Life of Johnson*, Coleridge's *Letters* and Rudyard
Kipling's *Kim*.

head east

De Vere Gardens

Henry James's address (1886–1902), no. 34
James moved into the fourth floor of this smart apartment block – 'my
small house seems most pleasant' he wrote – as *The Bostonians* (1886)
was coming out. In 1894, when Mark Twain, briefly living in Chelsea,
dropped by, James explained that he was teaching himself to dictate
directly to a typewriter (the term was then used both for the machine
and for the person who operated it). One Sunday afternoon that year
James was visited by Henry Harland and Aubrey Beardsley, who were
about to launch a new publication, what became the notorious *Yellow
Book*, the bible of the Aesthetic Movement (yellow being associated
with wicked French novels). Harland and Beardsley successfully
enlisted the celebrated author as a contributor, and James asked for £10
per 1,000 words (although he admitted he would make do with slightly
less for a very long piece).

For the first issue James came up with *The Death of the Lion*, an
essay on literature, but once the *Yellow Book* was established James
expressed his concern over the 'small square lemon-coloured quarterly'
that had shocked Victorian society. The *Yellow Book* fell from grace
after Oscar Wilde was convicted of homosexuality. In court he was
carrying a yellow-backed book and the public, mistaking this for *the
Yellow Book*, marched on the publication's editorial offices in Vigo
Street, Mayfair, and smashed the windows (see p. 193). In 1902 James
moved to Rye in Sussex after writing *The Tragic Muse* (1890), *What
Maisie Knew* (1897) and *The Ambassadors* (1903) here.

• Robert Browning's last English address was at no. 29 from 1888 to 1889,
returning to Italy where he died that year.

Maida Vale, w9

In *Books Do Furnish a Room*, the 1971 volume of Anthony Powell's *A Dance to the Music of Time* series, Maida Vale is described as consisting of 'time-honoured landladies, inveterate lodgers, immemorial whores'. The area is a little schizophrenic, combining the shabby bedsits around Shirland Road and Harrow Road with the stucco mansions of Little Venice on the north bank of the Grand Union Canal.

Maida Vale

Kingsley Amis's address (1965–7), no. 108, Maida Vale tube
Moving to an odd location as usual – the house, though grand, is on a noisy main road – Amis, who had just broken up with Hilly Bardwell (Martin Amis's mother), began a relationship with the novelist, Elizabeth Jane Howard. By this stage Amis had given up his teaching jobs in Cambridge and was relying solely on writing but, being a gregarious soul, was unhappy working at home; so, to ensure no slacking, he set himself a rigorous timetable which had to be adhered to even if he had the most miserable hangover. Each day a battle would rage within Amis's mind before he started work, and inevitably the lazy side would win, which meant that he would write all morning still in his dressing-gown. Howard, meanwhile, worked (dressed) in her study, and when they'd both done a fair day's slog (by about half-past eight in the evening) they'd stop and read the day's efforts to each other. Amis left when he went to Nashville to lecture.

North Kensington, w10

The area's name is something of a misnomer as Kensington proper is a couple of miles south, and North Kensington in contrast is bedevilled by rotting houses and uninspired redevelopment, bordered to the north by the grotty Harrow Road, to the west by the stark and windswept Wormwood Scrubs and to the south by the elevated Westway motorway. Before the Second World War North Kensington was a reasonably wealthy suburb of little interest, but it gradually became shabby as merchants began vacating the huge houses and, during the war, bombs flattened a number of streets. Decaying properties were then taken over by slum landlords, most notably Peter Rachman, and colonized by West Indian immigrants, which led to growing tension between the new residents and local poor whites and culminated in the 1958 race riots here and in Notting Hill to the south, as described by Colin MacInnes at the end of *Absolute Beginners* (1959). In the aftermath of the riots the West Indian community founded what is now the massive Notting Hill carnival (see Notting Hill introduction, below).

Harrow Road end to the Westway: roughly north to south

Harrow Road

Kensal Green Cemetery, Harrow Road opposite College Road
Best approached from the canal towpath, the cemetery contains the graves of Thomas Hood (died 1845), Sydney Smith (1845), Leigh Hunt (1859), William Makepeace Thackeray (1863), Harrison Ainsworth (1882), Anthony Trollope (1882) and Wilkie Collins (1889). Margaret Drabble's *The Radiant Way* (1987) features a psychopath who severs the heads of people walking along the canal by the Harrow Road. In Michael Moorcock's *Mother London* (1988), the Scaramanga sisters live in the fictitious Bank Cottage on the south side of the Grand Union Canal opposite the cemetery.

head south along Ladbroke Grove

Chesterton Road

Named after the area's greatest writer, G. K. Chesterton, Chesterton Road is where Keith Talent grows up in 'a low-rent basement flat' in Martin Amis's *London Fields* (1989). By the time Talent enters the novel, he is unaware whether his mother is still living on in Chesterton Road 'speechlessly'.

continue east

Golborne Road

While convalescing from a number of bad beatings, Keith Talent in Martin Amis's *London Fields* spends a considerable amount of time in the cafés of Golborne Road, where he ruminates on why one always saw 'black guys with white girls always blondes, always, presumably for maximum contrast gain and never saw white guys with black girls'.

Trellick Tower
In the same novel, Talent lives in this soaring block, London's most exciting skyscraper, built by flamboyant Hungarian émigré, Erno

Goldfinger, who is occasionally cited as inspiration for the James Bond villain of the same name.

The Westway

This two-mile-long elevated motorway is the setting for J. G. Ballard's *Concrete Island* (1973), in which a car crashes in the middle of the road but the driver is unable to flag down assistance from passing vehicles.

Notting Hill, W10, W11

'If I write about a hill that is rotting, it is because I deplore rot' from *Rotting Hill*, Wyndham Lewis, 1951

Brash, bold and thoroughly cosmopolitan, Notting Hill is in many respects the west London version of Islington – neglected in the 1960s, rediscovered in the '70s, gentrified in the '80s and indulged in the '90s. But Notting Hill has an even greater concentration of media outlets than Islington, with publishing firms, TV production companies and record labels dotted around the smart stucco terraces and with the huge Virgin organization based locally. The area is also renowned for the teeming milieu of Portobello Road market, which at weekends becomes one of the most crowded spots in the capital, and the annual Notting Hill carnival, which is now the largest street parade in Europe and attracts over a million people during the last weekend of August.

Notting Hill fascinated writers throughout the twentieth century, beginning with G. K. Chesterton's absurdist fable, *The Napoleon of Notting Hill* (1904). Chesterton, keen on the idea of the strong, proud, seemingly self-sufficient neighbourhood, dreamed up the fantasy romance while 'wandering about the streets telling [himself] stories of feudal sallies and sieges'. In the book, Chesterton painted an England of 1984 governed by monarchs chosen at random from the civil service who, when called, must serve, however unsuitable. More typical of Notting Hill are Wyndham Lewis's *Rotting Hill* (1951), Lynne Reid Banks's *The L-Shaped Room* (1960), Michael Moorcock's *Mother London* (1988), Mike Phillips's *Blood Rights* (1989) and Nicholas Royle's *Counterparts* (1993). The one recent book most closely identified with the area is Martin Amis's *London Fields* (1989) which, despite the irrelevant name – London Fields is in Hackney, east London (see p. 261) – is mainly set locally and features a group of fantastic characters probably drawn from unappetizing elements of Amis's psyche.

Philip Larkin clashed with Margaret Thatcher, then prime minister, at a 1982 dinner party held at the Ladbroke Grove home of Hugh Thomas, then head of the Conservative Party's Centre for Policy Studies. Larkin, upset to find he was surrounded by 'intellectuals', including Stephen Spender, Tom Stoppard, Anthony Powell and Isaiah Berlin, couldn't think of anything to say until Thatcher began talking about Germany. When the prime minister moaned about the Berlin Wall, Larkin turned to her and exclaimed, 'Surely you don't want to see a united Germany?' 'Well, no,' Thatcher agreed. 'Well then,' Larkin continued, 'what's all this hypocrisy about wanting the wall down then?'

Bookshops

Elgin Books, 6 Elgin Crescent, tel. 020 7229-2186, is a delightful shop, set over two floors.
Travel Bookshop, 13–15 Blenheim Crescent, tel. 020 7229-5260, has a huge cosmopolitan stock.

Westway end to Notting Hill Gate: roughly west to east

Elgin Crescent

Osbert Lancaster's address (1900s) and birthplace (1905), no. 79
In his memoirs, *All Done from Memory* (1963), the cartoonist, walking around Notting Hill during the Second World War, comes upon a street of dilapidated semis – 'all peeling paint and crumbling volutes' – and a group of sad-looking houses whose railings had been wrenched out to help the war effort. Lancaster notes the classical embellishments, the pillared portico and mouldings which mark it as a solid Victorian bourgeois home and is upset at the different ranges of net curtains which show it's now been turned into flats. Peering at the fading number and street sign on the wall, he soon realizes he's looking at the house where he was born, in 1905. Lancaster continues his wanderings around Notting Hill and is filled with melancholy at how the once grand square and terraces that had formed 'the very acropolis of Edwardian propriety' have suffered a severe decline, the rich city merchants having long ago fled to the suburbs, to be replaced by 'Viennese professors and Indian students and bed-sitter business girls'. These days Elgin Crescent has been restored to some of its former glory. Opposite Lancaster's house is the flat where Jawaharlal Nehru, the Indian leader, once lived.

head south along Ladbroke Grove

Lansdowne Crescent

In Martin Amis's *London Fields* (1989), Guy Clinch lives in this road, which Amis presumably chose because Jimi Hendrix died at no. 22, the former Samarkand Hotel.

Ladbroke Square

Ladbroke Square Gardens
In *The Information* (1995), Martin Amis describes this patch of greenery as Dogshit Park.

Holland Park Avenue

In Amis's *The Information*, Gwyn Barry, hated by the novel's hero, Richard Tull, and purveyor of literary 'trex', lives in splendour in this main road.

Ford Madox Ford's address (1907–10), no. 84
From above a poultry shop at this address in the last few years of Edward VII's reign, Ford edited *The English Review*, a hugely influential publication dedicated to the best new writing in England. Before he could publish, Ford needed to make the place more appetizing or, as Violet Hunt, with whom Ford later lived, wrote in her autobiography, *Those Flurried Years* (1926), 'the office was a maisonette above a poulterer's and fishmonger's combined. The sickly and depraved smell of chickens assailed me walking upstairs past the shop premise.' Ford couldn't do much about the smell, but he did line the stair walls with paintings by his grandfather, the Pre-Raphaelite, Ford Madox Brown. Unfortunately, these had to be sold after a year due to cash-flow problems.

Meanwhile *The English Review* took off culturally, if not commercially. The first issue premiered H. G. Wells's satire on advertising and quack medicines, *Tono-Bungay* (1909), and included contributions from Henry James and Tolstoy. Soon no. 84 was filled with would-be poets, hangers-on and beggars, and one day in 1909 a strange character wearing a long black coat and a multitude of scarves entered. Ford thought he must be a Continental refugee, or a Russian anarchist (there were lots around at the time), but the figure left a bundle of manuscripts and vanished, leaving no name or address. A few days later the mystery man returned and was amazed to find that Ford liked his work. It was Wyndham Lewis, who became an *English Review* regular. On a later occasion Lewis dropped by to get Ford's opinion on *The Pole*, a short story he had written, and, finding Ford in the bath, read the whole story to him while Ford washed. Also that year D. H. Lawrence sent in some poems that Nottingham University's magazine had rejected. When the office secretary asked Ford if he had discovered another genius, the editor replied, 'It's a big one this time.' Ford also published Conrad, who occasionally slept on the floor, and Ezra Pound.

In those days Ford was known by his original name, Ford Hermann Hueffer. For years his publisher had been suggesting that he change his name since no one could pronounce 'Hueffer', and so he chose Ford Madox Ford, partly in honour of Ford Madox Brown, and partly because Germanic names weren't popular in English society during the First World War. (Richard Aldington later claimed that 'Ford discovered that he was and always had been a patriotic Englishman'). Unsurprisingly, the new name aroused mockery. Ezra Pound affectionately called him 'Forty Mad-dogs Whoofer' and Osbert Sitwell 'Freud Madox Fraud'. Rebecca West described Ford as the author that 'people only recognized as he disappeared round the corner' and that being embraced by him was like being the toast under a poached egg. Anthony Burgess later claimed that Ford was the greatest novelist of the period.

head east and turn left at Pembridge Road

Portobello Road

London's most famous street market (along with Petticoat Lane), Portobello Road, unlike the other, overflows with enticing stalls and small permanent shops selling a mixture of antiques and interesting junk. In Martin Amis's *London Fields*, Keith Talent spends much of his time in the Mecca bookmakers by the market and in the nearby pubs, playing darts and plotting scams.

George Orwell's address (1927–8), no. 22
After resigning his commission in the Burmese police force and staying briefly with his family in Southwold, Suffolk, Orwell (then Eric Blair) decided to become a writer and move to London. In need of a place to stay he asked an old acquaintance, the poet Ruth Pitter, to find him lodgings; she came up with a sparsely furnished, freezing room in this unassuming little house at the southern end of Portobello Road, next to the pottery studio where she worked. The landlady, a Mrs Craig, had once been a maid to a titled lady and was an insufferable snob. One

day Orwell came back to find the occupants of the house locked out and staring hopefully at a window that was open on an upper floor. He suggested they borrow a ladder, visible in the front garden next door, no. 20, but Mrs Craig objected on the grounds that in fourteen years of living in the street she had never spoken to her working-class neighbour and could not bring herself to do so now. Orwell relented and had to walk a mile or so to one of Mrs Craig's relatives and borrow their ladder, which he then struggled to carry back. This vignette of the complications caused by middle-class respectability gave him much ammunition in later novels.

Pitter, meanwhile, was shocked at the idea that Blair/Orwell wanted to be a writer. She felt he was starting too late and had no income to fall back on, and her scepticism was reinforced when he let her look at his verse. She thought it naïve and amateurish, and later remembered how 'we used to laugh till we cried at some of the bits he showed us'. Nevertheless Orwell pressed on with his ambitions and chose to experience life as a tramp in the slum areas of east London, with some vague idea of collecting research for a book on the subject (what became *Down and Out in Paris and London*, 1933). Orwell used Pitter's pottery workshop (rather than nice Mrs Craig's rooms) to change into his tramping clothes, bought from charity shops in Lambeth, and then walked the seven miles east to Limehouse to begin his travails. He left the house for Paris in spring 1928.

head back south

Notting Hill Gate

Site of Wyndham Lewis's address (1940s), no. 27A

Lewis and his wife moved back to England after spending the Second World War in America and, when they re-entered the property, they found it had suffered minor bomb-damage. He used the flat as a microcosm for the shabby condition of post-war England in *Rotting Hill* (1951).

Shepherd's Bush, W12

Shepherd's Bush is Notting Hill without style and, like the latter, a popular media area (the BBC occupies a huge ugly site in the north of the area near Wormwood Scrubs); it has been randomly gentrified in recent years.

Du Cane Road

Hammersmith Hospital, East Acton tube
An 18-month-old Arab girl flown from the Gulf in 1977 for an operation to save her from a condition which had doctors baffled was cured when a nurse realized that the girl's symptoms were similar to those of a character in Agatha Christie's *The Pale Horse* (1961) who turned out to be dying of thallium poisoning. Tests proved that the nurse was right, and the girl recovered.

Wormwood Scrubs, East Acton tube
Joe Orton spent six months here in 1962 after being prosecuted for stealing books from Islington libraries (see p. 278).

West Kensington, w14

Like North Kensington, West Kensington bears little resemblance to Kensington proper, being composed largely of seedy hotels, dismal flats and roaring roads (it's the capital's worst area for carjacking). Muriel Spark's *A Far Cry from Kensington* (1988) deals with the seedy world of local bed-sits in the 1950s. In Hanif Kureishi's *The Buddha of Suburbia* (1990), Karim Amir, looking for action near, if not in, central London, moves here from bland suburban Bromley and notes in doing so the important people who once lived locally: 'Gandhi himself once had a room . . . Rachman kept a flat for the young Mandy Rice-Davies in the next street.'

● Landmarks can be reached from West Kensington tube.

railway end to Holland Park end: west to east

Addison Bridge Place

Samuel Taylor Coleridge's address (1811–12), no. 7
Coleridge lived opposite where the Olympia exhibition centre now stands when he was working on the political paper that became *The Friend* (1818).

Addison Road

Site of John Galsworthy's address (1905–12), no. 4
Joseph Conrad finished off *The Secret Agent* (1907) while staying
here with Galsworthy briefly in 1906. Conrad himself later lived at
99B.

Warwick Gardens

G. K. Chesterton's address (1877–1901), no. 11
Chesterton grew up in this cream-coloured stucco house, reading
avidly from the huge library, especially Macaulay's histories, later
describing how he was 'fascinated by the district of Kensington [which]
was, and is, laid out like a chart to illustrate Macaulay's Essays'. Here
he wrote his first book of poems, *The Wild Knight*.

FURTHER WEST

Hayes

This grey land of chemical works, dismal housing and arterial development was George Orwell's model for the suburban hell of West Bletchley in *Coming up for Air* (1939), in which the narrator, George Bowling, lives in the fictitious Ellesmere Road – 'even if you don't [know it] you know fifty others exactly like it . . . the stucco front, the creosoted gate, the privet hedge, the green front door'. Orwell chose Hayes after spending a couple of years here as a teacher in the early '30s, first at a private school, the Hawthorns at 116 Church Road (it is now a hotel), and then at Frays College at 65 Harefield Road, Uxbridge, leaving after nearly dying of pneumonia. Orwell described Hayes as 'one of the most godforsaken places I have ever struck. The population seems to be entirely made up of clerks who frequent tin-roofed chapels on Sundays and for the rest bolt themselves within doors.' Little has changed, except that nobody goes to church any longer. John Betjeman, predictably, found something of value in Hayes, ironically in Church Road where Orwell had taught, namely the parish church, St Mary's, which he claimed was one of the gems of Middlesex.

BIBLIOGRAPHY

The Oxford Literary Guide to the British Isles, edited by Dorothy Eagle and Hilary Carnell. Oxford at the Clarendon Press, Oxford, 1977.

The Wordsworth Book of Literary Anecdotes by Robert Hendrickson. Wordsworth, Hertfordshire, 1997.

The Woman's Travel Guide by Josie Barnard. Virago, London, 1993.

Our Sisters' London by Katherine Sturtevant. The Women's Press, London, 1990.

Dickens' London, An Imaginative Vision, introduced by Peter Ackroyd. Headline, London, 1987.

A Shakespeare Companion by F. E. Halliday. Penguin, London, 1964.

Betjeman's London, edited by Pennie Denton. John Murray, London, 1988.

London Lines: The Places and Faces of London in Poetry and Song. Selected by Kenneth Baker. Methuen, London, 1982.

A Literary Gazetteer of England by Lois H. Fisher. McGraw-Hill, New York, 1972.

A Sherlock Holmes Commentary by D. Martin Dakin. David & Charles, Newton Abbot, 1972.

The Encyclopaedia Sherlockiana by Jack Tracy. Doubleday, New York, 1977.

T. S. Eliot by Peter Ackroyd. Hamish Hamilton, London, 1984.

Philip Larkin, A Writer's Life by Andrew Motion. Faber & Faber, London, 1993.

A Reader's Guide to Writers' Britain by Sally Varlow. Prion, London, 1996.

You've Had Your Time by Anthony Burgess. Heinemann, London, 1990.

A Sultry Month, Scenes of London Literary Life in 1846 by Alethea Hayter. Faber & Faber, London, 1965.

The Oscar Wilde file, compiled by Jonathan Goodman. W. H. Allen & Co., London, 1988.

A Book of London, edited by Ivor Brown. Collins, London and Glasgow, 1961.

Ian Fleming by Andrew Lycett. Weidenfeld & Nicolson, London, 1995.

The Orton Diaries, edited by John Lahr. Methuen, London, 1986.

Literary London by Andrew Davies. Macmillan, London, 1988.

Poets London by Paddy Kitchen. Longman, London, 1980.

Soho in the Fifties and Sixties by Jonathan Fryer. National Portrait Gallery Publications, London, 1998.

W. B. Yeats: A New Biography by A. Norman Jeffares. Hutchinson, London, 1988.

Kenneth Grahame: An Innocent in the Wild Wood by Alison Prince. Allison & Busby, London, 1994.

Introduction to Dickens by Peter Ackroyd. Mandarin, London, 1991.

Graham Greene, The Man Within by Michael Shelden. Heinemann, London, 1994.

The London of Charles Dickens. London Transport and Midas Books, London, 1970.

Somerset Maugham and his World by Frederic Raphael. Thames & Hudson, London, 1976.

John Buchan and his World by Janet Adam Smith. Thames & Hudson, London, 1979.

Joseph Conrad and his World by Norman Sherry. Thames and Hudson, London, 1972.

The Life of Raymond Chandler by Frank MacShane. Jonathan Cape, London, 1976.

Lawrence of Arabia and his World by Richard Perceval Graves. Thames & Hudson, London, 1976.

Thomas Hardy's World by Molly Lefebure. Carlton, London, 1997.

The Charles Dickens Encyclopaedia, compiled by Michael and Mollie Hardwick. Osprey, Reading, 1973.

Kingsley Amis, A Biography by Eric Jacobs. Hodder & Stoughton, London, 1995.

The Exquisite Life of Oscar Wilde by Stephen Calloway and David Colvin. Orion Media, London, 1997.

The Time Traveller: The Life of H. G. Wells by Norman and Jeanne Mackenzie. Weidenfeld & Nicolson, London, 1973.

Somerset Maugham and the Maugham Dynasty by Bryan Cannon. Sinclair Stevenson, London, 1967.

Orwell: The Authorised Biography by Michael Shelden. Heinemann, London, 1991.

Writers and Hampstead edited by Ian Norrie. High Hill Press, London, 1987.

D. H. Lawrence and his Hampstead Circle by Christopher Wade. Hampstead Museum, London, 1985.

The Streets of Hampstead by Christopher Wade. High Hill Press, London, 1984.

Graham Greene Country by Paul Hogarth and Graham Greene. Pavilion, London, 1986.

The Brideshead Generation, Evelyn Waugh and his Friends by Humphrey Carpenter. Weidenfeld & Nicolson, London, 1989.

Under Siege: Literary Life in London 1939–45 by Robert Hewison. Readers Union Group of Book Clubs, Newton Abbot, 1978.

D. H. Lawrence and his World by Francis King. Thames & Hudson, London, 1978.

The Capital Companion by Peter Gibson. Webb & Bower, Devon, 1985.

Noel Coward by Clive Fisher. Weidenfeld & Nicolson, London, 1992.

London: A Literary Companion by Peter Vansittart. John Murray, London, 1992.

John Betjeman: A Life in Pictures by Bevis Hillier. John Murray, London, 1984.

Young Betjeman by Bevis Hillier. John Murray, London, 1988.

London and the Famous by Katy Carter. Frederick Muller, London, 1982.

Gilbert: The Man Who Was G. K. Chesterton by Michael Coren. Jonathan Cape, London, 1989.

Ezra Pound's Kensington by Patricia Hutchins. Faber & Faber, London, 1965.

Dylan: The Nine Lives of Dylan Thomas by Jonathan Fryer. Kyle Cathie, London, 1993.

Ezra Pound and his World by Peter Ackroyd. Thames & Hudson, London, 1980.

The Fitzroy by Sally Fiber. Temple House Books, Sussex, 1995.

East of Bloomsbury by David A. Hayes. Camden Historic Society, 1998.

The Life of Dylan Thomas by Constantine Fitzgibbon. J. M. Dent, London, 1965.

Aldous Huxley: A Biography, Volume 1 (1894–1939) by Sybille Bedford. Chatto & Windus, London, 1973.

The Life and Work of Ford Madox Ford by Frank MacShane. Routledge & Kegan Paul, London, 1965.

Literary London by Eric Lane. Dedalus, Cambridgeshire, 1988.

The Doctor, the Detective and Arthur Conan Doyle by Martin Booth. Hodder & Stoughton, London, 1997.

The Annotated Sherlock Holmes, edited by William S. Baring-Gould. John Murray, London, 1968.

Somerset Maugham by Anthony Curtis. Weidenfeld & Nicolson, London, 1977.

In the Fifties by Peter Vansittart. John Murray, London, 1995.

Curriculum Vitae by Muriel Spark. Constable, London, 1992.

The Life of Graham Greene Vol. 1 by Norman Sherry. Jonathan Cape, London, 1989.

The Opium Eater by Grevel Lindop. Oxford University Press, Oxford, 1985.

London Yankees: Portraits of American Writers and Artists in England 1894–1914 by Stanley Weintraub. W. H. Allen, London, 1979.

The London Encyclopaedia, edited by Ben Weinreb and Christopher Hibbert. Macmillan, London, 1983.

Oscar Wilde by Richard Ellmann. Hamish Hamilton, London, 1987.

Chelsea Today by Roger George Clark. Robert Hale, London, 1991.

Waterstone's Guide to London Writing, edited by Nick Rennison. Waterstone's, London, 1998.

Virginia Woolf's London by Dorothy Brewster. George Allen & Unwin Ltd, London, 1959.

Countless novels and poetry, but particularly inspiring were:

Novels

Julian Barnes *Metroland*, G. K. Chesterton *The Man Who Was Thursday*, Arthur Conan Doyle *The Adventures of Sherlock Holmes*, Joseph Conrad *The Secret Agent*, Charles Dickens *Barnaby Rudge*, Margaret Drabble *The Radiant Way*, Graham Greene *The Ministry of Fear*, George and Weedon Grossmith *The Diary of a Nobody*, Hanif Kureishi *The Buddha of Suburbia*, W. Somerset Maugham *Cakes and Ale*, George Orwell *Keep the Aspidistra Flying*, Iain Sinclair *Downriver*, Muriel Spark *The Ballad of Peckham Rye*, Bram Stoker *Dracula*, H. G. Wells *The Invisible Man*

Poetry

John Betjeman *Collected Poems*, William Blake *Collected Poems*, T. S. Eliot *The Waste Land*, Ezra Pound *The Cantos*

Other

James Boswell *London Journal*, Anthony Burgess *You've Had Your Time*, Iain Sinclair *Lights Out for the Territory*

INDEX OF WRITERS

INDEX OF PLACES

Buildings listed in italics are no longer in existence.

PENGUIN HISTORY

THE LONDON COMPENDIUM

ED GLINERT

The streets of London resonate with secret stories, from East End lore to Cold War espionage, from tales of riots, rakes, brothels, anarchy and grisly murders, to Rolling Stones gigs, gangland drinking-dens, Orwell's Fitzrovia and Lenin's haunts.

Londoner Ed Glinert has walked the city from Limehouse to Lambeth, Whitehall to Whitechapel, unravelling its mysteries along the way. Here he uncovers the tales of the hidden metropolis – street by street, area by area and building by building. Now updated and with a new subject index to help you discover the secret city, this book reveals London as you've never seen it before.

'One of those books, destined to be read until they fall apart, that map the unmappable and make it live' Iain Sinclair

'Splendid ... brings the underground to the surface, be it in the form of psychedelic rock clubs, suffragettes and political radicals, or the secret tunnels that link buildings across the capital in case of war' *Daily Telegraph*

PENGUIN CLASSICS

THE DIARY OF A NOBODY
GEORGE AND WEEDON GROSSMITH

'I fail to see – because I do not happen to be a "Somebody" – why my diary should not be interesting'

Mr Pooter is a man of modest ambitions, content with his ordinary life. Yet he always seems to be troubled by disagreeable tradesmen, impertinent young office clerks and wayward friends, not to mention his devil-may-care son Lupin's unsuitable choice of bride. Try as he might, he cannot avoid life's embarrassing mishaps. In the bumbling, absurd yet ultimately endearing figure of Pooter, the Grossmiths created an immortal comic character and a superb satire on the snobberies of middle-class suburbia – one which also sends up late Victorian crazes for Aestheticism, spiritualism and bicycling, as well as the fashion for publishing diaries by anybody and everybody.

This edition contains the original illustrations by Weedon Grossmith, further reading and an introduction by Ed Glinert discussing the novel's initial serialization in *Punch*, reactions to Pooter, the growth of suburbs and the figure of Mrs Pooter.

'The jewel at the heart of English comic literature' William Trevor

'The funniest book in the world' Evelyn Waugh

Edited with an introduction and notes by Ed Glinert

PENGUIN CLASSICS

THE DIARIES OF SAMUEL PEPYS: A SELECTION
SAMUEL PEPYS

'But Lord, what a sad sight it was by moonlight to see the whole City almost on fire'

The 1660s represent a turning point in English history, and for the main events – the Restoration, the Dutch War, the Great Plague and the Fire of London – Pepys provides a definitive eyewitness account. As well as recording public and historical events, Pepys paints a vivid picture of his personal life, from his socializing and amorous entanglements, to theatre going and his work at the Navy Board. Unequalled for its frankness, high spirits and sharp observations, the diary is both a literary masterpiece and a marvellous portrait of seventeenth-century life.

'This prince of Diarists, this most amiable and admirable of men, has at last been worthily served' Paul Johnson, *Spectator*

PREVIOUSLY PUBLISHED AS THE SHORTER PEPYS

Selected and edited by Robert Latham

PENGUIN CLASSICS

A JOURNAL OF THE PLAGUE YEAR
DANIEL DEFOE

'It was a most surprising thing, to see those Streets, which were usually so thronged, now grown desolate'

In 1665 the Great Plague swept through London, claiming nearly 100,000 lives. In *A Journal*, written nearly sixty years later, Defoe vividly chronicled the progress of the epidemic. We follow his fictional narrator through a city transformed: the streets and alleyways deserted; the houses of death with crosses daubed on their doors; the dead-carts on their way to the pits. And he recounts the horrifying stories of the citizens he encounters, as fear, isolation and hysteria take hold. *A Journal* is both a fascinating historical document and a supreme work of imaginative reconstruction.

This edition contains a new introduction, an appendix on the Plague, a topographical index and maps of contemporary London, and reproduces Anthony Burgess's original introduction.

'The most reliable and comprehensive account of the Great Plague that we possess' Anthony Burgess

'Within the texture of Defoe's prose London becomes a living and suffering being' Peter Ackroyd

Edited with an introduction by Cynthia Wall

PENGUIN CLASSICS

THE MOONSTONE   WILKIE COLLINS

'When you looked down into the stone, you looked into a yellow deep that drew your eyes into it so that they saw nothing else'

The Moonstone, a yellow diamond looted from an Indian temple and believed to bring bad luck to its owner, is bequeathed to Rachel Verinder on her eighteenth birthday. That very night the priceless stone is stolen again and when Sergeant Cuff is brought in to investigate the crime, he soon realizes that no one in Rachel's household is above suspicion. Hailed by T. S. Eliot as 'the first, the longest, and the best of modern English detective novels', *The Moonstone* is a marvellously taut and intricate tale of mystery, in which facts and memory can prove treacherous and not everyone is as they first appear.

Sandra Kemp's introduction examines *The Moonstone* as a work of Victorian sensation fiction and an early example of the detective genre, and discusses the technique of multiple narrators, the role of opium, and Collins's sources and autobiographical references.

'Enthralling and believable . . . evokes in vivid language the spirit of a place' P. D. James, *Sunday Times*

Edited with an introduction and notes by Sandra Kemp

PENGUIN CLASSICS

BLEAK HOUSE   CHARLES DICKENS

'Jarndyce and Jarndyce has passed into a joke. That is the only good that has ever come of it'

As the interminable case of Jarndyce and Jarndyce grinds its way through the Court of Chancery, it draws together a disparate group of people: Ada and Richard Clare, whose inheritance is gradually being devoured by legal costs; Esther Summerson, a ward of court, whose parentage is a source of deepening mystery; the menacing lawyer Tulkinghorn; the determined sleuth Inspector Bucket; and even Jo, the destitute little crossing-sweeper. A savage, but often comic, indictment of a society that is rotten to the core, *Bleak House* is one Dickens's most ambitious novels, with a range that extends from the drawing rooms of the aristocracy to the poorest of London slums.

This edition follows the first edition in book form of 1853. Terry Eagleton's preface examines characterization and considers *Bleak House* as an early work of detective fiction.

'Perhaps his best novel . . . when Dickens wrote *Bleak House* he had grown up' G. K. Chesterton

'One of the finest of all English satires' Terry Eagleton

Edited with an introduction and notes by Nicola Bradbury and with a new preface by Terry Eagleton

PENGUIN CLASSICS

OLIVER TWIST   CHARLES DICKENS

'Let him feel that he is one of us; once fill his mind with the idea that he has been a thief, and he's ours – ours for his life!'

The story of the orphan Oliver, who runs away from the workhouse only to be taken in by a den of thieves, shocked readers when it was first published. Dickens's tale of childhood innocence beset by evil depicts the dark criminal underworld of a London peopled by vivid and memorable characters – the arch-villain Fagin, the artful Dodger, the menacing Bill Sikes and the prostitute Nancy. Combining elements of Gothic Romance, the Newgate Novel and popular melodrama, in *Oliver Twist* Dickens created an entirely new kind of fiction, scathing in its indictment of a cruel society, and pervaded by an unforgettable sense of threat and mystery.

This is the first critical edition to use the *Bentley's Miscellany* serial text of 1837–9, showing Oliver Twist as it appeared to its earliest readers. It includes Dickens's 1841 introduction and 1850 preface, the original illustrations and a glossary of contemporary slang.

'The power of [Dickens] is so amazing, that the reader at once becomes his captive' William Makepeace Thackeray

Edited with an introduction and notes by Philip Horne

PENGUIN CLASSICS

PYGMALION   BERNARD SHAW

'Yes, you squashed cabbage leaf . . . you incarnate insult to the English language: I could pass you off as the Queen of Sheba'

Pygmalion both delighted and scandalized its first audiences in 1914. A brilliantly witty reworking of the classical tale of the sculptor Pygmalion, who falls in love with his perfect female statue, it is also a barbed attack on the British class system and a statement of Shaw's feminist views. In Shaw's hands, the phoneticist Henry Higgins is the Pygmalion figure who believes he can transform Eliza Doolittle, a cockney flower girl, into a duchess at ease in polite society. The one thing he overlooks is that his 'creation' has a mind of her own.

This is the definitive text under the editorial supervision of Dan H. Laurence, with an illuminating introduction by Nicholas Grene, discussing the language and politics of the play. Included in this volume is Shaw's preface, as well as his 'sequel' written for the first publication in 1916, to rebut public demand for a more conventionally romantic ending.

Edited by Dan H. Laurence with an introduction by Nicholas Grene

PENGUIN CLASSICS

THE IMPORTANCE OF BEING EARNEST AND OTHER PLAYS   OSCAR WILDE

LADY WINDERMERE'S FAN / SALOMÉ / A WOMAN OF NO IMPORTANCE / AN IDEAL HUSBAND / A FLORENTINE TRAGEDY / THE IMPORTANCE OF BEING EARNEST

'To lose one parent may be regarded as a misfortune; to lose both looks like carelessness'

The Importance of Being Earnest is a glorious comedy of mistaken identity, which ridicules codes of propriety and etiquette. Manners and morality are also victims of Wilde's sharp wit in *Lady Windermere's Fan*, *A Woman of No Importance* and *An Ideal Husband*, in which snobbery and hypocrisy are laid bare. In *Salomé* and *A Florentine Tragedy*, Wilde makes powerful use of historical settings to explore the complex relationship between sex and power. The range of these plays displays Wilde's delight in artifice, masks and disguises, and reveal the pretensions of the social world in which he himself played such a dazzlingly and precarious part.

Richard Allen Cave's introduction and notes discuss the themes of the plays and Wilde's innovative methods of staging. This edition includes the excised 'Gribsby' scene from *The Importance of Being Earnest*.

'Beneath the wit there is always an intense emotional reality. He criticized his audience while he entertained it' Peter Hall, *Guardian*

Edited with introduction, commentaries and notes by Richard Allen Cave

---

PENGUIN CLASSICS

THE HISTORY OF MR POLLY H. G. WELLS

'He had a curious feeling that it would be very satisfying to marry and have a wife – only somehow he wished it wasn't Miriam'

Mr Polly is an ordinary middle-aged man who is tired of his wife's nagging and his dreary job as the owner of a regional gentleman's outfitters. Faced with the threat of bankruptcy, he concludes that the only way to escape his frustrating existence is by burning his shop to the ground, and killing himself. Unexpected events, however, conspire at the last moment to lead the bewildered Mr Polly to a bright new future – after he saves a life, fakes his death, and escapes to a life of heroism, hope and ultimate happiness.

Widely regarded as Wells's funniest novel, *The History of Mr Polly* is a compelling account of one man's triumph against social obligation. Part of a brand new Penguin series of H. G. Wells's works, this edition includes a newly-established text, a full biographical essay on Wells, a further reading list and detailed notes. In his introduction John Sutherland considers the character of Mr Polly and his relevance to Wells's own life.

Introduced by John Sutherland

Textual Editing by Simon J. James

Notes by John Sutherland and Simon J. James

PENGUIN CLASSICS

LOVE AND MR LEWISHAM   H.G. WELLS

'He was no common Student, he was a man with a Secret Life'

Young, impoverished and ambitious, science student Mr Lewisham is locked in a struggle to further himself through academic achievement. But when his former sweetheart, Ethel Henderson, re-enters his life his strictly regimented existence is thrown into chaos by the resurgence of old passion. Driven by overwhelming desire, he pursues Ethel passionately, only to find that while she returns his love she also hides a dark secret. For she is involved in a plot of trickery that goes against his firmest beliefs, working as an assistant to her stepfather – a cynical charlatan 'mystic' who earns his living by deluding the weak-willed with sly trickery.

A biting critique on the spiritualist craze sweeping the nation, *Love and Mr Lewisham* is also an exploration of one man's conflict between love and ambition. Part of a brand-new Penguin series of H. G. Wells's works, this edition includes a newly established text, a full biographical essay on Wells, a further reading list and detailed notes. The introduction, by Gillian Beer, considers the book as the first of Wells's satires on social pretension in Edwardian England.

Introduction by Gillian Beer
Textual Editing by Simon J. James
Notes by Simon J. James

PENGUIN MODERN CLASSICS

DOWN AND OUT IN PARIS AND LONDON
GEORGE ORWELL

'The white-hot reaction of a sensitive, observant, compassionate young man to poverty' Dervla Murphy

George Orwell's vivid memoir of his time living among the desperately poor and destitute is a moving tour of the underworld of society.

Written when Orwell was a struggling writer in his twenties, it documents his 'first contact with poverty': sleeping in bug-infested hostels and doss-houses of last resort, working as a dishwasher in Paris, surviving on scraps and cigarette butts, living alongside tramps, a star-gazing pavement artist and a starving Russian ex-army captain. Exposing a shocking, previously hidden world to readers, Orwell gave a human face to the statistics of poverty for the first time. In doing so, he found his voice as a writer.

'Orwell was the great moral force of his age' *Spectator*

He just wanted a decent book to read ...

Not too much to ask, is it? It was in 1935 when Allen Lane, Managing Director of Bodley Head Publishers, stood on a platform at Exeter railway station looking for something good to read on his journey back to London. His choice was limited to popular magazines and poor-quality paperbacks – the same choice faced every day by the vast majority of readers, few of whom could afford hardbacks. Lane's disappointment and subsequent anger at the range of books generally available led him to found a company – and change the world.

'We believed in the existence in this country of a vast reading public for intelligent books at a low price, and staked everything on it'
Sir Allen Lane, 1902–1970, founder of Penguin Books

The quality paperback had arrived – and not just in bookshops. Lane was adamant that his Penguins should appear in chain stores and tobacconists, and should cost no more than a packet of cigarettes.

Reading habits (and cigarette prices) have changed since 1935, but Penguin still believes in publishing the best books for everybody to enjoy. We still believe that good design costs no more than bad design, and we still believe that quality books published passionately and responsibly make the world a better place.

So wherever you see the little bird – whether it's on a piece of prize-winning literary fiction or a celebrity autobiography, political tour de force or historical masterpiece, a serial-killer thriller, reference book, world classic or a piece of pure escapism – you can bet that it represents the very best that the genre has to offer.

Whatever you like to read – trust Penguin.